JAPAN AND GREATER CHINA

GREG AUSTIN

STUART HARRIS

Japan and Greater China

*Political Economy and Military
Power in the Asian Century*

HURST & COMPANY, LONDON

First published in the United Kingdom by
C. Hurst & Co. (Publishers) Ltd,
38 King Street, London WC2E 8JZ
© Greg Austin and Stuart Harris, 2001
All rights reserved.
Printed in Malaysia

ISBNs
1-85065-521-9 cased
1-85065-473-5 pbk

Dedicated to
Pamela Harris
and
Kay Diane Austin

ACKNOWLEDGEMENTS

This study is based on the collective research of the authors over five years, including numerous visits to Japan, China and neighbouring countries to discuss key issues and ideas and to interview selected officials and scholars. It draws heavily on the collective experience of the authors in analysis of international affairs over four decades, but it could not have come together without critical analysis and research support from many people. The authors acknowledge the critical comments on individual chapters by Dr Dong Dong Zhang, Dr Roger Farrell, Dr Richard Rigby, Dr Greg Noble, Dr Aurelia George, Dr Rafe de Crespigny, Dr Yang Jian, Dr Jennifer Amyx, Dr Takashi Terada, Ms Katherine Morton and Mr Hyroyasu Akatsu. Comments from Dr Phil Deans of the School of Oriental and African Studies, University of London, on the whole of the draft were greatly appreciated. Mr Keita Nishiyama and Mr Michio Diato of the Ministry of International Trade and Industry provided useful material on economic relations with China. Research assistance was provided by Lawrence Cremin, Richard Prosen, Michael Thomas, and Brendan Taylor. The authors also acknowledge the special support of Professor Liu Jiangyong of the China Institute for Contemporary International Relations and Dr Zhang Yunling of the Chinese Academy of Social Sciences. The authors also thank the East Asia Analytical Unit of the Australian Department of Foreign Affairs for permission to use small amounts of copyright material from their 1996 study *Asia's Global Powers*, to which the present authors made a substantial contribution. Finally, they thank Dr Pauline Kerr and Professor Andrew Mack for comments on drafts of that material.

CONTENTS

TABLES

MAP

INTRODUCTION

Asymmetries in the relative strategic and economic positions of Japan and China create considerable discomfort between them. China's population is ten times larger than Japan's and its military forces, armed with nuclear weapons, are ten times larger than Japan's forces which do not have nuclear weapons. On the other hand, Japan's economic wealth is probably ten times greater than China's on a per head basis and its technologies and level of development are far ahead of China's. Such asymmetries between any neighbouring states tend to create insecurities, but in the case of Japan and China, these insecurities are aggravated by remembrances from a bitter history of bilateral relations, by recurrent xenophobic impulses, and by sovereignty disputes.

In spite of these sharp asymmetries of power, neither Japan nor China has been in any comprehensive sense more powerful than the other in recent decades. But each is definitely looking to increase its power. Both see themselves already as great powers, and they regard with considerable pride their climb back in the late twentieth century from far less promising circumstances – defeat in war in Japan's case and civil war and revolutionary chaos in China's case. Both governments have sought to have their relative advance in power reflected in some changes to the structure or order of the international community. These ambitions for greater international influence have further fuelled mutual insecurities. This study of the Japan-China relationship therefore engages at the outset with questions of global and regional order.

In the 1990s, the sustained 'rise of China' and the peaking of Japan's economic growth gave rise to concerns about a fundamental change in regional order, and possibly even world order. In the late 1980s, similar concerns about change in world order existed but were

1

based on different scenarios or estimates – a stronger Japan and a declining USA. In the first years of this century, the concern about a shifting balance of power will almost certainly be based on yet another set of calculations. One could cite the possibility that China's massive domestic problems will have stifled its economic growth and brought about some domestic disorder. But in most imaginable circumstances, Japan and China will remain not only the most powerful countries in Asia, but will remain among the four or five most powerful countries in the world. Japan and China have certainly made that calculation about each other.

As aspiring global powers, the governments of Japan and China appreciate the world beyond their control, try to frame their policies accordingly, and achieve some measure of influence. Yet the two governments often misperceive the world at large. They react quite differently both to the outside world and to changing circumstances. Moreover, as China and Japan look to influence global order, so too does it influence them. At the very least, global and regional circumstances in a broad range of dimensions define the room for manoeuvre and the responses of the two governments in their mutual relations.[1] Thus, the shape of the bilateral relationship can depend more on factors external to it than any factors under the direct influence of either government. Many of the bitter conflicts between Japan and China, such as the two Sino-Japanese wars, the Korean war and Chinese support for communist insurgencies, were directly linked to the actions and omissions of other governments in many parts of the world, not only by more powerful governments but also by weaker ones. Equally, the extreme circumstances seen as possible causes of conflict between Japan and China are largely external to the two governments – an energy crisis in the Middle East or a declaration of independence by Taiwan.

Yet the bilateral relationship will not be the exclusive source of change or continuity in the positions of Japan or China relative to regional or global order. As important as Japan and China are to each other, their leaders have many domestic priorities that make the bilateral relationship pale into relative insignificance. And these other priorities, such as economic performance, are much more important

---

[1] Allen S. Whiting, *China Eyes Japan*, Berkeley: University of California Press, 1989, pp. 200–1, observed that the 'larger context of East Asian relations – specifically, the relative power and postures of the Soviet Union and the United States – will set the parameters of the relationship'.

for the political survival of each government than the bilateral relationship. The bilateral relationship has an important impact on the economic performance and strategic standing of each, but the extent of that impact is a question of some debate. Moreover, the outcomes in the bilateral relationship and in the way each country positions itself toward regional or global order may depend as much, if not more, on developments inside the two countries as on those directly concerned with foreign policy. If domestic political forces with sharply differing policy preferences came to power in just one of the two countries, then the prospects for bilateral relations, and the regional and global order that helps shape the bilateral relationship could be quite different. And the course of domestic political development is more often than not beyond the direct control of each government. This study of the Japan-China relationship does not provide a comprehensive account of the domestic foundations of the international policies of the two countries, but in many places takes these directly into account.

This book is an assessment of the bilateral relationship between Japan and China at the start of the twenty-first century, but it offers an assessment of how their mutual interactions have shaped, or have been shaped by, domestic and international circumstances. The book seeks to go beyond a documentation of what each of the two governments does with the other. It seeks to explain why the governments have pursued their respective policies in bilateral relations; and to ascertain how the relationship affects the domestic and international priorities of each, and how any adjustment of these priorities then feeds back into the bilateral relationship.

What is Japan? What is China?

In this study, the primary subjects are the governments of Japan and China. Interactions between non-governmental parts of the two societies are addressed with a view to determining how they affect the intergovernmental relationship. Thus, the study's analysis of trade between the two countries is not directed at documenting complementarities between the two economies; and the study of cultural relations is not directed at understanding the state of affinity between the two societies broadly defined. These sorts of relations are reviewed to understand how they affect the disposition of each government to the other; how they affect the domestic and international position of each government in material and social senses (the foundations of its power); and how they affect the perceptions of each government of its place in the world.

The study acknowledges that each government is not a static or unitary actor. A government is merely a legal entity in whose name various power holders are given the opportunity to act. Thus the China of 1978 was not the China of 1998. And changes have occurred with little warning. The China in 1989 that made the decision to use fatal force against demonstrators was not the same China that just ten months earlier signed an agreement with Japan on investment protection.

While some information in the study will reflect on the domestic politics of decision-making, it is not its purpose to analyse such issues. It aims first and foremost to document the state of the relationship between the governments of Japan and China in the late 1990s through a narrative analysis of its most important aspects. The study provides historical background only to the extent judged necessary to understand the contemporary significance of particular aspects of the relationship.

Greater China?

For the rest of this decade, as for the last two, Taiwan will be an important issue in relations between the national governments in Beijing and Tokyo. While there is considerable scope to debate the appropriate mix of realpolitik and morality in regard to Beijing's claims to be the legitimate national government of Taiwan, the study concentrates its attentions in this regard on how Taiwan affects Japan–China relations.

Equally importantly, in Hong Kong where the government in Beijing has yet to establish an enduring social contract with the majority of the people, Japan's support has been essential for the smooth political transition between 1984 and 1997. Japanese interests in Hong Kong have become even more substantial in recent years, and the atmosphere of Japan's relationship with China will influence Beijing's future relationship with Hong Kong. Japan's interactions with Hong Kong will remain an important subset of its relations with China.

'Greater China' has a broader significance for Japan–China relations than how it plays out directly in their dealing with each other.

The evolution of Taiwan's relations with China will have an important impact on how future governments of China position their country in the international system. China has been changing from a highly centralised, regionally homogeneous form of government to an increasingly decentralised system with diverse governmental sub-systems in different locations. The diversity is represented in the existence of special economic zones, a variety of other development zone regimes, and the creation of new municipalities independent of their previous provincial subordination. The decentralisation has been more visible in economic policy than in political forms, but effects in the latter area will be felt more sharply with the passage of time.

Political economy and military power?

The authors started this book project with the aim of providing a documentary and analytical study of the Japan-China bilateral relationship in the late 1990s. But in exposing the characteristics of the bilateral relationship of two of the world's great powers, a relationship profoundly influenced by the relationship of each with the sole superpower, the book's analysis must have an implication for theories about the moving forces of international relations. The relationships uncovered speak to issues of theory about world order, about regional order and about domestic regimes. The analysis speaks in particular to issues of theories of political economy and theories about military power. This comprehensive assessment of the multi-dimensional Japan-China relationship suggests quite strongly that traditional approaches to international relations theory that analyse military or security imperatives independently of domestic social and economic imperatives are inadequate to explain the complex relations that exist between great powers at the start of the twenty-first century.

An 'Asian Century'?

The term 'Asian century' is used in the title of this book merely to capture the essence of widespread debate about shifting foundations of international order under the very powerful influence of events in Asia. It recalls the debates over 'Asian values', and the idea of an 'Asian century' is certainly relevant to the manner in which the governments of Japan and China frame their policies.

1

JAPAN, CHINA
AND THE GLOBAL ORDER

The relationship between Japan and China has developed under the influence of their participation in the global order. This was as much the case for the first half of the twentieth century and the immediately preceding decades as it was during the Cold War from 1948 to 1989. Since then, both countries have sought a more direct influence on global order and therefore on their own international standing, including in respect of each other. By the mid-1990s, Japan sought to elevate its formal standing in the international system by seeking permanent membership of the United Nations Security Council. This was based on its position as the world's second largest economic power, its founding membership of the G-7 forum of leading world economies, and its strong support for United Nations programs and other forms of internationalism. At the same time, China had developed a much stronger sense of itself as operating on a global stage. Its rapid economic growth looked set to provide a durable material foundation to its existing formal position as a permanent member of the Security Council and its position as a second-tier nuclear power.

Both countries, however, have faced important constraints in satisfying their aspirations. Japan has been ambivalent about a global political role, and has not been able or willing to back its desire for influence with the appeal of soft power or the application of military force. China's international activities have been more concerned with East Asian affairs than with global order and, on more than a few occasions, characterised by a certain passivity. Thus both Japan and China face a problem of reconciling themselves to lesser degrees of influence on global order than each had been hoping for, yet needing to deal with higher levels of international ambition and activism on the part of the other than had been customary in the immediate past. This circumstance guarantees that the global order will continue to be an important influence on the relationship between Japan and China at the start of the twenty-first century.

Views differ over what should constitute global order, and the history of the twentieth century has been marked by violent and protracted contests over the right to shape that order. For much of this century, Japan and China followed quite distinct and divergent historical paths in positioning themselves relative to world order and in their conception of what it should be. Moreover, from an analytical perspective, it is possible to distinguish different co-existing global orders in seemingly separate domains, such as an international security order and an international economic order. For much of the second half of the twentieth century, Japan seemed more attuned to an economic world order and China to an international security order.

We ask in this chapter how far there has been a closing of the differences between Japan and China in respect of world order, how each reacts to the place of the other in that order, and how those things affect their bilateral relations. The positions of Japan and China relative to global order at the start of the new century are analysed around four major issues: interests, structures, institutions, and norms. The discussion would be incomplete or perhaps less comprehensible were it not preceded by a brief discussion of the received history in each country of its part in the global order and how this order shaped their bilateral relations throughout the twentieth century. For the first half of the century that bilateral history was for the most part confrontational and violent. The perceptions of that history remain a continuing influence on each country's approach to the other. Since historiography continues to play a special part in the relationship between Japan and China, particularly how they interpret and respond to each other's actions, an understanding of the lessons each has taken from history is critical to considering how they will react to each other in the global order of the twenty-first century. The problem is that both countries 'entertain very different notions about the debt of history'.[1]

However, the impact of historical lessons on Japan-China relations and the place of each in global order are not confined at this

---

[1] Takashi Inoguchi, *Japan's International Relations,* London: Pinter, 1991, p. 142.

juncture to those that arose in the bilateral relationship. For Japan, the national catastrophe that beset it because of its failed policies of authoritarianism at home and military expansion in Asia has left an enduring aversion in public policy in Japan to such paths. Japan's experience as the first and only target of nuclear weapons has also left a visceral objection to use of such weapons, and reinforced the anti-war and anti-military sentiments in Japan. China had bitter lessons of its own, not least of which was the nation-wide turmoil of the Cultural Revolution which was at its peak between 1966 and 1969.

For the Chinese people, however, a desire to avoid the excesses of the Cultural Revolution has become only part of two even sharper historical lessons. First, the domestic impact of the pursuit of communism by totalitarian methods and through isolation from the capitalist camp served only to entrench the country's backwardness and therefore its social instability. Second, the international pursuit of a new world order in which communism would overthrow the capitalist world would also serve to entrench the country's backwardness. By the Fifteenth Congress of the Chinese Communist Party in 1997, China's leaders all but admitted that such a goal was not achievable, and was probably not even desirable. Thus this chapter argues that by 2000, Japan and China had arrived at a position relative to world order that had something in common with where they had been 100 years earlier: both wanted to act and be recognised as great powers; both disposed of enormous reserves of power; but both had strong inclinations to work with the international order, rather than against it.

In this transition, there was a clear turning point – or at least a number of turning points – during the first half of the 1970s when the transition began to be consolidated. The opening by China to relations with the United States that began in 1970 and the vote by the UN General Assembly in 1971 to seat the Beijing-based national government as China were key turning points which set in train the eventual consolidation of the international order in which Japan and China now operate and now conduct their bilateral relations. This turning point is an important reference point for the discussion in this chapter.

The lessons of history

Participation in the global order was, for both countries, more than simply an unavoidable part of the modernisation sought by them.

When, in 1894, Japan and China went to war over which of them would dominate the Korean peninsula, it was a reflection of Japan's learning from the West that military power characterised nation states, and of its wish to join Western powers in colonialism and in the exercise of overseas spheres of influence. Japan sought to be part of the West rather than simply an Asian country under Chinese civilisational influence.[2] It was also concerned at the potential strategic danger of a unified China allied to a Western power. In the case of Japan, this meant forming alliances against these threats, as it did with Britain in the Anglo-Japanese treaty,[3] or competing directly with the Western powers for influence in China. Hence the Russo-Japanese War of 1904–5. Although the 1905 Treaty of Portsmouth, which brought the war to an end, created tension between Japan and the United States, the latter at this stage saw Japan's establishment in China as a useful counter to Russian expansionist ambitions in Asia.[4]

China's entry into the international system had taken place over a period roughly coincident with that of Japan.[5] This had been brought about largely as the result of reactions against increasing foreign penetration, but in resisting the European or Western world order, China moved away from its own Sino-centric conceptions of world order. Sun Yat-sen's wish for China to be a 'civilised nation', and to 'place China in a respectable place in international society' was a desire to be part of the Western global order and to obtain the associated rights. In China's transformation and learning from the West it absorbed a similar lesson to Japan about the desirability of strong military forces. In China, as in Japan, this gave rise to politically powerful military leaders. Unfortunately for it, China was less effective than Japan in developing a military capability. Not only was China divided and weak, despite its greater resource base, but there

[2] Or as Hamashita puts it, 'Japanese modernisation was an attempt to move the centre of the (Chinese) tributary trade structure to Japan'. Takeshi Hamashita, 'The Inter-regional System in East Asia' in Peter Katzenstein and Takashi Shiraishi (eds), *Network Power: Japan and Asia,* Ithaca, NY: Cornell University Press, 1997, p. 128.

[3] From 1902 to 1921, as well as agreements with the United States and Russia from 1907.

[4] James Pryzstup, 'China, Japan and the United States' in Michael Green and Patrick Cronin (eds), *The US-Japan Alliance: Past, Present and Future,* New York: Council for Foreign Relations Press, 1999, pp. 21–41.

[5] Diplomatic legations were established in the United Kingdom in 1877, in the United States in 1878 and in Russia in 1879. See Jeanette Greenfield, *China's Practice in the Law of the Sea,* Oxford: Clarendon Press, 1992, pp. 5–7.

was not the same entrenched military tradition in China as existed in Japan and China's elites had long seen China 'more as a culture (or civilisation) than as a military power'.[6]

Following the First World War, Japan emerged as a major military power and an accepted member of the global order.[7] In part that order reflected a fear of communism arising from the Russian revolution, a fear that the Japanese government shared, and Japan joined the major powers in sending troops in 1918 to fight the Bolshevik forces in Siberia. Japan's troops were not withdrawn until 1922. More generally, however, the global order began to reflect a widespread reaction to the devastating slaughter of the First World War, and a corresponding shift in beliefs in which military power lost its centrality in defining global order, power was increasingly defined in economic terms, and international cooperation was widely supported, including through the mechanism of arms control, notably at the 1921–2 Washington Conference.[8]

As a major military power along with the Western powers, Japan's continued extra-territorial exploitation of China did not run counter to the existing global order of the early post-war period, but a shift was underway in regard to the responsibilities of the great powers toward less developed or subjugated peoples and colonial territories. This shift towards more liberal beliefs was also taken up to a considerable degree by reform movements in Japan and China in the 1920s. Within Japan, however, the efforts of the reformers faced the problem that militarism remained the basis of Japan's great power identity. The consequent domestic divisions can be seen in, on the one hand, a response to a more internationalist global order that was reflected in Japan's recognition, along with that of other Western countries, of the Nationalist government which took power in China in 1928. On the other, Japan sent troops in the same year to China's Shandong province to counter Chiang Kai-shek's efforts at unification. Disaffection in some Western powers toward Japanese policy in China after the First World War was seen as price worth paying if it meant Japan's continued membership of the League of Nations.

---

[6] Akira Iriye, *China and Japan in the Global Setting,* Cambridge, MA: Harvard University Press, 1992, p. 9.

[7] Although, in company with China, it failed to gain a racial non-discrimination clause in the League of Nations Covenant, which helped to sow the seeds of anti-Western sentiment that burgeoned later in Japan in particular.

[8] Although mainly seen as a naval disarmament conference, one of its outcomes was a nine point treaty on China that Japan saw as protecting its China interests.

Although Japan had participated as a victor at Versailles, and had shared in the spoils (to China's disadvantage), it subsequently turned against the Western powers with the breakdown of the multilateral cooperation of the Washington Conference. The economic crises in the late 1920s, and the gradual emergence of disorder in the international system, led to a Japan that, like some in the West, increasingly rejected the internationalism of the existing global system. In Japan, it gave rise to ultranationalism and to the dominant influence of military leaders for whom international relations were tests of strength and who wished to prevent Chinese military modernisation and unification. Ultimately Japan left the League of Nations in 1933, thereby substantially isolating itself from the international community. Reflecting the strong anticommunist view of the Japanese government, and associated with the long held influence of things German, Japan formed an Anti-Comintern Pact with Germany in 1936, which Italy joined in 1937 and Spain in 1939. This was a fascist coalition with global militaristic ambitions, a fact attested by Japan's military leaders in northern China (the puppet state of Manchukuo) who undertook military provocations against the Soviet Union in 1937, 1938 and 1939 with a view to testing Soviet defences. For their pains, they were resoundingly rebuffed and defeated.

After the First World War, China felt badly let down by the West despite entering the war at United States suggestion in order to participate in the post-war settlement. In this way, and through member ship in the League of Nations, China had sought participation as an equal in the global order. Reform groups in China often reflected Western, universalist, ideas rather than simply nationalist themes.[9] Despite the continuing militaristic element in China's political debates, and in part to counter Japan's pan-Asianism and to gain global support against Japanese aggression, China continued for the most part to argue for universal Western ideas of liberalism and democracy in the 1930s. The liberal dispositions began to give way under the pressure of growing global disorder, an increase in the power and influence of the Chinese Communist Party, and an increase in the authoritarianism of the recognised Chinese government led by Chiang Kai-shek.

In the interwar years, economic interdependence and trade issues had been growing in importance in the bilateral relationship. Yet, these did not define the Sino-Japanese relationship as they came to

[9] Iriye, *China and Japan in the Global Setting*, pp. 46–7.

do after the Second World War. A divided and weak China was a tempting target for a Japan led by an authoritarian, militaristic government with concerns about the security of food and raw material supplies. Japan saw the opportunity to meet not only its pressing resource needs but also the strategic opportunity to prevent a modernised, nationalistic and unified China. Many Japanese came to believe that, 'the national involvement in China had an altruistic and even noble dimension',[10] that it was the manifest destiny of Japan to civilise China and to drive out Western imperialism, to develop an alternative Asian system, and for that purpose to create a co-prosperity sphere. Since initially Western reactions were mixed, some seeing Japan as a bulwark against Soviet communism, Western powers reacted only belatedly and quite ineffectively to Japan's war against China, which had been underway for a decade before Japan mounted a full-scale attack on the USA and other Allied powers in the Pacific in 1941.

During the course of the Pacific War (1941–5), the United States and its allies came to value China much more[11] and gave it a place in important wartime councils, a circumstance leading ultimately to its becoming one of the five permanent members of the United Nations Security Council established in 1945. Japan, as a defeated state in the war, was by contrast designated as an enemy state in the Charter of the United Nations, a status it sought to have amended only in the 1990s. China could look at Japan from its position as one of the Big Five victorious powers. China (at least the Nationalist government) had been a participant, if not an influential one, in the establishment of a global institutional framework. And the containment of Japan was a goal of that new global order.

As we discuss in Chapter 2, many in Japan, including those at the highest levels of government, have not been prepared to accept this lesson of history. The victorious Allies wanted Japan to see its defeat not just as a military defeat but as a moral defeat but this was not acceptable to many in Japan. Despite the guilt felt by many Japanese at the atrocities and suffering of the victims of Japanese imperialism,

[10] Michel Oksenberg, 'China and the Japanese-American Alliance' in Gerald L. Curtis (ed.), *The United States, Japan, and Asia: Challenges for US Policy*, New York: W.W. Norton, 1994, p. 102; see also J. Victor Koschman, 'Asianism's Ambivalent Legacy' in Katzenstein and Shiraishi, *Network Power*, pp. 83–110.

[11] As the United States and its European allies came to see China as a potential ally against Japan, they began to renegotiate and eventually abandon their extra-territorial concessions in China.

there was a widespread belief that their war in China had been a 'holy war' against communism,[12] and that their war against the United States and other Western powers had been necessary to avoid being 'swallowed up' by them.[13]

Following the Second World War, major changes emerged in the global order. Indeed, there emerged several layers of international order. There was a substantial multilateral frame to this global order which, however, rapidly became a largely Western order, with the emergence of an alternative order for many countries established from the late 1940s under the communist system. By the time the People's Republic of China was formally established in 1949, Cold War divisions were already in place in Europe, and the early postwar vision of an order based on the 'united' nations was soon replaced with an order characterised by marked division into two camps, both represented in the United Nations, but both locked in a struggle to define global order. Thus, from 1949 on, there was more than one vision of global order relevant to the bilateral relationship between China and Japan.

Goals and interests, 1949–71

In the eyes of the West, China's interests, as part of the communist order, constituted a major threat for much of the two decades or so to 1971. Its involvement in the Korean war confirmed Western beliefs that it was an active participant in the communist challenge to the Western order, while China's confrontations with Taiwan and its support for communist subversion in southeast Asia gave it the image of an aggressive regional actor. The Cultural Revolution in China reinforced views in the US-led camp, especially in Japan, of China as a country plagued by domestic instability and xenophobia.

In responding to its domestic anti-militarist tendencies, Japan had accepted the international order set by the United States and without too much difficulty the constraints on its military role. It put itself under the US security wing, denying itself a security role, and pursued a direct economic path. Japan substantially subordinated its policy towards China to the United States and the Western Cold War framework under the US defence alliance. Despite the West's

[12] How it was described by Prince Konoe, the Japanese prime minister, in 1940. Cited in Saburo Ienaga, *Japan's Last War: World War II and the Japanese, 1931–1945*, Canberra: Australian National University Press, 1979, p. 76.

[13] Inoguchi, *Japan's International Relations*, p. 142.

substantial trade embargo on China, however, Japan did not totally limit its relations with China in the economic field as we note later. Nevertheless, the extent of China's economic interdependence with Japan was small – as was true more generally.

From 1949 to 1971, despite its efforts to gain the UN 'China' seat, China was 'alienated'[14] or excluded from most of the Western institutions until it gained access to UN membership in 1971. Domestic issues dominated China's interests at this time but, in any case, it was not totally outside the international system, although it was excluded from participation in that part of the system under US control. While part of the communist order for some of that time, it developed economic links with some European countries and economic and political links with the Third World. These started with the non-aligned movement beginning at Bandung in 1955 among countries wanting to stay apart from the existing bipolar division of the international system. China sought leadership of the developing world as reflected in its articulation of the 'three worlds' concept. For China, this was partly ideological and in part a practical counter to superpower pressures.[15]

Within its policy of containment of global communism, the United States had considered China as a potential point of communist attack against Japan. China, while critical of Japanese militarism and its encouragement by the United States, did not have Japan high on its agenda. Although Mao Zedong was hopeful in the 1950s and 1960s of encouraging Japan to recognise the PRC rather than the Nationalists on Taiwan, he had long viewed Japan less in terms of the bilateral relationship than 'in terms of the global strategic situation', and in the context of US hostility. Thus when China tilted towards the United States, its strategic interest in Japan was as a potential candidate for a united front against the Soviet Union.[16]

In practice, despite various differences and periodic tensions

---

[14] The term used by Yongjin Zhang in his *China in International Society Since 1949: Alienation and Beyond,* London and New York: Macmillan and St Martin's Press, 1998. Zhang argues against the view that China was isolated diplomatically for the two decades following 1949 (or at least following the Korean war).

[15] The motivations are discussed in Peter Van Ness, 'China and the Third World: Patterns of Engagement and Indifference' in Samuel Kim (ed.), *China and the World: Chinese Foreign Policy Faces the New Millenium,* Boulder, CO: Westview Press, 1998, pp. 151–68.

[16] Ross Terrill, *A Biography: Mao,* New York: Harper and Row, 1980, p. 340. After the rapprochement with the United States, Kissinger was urged by Mao to maintain

between the two countries, the bilateral relationship did not, in this period, reflect major differences or antagonisms arising from different goals or interests in their participation in their respective international orders. This might seem surprising given that, within the bipolar global order, Japan was clearly part of the US-led Western order and China was not, having formally allied itself with the Soviet Union in 1950. Moreover, the West was trying to isolate and contain the Soviet-led communist order, of which China was a member for some two decades, and what it saw as communist expansion in Asia. Although it was not involved in the Korean war, and gave only minimal support to the United States and South Vietnam in the Vietnam war, Japan was an important part of that containment process; not only was Japan part of the regional alliance framework but the United States obtained permanent military bases in Japan and allowed Japan to establish a military capability despite contrary constitutional provisions.

In part, this limited impact bilaterally of the superpower confrontation was a response to the reality that at least following the resolution of the Cuban crisis, the Cold War had become a system in itself, with rules of behaviour largely accepted on both sides with the shared goal of preventing a Third World War.[17] In part the reason is that Japan and China had common economic interests and as a consequence neither adhered fully to the conditions of their particular international order with respect to each other.

Goals and interests after 1971

Mutual interests of China and the United States led to their decision to re-open political dialogue in 1970 and 1971. Through the 1960s, China had been hostile to the United States-led international system and, in that respect, its interests differed fundamentally from those of Japan. Moreover, although it had become a nuclear power in 1964, China saw itself facing threats from both the United States and the Soviet Union. By 1969, the threat perceptions of both China and the USA had changed. In that year, China had been dealt a decisive

---

good relations with Japan. See Henry Kissinger, *The White House Years*, London: Weidenfeld and Nicolson and Michael Joseph, 1979, p. 1062.

[17] Gordon Craig and Alexander George, *Force and Statecraft: Diplomatic Problems of Our Time*, New York: Oxford University Press, 1983, p. 117.

military defeat at Damanskii Island on the disputed border with the Soviet Union, and the Soviet Union had threatened use of nuclear weapons against China. For its part, the concern of the United States had changed from communism in general to Soviet communism in particular and its newfound and expanding military power. The mutual concerns about the Soviet Union were one of the primary foundations for the eventual normalisation of diplomatic relations between China and the United States. This was to lead to a convergence of interests on the part of China and Japan over the Soviet threat, but Japan was trying an omnidirectional policy that was designed not to be antagonistic to the Soviet Union.

Although Japan was taken by surprise by the US decision to move toward normalisation of relations with China, its own thinking had already moved in that direction. It was able, therefore, to respond rapidly in taking advantage of the shift in Western attitudes to expand its own links with China. China's growing common interest with Japan as a partner in economic development, as well as a strategic support, meant that they had shared interests in relations with the United States. These were only marginally competitive at this stage, a condition due as much to the United States as to themselves: the United States under Nixon had initially put its weight on the link with China but the Reagan administration saw Japan as the more important.[18]

In 1978, China signed a peace treaty with Japan. It gained from this a reluctant Japanese condemnation of 'hegemony', implicitly aimed at the Soviet Union.[19] The successful conclusion through the 1970s of a strategic relationship involving China, the United States and Japan may have contributed to the easing of direct Sino-Soviet tensions along their shared border, but the most decisive factor had been the abandonment by China of its belligerent international policies both in general and along the Soviet border in particular. The Soviet Union was not well positioned to respond to the change in China's policy, in part because it could not trust China and in part because it had bigger global ambitions in confronting US military power. The Soviet Union continued to build up its air and naval power in its eastern territories bordering China and the Pacific Ocean. This build-up, along with a military build-up in Central

[18] William Tow, 'China and the International Strategic System' in Thomas Robinson and David Shambaugh (eds), *China's Foreign Policy: Theory and Practice*, Oxford University Press, pp. 138–9.

[19] But Japan was able to maintain its position on economic links with Taiwan.

Europe and the expansion of Soviet influence world-wide, only added to the security concerns of China and Japan and intensified their mutual interests in a common strategic front.

Countering the Soviet threat was China's overwhelming international priority in the 1970s and early 1980s. Despite its continuing rhetorical support for its 'three worlds' concept, which positioned China in the camp of the 'Third World' of developing countries working against the exploitative and militaristic policies of both the capitalist and socialist (Soviet-led) worlds, the willingness of the developing countries to accept the leadership of China had diminished after the thaw in its relations with the major capitalist powers in the early 1970s. Similarly, China's interest in the Third World also diminished, and China abandoned both its support for communist insurgencies in Southeast Asia and its policies of trying to compete with the Soviet Union in delivering aid to the Third World. China scaled down its aid but its trade links with developing countries expanded. Through the 1970s, China began to set itself new objectives of domestic modernisation in which the Third World had little to offer and the First World much to offer, especially the most advanced technology. Yet even though the revolutionary and class war thinking was no longer part of China's international objectives in the Third World, China still needed to perpetuate the good relations it had built up there for two reasons. It wanted support from developing countries for China's emerging global interests, and it needed to ensure continued support for the one-China policy to counter Taiwan's vigorous efforts to regain international recognition. As we note below, Japan also had interests in the developing countries but in ways that were not greatly competitive with those of China.

By the mid-1980s, the Soviet threat seemed less ominous. In 1982, China signalled a move back from its links with the United States towards an 'independent' policy. There were a number of reasons for this. One was China's assessment of a shift in the international balance of forces more in favour of the United States and to the disadvantage of the Soviet Union, particularly as a result of the Reagan administration's increased anti-Soviet posture. A more important reason may have been the re-emergence of tensions in its US relationship over Taiwan. Nevertheless, China still maintained its 'tilt' towards the United States and Japan for security and for economic reasons.

By this time, Japan had achieved an economic position and status that the West saw as approaching that of the United States. Having experienced two oil shocks in the 1970s and with a continuing dependence on resource imports, Japan's interest was to avoid partisan involvement in international disputes, like the Arab-Israel confrontation, that might put at risk access to such imports. Moreover, Japan had long been fearful that its alliance with the United States might draw it into destructive regional military conflicts and though this concern diminished to some extent with the settlement of the Vietnam war, it remained an important influence on Japan's approach to international order.

Ultimately, however, Japan's international timidity led to criticism of it by its allies[20] for failing to accept global responsibilities, particularly at a time when Japan's economic power had surpassed that of all of the allies except the United States, and in a situation where Japan's new economic power was heavily dependent on access to markets in the wealthy economies of its allies. Such considerations lessened the strength of the US-Japan relationship, with consequences for Japan's position elsewhere, while China had come closer to the Western alliance both for strategic and economic reasons. When, after 1989 and the end of the Cold War in Europe, the US interest in China's strategic value declined, China, as we note elsewhere, tried to loosen the links between Japan and the United States. This became less feasible as Japan reacted to the Gulf War, then to North Korea's nuclear developments, and then to the Taiwan Strait crisis of 1996.

The Gulf crisis, which exposed Japan's 'still low level of real internationalisation',[21] sparked an intense re-examination within Japan of its global interests. Up to that time, Japan had been basically secure under the US umbrella even though the Ohira concept of comprehensive security of 1980 was based on a belief that the United States would not be able economically to carry the burden of hegemonic leadership in the future. The end of the Cold War, however, led

---

[20] Japan did not have a formal military alliance with any other country apart from the United States but through the late 1970s and 1980s, it was regarded as an unofficial 'sixteenth' member of NATO based in part on the commonality of strategic interests and in part on the inevitability of Japanese military involvement in any war between the United States and the Soviet Union.

[21] Yoichi Funabashi, 'Introduction: Japan's International Agenda for the 1990s' in Yoichi Funabashi (ed.), *Japan's International Agenda*, New York: New York University Press, p. 2.

to a different, less threatening, situation. Japan initially was talking in terms of its own leadership role in Asia and an ability to be less subject to the direct control of the United States. The Gulf War, however, effectively reminded Japan that it still had global security concerns, that it depended on the United States to handle those concerns and, moreover, that the international community expected Japan to contribute to the maintenance of global order. The response in Japan as the Gulf crisis emerged was one of a public reluctance in the face of official desires to participate.[22] The subsequent Japanese response in the light of international criticism of this reluctance has been mixed. Japan has accepted a role in UN peacekeeping activities, it has sought to lead in international environmental issues and in addition to its global aid program, has contributed to the funding of reserve packages for countries affected by the East Asian economic crisis. Yet it has not done what is seen as an important element of leadership at the global level – provided markets for exports from affected countries.

A continuing problem for each country, though probably more so for Japan than China, has been the tension between its regional Asian interests and roles and its global interests. Japan has on many occasions indicated its desire to contribute to international leadership at the global level, and the reality of its economic growth suggested that this was an obvious influence it could have. The global economic area was one where Japan had started to exercise some initiative, as with the Nakasone high yen policy associated with the Plaza Accord in 1985 and the fiscal expansion of 1987 designed to support the global economic system. In 1990, in the context of support for Eastern European reform after the Soviet collapse, Prime Minister Kaifu, on a visit to Eastern Europe, expressed the hope that it would be seen 'as our first move in meeting the real challenge of our global role'.[23] Yet, in responding to the Asian economic crisis of 1997 and 1998, even though Japan made a significant contribution through the provision of financial support, it was less able to meet the real challenge of a leadership role, illustrating that it has less influence on the global order than even its material position in the East Asian region might have suggested.

China's regional interests are made complex by its unresolved

[22] Thomas Berger, 'Norms, Identity and National Security in Germany and Japan' in Peter Katzenstein (ed.), *The Culture of National Security: Norms and Identity in World Politics,* New York: Columbia University Press, 1996, pp. 317–56.

[23] Reuters, 17 Jan. 1990.

sovereignty issues – Taiwan and islands in the South China Seas.[24] These, rather than similar unresolved sovereignties in the East China Sea, represent the major focus of China's regional interests, and largely distort its relations with the region. Its assertion of its position in the associated disputes generates often hostile responses, or at least raises fears, among its regional neighbours, including Japan, and seriously complicates its image in global affairs. For these reasons China has been more active in the 1990s in regional cooperation and dialogue processes.

China's participation in regional activities reflects also its desire over the same period to achieve greater acceptability in the international system. As we discuss more fully when looking at institutions, it has taken for the most part a constructive, though not uncritical, attitude to the international arrangements underpinning global order. In particular, it is seeking to increase its own influence in that international system. This more constructive approach has represented a substantial shift in the thinking of China's leaders with major, and generally positive, implications for global order.

Japanese leaders have often said that their diplomacy toward the United States and China are just two tracks of a more or less similar type. However a Chinese author has argued for a different interpretation, suggesting that the two tracks are fundamentally different. He sees Japan's diplomacy toward the United States as running on a global order track, while Japan's relations with China are conducted on a regional order track. For Japan to become a world order power it has to become an Asian order political power and that depends upon China accepting Japan in that role.[25] A senior Japanese diplomat also echoed the importance of good Japanese relations with China as a prerequisite for a Japanese leadership role in Asia.[26]

There has been a degree of convergence of Japanese and Chinese interests in the international order, based on shared interests in economic matters and increased participation by them both in the global system. On global issues their interests often differ but are not necessarily in conflict depending on how they are perceived. As we discuss below, although both generally support the international

[24] Its sovereignty problems in the South and East China Sea are discussed in Greg Austin, *China's Ocean Frontier: International Law, Military Force and National Development*, Sydney: Allen and Unwin, 1998.

[25] Zhou Jihai, 'A Chinese Perspective' in Tsuneo Akaha and Frank Langdon (eds), *Japan in the Post Hegemonic World*, Boulder, CO: Lynne Rienner, 1993, pp. 196.

[26] Yosuke Nakae, cited in David Arase, 'Japan in East Asia' in Akaha and Langdon, *Japan in the Post Hegemonic World*, p. 123.

institutional arrangements, there are differences that come in part from the role and activities of the United States.

Structure

For much of the postwar period, the overriding structural feature of the international system was a bipolarity that emerged rapidly at the end of the Second World War. There were different layers of international order, based on different organising principles. The bipolar structure between the United States and the Soviet Union was based on the balancing of military power. Yet Europe developed its own structure based on cooperation. Moreover, with Europe's economic recovery, the structure of the international system in terms of economic power became more pluralistic. Japan's economic growth also changed the economic underpinnings of the global order. From being a marginal actor in the early postwar decades, it became a major factor in the global economy. Yet the growing pluralism in economic terms made little difference to the overall strategic structure which essentially remained bipolar until the collapse of the Soviet Union in 1991.

While the strategic structure is based on the relative power of states and what that can mean for interactions between states, economic structures are influenced by non-state factors, such as capital markets and transnational corporations (TNCs) operating within a largely, and increasingly, capitalistic economic system. Also, the internationalising or complex interdependence processes commonly known as globalisation affect increasingly the implications of those structures for inter-state relations. These globalising processes impinge directly not just on trade but on investment, financial flows, transport and communications systems, energy networks and the like. These developments and the interdependence they imply put great weight on cooperation or at least imply constraints on non-cooperation.

Moreover, internationalisation implies broader qualitative changes in any bilateral relationship primarily because a whole range of domestic factors are being transformed by the globalising influences. Because these transformative influences limit the extent of control that national governments can exercise directly on a wide range of activities, and cut across state groupings or alliances and subsystems, they have particular importance for the structural environment of Japan-China relations especially in the light of the rapid economic development that took place in both countries. Second, bilateral relationships are less and less able to develop without having implications on the regional or global levels. In particular, bilateral relations are increasingly enmeshed in multilateral frameworks that have developed under the influence of the internationalisation of global society.

This new interplay of strategic and economic structures can be seen in the changes in recent decades in how China and Japan have been viewed relative to the West. From the 1970s on, while China gradually became more closely linked with the West, Japan's economic development had led to growing trade conflicts with the West. In 1989, this relative position was reversed. China's strategic value had declined as the Cold War moved towards its end, while Tiananmen Square was regarded by the West (although less so by its Asian neighbours) as a rejection of the norms of international society. Yet, in a world in which economic capabilities were seen increasingly as the key to power, by the end of the 1980s China, perhaps prematurely, was perceived as having joined Japan as one of the major global power centres, along with the United States and Europe. (Russia at least temporarily had dropped from the list.)

At the start of the twenty-first century there is wide acceptance that because of the collapse of the Soviet Union and the end of the Cold War, the dominant structural aspect of global order is unipolarity. This view is based on the recognition that the US military pre-eminence likely to be maintained through at least the early part of the century, and that strength – alongside its economic power, technological advantages and cultural appeal – places it in a class well apart from other great powers. US strategic pre-eminence is based on a combination of vital factors: a global foreign policy; a will and the capacity to mobilise significant assets to prevent the emergence of threats to US interests; and the will to shape its own foreign policy and military activities to a fairly coherent and in most cases enlightened conception of global order. US assets include not only military forces in the field but the full range of international instruments, including strong diplomatic representation and intelligence services. No other country possesses the military power and the economic weight of the United States nor has its willingness to apply them internationally. Underpinning this US position is a global network of alliances, sustained not by force, but by common consent.

One particular strength of the US position of strategic pre-eminence is that it is not dominance, and to the extent that the United States is seen to be disavowing that goal, there will be less likelihood that other great powers would unite to challenge US power (and global order). While the United States does not seek world dominance, one reason why it would be difficult to aspire to this goal is that its lead in military power over other countries is not matched in the economic sphere. There are other centres of economic and technological power, and other sources of international diplomatic power. Britain and France may not be able to match the United States in military or economic weight, but their status as permanent members of the UN Security Council, along with China and Russia, guarantees that the United States will not be given a free hand. While US economic power and technological leadership will also be sustained through the early part of the twenty-first century, the relative strengths of Japan and Europe, and the rising power of China, are reliable indicators that the US lead in these dimensions of power cannot be as dominating as it is in military power. But the essence of US power cannot be calculated simply in measurable material terms where the figures for it are compared with those for another. The exercise of US power has as much to do with the fit between the levers of power available to it and the structures of the international society in which they are applied. US foreign policy in the 1990s has for the most part been characterised by consensus building in the international community – notwithstanding occasional flashes of unilateralism. In important respects, in spite of the US position as sole superpower, world order has through the 1990s become more reliant on multilateral approaches to major problems.

Japan and China sit on different sides of the fence in their policy reactions to the US position in world order. Japan is broadly comfortable with the US position as sole superpower since a security treaty links the two countries, since the economic ties are unequalled in scale and scope by any other pair of countries, and since there is a robust political relationship. At the same time Japan has expressed its wish to participate in building a new international order and it will no doubt continue to seek a greater political role internationally. Deep down, many Japanese politicians would like to see an international system influenced largely by a concert of great powers, of which it is one, working harmoniously together through the UN system more or less as equals, and so without a clear leading power.

China is uncomfortable with an international structure so dominated by the United States. Chinese leaders see the United States using its position of power to China's disadvantage. They deeply resent the unrelenting campaign by the US government and by US-based groups to revise the domestic political order in China through a variety of international institutions. One Chinese government minister described this sort of campaign as 'WorldWarThree without smoke'.[27] They resent just as much the commitment of the United States to defence ofTaiwan. Chinese leaders are jealous of US wealth and power, and they believe their country has some sort of historic right or destiny to be just as powerful. They are distrustful of US military forces deployed in Korea and Japan. But, as uncomfortable as Chinese leaders are with a global order in which US power is pre-eminent, they are not intimidated by it. China has effective diplomatic levers at its disposal to deal with US pre-eminence and a fairly impressive record of doing just that. Although the only major security threat conceivable to China is the United States, it has no sense that the United States is seeking one final confrontation with it, and it does have a sense that the United States is prepared to deal with China most of the time on mutually satisfactory terms.

The strong commercial interests of US firms in China and the evolving economic relationship between the two countries provide powerful disincentives against rash actions by the United States. Chinese leaders have made a strategic calculation that the imperatives of economic development at home, particularly the acquisition of advanced technology and access to foreign funds, give them little choice but to put up with the interference from the United States. There is also a strong awareness in the leadership that the most powerful destabilising forces in domestic society come not from external interference but from domestic sources. China sees itself as increasingly influential in the institutions of world order, not least through the attention paid by most countries of the world to the potential of good economic and political relations with China.Thus, for a variety of reasons, China in recent decades has not seen any pressing strategic necessity to challenge the US position of pre-eminence.

Given China's ambitions to match US power and to have a strong influence on world order, its relative confidence in dealing with the US position in global order bears out the suggestion above that the unipolar aspect of this order is only one characteristic of it and not an overwhelming one. The world may be experiencing a unipolar moment but there are strong countervailing multipolar moments and reserves of national strength and independence that dilute the

---

[27] See Greg Austin, 'The Strategic Implications of China's Public Order Crisis', *Survival*, winter 1995, pp. 7–23.

unipolar effect. The triangular relationship between Japan, China and the United States is as much an underpinning of world order at the start of the twenty-first century as is the US position as sole superpower – as discussion in subsequent chapters of this study reveals. The ability of China (or Japan for that matter) to reach out to other great powers for support in its diplomacy or for access to technology and investments has demonstrated just how fine the balance is between the unipolarity and the multipolarity. Some 14% of China's total trade is with Europe, and this helps to temper the impact of major US economic actions against China. But in other diplomatic areas, especially in the battle over human rights, there are some limitations to the value of European countries as a counter to US power and pressure. China has made overtures to Russia, and through the 1990s looked to import Russian military technologies as a substitute for US military technologies that had been offered in the 1980s but then refused after the Tiananmen Square incident in 1989. China has even used the term strategic partnership to describe its relations with Russia aimed at achieving some form of multipolarity. Yet, it is not clear that China believes that Russia has great value as a strategic partner, except on particular issues on which both China and Russia have problems with the US position, such as the 1998 crisis over arms inspections in Iraq, or the 1999 NATO war against Yugoslavia.

China's confidence that its interests are not threatened significantly by the current structure of international order is also borne out by its approaches to what should be done to amend the current structure. China has called for a 'genuinely' multipolar world, in which the great powers of broadly equal strength might form the security directorate for world affairs much as envisioned in the provisions for the UN Security Council in the UN Charter.[28] China, however, has not shown much interest in working aggressively or even vigorously to bring this about. At the end of the 1990s, China has not sought to balance US power through a vigorous military build-up or through the development of new anti-US alliance relationships.

That said, the domestic pressures in China for change in policy to

---

[28] See, for example, the summary of the Chinese contribution in *Sino-American Cooperation on the Korean Peninsula,* conference report, Asia Pacific Centre for Security Studies, Honolulu, May 1998, p. 6.

a comprehensive, potentially combative partnership with countries like Russia against the United States will probably continue to gain ground. The political ideologies that could bring about a major shift in policy are well formed and have significant if still relatively small support. The political situation in China is sufficiently unstable or polarised to throw up such a change with relatively little warning. It is easy to identify credible scenarios that might push China to such a position. At the end of the 1990s, China had already been on the cusp of a political crisis. It would be pushed to a strong anti-US position if Japan made more substantial moves toward planning joint combat operations with the United States, theatre missile defence, or forward deployment of Japanese military forces. If Taiwan provoked a major confrontation with the mainland, China and the United States would quickly be at loggerheads and China may well seek Russian support.

Nevertheless, the threat of a new China-centred military alliance directed at US global interests remains distant, and a number of powerful constraints remain in place even for quite limited coordination of anti-US positions by China. Yet, the prospects must be for an increase in efforts by China in partnership with whoever is willing to hobble the accretion of US power and to contain the cultural onslaught of internationalising influences identified with the United States. The United States shows no signs of abating the determined, often aggressive, pursuit of its foreign policy objectives, so an escalating spiral of reaction and counter-action with China may well be inevitable. The intensity and consequences of this inevitable spiral of reaction will depend on the ability of major players, including the United States, the European Union, and Japan to provide necessary circuit-breaking measures or incentives for China to step back from sustained and damaging confrontations. The record by end-1999 was that the governments of China, Japan and the United States were prepared in almost all circumstances to do just that.

Institutions

Global institutions, and the treaties, agreements and arrangements related to them, provide a framework for functional cooperation globally and are substantially the basis for maintaining and, at times, enforcing norms and rules on international interactions. Membership of global institutions is one indicator of participation in the global system. Global institutions also perform an important socialising function, by which members move gradually to develop new norms and to accept or conform to existing norms. This has been important for both Japan and China.

The major global involvement for both countries now is through the United Nations and the Bretton Woods institutions. Japan regained formal independence in 1951, after the signing of the peace treaty, but it was outside the major institutional arrangements buttressing the Western order until it was able to establish its credentials for admittance to the international community, the GATT in 1955 and the UN in 1956. In 1945, China was no serious threat to the international order, despite the ongoing civil war. Nationalist China was a founding member of the UN and a permanent member of the Security Council. It was the only Permanent 5 country to recognise the compulsory jurisdiction of the International Court of Justice, which it did in 1946. From 1949 to 1971, the PRC was outside the UN, China's place being held by Nationalist Taiwan with US support. Although Japan had, within the constraints provided by its links with the United States, been rather more positive in developing economic links with China, in political terms it adhered closely to US wishes. Thus it cooperated closely with the United States in voting consistently against moves to unseat Taiwan and seat the PRC in its place.

During the period of 'alienation', China was essentially excluded (or it excluded itself) from participation in international institutions. After gaining its UN seat in 1971, it moved at first only slowly to participate more widely; but, after Mao's death and the removal of the 'gang of four', it took a more active approach. We noted earlier that it is now a major international trader, working within the capitalist structure of much of the international economy. Like Japan, it is a participant in most UN organisations, and a member of 30 intergovernmental organisations with a universal membership, compared with 36 for Japan (but only 31 for the United States). It is a member of almost all the functional international organisations – ranging from the Universal Postal Union to the International Air Transport Association; and follows their rules and practices, generally as a constructive if status quo oriented power. Chinese participants are involved in a surprisingly large number of the international NGOs (552), even if substantially less than Japan (935).[29]

[29] Data from *Yearbook of International Organisations,* Munich: K.G.Sauer, 35th edn, 1998/9, vol. 2, tables 4 and 5.

China is also a member of the major international financial institutions. It joined the World Bank and the IMF in 1980 where 'the Chinese posture has been to facilitate the work of the World Bank and the International Monetary Fund by espousing and adhering to their norms'.[30] In 1999, a bilateral agreement with the United States on the terms of China's accession to the WTO removed perhaps the major impediment to its membership of that organisation. China has become increasingly active in international environmental affairs, having signed most of the major international environmental agreements, including the important global ones on ozone depletion, climate change, ocean dumping of hazardous wastes, endangered species, heritage and tropical timber.

Japan has taken a high profile on international environmental issues, seeing this as an area on which it can pursue an international leadership role as it sought to do at Rio de Janeiro in 1992 and in hosting the 1997 meeting in Kyoto of the Framework Convention on Climate Change.

When China joined the IMF there were fears that it would bring its own agendas and ideas with its membership and try to impose them, yet China's involvement has been basically to accept and work within the existing framework.[31] Similarly when the PRC took its UN seat there had been concerns among some Western powers that it would be a disruptive influence. In practice, however, it followed substantially a learning process, although being willing to argue in a generally moderate way the case of the developing countries on issues such as the international economic system and the law of the sea. Gradually, it came to fit in with an international order accepted by the majority of states in the international system. Conformity by China with this system was to a degree grudging, yet it was accepted in order to argue for change from within. In committing itself to that order, however, China found that it needed to make modifications and adjustments to its international policies in many sensitive areas.[32]

Both China and Japan have generally been constructive if not

[30] Harold Jacobsen and Michel Oksenberg, *China's Participation in the IMF, the World Bank and the GATT: Towards a Global Economic Order,* Ann Arbor: University of Michigan Press, 1990, p. 149.

[31] Jacobsen and Oksenberg, *China's Participation in the IMF, World Bank and the GATT,* p. 127.

[32] Zhang, *China in International Society,* p. 126.

especially active participants in international organisations. Samuel Kim observed of China's early UN years that China was modest and self-effacing, showing 'a respect for sovereignty and independence of other member states, irrespective of their size and status in the international system' and never bullying small powers.[33] Discussions with diplomatic representatives at the UN suggest that this attitude has not changed significantly. China has put increasing weight on the role of the UN as a means of managing international affairs, in part as a counter to US unilateral actions, and for enhancing global multipolarity.[34]

From one perspective, for a long time Japan's diplomacy in the UN was 'ambivalent and pragmatic' consistent with its minimalist approach to foreign policy.[35] From another, Japan sees its security policy as increasingly UN centred. Indeed Ichiro Ozawa argued that during the Cold War, 'Japan's security policy was in principle centered on the United Nations'.[36] What this means in practice is unclear but certainly in seeking to expand the role of the Self-Defense Force, through participation in peace keeping operations, Japan continues to stress the central UN role. China was initially critical of Japan's moves to be involved in peacekeeping, involving the overseas positioning of Japanese soldiers. It categorised this activity as a design for resurgent militarism. It continues to watch suspiciously Japanese activities of this kind, although it eventually supported Japan's participation in the Cambodian peacekeeping operations, to which China also contributed military personnel.

China continues to see itself as the leader of the Third World. It has not been a member of any developing country grouping, whether the NAM, the G77 or the developing country grouping within major organisations such the IMF, but has pursued an

[33] Samuel Kim, 'Behavioral Dimensions of Chinese Multilateral Diplomacy', *China Quarterly*, no. 72, Dec. 1977, p. 740.

[34] The communiqué from the China-Russia summit in November 1998 saw UN action as displaying 'more fully and promoting the increasing multipolar potential of the world', *Xinhua*, 23 Nov. 1998 (FBIS-CHI-98–327). See also Li Luye, 'The United Nations at the Turn of the Century', *CCIS International Review*, no. 3, 1996, pp. 1–18.

[35] Yasuhiro Ueki, 'Japan's UN Diplomacy: Sources of Passivism and Activism' in Gerald Curtis (ed.), *Japan's Foreign Policy After the Cold War: Coping with Change*, Armonk, NY: M.E. Sharpe, 1993, p. 347.

[36] Ichiro Ozawa, *Blueprint for a New Japan: The Rethinking of a Nation*, Tokyo: Kodansha International, 1994, p. 106.

autonomous position, a practice which it still follows more generally in its diplomacy. Although not clearly accepted in a leadership role by the developing countries, which are less well coordinated than in the past, it is the only permanent Security Council member able to represent Third World positions. An area where it has assumed an increased leadership role among developing countries is in environmental matters, particularly those concerned with global issues such as ozone depletion and climate change.[37]

Yet Japan also has claims to represent part of the developing world, apart from its particular interest in regional developing countries reflected most notably in its heavy involvement in the establishment of the Asian Development Bank and its initiatives in the 1997–9 economic crisis. It has seen itself as representing Asian countries in the G7 summits, including, since the Houston summit in 1990, China. In the UN it has been argued that, by the mid-1980s, Japan voted with the United States on little more than one in three occasions, its voting records 'coinciding to a considerable degree with those of the non-aligned movement'.[38] A tendency to follow America's lead became more prominent in the 1990s.[39]

China has always denied that it will ever become a superpower, yet its position as a permanent member of the Security Council poses something of a dilemma since it suggests the contrary. To reconcile the two positions, China has used its veto infrequently, distinguishing between its in principle opposition, which it expresses often quite strongly and its unwillingness to obstruct the will of the majority. Non-participation in the vote thus has become the device it has developed and continues to use – as it did, for example, in the Gulf War.

A controversial issue was China's strong criticism of UN peace-keeping activities before, but even for a decade after, it gained its UN seat, its memories of UN involvement in the Korean war remaining a strong influence. As a member of the Security Council, it could have vetoed peacekeeping activities. In practice, it did not use its veto over peacekeeping activities, on the grounds that the majority

[37] Elizabeth Economy, 'China's Environmental Diplomacy' in Kim, *China and the World,* pp. 272–3.

[38] Sadako Ogata, 'The United Nations and Japanese Diplomacy', *Japanese Review of International Affairs,* 4 (2), fall/winter 1990, p. 156.

[39] Yozo Yokata, "Rethinking Japan's UN Diplomacy', *Japan Review of International Affairs,* 13(2), summer 1999, pp. 81–92.

wanted them. Eventually, in 1981 it changed its position to support, thenceforth, UN involvement in peacekeeping. In fact, both countries had problems with peacekeeping although the difficulties were unrelated. Japan's difficulties are largely domestically based, concerned with the interpretation of its constitution but also the regional reaction to any Japanese military involvement in peacekeeping activities.

As noted earlier, Japan's 1945 status as an outlaw state remained long entrenched in the 'enemy state' clauses of the UN Charter. This Japan saw as an important symbolic disadvantage in its quest to obtain permanent membership of the Security Council. By 1995, however, Japan was confident enough of its position to push successfully for deletion of these clauses. It has not progressed far as yet, however, with its desire to become a permanent Security Council member. That is unlikely to be achievable in the near future, given both the difficulties of UN reform and the competition from others who see themselves equally qualified for such membership. Although Japan is both a major economic power and the second largest contributor to the UN budget, the hurdles to be surmounted are large. China has indicated that it supports Japan's membership but in a context of overall UN reforms which both, perhaps nominally in the case of China, support.

Japan has seen multilateral institutions as a way to reflect its interests in global as well as regional interests and as a way of demonstrating a foreign policy not set totally by the United States. Japan also prefers multilateral to bilateral approaches to potentially contentious problems, such as human rights that, with the end of the Cold War, have become a basic component of relations between states. Yet its role in the UN Human Rights Commission (UNHRC) was for a long time, and to a considerable degree still is, mainly defensive, reflecting international criticism of its record on such things as its minorities, women, trades unions, and refugees. While bilaterally, as we note later, Japan limited its comments on China's human rights record following the Tiananmen Square tragedy, it was more active in the multilateral arena. In each year from 1990 to 1996 it supported the United States by co-sponsoring resolutions critical of China in the UNHRC. This could indicate its sensitivity to global opinion over Tiananmen Square or a growing interest in human rights as such. In any case, it also reflected a balancing of the requirements of the relationship with the United States, which were met multilaterally by its support for the United States in the UNHRC, with its relationship with China, leading to a softer bilateral approach.[40] Like a number of Western countries, however, it did not co-sponsor the UNHRC resolution in 1997, the last in the 1990s, although it voted for it.

Compared with the UN, membership of the economic institutions tends to be more complex with conditions usually applicable for membership. For both countries, membership of these institutions has been important in ways beyond the immediate benefits. Although in different ways, membership also helped their closer participation in, and socialised them into the ways of, the international community.

Nevertheless, although Japan became a member of the GATT in 1955, for nearly a decade after that a number of countries declined to apply the provisions of the GATT to Japan, among them the United States. Subsequently, given Japan's concentration on the international economic order, and the benefits it receives from open international markets, it has naturally been a strong supporter of GATT efforts to liberalise international trade.

Japan has been more reluctant to follow the spirit of trade liberalisation imbuing the GATT's efforts and has certainly been slow to contribute to initiating trade reforms. It has often been accused of following a neo-mercantilist trade policy: despite espousing the promotion of trade in the early postwar decades, 'this was more accurately meant as promotion of exports'.[41] There was subsequently a shift in Japan's trade philosophy to accept, if still not completely, the mutual benefits of trade liberalisation, including imports as well as exports, and to respond to the international anger at its trade policy. Yet it remains a reluctant actor. Thus it has tended to be the last major country to come aboard in trade negotiations, using international pressure as a way to overcome domestic resistances. Only in recent years has it made effective use of trade dispute mechanisms in the GATT/WTO.

Since 1978, when China first looked for aid from UNDP, it has sought or accepted membership in most international economic or

[40] Ming Wan, 'Human Rights and US-Japan Relations in Asia: Divergent Allies', *East Asia: An International Journal*, 16 (3/4), autumn–winter 1998, p. 157.

[41] Ryutaro Komiya and Motoshige Itoh, 'Japan's International Trade Policy 1955–1984' in Takashi Inoguchi and Daniel Okimoto (eds), *The Political Economy of Japan*, vol. 2: *The Changing International Context*, Stanford University Press, 1988, p. 176.

financial institutions, its central bank becoming a member of the Swiss-based Bank for International Settlements in 1996. It has clearly benefited substantially from those memberships directly through aid and through technological advice and training as well as indirectly through confidence given to international traders and investors. They have also generated a basic process of cognitive learning, however, leading both to changed views on how the world works and how national interests can best be pursued within that international context, and to changes in policy, policy processes and institutions in China.[42]

China was an applicant for GATT membership from 1986 onwards and this was the subject of an extremely long negotiation with the United States as the principal negotiator, where it is hard to accept that domestic politics did not have an important bearing on the outcome. In that context, Japan was a strong supporter of Chinese accession to the (now) World Trade Organisation and, by 1999, had reached agreement with China on the necessary bilateral negotiations.

Overall, Japan is comfortable with the existing international institutional framework if not totally with its place in it. Since the mid-1950s, it has joined most IGOs relevant to it and is a member of a large number of international NGOs. It has seldom sought to be a rule maker. Yet it also has limited opportunities. It is not a Security Council member as of right; the G7, the major global institution to which it belongs, has a limited, mainly economic, agenda; and although the OECD, which it joined in 1964, does shape some rules, it is predominantly a dialogue forum for developed countries. Japan, as an established member of the West, has been a participant in most of the significant international arms control treaties and arrangements, with acceptance of the principles encompassed in them, including the NPT, which it ratified in 1976. It has pursued particular arms control interests; with the European Union (EU) it proposed the UN conventional arms registry established in 1991.[43]

For its part, China has also increasingly accepted global institutional arrangements to handle the range of overlapping interests that

[42] Jacobsen and Oksenberg, op. cit., pp. 139–52; Stuart Harris, 'China's role in the WTO and APEC' in David Goodman and Gerald Segal (eds), *China Rising: Nationalism and Interdependence,* London and New York: Routledge, 1997, esp. pp. 148–52.

[43] It also initiated the establishment of a UN panel of government experts on small arms in 1996.

reflect its involvement in the international system today. China, with its more recent involvement with the West, has nevertheless made rapid progress in adhering extensively to ongoing treaty arrangements. Already a member of the NPT, in the 1990s it signed on to the Comprehensive Test Ban Treaty (CTBT) and the biological and chemical weapons conventions (BWC and CWC). It has also indicated compliance with the principles of the Missile Technology Control Regime (MTCR); though continuing differences over coverage have rendered negotiations with the United States unsuccessful to date but differences be-tween the two sides have substantially narrowed.

While Japan is a firm participant in and supporter of the existing international order, the United States and some of its followers tend to see China as in some sense external to the international system. For them, the policy question is how to bring China into the international system. Iain Johnston has observed that this is based on a dubious assumption – which is that China is somehow currently outside the international system.[44] If we judge in terms of participation in international institutions, it is evident that China is already a major participant in the existing global order and is substantially a complying part of that order. Its international involvement in global institutions is very extensive. Johnston has argued that given its level of development, it is over involved in IGOs.[45] That, together with its substantial involvement in international NGOs, may simply reflect China's view of the position as a great power in the international system to which it aspires.

Norms

Norms[46] may not be the primary determinant of how Japan and China view each other and their place in global order. Norms are

---

[44] Alastair Iain Johnston, 'Engaging Myths: Misconceptions about China and its global role', *Harvard Asia-Pacific Review*, 1997-98 (www.hcs.harvard.edu/hapr).

[45] Ibid.

[46] Within the given global structure, and reflected in the related institutional arrangements are the norms, rules and practices that are commonly accepted by the international community to govern international (and increasingly domestic) behaviour by states. The word 'norm' has several meanings. It is used here to mean both what must be done (the rules as they exist in a concrete and articulated sense in international law) and what should be done (an expectation in a moral sense of what is fair, appropriate or simply right). This dichotomy is recognised to some degree in international law specifically through the principle of equity in the statute of the

certainly not as powerful an influence as the perceptions of each other's material capabilities: their military, economic and technological strengths and weaknesses. But how Japan and China perceive the other's acceptance or otherwise of norms, rules and practices governing international behaviour is a powerful influence on relations because their perceptions of norm-adherence by the other forms a central part of how each perceives the intentions of the other. Because of the record of breach of international norms by Japan and China at different times this century, each country looks closely at the other to see how firmly the international norms have been internalised in its society.

We began this chapter by noting that Japan and China, in their initial efforts to be part of the international community late last century, adopted the normative patterns in force. Aggressive war was not outlawed, states accorded primacy to military power and colonialism was a normal activity. As this normative framework developed in the subsequent century, so too has it changed for Japan and China. Aggressive war and the taking of colonies are now outlawed in international law. There are many constraints on the development and use of military power that did not exist a century ago. And there has been a massive expansion of international regimes that have changed the incentive structures for war and that have advanced the cause of economic integration among states. Although contemporary international society, like any society, reflects elements of coercion, as well as interests and values, coercion through military force has come to be seen as less desirable than other forms of compulsion and therefore as something to be used only as a last resort. A general acceptance has emerged of the principle of peaceful settlement of international disputes rather than through military action. The nominal collective security mechanisms established in the UN system have become increasingly attractive to the great powers through the 1990s. In Japan's case, the support for war avoidance evident in its public opinion is codified in its constitution.

It is fair to conclude that just as Japan and China had accepted and internalised the Western norms governing international relations at the beginning of the twentieth century, so they have come to

---

International Court of Justice and the principle of *jus cogens* (peremptory norms said to derive from the 'law of civilised nations', such as the prohibition on genocide or racial discrimination). See Ian Brownlie, *Principles of Public International Law*, 3rd edn, Oxford University Press, 1973, pp. 512–15.

internalise, basically, the extant norms of the international community one hundred years later. This does not mean that all norms are interpreted identically in each country but it does imply a fairly close degree of conformity in broad outcomes and major policy settings in respect of the fundamental norms, such as non-use of force except in self-defence or as authorised by the UN Security Council. The degree to which the non-aggression norm has been embedded in Japan-China relations is discussed at some length in Chapter 3.

The fundamental norm of respect by the international community for the domestic sovereignty of a state, and its associated obligation of non-interference in its internal affairs, is one that has created more difficulties for Japan and China in recent decades. This norm has been undergoing constant and fairly profound evolution since 1945, evidenced not least by NATO claims in 1999 that it had a right and a duty to interfere in the internal affairs of Yugoslavia by intervening militarily to prevent genocide in its province of Kosovo. For China, the norm of domestic sovereignty has been regarded as absolute for most of the time since 1949.[47] This position reflected extreme sensitivity to any repetition of the extra-territorial concessions and interference of the Western powers that China suffered for over a century, but it also had strong foundations in China's need to protect its domestic political order from Western attempts to impose democratic pluralism. But there has been an even more important consideration. The Chinese government in Beijing has seen its legitimacy as dependent upon preventing Taiwan from declaring itself independent or having that recognised by the international community. China also sees a similar requirement in the cases of Tibet and Xinjiang, both of which are subject to independence claims or separatist pressures.

Japan has not had similar concerns to China about domestic sovereignty since 1945 because its domestic order has not been so visibly at odds with the image demanded by the major Western powers. For most of the time since 1951, the Japanese government has not faced threats to its sovereignty of the sort faced by China, apart from the successfully resolved issue of the Kurile Islands and the unresolved issue of the northern territories. But Japan's post-war political order

---

[47] Although China is portrayed as being uncharacteristically sensitive to intrusions by the international community on its domestic order, China is probably no more sensitive in practice than other countries, including the United States.

was imposed through an intrusion on domestic order as great in scope, if not duration, as anything China had experienced. And the communist powers were relatively united in support of the right of the victorious allies to redefine Japan's domestic order – even as they differed on what its desirable form should be. Japan's history of occupation and reorientation of domestic order under that occupation has left its own psychological dispositions against external pressure. In the realm of human rights, Japan has certainly developed its own strict interpretation of national sovereignty, defending its internal practices against external pressure rather than actively seeking out common interests;[48] the same has been true of its economic policy in the face of growing pressures through the 1990s for liberalisation. Interference in its national sovereignty was also a defence advanced by Japan's education department supporters in the textbook issue discussed in Chapter 2. Thus, Japan has often been closer in its instincts to China's position on non–interference in domestic order than the United States or other Western allies would prefer.

The different approaches by Japan and China to these two norms (non–use of force and non–intervention) have led the two countries to quite different approaches to global order. Japan has been less inclined to favour military solutions than others in the West, but has generally supported US use of force as a last resort and where there was a strong international consensus, as in the UN-sponsored operations against Iraq in 1990 (sanctions and associated enforced inspections) and 1991 (military operations to evict Iraq from Kuwait). By contrast, although China did not use its veto to oppose those UN-sponsored operations in the case of Iraq's aggression against Kuwait, China has been careful to make plain its continued opposition to any action that is not in response to such a clear breach of international law, as the Iraqi invasion of Kuwait. China remains fearful that use of force in cases like Kosovo in 1999 might provide precedents to override sovereignty that could, at some stage, have direct application to China. It has also supported Russia's right to take action over Chechnya for domestic sovereignty reasons. China has been relatively consistent in reflecting a high degree of sensitivity on domestic sovereignty, for many years a disposition shared by other governments in Asia.

In practice, China has increasingly made compromises over its

---

[48] John Peek, 'Japan, the United Nations, and Human Rights', *Asian Survey*, XXXII (3), Mar. 1992, pp. 217–29.

sovereignty and its concern over non-interference in domestic affairs. It has accepted conditionality on IMF loans and US inspections of compliance with intellectual property rights agreements. It recognises that WTO membership also involves domestic intrusions, as does verification of arms control agreements. It has gradually accepted a legitimate international interest in its human rights policies and practice, although this acceptance is begrudging and limited in scope. In a process in which double standards abound, China put its human rights performance during the 1989 crackdown in Tiananmen Square under critical scrutiny internationally. In response to critical resolutions in the UNHRC and a range of other criticisms, China allowed international groups to examine its human rights and published a white paper on China's human rights.[49] While China differs basically on some basic Western human rights principles, it often shares the views of some other Asian states such as Singapore and Malaysia, although not Japan. Nevertheless, its acceptance that human rights are a valid matter of international interest has been further reflected in its ratification of the UN Convention on Economic, Social and Cultural Rights, and the UN Convention on Civil and Political Rights.

More remarkable though is the consideration that as a price for joining the international community of states and maintaining good relations with the United States and Japan, China has actually tolerated continued interference in its domestic affairs in respect of Taiwan. As much as China has railed against the military relationship between the United States and Taiwan as a gross interference in China's domestic affairs, successive Chinese governments have not been prepared to challenge the Americans to end that policy. In 1999, the US commitment to defend Taiwan against any use of force by China is probably as strong as at any time since 1950, the year the United States took a firm stand on the issue. Thus even on this sensitive issue of Taiwan, China has been prepared to accommodate a degree of intrusiveness in its domestic affairs that is contrary to what its rhetoric would suggest.

Japan's constitution reflects the universal values embodied in it by the Western occupation forces. Japan's interest in human rights in China emerged only after the Tiananmen Square events. Yet here it

[49] Although widely criticised as an inadequate defence of China's performance, much of the criticism missed the significance it reflects of China's growing, if still very inadequate, socialisation on human rights. Zhang, *China in International Society*.

was more restrained than the West and it subsequently argued against the US' linking of China's MFN (now NTR) trading status with human rights.[50] It has also at times reflected a view of human rights that needs to take into account the circumstances of the country concerned.[51] In this, it has been more sympathetic to China's view of human rights than others in the West. Yet both countries have indicated their support for the universality of human rights arguing, more particularly in China's case, in terms of priorities and ways of approaching human rights outcomes than denying their validity.

Although Japan's human rights NGOs remain weak, there is a slowly growing Japanese domestic interest in its human rights diplomacy, and in 1994 Japan cut its aid to a number of African countries on human rights grounds. Funabashi argues that unless Japan more effectively reminds Chinese authorities, and the Chinese people, of Japan's interests in human rights, both the Chinese and the Japanese people will regard the relationship more negatively.[52] Yet it is not clear that Japanese views on human rights coincide fully with those of the activist Western states and the strength of Japan's future pursuit of the issue internationally, including bilaterally with China, could well result more from political than substantive interests.

On pursuing human rights internationally, Japan has been equivocal: in part because of its own human rights limitations; in part because its wartime history acts as a major constraint with respect to its regional neighbours in Southeast Asia as well as China and Korea; and in part because for broader policy reasons it is reluctant to confront its Asian neighbours on the issue. Japan, like other Western powers, also restrains its pursuit of human rights on the international stage according to the sensitivities of countries important to it, such as Saudi Arabia on which it depends for oil. Japan's occasional lapses in taking full responsibility for its wartime conduct also affect international views on both its human rights history and its capacity for international leadership on this and other issues.

The interactions between Japan and China have for the whole of this century involved and affected the aspirations of each to be a major player in the global order. Since both retain that objective, the problem is how far each is comfortable with the other's vision of that

---

[50] Wan, 'Human Rights and US-Japan relations in Asia', p. 144.

[51] Peek, 'Japan, the United Nations, and Human Rights'.

[52] Funabashi, 'Introduction: Japan's International Agenda for the 1990s', p. 15.

order and the other's place in it. In this chapter, a review of the interactions between the interests of Japan and China and the structures,
institutions, and norms of global order suggests strongly that by 2000
the two countries had become very much status quo powers willing
to work within the system even as each seeks important adjustments
in certain aspects of it. The chapter also demonstrated that there are
important differences between Japan and China on the future role of
the other in global order, but that these differences are probably muted or contained sufficiently by the existing structure of world order –
not only the special position of the United States as sole superpower,
but also the strong countervailing tendencies toward multilateralism or concerting among the great powers. China's assessment of its
domestic economic development priorities is also a major constraining force on any differences or insecurities between the two.

Although Japan and China have become increasingly significant
participants in the global order, so far neither has aggressively pursued or been able to play a major agenda-setting role. Moreover, for
both, their involvement at the global level and in global institutions
has not been a major basis of contention between them. Since the late
1970s, China has accepted that participation in the global economy
implies economic interdependence and that may in due course lead
to increased competition between them. Political liberalisation in
China, as it emerges, may give rise to greater Chinese criticism of
Japan since until now such criticism has been restrained because of
China's economic dependence on Japan. In seeking to play an influential role in the global economy, one limitation for Japan is that
it may have reached or passed its economic peak in relative terms. The
start of a new century highlights not only Japan's economic malaise
but also the limits on future economic growth imposed by its aging
and prospectively declining population. Japan's disposition to look
inwards may constrain it from making the necessary reforms to get
itself out of this long term if gradual relative decline. Nevertheless,
Japan may play a more important role in areas of growing international importance – macroeconomic policy, the environment, and
economic aid, for example. Japan has particular advantages apart
from its great economic strength, including its anti-militarism and its
non-assertive approach in global (and regional) affairs. It will be able
to benefit fully from these advantages, however, only if it can overcome its leadership problems.

China can expect to have more influence globally in the future despite a degree of reluctance on the part of the United States and some other major powers to welcome this. For much of the international community outside of that small group, China commands respect and influence for a number of reasons: it does sit outside the group of traditional great powers; it has not sought in recent decades at least to impose its views unduly on the international community; it has huge economic attraction; it has a significant share of the world's population; and the international community cannot deal effectively with many global problems unless it has China's cooperation.

2

IMAGES AND ATTITUDES

In 1997, as an aspiring prime minister of Japan, Ichiro Ozawa, made plain his view that Japan and China have little in common:

All China wants from Japan is money. All Japan wants from China is the Chinese market. . . . A relationship based solely on financial considerations is a fragile one. If ours remains the way it is now, it is bound to sour in the future.[1]

Yet it is customary for both sides to emphasise the common heritage between the two countries. Certainly, Japan and China's common cultural heritage can be traced back 2,000 years; both are Confucian societies; and both have been influenced by Buddhism. Japan borrowed China's writing system and Chinese medicine. The Japanese still read Chinese classics and are familiar with Chinese history. Despite this, and as much as the two governments and some scholars might talk about the common cultural heritage and replay mantras of propaganda about growing ties between the two countries, there are important gulfs of sentiment, experience and wealth between people in the two societies.

There are many obstacles to warmer relations between Japan and China. One is the lack of close personal ties between Chinese and Japanese government officials.[2] The growth of stronger personal ties between senior government leaders in both countries remains

[1] Ichiro Ozawa, then chairman of the Shinshinto Party (subsequently chairman of the Liberal Party), *Shokun*, Dec. 1997, pp. 26–33 (FBIS-EAS-97-346, 12 Dec. 1997).

[2] A view expressed by the Japanese scholar Ryosei Kokubun on relations with China. See *Nikkei Weekly*, 24 Feb. 1997, p. 3 (NDB). The former Prime Minister of Singapore Lee Kuan Yew has made a similar observation.

inhibited, in part reflecting ambivalence in the views that the public in each country has of the other. That ambivalence has deep roots in several major sources. These include the history of Japan's war and aggression against China, and the divide between their social and political systems for most of the period since the Second World War. The negative impact of these influences may decline over time but such a decline in itself does not provide a positive foundation for closer relations. The passing of time is also reducing the number of people in both countries with personal experience and established associations in the other. In Japan in particular, much of the sympathy for China came from those directly aware of the suffering caused by Japan in China and who understood how sensitive the issues were for the Chinese; the numbers of Japanese now who know anything about the war in China from direct experience is small. Many in Japan and China know little of the other apart from reliance on stereotypes. Considerable mutual ignorance remains; there is only a limited cultural appeal in either society toward the other; and a largely negative public opinion has developed in each country toward the other. Moreover, on both sides there are sentiments of insecurity and feelings of national inferiority that co-exist with sentiments of national superiority.

We deal in later chapters with the growing economic and other ties between the two countries that could draw them together, as well as with the political and strategic issues on which the interests of the two countries differ and which serve to maintain the divide. In this chapter our interest is in the underlying attitudes and images that affect the development of relations between the two governments and the influence of the two governments on these images and attitudes. The chapter comments briefly on the issue of common cultural foundations of the two societies, before treating the issue of war history at some length. After a brief overview of public opinion in each country an assessment is made of the place of cultural diplomacy and cultural relations in shaping mutual images and attitudes.

Common and uncommon cultures

Both governments encourage increased cultural ties between the two countries in order to achieve a generational change in mutual perceptions. In this process, the two governments attempt to give a positive impetus to closer relations by building, often quite tenuously, on their common cultural roots. Almost every high level visit by senior political figures from one country to the other is accompanied by reference to the tea ceremony borrowed by Japan from China, the Buddhist religion brought via China to Japan, or the writing system Japan borrowed from China. For example, in November 1997, when the then Chinese premier, Li Peng, visited Japan the Japanese government included in his itinerary a Buddhist monastery founded in the eighth century by a Chinese monk. On visiting the monastery, Li remarked in a far from accurate interpretation both of history and Buddhism that he was honoured to visit a temple in Japan founded by a Chinese monk who devoted himself to fostering friendly relations between Japan and China.[3] There is no evidence that the monk in question saw himself as performing any such function, and Buddhism does not relate centrally to Japanese culture. During Jiang Zemin's 1998 visit to Japan, he made a pilgrimage to Sendai in a tribute to the Chinese writer Lu Xun who had studied there. There is irony in this, too, in the light of the troubled 1998 Jiang-Obuchi meeting discussed below, since Lu Xun, writing in 1918, had been critical of China's failure to face its own history of aggression and expansionism in building up its empire. [4]

Appeals to common Japanese and Chinese cultural roots are useful politically when searching for something positive to refer to in a relationship with such a tortured modern history. But they are unlikely to be successful in mobilising popular enthusiasm in one population toward the other for various reasons. Common roots can only be found from periods largely hidden in distant history, so any cultural similarities are largely superficial. Many Chinese think that Japan inherited most of its culture from Chinese sources and consequently have shown little interest in Japanese history or in traditional Japanese culture as something unique or comparable in importance to that of China. At the beginning of the twentieth century, some Chinese historians developed an interest in Japanese culture as a unique, non-Chinese culture, but this perspective had achieved little penetration in late twentieth century Chinese popular perceptions. In Japan, the subsequent improvement or adaptation of the many aspects of Chinese culture – art, poetry, language, calligraphy, ethics – that came from China directly or through Korea in past

---

[3] *Xinhua*, 16 Nov. 1997.

[4] Geoff Wade, 'Facing History', *Far Eastern Economic Review*, 24 Dec. 1998, p. 29.

centuries, was often so profound that their Chinese origin was either forgotten or considered irrelevant.

As Rupert Hodder has remarked, the 'Japanese early regarded themselves as being very different from the Chinese, a distinct people with a quite separate destiny.'[5] The Shinto religion, for example, may be said to mark out Japanese society as having followed a unique path of social and religious development thereby weakening the strength of claims about a common cultural heritage with China that might underpin closer interactions now.

Moreover, most people in the two countries see the implied claim that surviving cultural similarities could underpin friendly relations as empty when set alongside the events of the last 100 years. For the most part, long-standing elements of mutual disdain survive in each country towards the other. 'The Sino-Japanese War changed the Japanese image of China as a great centre of classical culture, a powerful nation . . .',[6] a change now echoed in Japanese textbooks.[7] Much of the subsequent propaganda justifying the Japanese invasion and occupation of China inculcated in schools and elsewhere notions of Chinese inferiority in racial terms.[8] Substantial elements in Japan continue to look down on China's technical and economic capabilities. Yet, as in Japan, there is a sense of superiority within the Chinese population based on the view that their country is more culturally oriented than what they see as the materialistic Japanese.

In the older generation in Japan there are those who warn that 'ethnic' differences between Japanese and Chinese could provide a basis for conflict. For example, the brother of the late Emperor Hirohito, Prince Mikasa, noted:

. . . we must bear in mind that we are not Europeans but Asians, and even among Asian neighbours there are major ethnic differences, in terms of traits,

[5] Rupert Hodder, *The West Pacific Rim: An Introduction*, London: Belhaven Press, 1992, p. 37.

[6] Saburo Ienaga, *Japan's Last War*, Canberra: Australian National University Press, 1979, p. 6.

[7] See Tokyo Shoseki Junior High School Textbook, published in translation by the International Society for Educational Information Inc., Tokyo 1994, p. 67: '. . . strengthened by the defeat of China (in the 1894 Sino-Japanese War), the Japanese acquired a sense of superiority, looking down on the Chinese . . .'. The comparable Osaka text refers to 'a growing sense of disdain for the Chinese' for the same reason (p. 255).

[8] Ienaga, *Japan's Last War*, pp. 6–7.

manners and customs. We must not forget this and do our utmost to build friendly relations and peacefully coexist with our neighbours.[9]

This view of relations with China is not confined to the older generation and is often addressed less sympathetically. In 1992, a group of twenty-six 'young Turks' in the LDP were among those most opposed to the proposed visit to China by the Emperor.[10] These parliamentarians, mostly middle-aged, cited as one of their reasons the assertion that China sees itself as the centre of world civilisation and might therefore see the visits as a renewal of tribute diplomacy. Just as many in Western societies had – and to a degree may still have – a supremacist attitude towards the Japanese (and Chinese), Japan had a racially based sense of superiority to the Chinese. This was played up strongly during the Pacific War. It has since softened, an open and non-judgmental approach to non-Japanese people now being more widely reflected in Japanese society.[11] Thus, while the sympathy of many Japanese people for China is reflected in a variety of ways, many of these owe little to the broader historical and cultural links usually written about, and are attenuated by some powerful negative influences.

The modern political and social cultures of Japan and China have been markedly different. One can find commonalities in social norms, such as deference to the community or group, in contrast to some European or US political cultures. The underlying incompatibility, however, of a communist system that consciously rejected its traditional culture on the one hand, and a democratic and modernising society on the other, the state of affairs in Japan for most of the period since the Second World War, may have had more impact on the cultural orientations and receptivity of the two societies in respect of each other than any more enduring social traditions. While the playing out in international affairs of these differences in domestic

<hr />

[9] *Daily Yomiuri*, 6 July 1994, p. 7 (NDB).

[10] *Mainichi Daily News*, 9 Aug. 1992 (NDB).

[11] Dower suggests that compared with Western racial attitudes that tend to emphasise the inferiority of the non-white races, Japanese racial attitudes tend to emphasise their own hierarchical superiority stemming from a sense of the purity of the Yamato race. John Dower, *Japan in War and Peace,* London: Fontana, 1993, pp. 257–85. (Yamato is the mythic birthplace in the sixth century BC of the emperor). The factual basis of the racial purity argument, used for example by Prime Minister Nakasone in 1986, is contested in Japan; see Yoichi Kibata, Japan's Search for Identity in Asia', paper to a University of Tokyo/University of Sydney international symposium, Sydney, 2–3 Oct. 1998.

systems within the global Cold War confrontation exacerbated the differences in world view between the Japanese and Chinese governments, their importance weakened after the early 1970s when the governments of both countries acknowledged each other as an ally against the Soviet Union. To a degree, the broader social and political differences have similarly diminished in importance as China has opened up its economy and allowed a greater degree of political relaxation.

While discussions of differences between Japan and China tend to focus on the question of history, they need to be seen against a broader background. The substantial differences between the stage of development and wealth of the two countries have also contributed to this gulf of sentiment. These background influences, in themselves, need not have been so influential individually but, when taken with the war history between the two countries, seem to have been an important factor in popular perceptions through the 1970s and 1980s. In Japan, the wealth and success of the economy reinforced feelings of superiority toward the Chinese. China's relative backwardness compared with Japan led to China questioning the justice of the outcome of the allied victory over the aggressive Japan. Concurrently in China, the wealth of Japan provided some solace to those who thought the 'Western' powers needed to be taught a lesson and put in their place; if a wealthy 'Asian' country, even Japan, could do it that made Japan something of a role model for China. Moreover, while Japan's economic success compared with China's relative backwardness provided some grounds for jealousy in China in the past, this has declined in importance given Japan's economic difficulties and China's economic progress.

Victor-vanquished and the issue of war history

When the Chinese President Jiang Zemin met with the Japanese Prime Minister Keizo Obuchi in November 1998 in Tokyo, it was hoped that it would provide the basis for a smoother bilateral relationship in the future. That meeting will no doubt have some beneficial consequences including agreements for closer cooperation in a number of subject areas in the twenty-first century. The reporting on the event, however, was dominated by the controversy over the failure of Japan to apologise to China for its actions in the 1930s and 1940s, similar to the apology given only weeks earlier to the South

Korean president Kim Dae Jung. The failure of Japan to give such a formal written apology to China was believed to be due to the strength of nationalist opposition. At the time of the Jiang visit, Obuchi's party, the LDP, was negotiating a coalition arrangement with the conservative Liberal Party, the other party embracing nationalist politicians, to enhance his government's legislative capability. The outcome indicates, however, that although more than fifty years have passed since the end of Japan's conflict with China, relations between Japan and China continue to be overshadowed by the history of war between them.

When the China-Japan Peace and Friendship Treaty was signed in 1978, Japan and China sought in their official relations to bury the past. This desire had been reflected earlier in, for example, the lenient treatment by China of Japanese prisoners of war, including some convicted of war crimes, compared with other involved protagonists, and the decision by China not to seek reparations. Rather than emphasise the legacy of the Pacific War, officials of both countries sought to pursue a policy stance that emphasised common cultural roots. This remained an influence. For example, on the twentieth anniversary in September 1992 of the normalisation of Sino-Japanese relations, while acknowledging the need not to forget the 'unfortunate' 1930s, Chinese commentators chose to give priority to the two thousand-year-old cultural links between the two countries.[12]

The war might have faded as an issue for many in China had it not been for subsequent developments that have fanned the bitterness and kept personal animosities alive. Indeed, rather than fade, the question of history seemed to intensify in the relationship as the twentieth century ended. Among the diplomatic discords surfacing in the 1980s and 1990s were those over Japanese school textbooks; provocative statements by Japanese ministers playing down or denying Japan's responsibilities for war crimes (almost ritually followed by avowals that they did not mean them); disputes over not just the magnitude of the Nanjing massacre but also its very existence; official visits by senior Japanese leaders to the Yasukuni Shrine (war cemetery) in which a number of major convicted Japanese war criminals are buried; the unsympathetic response to the claims of 'comfort women'; and the limited political support for a Diet resolution on

---

[12] 'Sino-Japanese Relations: Achievements and Prospects', *China News Analysis*, 15 Feb. 1993, p. 5.

the fiftieth anniversary of the end of hostilities. From Japan's perspective on the war history, the Tianamen Square incident offset some of China's seeming moral superiority, while China's testing of nuclear weapons in the 1990s generated a particularly adverse reaction.

Not all the issues arose directly as a result of Japanese governmental actions. Japan's earlier lack of systematic debate over its war history reflected among other things a strong United States interest, backed up by its exercise of censorship during the Occupation. This was noticeably the case over the biological and chemical warfare experiments in China of Japan's Unit 731. It was reinforced by the US reliance on the conservative successors of the wartime leadership (and often the leaders themselves) in order to face the new threat of communism in which Japan was to be the West's bulwark. The leftist elements seeking to raise the war history issue in opposition to militarism were suppressed.[13] The school textbook issue arose as an international issue in somewhat confused circumstances in 1982 when some Japanese newspapers claimed that Japanese school texts had been altered in that year to describe the Japanese action not as an 'invasion of' China but as an 'advance into' China. These particular claims were inaccurate but it became clear that this and other comparable changes had been made much earlier and were still being required by the education ministry. In its strong reaction to these changes China was joined by South Korea and other Asian governments, and by a substantial body of Japanese scholars and historians. The distinguished historian, Saburo Ienaga, himself an author of a school textbook the subject of this censorship, pursued a series of legal challenges to the ministry that began in 1964 and continued well into the 1990s.[14] Finally, in 1997, the Tokyo High Court ruled that the ministry had exceeded its constitutional role.

The 1937 Nanjing massacre reemerged[15] in the 1990s as a major issue but not through direct governmental action. Its profile was

---

[13] George Hicks, *Japan's War Memories: Amnesia or Concealment,* Aldershot: Ashgate, 1997.

[14] See, for example, Ian Buruma, *Wages of Guilt: Memories of War in Germany and Japan,* London: Vintage, 1995, pp. 189–97.

[15] The Nanjing massacre had been raised during the Tokyo war crimes trials (the International Military Tribunal for the Far East) although not as a major issue on its own; it surfaced again in Japan in the early 1970s, with right wing writers arguing that it was a myth; and the ministry of education's direction on how it was to be reported was part of the subject matter of the text book crisis in the early 1980s.

raised, however, by nationalists downplaying its importance or, like Shintaro Ishihara, denying to an international audience that the Nanjing massacre ever occurred. Ishihara asserted that it was 'made up by the Chinese,[16] an argument repeated publicly by a Japanese consular official in Houston in the same year. It subsequently received considerable international attention through a widely publicised book by Iris Chang.[17] If that had not been sufficient to bring the issue to public attention, in 1998, Seisuke Okuno, member of Japan's lower house of Parliament and a former justice minister, also argued that Nanjing was a 'fabrication'.[18] The issue emerged again in a court case when a Japanese veteran, whose diary, when published, described his involvement in the massacre, was sued successfully for libel by a fellow veteran whom he also implicated, on grounds argued as controversial. The libel suit was supported by nationalist organisations.[19] Nationalist groups also held a rally in Osaka in January 2000 to 'disprove' the occurrence of the Nanjing massacre.[20]

Although reportedly the emperor resumed his annual visits to the Yasukuni Shrine in 1948,[21] such visits became an international issue following the 1985 visit by Prime Minister Nakasone, which he undertook in his official capacity. The significance of this visit to what was a major symbol of Japanese militarism and the emperor cult was enhanced by the suspicions of Nakasone held by the Chinese as more nationalistic than his immediate predecessors. It was clearly a political gesture by Nakasone, and a template against which subsequent prime ministers are judged by both nationalists and pacifists from their differing perspectives. As Arthur Stockwin notes, however, neither the administration of the Shrine, nor some members of ex-service organisations, were happy with the political use of the shrine by Nakasone at that time.[22]

The Socialist Party leader and Prime Minister, Murayama, sought to obtain a parliamentary resolution ahead of the fiftieth anniversary

---

[16] In *Playboy Magazine* (US edition), Oct. 1990; he subsequently repeated it in the Japanese edition. Ishihara, an ex-transport minister, was well known as the author (at times co-author) of the book widely read in the West, *The Japan That Can Say No*.

[17] Iris Chang, *The Rape of Nanking*, New York: Basic Books, 1997.

[18] Reuters, Tokyo, 5 Nov. 1998.

[19] *Detroit News*, 14 Aug. 1995; *Mainichi News*, 25 July 1998; *CND*, 12 Dec. 1998.

[20] *The Daily Yomiuri*, 19 Jan. 2000.

[21] Ian Buruma, *Wages of Guilt*, p. 64.

[22] J. A. A. Stockwin, *Governing Japan: Divided Politics in a Major Economy*, Oxford, 1999, p. 198.

of the war's end, partly to anticipate his visit to China, with a formal expression of apology by Japan and partly to reflect his party's opposition to Japan's military policies.[23] The move caused serious conflict within the coalition government. Half the cabinet was opposed to any formal apology by Japan. Although the resolution was ultimately passed, he failed to obtain more than limited parliamentary support for what was already a heavily qualified resolution. The Japanese Cabinet did approve his expression of 'profound remorse for these acts of aggression, colonial rule and the like . . .'.[24]

The issue of 'comfort women' emerged in the 1990s, as did the question of compensation for victims of the Japanese chemical experiments. Although most comfort women were Korean, in November 1998, three Chinese and subsequently nine Taiwanese comfort women filed lawsuits in Tokyo against the Japanese government seeking an apology and compensation.[25] After many years of denials by the Japanese government of any official involvement in the organised provision of 'comfort women', a Japanese historian found documentary evidence in Japanese archives of such involvement. From 1993 on, the Japanese government accepted the involvement of the Japanese military authorities and acknowledged its moral responsibility. In Murayama's Cabinet-approved statement, he had expressed his 'profound and sincere remorse and apologies' on the issue. The limited compensation paid, however, has been organised through semi-private funding arrangements rather than directly from government funds.

In responding to these diplomatic problems, both governments accept that a correct understanding of history should be part of the basis of mutual trust in bilateral relations.[26] But in Jiang Zemin's appearance at the Japanese National Press Club in December 1998, he noted that 'there are always some people in Japan, including some people in high positions, who often distort history, beautify history, and hurt the feelings of the people, including Chinese people, of victimised Asian Countries . . . taking a correct attitude towards history has always been a problem that has not been properly solved in Japan.'[27]

[23] *China Daily*, 16 Nov. 1998; Associated Press, Tokyo, 14 July 1999.

[24] Statement by Prime Minister Tomiichi Murayama (approved by his Cabinet), 31 Aug. 1994 (copy provided by Japanese Embassy, Canberra).

[25] *China Daily*, 16 Nov. 1998; Associated Press, Tokyo, 14 July 1999.

[26] *Gaiko Forum*, 30 Sep. 997, pp. 24–35 (FBIS-EAS-97-288, 15 Oct. 1997).

[27] *Xinhua Domestic Service* (FBIS-CHI-98-133, 1 Dec. 1998).

The Japanese position is complex. Perceptions of the history of the war differ markedly among Japanese. Even the use of one term rather than another to refer to the war period commonly denotes a political judgement about the history. The choice is usually between the term Pacific War or the official Japanese term (from 1941) the Greater East Asian War,[28] now favoured by conservatives. Both terms, however, relate to a war that extended well beyond the war in China which is often referred to, particularly by nationalists, merely as the China Incident, while by others as the Fifteen-Year War.

Even if, as we suggest later, a substantial part of the Japanese population accepts a sense of guilt arising from the actions of the Japanese militarists,[29] this does not necessarily translate into a position favourable to China. There are a number of reasons for this but the consequence is that, in Japan, the war period remains a divisive issue with no consensus in favour of further apologies to China for the war.

Among the reasons are, first, many opinion leaders in Japan and high ranking government figures simply do not agree with the moral judgement on the war that has been made in China, the rest of Asia and, indeed, much of the world. In a variety of formulations, many argue that they were fighting a war to liberate Asia from Western colonialism and Soviet communism.[30] Consequently, these leaders have not internalised regret for the effects on others of the war sufficiently to feel the need to apologise. Many do not feel that Japan committed a moral wrong, do not acknowledge Japanese guilt over the war and are not reluctant to say so. Moreover, for many nationalists, the war was essentially the war with the United States, responding to pressures which would otherwise have forced Japan out of all of its overseas possessions and especially Manchuria (Manchukuo). The war with China and what happened there is often not remembered as central.

[28] The official designation of the war by this title by the Japanese authorities in 1941 included the fighting in China from 1937. Ienaga, *Japan's Last War*, p. 247.

[29] Given the difficulties that current generations in many countries have in reacting to historical mistreatment of others, including as well, minorities or indigenous populations, this is perhaps more usefully thought of as a 'sense of obligation' rather than 'guilt'.

[30] Or, as the Imperial Rescript declaring Japan's surrender said on 12 July 1945, war was declared by Japan '. . . out of Our sincere desire to assure Japan's self-preservation and the stabilisation of East Asia' and not to impinge on the sovereignty of other nations or for territorial aggrandisement.

The continuing strength of views supporting Japan's pre-1941 perceptions of the war with China may in part be due to the considerable degree of postwar continuity in the Japanese governmental process. Not only did the emperor remain in office, but many of the political leaders and senior bureaucrats of the prewar years also remained in or came to leadership positions.[31] For example, Nobusuke Kishi, minister in the Tojo cabinet during the war and held as a war criminal but released in 1948, became prime minister in 1957. He reportedly said in 1978 that he did not think the idea of the Great East Asian Co-Prosperity Sphere was basically wrong.[32] While this generation has now largely passed from the scene, their view was substantially maintained in various ways, including through the school texts that helped shape the views of subsequent generations.

A second reason for reluctance to apologise to China is the view that even if Japan was aggressive, this was no different from the behaviour of other great powers. In 1997, the Japanese ambassador to China told China's then vice-minister of foreign affairs, later appointed foreign minister in 1998, that for Japan the correct view of history included acknowledgement by China that the policies of Japan that pushed it toward war in the 1930s were no different from those of other imperialist powers at the time. There is a measure of truth in this claim, made by the Japanese government and many Japanese historians: that what Japan did in the 1930s and 1940s merely imitated in form, and perhaps in nature, what the major powers did in Africa and Asia over the previous century. The Japanese argument has been extended in some cases to the view that while Japanese soldiers may have committed some cruel acts, this is inevitable in war. These are views, however, that most in China and many other countries have rejected. Global norms had already changed both about the initiation of conflict and about the way in which conflict should be pursued.

A third argument, even where there is no total denial of the overall picture of events, is based on a belief that the war history issue is being

<hr>

[31] Haruhiro Fukui, *Party in Power: The Japanese Liberal Democrats and Policy Making,* Canberra: Australian National University Press, 1970, especially chapter 2. Ian Buruma, *Wages of Guilt,* pp. 60–3, notes by comparison that in Germany the whole governmental system was changed.

[32] Misuhiko Shiota, Tajiri Ikuzo and Yoshio Takemura, 'Kishi Nobusuke Kenkyu (Studies on Kishi Nobusuke: Ambitions for Power)', *Bungei Shunjyu,* July 1978, p. 145. Our thanks to Takashi Terada for drawing our attention to this reference.

manipulated for political reasons. In part this argues that numbers, as of casualties, are part of a political game being played over the extent of the Japanese impact on China. Both Japanese and Chinese see the other manipulating the figures, particularly those of casualties in the 'China Incident' and the Nanjing massacre. In such a politicised climate where precise figures are unlikely to be available, some variation is to be expected but the differences are large. In 1985, published Japanese estimates of Chinese casualties due to the Japanese were 21.8 million civilian and military dead or wounded.[33] Subsequently, Jiang Zemin, in a 1995 speech commemorating the fiftieth anniversary of the end of the war, spoke of 35 million killed or injured.[34] He repeated the figure in his speech at Waseda University during his 1998 visit.[35] In the case of the Nanjing massacre, Jiang's 1995 speech referred to over 300,000 people being killed. This is a commonly used but disputed figure.[36] Japanese nationalists either deny the massacre or argue that the numbers were small and incidental to the battle for Nanjing. The Japanese schoolbooks, since 1993, have noted that 'It has been said that 200,000 people were slaughtered by the Japanese army in (an) incident which was condemned internationally as the 'Nanjing Massacre'.[37] Whatever the actual figures, the school book figure of 200,000 seems to give a reasonable perspective on the clearly substantial and brutal events. Within certain limits, the precise figures are not that important in themselves although they can be and are used for comparisons between other events, including the casualties suffered by Japan at Hiroshima and Nagasaki.[38]

[33] Wu Jingsheng, 'Reassessing the War In China,' *Beijing Review*, 12 Aug. 1985, p. 221. The war of 1937–45 surpassed any other foreign aggression or depredation in modern Chinese history (but probably not the depredations forced on the Chinese by their own governments).

[34] *Beijing Central Television (Program One) Network* (FBIS-CHI-95-171).

[35] *Associated Press,* Tokyo, 28 Nov. 1998.

[36] Ikuhiko Hata has published a list of the various estimates in 'The Nanking Atrocities: Fact and Fable', *Japan Echo,* Aug. 1998, p. 49 that shows a range from 'very few' to 300,000–340,000. He does not include a figure of 300,000 reportedly given in 1938 by Hirota Koki, the then minister of foreign affairs (and previously prime minister) in what is described as a recently declassified cable from Tokyo to Washington. (CND).

[37] Osaka Shoseki Junior High School Textbook, International Society for Educational Information Inc., op. cit., p. 254 (p. 321 in the consolidated translation). A similar figure is given in the Tokyo Shoseki text, p. 274 (p. 131).

[38] Hata (see footnote 33) suggests that 'People like Allen Whiting say that this number is used to give the impression that the Nanking atrocities were far worse

A more general argument is that the war history is simply used for its instrumental value to China to put economic pressure on Japan, as frequently asserted by Japanese (and Western) writers.[39] China finds these arguments useful in domestic Chinese politics and in expressing its concern at Japanese international actions.[40] This was argued during the textbook crisis in the 1980s, but also more recently, as in 1998 after a Jiang-Obuchi meeting, when again some commentators concluded that the issue of war history was useful for China because it kept alive the historical irritant to use against its regional rival and helped in China's internal politics.[41] This commonly held view in Japan adds to the strength of those opposed to any concessions. Some other analysts, however, starting from similar premises, conclude that Japan would have been wiser to have given a formal apology to close the issue, thereby on the one hand avoiding the appearance of insincerity, and on the other making it more difficult for China to use those arguments in the future.[42]

China has undeniably introduced the history argument when it has felt disadvantaged by Japanese actions. It has exploited the war issue during its negotiations with Japan over loans or grant aid. China has not failed to remind Japan on many occasions of its moral debt to atone for its wartime devastation of China when it felt development assistance packages were insufficiently generous or direct investment levels inadequate. In particular, when Japan froze grant aid in 1995 and changed the conditions for ODA in an attempt to pressure China to stop its nuclear testing, China reacted by portraying Japan's policies as evidence of a revival of strategic pressure associated with wartime militarism. At other times, its government was much quieter on war issues. This was the case in the first few years after the Tiananmen Square repression in 1989, when China was

than the atomic bombings of Hiroshima and Nagasaki', citing Allen Whiting's *China Eyes Japan*, Berkeley: University of California Press, 1989, p. 187. In fact the reference in Whiting merely notes (on p. 187) that the 'reluctance (of Japan) to deal with the guilt of aggression and atrocities in China while dwelling on the Hiroshima and Nagasaki atomic casualties both frustrates and infuriates the Chinese'. Numbers of casualties are not mentioned.

[39] See, for example, Ijiri Hidenori, 'Sino-Japanese controversy since the 1972 diplomatic normalization', *China Quarterly*, no. 124, Dec. 1990, pp. 639–62.

[40] Caroline Rose, *Interpreting History in Sino-Japanese Relations: A case study in political ecision making*, London and New York: Routledge, chapter 6.

[41] See, for example, Agence France-Presse, Hong Kong, 28 Nov. 1998; Reuters, Tokyo, 29 Nov. 1998.

[42] Mike Mochizuki, *Tokyo Shimbun*, 7 Dec. 1998.

internationally isolated, in a bid not to upset Japan while other major powers were still unwilling to deal with China on a normal basis. David Gries in his study of face nationalism (a nationalism seeking status and respect), however, has argued that, contrary to the belief that China's actions are simply instrumental, motivations for anti-Japanese behaviour on the part of the Chinese are neither simply instrumental nor purely an emotional response by the Chinese people but are tightly bound to identity dynamics.

A further argument used increasingly in Japan against an apology is that Japan has already apologised enough and has made sufficient amends. The Japanese note that in the joint declaration at the time of resumption of diplomatic relations in 1972 Japan expressed 'deep remorse' to China for the war. They also note the particular significance of the visit of the Japanese emperor to China in 1992 where he also expressed 'deep remorse'.

When Japan's Prime Minister Hosokawa visited China in March 1994, his personal statement included what was then the most fulsome apology delivered by a Japanese leader: he offered 'deep remorse and apologies for the fact that past Japanese actions, including aggression and colonial rule, caused unbearable suffering and sorrow for so many people'. This was the first time a Japanese prime minister had used the words 'aggression' and 'colonial rule'. Premier Li Peng described Hosokawa's remarks as the 'most frank and sincere attitude' he had ever heard.[43] Hosokawa symbolised this approach by laying flowers at the Monument to the People's Heroes in Tiananmen Square on the same day.

Yet shortly after Hosokawa's visit, the issue of a correct appreciation of history flared again, with an LDP minister in the Murayama coalition government describing Japan's war policy as having liberated Asia and popularised education and literacy there. This provoked a call from China for Japan to 'attach importance to this issue', leading to the resignation of the minister (the second to resign over this issue in three months and the fourth in eight years).[44] Murayama, who had succeeded Hosokawa, used the occasion to assert that 'all Japanese need to understand Japan's war responsibility deeply'.[45]

Prime Minister Hashimoto, in what was seen by the Chinese government as a very positive trip to China in 1997, visited a war museum in Shenyang and said that the Murayama statement of profound

[43] *Kyodo*, 20 Mar. 1994 (FBIS-CHI-94-054, 21 Mar. 1994, p. 13).

[44] *Xinhua*, 13 Aug. 1994 (FBIS-CHI-94-157, 15 Aug. 1994).

[45] Ibid.

remorse, endorsed by the Japanese Cabinet in August 1994, and made during Murayama's visit to China in that month, reflected Japan's official view of its wartime atrocities.[46] Nevertheless, the Chinese government, while welcoming the Murayama statement, had seen it as falling short of the apology they sought, but Hashimoto declined to make an official apology.

In addition, it is at times argued that an apology could lay Japan open to added compensation claims. Already, as well as comfort women, many prisoners of war of the Japanese have also sought compensation from the Japanese government in the Japanese courts. One political commentator, Hisayuki Miyake argued that 'if they start paying compensation and acknowledging the guilt, there will never be an end to it.'[47]

Finally, a source of reluctance comes from those who believe that Japan was also a victim in the war because of the bombs on Hiroshima and Nagasaki. The use of nuclear weapons against two Japanese cities in the war further complicates the ambivalent and confused psychological instincts in Japan toward the historical record. For many Japanese, Hiroshima in particular is the supreme symbol of the war and reinforces the views of the conservatives who saw Japan as confronting a dominating west but also those on the left with incipient anti–US attitudes. Although it was not related directly to the 'China Incident', the question is often asked why, if Japan should apologise for Nanjing, should not the West (or the Americans) apologise for Hiroshima.

Given the complexities of the reactions within Japan to its history, the Japanese government faces strong domestic pressures in its handling of war issues, often from two opposing constituencies. Those with conservative or 'rightist' political leanings tend to defend Japan's 'history', while those of a more liberal or 'leftist' bent, especially within the Socialist Party, tend to side with those wanting to acknowledge the country's war crimes. In many respects, however, just as the history issue in China reflected identity dynamics in a changing domestic and international environment, so in Japan it was a proxy for Japan's domestic debate between competing ideologies.

Moreover, many on the conservative side often depend for their election upon substantial support from veterans' or veterans'

---

[46] Agence France-Presse, 6 Sep. 1997 (CND). This was not expected of Hashimoto who, when leader of a group representing children of the war dead, had been highly critical of the Hosakawa statement.
[47] Reuters, Tokyo, 26 Nov. 1998.

families' organisations who would see an acknowledgement of guilt as diminishing the value of the sacrifice of those who fought and died for Japan, particularly important given the particular cultural symbolism of family relationships. For various reasons, conservative governments in particular have not been prepared until recently to work to bring public opinion around to a position more responsive to China. Stronger leadership on this issue, requiring the expenditure of political capital, will be needed before China and many Chinese people are convinced that Japan as a state has accepted the moral judgement China believes appropriate.

Many opinion leaders in Japan claim to be tiring of pressure on Japan to conduct 'apology diplomacy' and to resent governments like China for insisting on it. In 1996, after China's protests about a visit by Prime Minister Hashimoto to the Yasukuni Shrine, and before his visit to China, Hashimoto is reported to have expressed the view: 'why should it matter anymore'.[48] The influential chief cabinet secretary and government spokesperson Hiromu Nonaka was reported as asking at the time of the 1998 Jiang-Obuchi meeting, 'Isn't this a finished problem? There is a school of thought that Japan has already reflected on its part and apologised to China any number of times before.'[49] He subsequently claimed to have been misquoted and that he was simply reporting others' views, which did not reflect his personal opinion.[50]

There has been an increasing willingness by Japan to acknowledge that it instigated a war of aggression against China and to express regret. The problem for Japan has been that the gradual public purging of war guilt in Japan by the government has been so slow, so grudging and so contested that any apologies or other acts of atonement and contrition have lost much of their impact.[51] The

[48] *Mainichi Daily,* 3 Dec. 1996 (NDB). Hashimoto subsequently refrained from publicly announced visits to the Shrine.

[49] Reuters, Tokyo, 29 Nov. 1998.

[50] Reuters, Tokyo, 2 Dec. 1998.

[51] According to one analysis, part of the problem has also been in the expressions used. The Japanese term *owabi* (apology) was used in the written apology to Kim Dae Jung but not in other cases. Yoshida in 1972 used the weaker term *hansei* (remorse or self-reflection, as did the Japanese emperor in his 1992 visit to China). During the 1998 Jiang visit to Tokyo, Obuchi used *owabi* in his oral presentation but declined to use it in written form. See Peter Lander and Susan V. Lawrence, 'Sorry, No Apology: Summit May Have Pushed China and Japan Further Apart', *Far Eastern Economic Review,* 10 Dec. 1998, p. 21.

willingness to discuss publicly historical events has improved as the change in the presentation in the school texts indicates, although those changes will take a long time to have an influence on a substantial proportion of the population. Yet as one side of the debate presses the acceptance of guilt the other side denies it more strongly and the various changes 'deepened the sense of crisis of the right-wing people'.[52] Consequently, a nationalist backlash is in evidence.

This was evident in the nationalist-backed film *Pride-The Fateful Moment* released in November 1998, about Hideki Tojo, Prime Minister of Japan in 1941–4, and centering on the Tokyo war crimes trials, which seeks to paint him as a patriotic hero.[53] It was also evident in the extensive public campaign by Nobukatsu Fujioka, a professor of education at Tokyo University, to have the school textbooks revised to exclude any material critical of the Japanese actions during the war, and in particular to remove the description of the 'comfort women', arguing that they were ordinary prostitutes.[54]

Fujioka, like many others, is arguing from a concern about Japanese identity. National identities emerge from histories and Japan's history provides an uncomfortable basis for establishing a clear identity. This is accentuated for Japan as it moves into the twenty-first century by its added uncertainties arising from the impact of globalisation, the indistinct post-cold war regional order, Japan's shaken economic confidence, its conflicted and semi-dependent relationship with the United States and the future of Japan's aging society. Fujioka wants the textbooks revised so that Japanese people can have pride in their history.[55] According to one of his academic colleagues, the historian Takao Sakamoto, the basis of a country's identity is what is unique in its long history and the story of modern Japan is that of its effort to resist the advancement of European powers into Asia and to build up a unique position in the history of international society.[56]

---

[52] Yoichi Kibata, 'Japan's Search For Identity in Asia', paper to a University of Tokyo/University of Sydney international symposium, 2–3 Oct. 1998, p. 6.

[53] Eriko Amaha, 'Pride and Prejudice', *Far Eastern Economic Review,* 21, 1998, pp. 46–7; China was reportedly planning to make a film ('its own Schindler's List') to publicise the Nanjing massacre. *The Australian,* 11 Jan. 1999.

[54] Sonni Efron, 'Defender of Japan's War Past', *Los Angeles Times,* 9 May 1997.

[55] Having been criticised extensively in the past for their censorship activities, education officials are now the butt of attacks for the more accurate representation of Japanese history in school texts, including in an extensively read manga comic in which Yoshinori Kobayashi popularises Fujioka's ideas.

[56] Cited in Kibata, 'Japan's Search for Identity in Asia', p. 7.

The problem with this argument, as his Japanese critics point out, is that it is based on a process of excluding, concealing and forgetting as well as one of remembering, and what Japan excludes in particular are its past relations with its neighbours. This is an essential component of identity but Japan's perception of its identity has not involved a close relationship with Asian neighbours in the postwar years in part because until the 1970s at least, its international efforts were largely subordinated to US policy, and in part because its failure to come to terms with its history kept it apart in any case.

Nevertheless, the level of argument by the nationalists is now more sophisticated, extending beyond the simple denial of difficult to deny events in defence of Japan's wartime role. This attempt at a more positive interpretation encourages the outspoken provocative comments by leading Japanese that in turn places the subject on China's agenda from time to time.

Yet the trend in Japan is toward a position more acceptable to China although for many observers in both Japan and in China the pace is slow. As a 1992 editorial in Japan put it:

Although Japanese textbooks are making more open and honest references to our outrages as a result of prodding from China and South Korea, teaching fragmentary facts of the past does not amount to facing up to history.[57]

Disagreements between Japan and China over public presentation of war history continue at the political level and among scholars as to what the unfortunate 1930s really represent. There remain genuine and substantial differences of view about the events of the period and the motivations involved. Nevertheless, active collaboration between Chinese and Japanese academics, journalists, and others in many fields shows a growing awareness that recent history should be scrutinised by both sides in a search for understanding, based on joint, and not simply individual research efforts. Particularly significant have been joint projects examining the modern history of Sino-Japanese relations. Historians from both countries have organised symposia on the war, undertaken research into the 'rape of Nanking', and translated each other's work.[58]

While critics within Japan of the Japanese government's position remain active, the war issue is likely to continue as an irritant to

---

[57] Editorial, *Mainichi Shimbun*, 16 Aug. 1992 (NDB).
[58] Akira Iriye, *China and Japan in the Global Setting*, Cambridge, MA: Harvard University Press, 1992, p. 133.

governmental relations given the increased conservatism in Japanese politics. A Japanese magazine referred to Japan fighting – and losing – a spiritual battle to rid itself of its militaristic mentality.[59] Yet other views tend towards greater optimism. One Chinese analyst argued that public opinion in Japan now had a basically clear (and correct) understanding of the war.[60] A similar view was expressed by Japan's foreign minister in 1998.[61] On the other hand, it could be argued that attitudes of the two countries will remain in conflict since Japan, for reasons of identity, wants to forget while China wants to remember. The conflict of these two attitudes poses a significant obstacle to the stable, close, and enduring relationship based on trust and friendship that is officially advocated in Beijing.

There is some basis for seeing different cultural responses to the history. Allen Whiting referred to the professed proclivity of the Japanese to live in the present with little interest in the past, particularly if it reflects unfavourably on the nation.[62] A similar view was expressed after Jiang's 1998 visit by Japanese Foreign Minister Komura who explained the lack of a written apology for Japan's war crime atrocities in China by reference to a Japanese cultural tradition of letting bygones be bygones.[63] Irrespective of any such cultural difference, and it is not clear that it applies equally in Japan to Hiroshima, it is not hard to understand why the Japanese government would wish to forget.

A question remains, however, why the Chinese government wants to remember and, in remembering, to obtain a formal apology from Japan. It may in part stem from a cultural tradition of looking back at the history. Even so, an obvious underlying domestic political basis is that there are still many in China who were victims of the Japanese occupation with unhappy memories of that period, and these include Jiang Zemin and some of his colleagues. Chinese leaders in their 60s and 70s would have childhood memories of the most bitter period of the war, and are therefore likely to be less forgiving of Japan than younger Chinese with little direct experience

[59] *Senkai* quoted in the *China Daily,* 5 Sep. 1996, p. 4.

[60] See, for example, Liu Jiangyong in Greg Austin, 'Japan and China in the Asia Pacific Region – The Southeast Asia Dimension', *A Conference Report,* Australia-Japan Research Centre, Canberra, ACT, 1997, p. 2.

[61] Masahako Komura said that 'ordinary Japanese who are ideologically neither on the right nor left all feel they were wrong'. Agence France-Presse, 21 Dec. 1998.

[62] Allen Whiting, *China Eyes Japan,* p. 187.

[63] Agence France-Presse, Tokyo, 21 Dec. 1998.

of the war, or even than older Chinese, like former Prime Minister Zhou Enlai, who had known a kinder, more inspirational Japan. For those affected by the events of the past an apology is a recognition of their hurt and a prerequisite step towards reconciliation.

Consequently, within China, as in Japan, the domestic political pressures are substantial. Hu Yaobang, the political leader most closely identified with Japan fever in the mid-1980s, was deposed from his post as Secretary General of the Chinese Communist Party over many issues, but an important one may have been his desire to make rapid breakthroughs in the relationship with Japan. As Hu pointed out in 1985, party cadres who joined during the anti-Japanese war from 1937 to 1945 formed the backbone of leading bodies at the central, provincial and municipality levels at that time, and they were therefore less enthusiastic than he was about the relationship.[64]

While China's leaders have generally tried to control expressions of anti-Japanese feelings, it has not always found this totally feasible. For example, in March 1994, Shanghai-based dissident Bao Ge accused the Chinese Government of having violated the constitution and acting against the wishes of its people when it renounced the right to war reparations in the 1972 joint statement on normalisation of relations.[65] Bao, who has been jailed several times for his stand on war reparations and democratisation, also called for Japan to make an apology as well as provide reparations on the eve of Prime Minister Hosokawa's visit to China on 1994. Bao was detained for the duration of Hosokawa's visit to Shanghai. A private group called the Preparatory Committee for Japanese War Reparations, which has supported Bao's work, enjoys some personal support in the Chinese leadership. This group, like Bao Ge, accuses the Chinese government of violating the constitution and acting against the wishes of its people in renouncing war reparations in 1972.

Yet in itself all this may not be a sufficient explanation. The experience makes clear that an intensity of feeling exists that will emerge when the occasion warrants or when it is called upon. Experience

[64] *Ming Pao* (Hong Kong), 6 Dec. 1985.

[65] *South China Morning Post*, 17 Mar. 1994, p. 11 (FBIS-CHI-94-053). In Nanjing (Nanking) in Dec. 1994, on the 57th anniversary of the massacre, about 1,000 provincial level officials who were veterans of the massacre or soldiers during the war took part in ceremonies to commemorate the event. At the same time, an international conference was held in San Francisco for the same purpose, and many participants called on Japan to atone more appropriately.

also shows, however, that generally the authorities can, and have been willing to, dampen any such surge of anti-Japanese feelings. Nevertheless, China's leaders question whether Japan has really changed its basic view of the war and the militaristic instincts that underpinned them. This it sees reflected in Japan's failure as a country, a government and a society to be appropriately contrite for the wars of aggression against many communities in Asia. Underlying this is a concern that while the country rapidly became pacifist at the end of the Second World War, such a rapidity of change from a militarist society to a pacifist society could conceivably as quickly be reversed. Given the history, there is a deep-seated uncertainty in China about the ability of the Japanese to control their military forces, an uncertainty shared with a substantial body of Japanese opinion. For this reason, fears of a resurgent Japanese nationalism and rise of militarism remain in China, and are accentuated in particular by what they judge to be Japan's closer military relations with the United States.

Nevertheless, it is not clear how far, in the absence of provocation, China would use the history card. The difference in the two governing systems complicates a judgement. Given the underlying antipathies among the Chinese, it is largely a question of the Chinese government, rather than stirring domestic anti-Japanese responses, containing those responses except when it finds it convenient not to do so. It seemed to relax such constraints at the time of the fiftieth anniversary of the end of the war, reflecting a somewhat contradictory set of objectives for China. Instead of trying primarily to subordinate the war issue to the goal of China-Japan cooperation at that time, Chinese leaders undertook a widespread program of education about the war in order to revive patriotism to counteract the declining political authority of the Communist Party and declining public order. In viewing the balance between the propaganda value for domestic purposes of reminders of how the Communist Party had led the war against the cruel Japanese army on the one hand, and on the other the need not to offend China's principal aid donor too much, China clearly came down on the side of its domestic objectives.

As we noted earlier, on balance, the Chinese government tries to limit public demonstrations of anti-Japanese feeling. It tried to tone down a civil campaign asking the Japanese for an apology at the time of the sixtieth anniversary of the Nanjing massacre.[66] Similarly, in the

[66] *Hong Kong Standard*, 13 Dec. 1997.

dispute between China and Japan over the Senkakus, it restrained street demonstrations, in part because of the importance of the economic links with Jaipur although also because nationalist demonstrations can often turn into criticism of the Chinese government.

The divisions on the question of Japan's war history apply more widely than simply to China. Japan has been seeking to come to terms with other countries that were its wartime victims. Apparently, at government to government levels at least, the history issue has been put to rest with South Korea, which until recently had shared with China its feelings of the inadequacy of the Japanese position on its colonial and wartime history.

From China's viewpoint, the question arises why Japan can give a written apology to South Korea and not China. Japan says that Korea was a colony and therefore the issues are different. Moreover, an arrangement was accepted that this would finally settle the matter and it would not be raised again. Arrangements for Korea to lift restrictions on cultural imports, such as films and television programs, from Japan were also part of the deal. Whether an apology that is simply part of a deal in the hope of taking it off the official agenda will hold for the Korean public is unclear. How far it involves moral judgements is open to question and it may not represent an effective internalisation of any sense of guilt. Whether such a deal in the case of China would meet its needs is similarly questionable.

The occasional manipulation, perceived or real, of war issues for politically expedient purposes in domestic politics or bilateral relations has further complicated any resolution of the issue and undermined efforts at reconciliation and bridge-building. Just as, for the Chinese, the history issue rises in importance whenever a Japanese leader or media personality downplays the issue, in Japan domestic divisions intensify when, often on politically opportune occasions, or as coded references to other points of difference, China protests against them.

In looking at where this process might go in the future, it is likely that in spite of the efforts of the two governments to subordinate memories of the war to the broader diplomatic goal of peaceful cooperation, Japan's invasion of China will continue to thwart the development of any real intimacy in government to government relations for some time to come. Regardless of a Diet resolution, the Murayama Statement and the various personal apologies by the Japanese emperor and individual prime ministers from Prime Minister

Hosokawa onwards, some senior Japanese political, business and community leaders remain unwilling to 'concede' to China. China is clearly not yet satisfied with the Japanese government's determination in handling this matter. It may only be when the Japanese government can show consistency and sustained leadership on this issue that, as one Chinese analyst observed: 'A full stop can be put to the past.'[67]

Yet the problem arises on both sides of the relationship. Given that the Japanese as a whole have not internalised feelings of guilt for their military role in China during the Fifteen Year War, the continuing refusal of many in Japan to accept the moral judgement China wants means that the issue will not die lightly. This is also true given that the bulk of Chinese people have not internalised the Chinese government's hopes of moving on from the past. As one Chinese scholar put it:

Poor innocent Chinese leadership, they believe in harbouring and nurturing the friendship of Japanese at the expense of the Chinese ordinaries. They want to show that they were (and they are still doing it) the generous host. A typical chauvinism attitude. I hope the new generation among Chinese leadership can shake off this kind of stupid style.[68]

Nevertheless, there are some positive signs. Despite the difficulties over history in the 1998 Jiang-Obuchi meeting in Tokyo, these did not recur in the 1999 Obuchi visit to Beijing. China seemed keen to downplay the issue and to put a favourable interpretation on the visit's outcome and Obuchi wanted to be constructive without offering further concessions on the issue. According to a Xinhua report, in commenting on the issue of history, Zhu Rongji said of the Obuchi visit that 'For the first time, the Japanese Government acknowledged its aggression against China and expressed its remorse and apology.'[69] While not an especially accurate gloss, if sustained elsewhere in the leadership it could be a helpful step in reducing the two countries concerns about their histories. In 2000 the Japanese government responded to a planned rally on the Nanjing massacre by disassociating Japanese authorities from it. A Japanese official

---

[67] *Tangtai* (Hong Kong), no. 25, 15 Apr. 1993, pp. 90, 91 (FBIS-CHI-93-084, 4 May 1993).

[68] Tomoyuki Kojima, *Nikkei Weekly*, 19 Oct. 1992, p. 7.

[69] Beijing: Xinhua Domestic (and English) Service, in FBIS-CHI-1999-0709, 12 July 1999.

reportedly told a Xinhua correspondent that Japan accepted the fact of the Nanjing incident and reaffirmed Prime Minister Murayama's 1994 statement on Japan's war history.[70]

If leaders in the two countries wish in the future, as often in the past, to put their view of their nation's interests ahead of public responses to the history issue, to do so will require greater political persuasiveness than before. In both countries, the governments are increasingly obliged to be sensitive to public opinion. In recent decades, the history issue has been important in the domestic politics of both and, when the almost inevitable periodic tensions in such an interdependent relationship have occurred, has been an important part of the ritualistic outward manifestation of those tensions.[71] In each country, history is not the only determinant of public images of and attitudes toward the other, but it is an important one. Yet in the past the two governments have generally not let history dominate the relationship or their decisions. Each government's response to the other will, nevertheless, be constrained by developments in the broader aspects of public opinion in the two countries. Public opinion is, however, not immune to persuasion nor to manipulation. The question is whether in both countries the domestic political aspects will be as readily managed in favour of longer term national interests in the future as in the past.

Public opinion

When bilateral relations were normalised in 1972, there was a large reservoir of goodwill in Japan toward China. Much of this has continued although it is seemingly declining. The MP elected as chairman of the Dietmen's League for Japan-China Friendship in November 1993 had visited China more than twenty times. Former Prime Minister Hosokawa, on the eve of his departure for China, reported that his wife had visited China nearly ten times, and that his daughter was touring Shanghai as he spoke.[72] Foreign Minister Hata reported in January 1994 that he visited China every two or three

[70] *Daily Yomiuri*, 19 Jan. 2000; *People's Daily*, 20 Jan. 2000; *People's Daily*, 24 Jan. 2000.

[71] Caroline Rose' study of the text book crisis emphasises the ritualistic nature of the history issue in China-Japan relations, largely responding to, rather than causing, major relationship difficulties. Rose, *Interpreting History in Sino-Japanese Relations*.

[72] *Xinhua*, 18 Mar. 1994, in FBIS-CHI-94-054, 21 Mar. 994, p. 10.

years, having first visited in 1973.[73] By the mid-1990s, Japanese tourists and business travelers outnumbered any other foreign nationality in China, coming ahead of South Korea and the United States.[74] This is a dramatic turn-around from a decade earlier when Japanese tourists were not so common and Japanese businessmen were less visible than their US counterparts.

However, there is a considerable awareness in Japan of the gulf that still divides the people of the two countries. As an editorial put it in 1992 writing in support of the emperor's visit:

> Every thinking Japanese has long believed that despite normalisation of ties twentieth years ago, this nation will have to take a step of historic significance to help further encourage the Chinese people, not the government, to open up their hearts and minds to us.[75]

By 1996, Japanese sympathy toward China had declined considerably from previous levels. In a regular prime minister's office poll, only 49% of respondents in 1996 had recorded warm feelings for China compared with 79% in 1980. By 1997, this figure was down to 46%.[76] In the 1996 poll, there was a sharp rise (12%) over the two years in those seeing Japan-China relation as in bad shape (a record 46%).[77] In a survey over two years in the mid-early 1990s, Japanese travelers surveyed did not include China in the top ten of countries or regions they regarded as friendly.[78] No Chinese city was included in the top ten that Japanese like to visit.[79] These results were repeated in a 1997 survey.[80] But in 1997, China (with 633,000 visits) was for Japanese the fourth most frequented tourism destination, after the United States (4.7 million visits), South Korea (1.37 million visits), and

[73] *Xinhua*, 7 Jan. 1994, in FBIS-CHI-94-006, 10 Jan. 1994, p. 7.

[74] Mark O'Neill, 'China: China Sees More Tourist from Asia', Reuters, 17 Jan. 1995, citing official Chinese statistics of the China International Travel Service which handles most foreign visitors entering China. No figures were given for the number of Japanese visitors.

[75] *Japan Times*, 1 Sep. 1992 (NDB): 'Meaning of Historic China Visit'.

[76] Public Relations Office, Prime Minister's Office, 'Opinion Survey on Foreign Affairs', Jan. 1998, accessed on on 12 July 1999.

[77] *Kyodo*, 21 Jan. 1996, in FBIS-EAS-96-014, 21 Jan. 1996.

[78] Japan Information Network, 'On Japanese Overseas Air Travellers', Advertising Department of Mainichi Newspapers, 1994 (electronic source).

[79] Japan Information Network, 'Cities that Japanese desire to Visit Sometime, as of 1994', Rikuruto KK, Tokyo, 1994 (electronic source).

[80] Japan Information Network, 'On Japanese Overseas Air Travellers', Advertising Department of Mainichi Newspapers, 1997 (electronic source).

Hong Kong (707,00 visits).[81] For Japanese tourists travelling in mid-1998, China was rated highly as a country that they regard as 'cultural or historical', second after Italy.[82]

In China, substantial resentment persists toward Japan and this reached quite high levels in 1995 and has stayed high. That year, the *China Youth Daily* published results of a survey which instantly became famous in the China-watching community because it recorded high levels of dissatisfaction with US policies toward China – 57% of respondents regarded the United States as the most unfriendly country toward China.[83] The same survey however carried some salutary lessons for Japan since its results on Chinese youth attitudes toward Japan were a little more out of step with government stated aims at the time, although presumably affected by the fifty-year anniversary propaganda. Japan was recorded as the 'most disliked country' after the USA. More interestingly, 22% of respondents selected Japan as the country toward which they had the 'most unpleasant feelings', only second after the United States. The results in the youth survey of graduate students, a group who may be considered to have 'informed opinion', were even more interesting. Among this group,

---

[81] Japan Information Network, 'Top 10 Overseas Travel Destinations, as of 1994', *Annual Report of Statistics on Legal Migrants*, Judicial and Research Dept, Ministry of Justice, Tokyo, 1994 (electronic source).

[82] Advertising Department of the Mainichi Newspapers, 'On Japanese Overseas Air Travelers', Dec. 1998.

[83] Wang Xiaodong and Wu Luping (edited by Ma Mingjie), *Zhongguo qingnian bao* [China Youth Daily], 21 Jan. 1995, FBIS-CHI-95-050, 21 Jan. 1995. The survey recorded that only 31% of those surveyed actually nominated the United States as the country most disliked. The figure of 57% has been erroneously reported in other Chinese sources. For example, one source reported it as 87%. See Guan Fu, *Zhongguo qingnian* [China Youth], 22 July 1995, p. 1 (FBIS-CHI-95-184, 22 Aug. 1995). The Chinese propaganda officials who published it in order to maximise the perception of damage to US-China relations interpreted this survey in a highly politicised fashion. (The one result the analysts of the poll had most difficulty coming to terms with was the result recorded that President Clinton was the sixth most admired Chinese or foreign leader, after four Chinese leaders and Nelson Mandela.) This result is only evident after a close reading of the reporting of the survey. The first four were Mao Zedong (40%); Zhou Enlai (27%); Deng Xiaoping (10%); Nelson Mandela (4.5%). The fifth was not identified, but may have been Hu Yaobang. Bill Clinton received 1.9%. Given that most respondents in this survey had identified economic might, social stability and living standards as the criteria by which a country should be judged, it is fairly clear that had the question been put to the respondents about which government they disliked most and if the Chinese government had been included, then the latter might have been even more disliked than the US and Japanese governments.

Japan took the place of the United States as the country for which the respondents had the 'most unpleasant feelings' – Japan with 46% and the United States with 29%.[84] And the war with Japan will not go away. Some 97% of respondents 'still felt indignation' and 99% remembered very well the suffering of the Chinese people in the Japanese occupation and war. An upsurge in anti-Japanese sentiment was predictable in 1995, which was the fiftieth anniversary of the end of the war, given the intensity of official and unofficial reminiscences and memorial events.[85] But the fact remains that more voices are now being raised within China for the government of Japan to do much more to atone for its actions during the war. A late 1996 poll by the *China Youth Daily* reported similarly high levels of youth disaffection with Japan.[86] A news report of late 1998 reported a later Youth League opinion survey in China that showed an 82% level of opposition to China's policies toward Japan.[87]

The Chinese government has worked hard to suppress dissent within China against its polices toward Japan but not always successfully. For example, although it had opposed claims by Chinese individuals for reparations or damages from Japan, it was forced in 1992 under pressure from a proposed bill in the National People's Congress to stand aside to allow private citizens to pursue such claims through the Japanese courts. China's arrest of about 100 demonstrators in front of the Japanese embassy in Beijing in March 1994 provoked a call from a group of 500 Chinese intellectuals for their release and the release of a leader of the compensation movement in China, Tong Zeng.[88] The release of previously hidden information about Japan's wartime activities serves to fuel the issue. For example, in November 1994, a Chinese historian claimed that up to 20,000 refugees died in biological warfare experiments conducted by Japan in China.[89] By the late 1990s, the Chinese government was coming under increasing pressure to be firmer with Japan on a range of issues, including Taiwan, interpretation of history, the territorial dispute

---

[84] Ibid.

[85] Chinese film studios used the fiftieth anniversary of the end of the war as an opportunity to make a number of films about the war, including the Nanking massacre.

[86] *Zhongguo qingnian bao*, 18 Mar. 1997, p. 1 (FBIS-CHI-97-094, 18 Mar. 1997).

[87] *Cheng ming*, no. 253, 1 Nov. 1998, p. 30 (FBIS-CHI-98-307, 3 Nov. 1998).

[88] *Kyodo*, 21 Mar. 1994, carried in FBIS-CHI-94-054, 21 Mar. 1994, p. 23. The demonstrators had been released by the time the open letter was published.

[89] Cited in Kevin Rafferty, *The Guardian*, carried in Reuters, 24 Nov. 1994.

over the Senkaku Islands, and unsettled maritime resource jurisdiction in the East China Sea. In November 1998, a Chinese dissident, Qin Yongmin, criticised President Jiang for his concessions to Japan which 'undermine the national dignity of China'.[90]

In China, it would appear that older officers in the PLA have a particularly strong view of the war record of Japan and its contemporary relevance. Apart from evidence obtained in personal interviews, this is apparent from time to time in military related press. In 1994, a magazine linked to the PLA Navy claimed that Japan's defence forces were no longer defensively oriented and that Japan had embarked on a 'new militaristic path'.[91] This type of propaganda could be dismissed as formulaic, but as a Japanese News Agency suggested in reporting the article, it indicated that the Chinese military leadership still harbours strong doubts about Japan's intentions.

This view might be expected in military academies. For example, in August 1994, on the 100th anniversary of the outbreak of the 1894–5 Sino-Japanese war, two sections of the PLA sponsored a symposium on the conflict. In his speech to the symposium, the vice-chairman of the Central Military Commission, Liu Huaqing, said the war set off a new round of imperialist carve-ups of China and hastened the process of making China a semi-colony. He went on to say: 'Marking the Sino-Japanese War of 1894 is meant to remind people of our past national humiliation and to learn from historical experiences and lessons.'[92] A large group of PLA leaders reportedly petitioned the Politburo for a review of China's relations with Japan (and the USA) citing Japan's position on Taiwan, war issues, and the territorial dispute with Japan.[93]

Yet the general mood was quite measured for most of the 1990s. An article in the *People's Daily* in August 1994 decried a recent visit to the Yasukuni shrine by serving cabinet ministers and what it said were other signs of resurgent militarism in Japan, but it concluded with the observation that 'only a handful of people' cling to these ideas which 'have found very little support among the people or within the government'.[94] A 1997 article citing the views of a Japan

[90] Agence France-Presse, 26 Nov. 1998.

[91] *Kyodo*, 2 June 1994, carried in FBIS-CHI-94-106, 2 June 1994, pp. 6–7.

[92] *Xinhua*, 18 Aug. 1994, carried in FBIS-CHI-94-162, 22 Aug. 1994, p. 5.

[93] Lo Ping, *Cheng ming*, no. 254, 1 Dec. 1998 (FBIS-CHI-98-342, 8 Dec. 1998.)

[94] Gu Ping, *Renmin Ribao*, 18 Aug. 1994, p. 6 (FBIS-CHI-94-163, 23 Aug. 1994, p. 3).

specialist noted that 'we will not mistakenly assume that the whole of Japan is practising militarism simply because of the words and deeds of the minority of right-wingers'.[95] This appears to be the assessment of the Chinese government, as the Jiang comment in Tokyo noted earlier seems to indicate.

Place of cultural diplomacy and cultural relations

In the Japan-China relationship, cultural diplomacy has been a fairly narrow, relatively uninspired one-way street – from the government of Japan toward China.[96] Funding has been relatively low, activities have been confined largely to traditional culture, and impacts in China have been minimal. Beyond the efforts by governments to use cultural relations as a tool of diplomacy, however, the interaction between the two societies has developed on a broader and more productive front. Yet even here, there have been substantial constraints. Both Japan and China attach considerable importance in their public posturing to the need to enhance understanding and increase interaction between their two societies, but until the late 1990s had not given supportive activity any sustained government attention. In China's case, efforts to make a dramatic advance in contacts fell foul of domestic politics, as we discuss below.

For its part, the Japanese government has accepted that an important part of its cultural diplomacy toward other East Asian countries, and an important part of their societies' interactions, must be directed toward overcoming the bitter legacy of invasion, military occupation and war.[97] In Japan, cultural diplomacy is seen as having become more important since the end of the Cold War because fading ideological confrontations have been replaced by 'differences in ways of thinking or in social systems arising from ethnic, religious and historical differences'. The Japanese government is also looking to flesh out the country's image as something more than an economic powerhouse, an image which the government feels is too narrow and not representative of the country or its aspirations. Japan has also

---

[95] Li Zhanjun, *Guangming ribao*, 17 July 1997, p. 2 (FBIS-CHI-97-220, 8 Aug. 1997).

[96] For a comprehensive assessment of this subject, see Greg Austin and Diana Betzler, 'Gulfs in Sino-Japanese Relations: An Evaluation of Japan's Cultural Diplomacy toward China', *Journal of East Asian Affairs*, summer/fall 1997, pp. 570–613.

[97] Foreign Ministry of Japan, *Diplomatic Blue Book 1995* (electronic version).

identified the emergence of a global or universal culture premised on common values of humanity and environmental protection as an important new target of its cultural diplomacy. After 1995, the goals of Japan's cultural diplomacy had become quite complex, involving not only the dissemination of knowledge about Japan but also the dissemination of knowledge inside Japan about foreign cultures as part of the country's goal of internationalisation.[98]

Although cultural diplomacy by Japan toward China became significant in 1972 when the two countries normalised diplomatic relations, it was not until 1984 that a substantial program emerged, with the support of the Secretary General of the Chinese Communist Party, Hu Yaobang. This allowed the visit of a delegation of 3,000 Japanese young people to China for a fifteen-day gathering.[99] The assembly was organised by the newly created Twenty-first Century Committee for Sino-Japanese Friendship, with the intention of developing mutual understanding between youth of both countries with regard to the future.[100] Japan in return invited 300 young people in 1985.[101]

Cultural diplomacy on the scale foreshadowed in 1985 lost momentum in the wake of the resignation of Hu Yaobang in 1987 and the freeze in relations after the Tiananmen Square incident in 1989. An opportunity to restore momentum to cultural diplomacy and exchanges came in 1992, just several months after the G-7 had agreed in 1991 to restore links with China – the twentieth anniversary of the normalisation of diplomatic relations between the two countries. The Japan Foundation participated in many events that year[102] but the most important single event of 1992, both from the point of view of bilateral relations and from the perspective of cultural diplomacy, was the emperor's visit to China, the first ever such visit.

[98] Foreign Ministry of Japan, *Diplomatic Blue Book, 1995* (source: *Japan's Foreign Policy on CD-ROM*).

[99] *China Pictorial*, Dec. 1984, p. 40

[100] 'Sino-Japanese Friendship looks to the Future', *Beijing Review*, 1984, vol. 27, no. 39, p. 16.

[101] Allen S. Whiting, *China Eyes Japan* (Berkeley: University of California Press, 1989), p. 150.

[102] *The Japan Foundation, Overview of Programs for Fiscal 1991*, p. 91. Exhibitions of: contemporary Nihonga, contemporary Japanese posters; performance tours of: Shiki Theatrical Company's musical *Rikoran*, Peking Opera's *Sakamoto Ryoma*, Southern All Stars, Matsuyama Ballet Company, and Japanese classical (traditional) music; and a celebratory film festival.

Notwithstanding enthusiastic rhetoric about deepening mutual understanding that surrounds such Japan–China events, the high profile of such publicity at the time does not say much about the overall priority accorded China in Japanese cultural diplomacy. While cultural diplomacy directed to China represents the second largest amount spent on individual countries in Japan's cultural diplomacy spending, it seems not to attract a level of effort or a focussing of that effort commensurate with the need to redress the sad history between the two countries. The numbers travelling between Japan and China on Japan Foundation programs remain small.[103] There were more funded exchange visitors between Japan and Southeast Asia in 1996 than between Japan and East Asia and expenditure by the Foundation on Southeast Asia was double that for East Asia for most of the decade.[104] The Japanese government views China merely as one of several important countries in the Asia region, and not one to be singled out as the recipient of a disproportionate amount of cultural capital or effort.

Nevertheless, often quite independently of government direction, the volume and variety of cultural ties between China and Japan has steadily increased,[105] an outcome which both governments hope will bring a generational change in how people perceive each other's country. Both the Japanese and Chinese governments see Japan-trained Chinese students as well placed to progress to influential positions in government and economic planning, not least because many of them are dependents of people with high level influence in the Chinese government.

[103] See Austin and Betzler, 'Gulfs in Sino-Japanese Relations'.

[104] *The Japan Foundation Annual Report 1997*, pp. 156–7, 160.

[105] Numerous organisations have been formed to promote Sino-Japanese friendship. In China, these include the China-Japan Friendship Association, Japan-China Science Technology and Cultural Centre, Twenty-first Century Committee for China-Japan Friendship, Annual Conference on Sino-Japanese Economic Coordination, China-Japan Youth Exchange Centre, Chinese-Japanese Non-Governmental Personages Meeting. In Japan, these include the Japan-China Friendship Association, Japan-China Society, Japan-China Cultural Exchange Association, Japan-China Youth Exchange Association, Diet Members' League for Sino-Japanese Friendship, Japanese Chinese Friendship Hall, Japan-China Association of Economy and Trade, Japan-China Economic Exchange Association, Japan-China Science Technology and Cultural Centre, Tokyo Japan-China Friendship Association, Tokyo Prefectural Sino-Japanese Friendship Association, Fukuoka Prefectural Sino-Japanese Friendship Association (twinned with China's Jiangsu province), and the 'China Tour'.

By the early 1990s, Chinese students in Japan numbered 20,000, and the number remained around that level through the decade, although beginning to decline from a 1995 peak of 24,000.[106] Although mostly not on government sponsored programs – most government sponsored students coming from elsewhere – Chinese students in Japan were the biggest foreign national group; by 1997, they constituted 44% of the total foreign student population, compared with 26% in 1987.[107] There is also a sizable and increasingly visibly contingent of young Chinese scholars in Japan, probably about 5,000 in 1998, and twelve awardwinning books have been written in Japanese by Chinese scholars.[108]

For Japanese students it has become increasingly popular to go to China. Between 1983 and 1997, the number of Japanese students[109] in China each year grew from 349 to 15,284.[110] The 1997 figure for China compared with 46,616 in Europe, and 83,154 in the United States. The United States enjoyed a bigger growth rate in popularity for Japanese students in the period 1983 to 1997 than China, while Europe enjoyed a lower growth rate than China.

Beyond the student or academic populations, the picture is a little more one-sided. In 1997, there were 252,164 Chinese residents in Japan, making them the biggest nationality after Korean (North and South) living in Japan.[111] The Chinese community was six times higher than the US community in Japan in the same year. By contrast, only 46,821 Japanese resided in China in 1997, compared with 284,006 Japanese in the United States. More Japanese lived in Brazil and Britain in 1997 than in China, and only 20,000 more Japanese lived in China in 1997 than in Australia.

Sino-Japanese cultural ties have increased substantially in the last

---

[106] Duan Yue Zhong, 'China in Japan', *Look Japan*, Oct. 1998, p. 5. The figure for 1997 was 22,323.

[107] Foreign Ministry of Japan, *Diplomatic Blue Book, 1995* (source: *Japan's Foreign Policy on CD-ROM*).

[108] Duan, 'China in Japan', p. 7.

[109] People studying in China for educational or training purposes or to learn technical skills.

[110] Japan. Ministry of Justice. Judicial System and Research Department, 'Annual Report of Statistics on Legal Migrants', 30 June 1998, http//:jin.jcic.or.jp/stat/stats/16EDU62.html.

[111] Japan. Ministry of Foreign Affairs. Consular and Migration Affairs Department, 'Annual Report of Statistics on Japanese Nationals Overseas', Nov. 1998, http//:jin.jcic.or.jp/stat/stats/21MIG33html.

few years, although the level and extent of these appear often to support commercial ties rather than reflecting a 'natural' expansion of cultural ties, of the sort both Japanese and Chinese society experience with the United States. In the last decade, Chinese society became 'more porous and open to the outside world', with greater freedom of expression tolerated, especially in large cities close to the coast, such as Guangzhou, Shanghai and Beijing. Japanese movies and TV series, especially cartoons, are popular in China. People in South China receive Hong Kong TV, which shows many Japanese movies and TV series. (In Japan, some Chinese movies have become famous, and there are 'cult cliques' for some Chinese comedy movies.) This is all part of a generational change in how people in both countries show interest in and perceive each other.

Japanese of the older generations were fascinated by Chinese culture but younger Japanese show more interest in Western culture and tend to show interest in China more for commercial reasons. Young Chinese people are becoming more interested, however, in Japanese culture. Karaoke, an entertainment from Japan, and comics and video games are popular.[112] Many of these cultural exports, however, are not purely Japanese. Because of the strong influence of Western countries, Japan has taken on the role of a transmitter of Western culture. In the final analysis, young Chinese are more interested in Western culture than in Japanese culture, while many in the older Chinese generations, still remembering the wartime actions of the Japanese, do not want contact with Japan.

Despite these mostly positive developments by the late 1990s, Japanese cultural diplomacy in China had simply been inadequate in the light of the gulfs of sentiment and experience between the two countries. For its part, China had been prepared to go slow on cultural diplomacy. Chinese leaders were prepared to advance economic relations with Japan but seem unwilling to forge more intimate ties. On a visit to Japan in November 1994, Rong Yiren, Vice Premier of China, said: 'China is willing to conduct more cooperation and exchanges in the economic sector . . . to jointly endeavour to promote Sino-Japanese economic cooperation to a new level', having said earlier in the speech that he was satisfied with progress in the cultural field – notwithstanding its extremely low level.[113] This seemed to

[112] Keji Ribao, 'Views on Values Among Youth', *Beijing Review*, 1994, no. 40, 3–9 Oct., p. 27.
[113] *Xinhua*, 1 Nov. 1994, carried in FBIS-CHI-94-054, 21 Mar. 1994, p. 16.

remain the position for some time but eventually the two governments had to acknowledge that there had been a serious slide in popular sympathies within each country toward the other. They concluded therefore that they needed to do more to promote exchanges. The two governments agreed through 1997 and 1998 on a renewed concentration on youth exchanges. China specifically acknowledged the need to overcome negative sentiment toward Japan among its young people demonstrated in opinion polls.[114] In November 1998, Japan and China signed a Youth Exchange Framework Agreement pledging exchanges of 15,000 young people between 1999 and 2003.[115]

The images and attitudes in Japan and China towards each other have quite different starting points. The Japanese viewpoint is one of continuing superiority emerging in part from past indoctrination and in part from their economic and technological achievements; but this is tinged with a sense of guilt about the past. Japan also has, however, a resentful sense of being manipulated, and some fear of a more powerful China that might engage one day in strategic payback for the fifteen years of brutal aggression from 1931 to 1945, even though there is little evident basis for such fears. Chinese self-perceptions take a number of forms: that of victim who sees those under whom it suffered as unwilling to acknowledge responsibility; that of a country once superior to the other yet remaining long the inferior; and that of a country rapidly escaping from economic backwardness but uncomfortable at the prospect of too great an economic dependence on Japan.

From Japan's perspective, China appears either self-serving in its use of history or increasingly assertive politically. Yet China sees insensitivity in Japan's failure to appreciate the external consequences of its actions, past and present. The likelihood of rapid change in these underlying feelings is small and the potential for sustained differences among both populations remains. As Allen Whiting wrote of the Japan-China relationship in the late 1980s, the 'mutually avowed goal of friendship in the twenty-first century reflects rhetoric, not reality, at the level of state-to state interaction. Governments pursue national interests, as they perceive them, free of those bonds and obligations

---

[114] *Gaiko Forum*, 30 Sep. 1997, pp. 24-35 (FBIS-EAS-97-288, 16 Oct. 1997).
[115] Japan-China Joint Communiqué, Xinhua, 26 Nov. 1998.

inherent in personal friendships'.[116] Friendship between two countries is not a precondition for effective bilateral relations, and at least
at the general level, mutual perceptions do support a business-like
approach to relations for various pragmatic reasons. Yet a degree of
warmth in a relationship makes pursuing bilateral relations easier for
the governments involved and enables small disputes to be handled
without becoming a test of the whole relationship.

For most Japanese and Chinese citizens, the other country is not
seen as a positive or even powerful spiritual influence determining
the main directions of public policy. Therefore, the main impulses for
official interaction between the two countries remain outside what
might be called the popular imagination. The impulses for closer official ties lie very squarely within the government sector. In practice,
the policies between the two countries are likely to be driven primarily by practical interests. To the extent that government actions are
influenced by public opinion, however, the influence is mostly a
negative or limiting one.

Likely trends in domestic politics and social development in both
Japan and China do not encourage expectations for a rapid change
in this situation in a positive direction. The Tiananmen Square incident and China's testing of nuclear weapons and its missile diplomacy
across the Taiwan Straits, reinforced negative views of China in Japan,
and Japan's periodic imposition of political restrictions is likely to
sustain those views for some time. This then will have a response effect in China stimulating more negative views of Japan. Japan's continuous nationalist propaganda, propagated by a small but publicly
articulate minority, and its increased security links with the United
States, given the volatile US relationship with China, intensify the
lack of trust of Japan in China.

There is a wide variety of public perceptions and a growing
sophisticated public commentary in Japan and China about the other
but the sophisticated commentary has yet to provide any political
constituency for significantly closer relations between the two countries. Attitudes in each country toward the other remain heavily
influenced by stereotypes. Moreover, while the changing political
system in China has reduced the ideological differences in the relationship, the difference in governmental systems continues to be
misunderstood on either side and, as a result, the expectations of both
are unrealistic.

[116] Whiting, *China Eyes Japan*, p. 181.

In the five- to ten-year time frame, as for the short term, there is little likelihood that there will be any sizeable domestic constituency in Japan or China for particularly warmer political relations between the two countries. One obstacle that has increased in significance is that many in Japan believe that Japan has apologised enough for the war; Japan will be increasingly resistant to Chinese demands to do more should they persist. Another obstacle is the lack of firm leadership in either country for a new approach in domestic politics to the war issue. Yet another obstacle for the Chinese exists on the Japanese side. Japan is now the only country in the region where a foreign government is host to a substantial military presence that has a direct unbroken link to the end of war military occupation by the victor. This has implications for its identity – its sovereignty and its national goals or purposes. It tells much about where Japan in particular fits in the region and the global order.[117] Despite feelings of subordination toward the United States, and although Japan may have rebuilt itself after the war, it has so far failed to break the psychological link of its identity arising from the US occupation and subsequent alliance.

Given not just the differences of interest between the two countries but the continuing misperceptions and the critical need to provide more than just a fragile underpinning of people to people relationships to buttress what will inevitably be a continuing difficult relationship, one might have expected conscious efforts by the two governments to strengthen and broaden the relationship. Cultural diplomacy, defined broadly, would have seemed a matter of high priority on both sides. In practice, official cultural diplomacy by Japan toward China seems to be a meagre, faltering or misguided effort. Public diplomacy from China to Japan has been negligible by comparison. Yet links between the two societies are growing steadily regardless of persistently negative or indifferent attitudes in one country toward the other. In addition to expanding business links, private friendship organisations, private initiatives, regional governments and universities are now enhancing non-governmental ties. Few obstacles are likely to emerge that would prevent continued growth in such contacts in an expanding range of activities. This does

---

[117] As Ozawa has commented, the region's reluctance to see Japan act independently meant that Japan increasingly needed to act in collaboration with the Unisted States, Ichiro Ozawa, *Blueprint for a New Japan*, Tokyo: Kodansha International, 1994, p. 104.

not mean, however, that in five to ten years either Japan or China will be the country of first call for that small percentage of each population that actively looks outside its borders for intellectual stimulation, entertainment or political inspiration.

Japanese officials, business people and technocrats will have an increasingly powerful influence in China's society through economic interchanges, education and training activities, but the values that will be transmitted through these channels will not vary in significant ways from those transmitted through similar activities by nationals from the United States, Australia, Britain or Germany. Thus, while the numbers of Japanese nationals participating in rejuvenating China's public infrastructure may become greater than those from any other country, this is unlikely to bring about a broad reorientation of Chinese political life toward some distinctly Japanese political model.

Yet, apart from any impact of cultural diplomacy by governments, broadly-based relations between individual components of the two societies can have a longer-term impact. The full social multiplier impact of a cultural relations advance, can, with 'generational change', be expected to be felt after 20–30 years. It is to this time frame that one may have to look for any intensification of trust between the two governments and a greater intimacy between the two societies. The war issue, the Taiwan issue, and the question of differences in domestic political organisation and economic development would have to be ameliorated or attenuated before there is any significant improvement in trust.

The universalising influences of cultural activities not specifically identified as Japanese or Chinese, and the intensification of Chinese economic integration into the world economy, may be more powerful and work more quickly in bringing people of the two societies to a more trusting position. In this respect, the amount of money spent by Japan on cultural diplomacy in China may not turn out to be as significant as the larger effort by Japan to open up its own society and to define its identity more clearly in international rather than national terms.

3

BILATERAL
SECURITY RELATIONS

In the five decades since 1949, security interactions between China and Japan have operated across the spectrum from confrontation to cooperation, with negative interactions often coexisting with more positive ones. In the early post war decades, the balance between these different aspects was unstable, as the Korean War (1950–3) and the 1950s Taiwan Strait crises showed. In more recent times, the balance has had elements of instability, as incidents over the Senkakus and China's missile diplomacy over Taiwan in 1995 and 1996 demonstrated. In the past quarter century, however, this instability has not threatened hostilities between the two countries. The governments of Japan and China have been determined to avoid not only direct military confrontation but also hostile posturing that might lead to a confrontation with each other. In the last decade, this attitude has been complemented by moves toward overt bilateral security cooperation and joint participation in region-wide security initiatives, such as the ASEAN Regional Forum (ARF).

The main question about the security relationship between Japan and China is whether either government will be inclined to abandon the five decades of peace for some pressing military necessity or perceived strategic opportunity. As we saw in Chapter 2, as well as emotional tensions between the two societies, there are continuing causes for disaffection between the two countries. These include the territorial dispute over the Senkaku Islands, suspicions of each other's military policies, and resentments in China over lack of technology transfer, wealth differences, and lack of appropriate Japanese responses to a variety of matters arising from the Second World War.

These irritants are matched by equally powerful insecurities in Japan about the potential size of China and its history of unpredictability. Yet, in spite of important political differences and frequent exploitation of opportunities to needle each other, both governments have displayed a sophisticated appreciation of the costs that a military confrontation would involve. Each government appears confident that the other is not undertaking active military preparations for such a confrontation.

This chapter assesses how in Japan and China the components of security posture – beliefs, dispositions and actions – interact with each other as the two countries enter the new century. We examine first the two most important influences on the bilateral security relationship: the gradual acceptance by both of an effective norm of non-aggression, and the US-Japan security alliance.[1] We then consider other factors and events that influence how each government shapes its strategic policy toward the other. These include trends in perceptions of the other's strategic capacities, and their disputes over specific aspects of strategic policy (maritime issues, testing weapons of mass destruction, and US plans to deploy a theatre missile defence system in East Asia). Finally, we assess the likely impact on mutual perceptions of the increased bilateral security contacts since 1993.

Non-aggression, mutual interest and military power

A defining characteristic of security relations between Japan and China as they enter the twenty-first century is that the international principle of non-aggression, basic to the global order discussed in Chapter 1, has been buttressed by the specific strategic, political and historical circumstances of the two countries.[2] Two enduring political factors contributing to this process have been mutually reinforcing: the US role as a power balancer in East Asia and the strong anti-war norm in Japanese domestic politics. Neither has remained static, but other powerful forces have emerged to reinforce the peace between Japan and China: gradual reinterpretation of the war history

---

[1] Since the following chapter suggests that the dynamics of security interaction between Japan and China have developed largely under the influence of factors apart from Taiwan, the focus on the US-Japan alliance in this chapter is largely on the how it plays out on the broader security perceptions independently of the Taiwan issue.

[2] International law does not prohibit use of force, the principle circumstance in which use of force is sanctioned being self-defence, but it does prohibit launching aggressive war.

to the point where its main significance has become the view that the 'tragedy of the past must not be repeated';[3] China's turning away from a belligerent international posture to one that gives highest priority to domestic economic development; and the consequent entrenchment in Japan-China relations of patterns of bilateral cooperation, dispute resolution and mutual predictability.

Geographic separation by hundreds of miles of sea was physically important in dampening any potential for military conflict between Japan and China for most of the time since 1949. In recent decades, the geography factor has diminished in importance as China now has ballistic missiles capable of delivering a nuclear warhead to Japan. This has provided an underlying level of concern in Japan for some time. So did China's promulgation of its territorial waters law in 1992, and reassertion of its claim to the Diaoyu Islands, while the 1996 ratification of the Law of the Sea by China and Japan, also ratified their overlapping claims in the East China Sea. This seeming assertiveness underscored for successive Japanese governments China's longer term potential to develop conventional military forces able to threaten Japan for the first time in six centuries. Japan has also shown an increased assertiveness in criticising China. These influences on the bilateral security relationship are discussed below.

Mutual trust is still lacking. Both sides assume the other will trust them. Otherwise the repeated statements of reassurance – by China that it will not use nuclear weapons against non-nuclear states, or that it does not intend to be a hegemon; or in Japan's case that its strategic posture will remain defensive and it will not support Taiwan's independence – have limited purpose. Yet Japan lacks trust of China over its nuclear testing and its use of missile diplomacy. China lacks trust of a Japan that can so reinterpret its constitutional provision against a military that it now has the most modern military in Asia and, despite its three non-nuclear principles had nuclear weapons stored for decades on its soil.

Yet, just as China's accession to the Comprehensive Test Ban Treaty (CTBT) has eased Japan's concerns, so Article 9 of Japan's constitution and the three non-nuclear principles, as well as the sometimes breached 1% of GDP ceiling on military expenditure, remain important constraining factors on Japan. While trust will be long in developing, overall most interactions reinforce the determination of

---

[3] Ryosei Kokubun, 'The Delicate Triangle in the Post-Cold War Era: Sino-Japanese Relations and the United States', manuscript, p. 11.

both governments to avoid war at almost any cost; and nothing has yet emerged with sufficient weight to threaten that determination.

Reinterpreting the war: 'Never Again' as a classic no-war principle

The balance among the factors reinforcing the norm of non-aggression between the two countries has changed in the fifty years since the end of the war. The reinterpretation of the historical significance of the 1931–45 Sino-Japanese War is especially important. The previous chapter showed that the war has fed powerful suspicions and animosities. A more positive influence, however, has probably been at least as strong. Both governments have used the war history to entrench progressively an implicit 'no-war' or non-aggression agreement in their relationship. This process began explicitly. On 12 August 1978 the two countries signed a Treaty of Peace and Friendship.[4] The treaty went beyond formally marking of the end of war between Japan and the 'China' it had recognised only since 1972. It included a clause on peaceful resolution of disputes. This commitment, which replays a similar one in the UN Charter, has been interpreted by both governments as a non-aggression principle, providing each signatory with an implicit security guarantee – freedom from threat of attack by the other.[5]

At time of signature, the non-aggression commitment contained in the treaty was not regarded by many as a particularly durable security guarantee. One reason was that many similar treaties between great powers prior to the Second World War, and in previous centuries, have been little more than temporary commitments to be abrogated when geopolitical circumstances or domestic political interests changed: the Soviet Union breached its non-aggression pact with Japan on declaring war on Japan in 1945. Another reason was that China had spent much of the post revolution period before 1978 promoting armed confrontation either against the interests of Japan's major ally, the United States, or against democratic, capitalist systems

---

[4] The treaty entered into force on 23 Oct. 1978.

[5] The commitment to peaceful resolution of disputes could be seen by some as more than a non-aggression pact. A treaty obligation to peaceful resolution of disputes implies an obligation to respond without resort to force even where the other party has not shown good faith through initiation of combat operations (presumably small scale). A simple non-aggression pact would imply no obligation to refrain from use of force if the other party initiated military hostilities of any sort.

as practised in Japan. In 1978, China still maintained large defence forces, a robust military posture, and a high degree of militarisation in an authoritarian society. A large share of Chinese government spending was on the military. Lack of faith in the non-aggression commitment in the 1978 treaty was aggravated by China's unfinished civil war, and reflected in the backing within Japan's ruling party for US support of Taiwan. A confrontation involving armed Chinese fishing boats and Japanese coastguard units near the disputed Senkaku Islands in the East China Sea during the 1978 peace treaty negotiations gave an edge to concerns that the non-aggression commitment was fairly thinly-based.

Thus in 1978 most observers, and probably many officials inside the governments of Japan and China, saw the peace treaty and its commitment to non-aggression as a largely symbolic requirement for a document establishing diplomatic relations between the two countries. Few believed in 1978, however, given such a bitter history and such different social systems, that the non-aggression commitment could become a normative corner-stone for bilateral relations, let alone of international order in the region. Grounds for sustained scepticism were revealed within six months of the signing of the treaty when China invaded Vietnam.

Yet some twenty or so years later, at the end of the 1990s, the principle of peaceful resolution of disputes between Japan and China had acquired considerable normative force.[6] The implicit bilateral security agreement has been strengthened by the emergence of a stronger sense of common interests and mutual dependencies than existed in 1978. That agreement, and the subsequent patterns of conflict

[6] Scholars and government leaders alike disagree on what gives treaty commitments their normative force, but practitioners of international affairs such as government leaders generally place considerable value on a long record of observance, continued rhetorical support for observance, the presence of high diplomatic costs for breach, and the presence of high domestic, economic and social costs for breach. But in this sense, practitioners are not looking for an absolute normative force in principle but a conditional normative effect that can be sustained and nurtured. Most practitioners, while alert to a prospect of breach, believe that the more nurturing or conditioning of a treaty commitment against breach, the higher the prospect of sustained observance. Most practitioners, like scholars, do not have a standard view of how much economic interdependence is enough to entrench a non-aggression treaty, but most accept that sustained, deepening and high levels of economic interdependence are a good buffer against breach of a non-aggression commitment because they substantially raise the costs of aggression between great powers.

avoidance, have been enmeshed in increasingly complex commercial, social, political and strategic interactions. China's reforms since 1978 in particular have facilitated the entrenchment of perceptions in Japan and China that the two governments are increasingly following common rules in their efforts to gain a share of the world's economic potential for the benefit of their societies. China has also come to see security in a broader, more comprehensive, sense and effective power as extending well beyond the military.

China's increasingly predictable and constructive responses to its domestic and international problems strengthened Japan's confidence in dealings with China. More importantly, the two governments have actively promoted the peaceful resolution of disputes as the only feasible foundation of bilateral relations. In China's case, negative propaganda images of Japan have been greatly modified. Japan has long been careful in its public comments on China. Although it has become more assertive in stating its views on particular issues, it has consistently sought to quarantine the overall relationship from often negative criticism on particular matters. There are also signs that both governments want to move on from the negative issue of history.

This increasingly cooperative approach to the relationship, despite continuing differences and competitive urges and despite considerable faith in the *realpolitik* approach to international relations, has been facilitated by their common participation in international institutions. At the global level, this includes the UN and the Bretton Woods institutions and at the regional level, participation in various economic institutions such as APEC and in the ARF has been influential. It has also been helped by the growing economic interdependence of the two countries. While this is not large, neither has a dependence developed that is sufficient to raise serious concerns about vulnerabilities.

Moreover, other factors have been at work. Two decades of visits, informal discussions and formal negotiations over often difficult policy disputes have softened much of the suspicion and mistrust among the elites involved, engendering a degree of confidence in peaceful approaches to dispute resolution. Japan's commitment to clearing up chemicals weapons left over from the war has been a symbolically significant example.

Both governments have been increasingly guided by pragmatism. Neither holds an ideology of expansion and neither supports an ideology or doctrine of security involving an offensive strategic posture. Even within the framework of pragmatism, levels of risk in decision-making are important, but Japan and China in the last decade have not for the most part pursued high risk negotiating strategies. There are some possible exceptions to this record as we note below. But these exceptions have not been significant enough to destabilise the underlying commitment by both countries to the presently held view that war between them is unthinkable.

Consequently it is now possible to talk about a mutual confidence that neither is likely to resort to large-scale military hostilities against the other. The basis of this last judgement is in terms of capabilities as well as intentions. Both countries keep a wary eye on the other's military developments, and both have the capability to engage in large-scale hostilities. Given the clear lack of preparations by either for such hostilities, however, neither government believes the other is actively preparing its armed forces for military conflict with it.[7]

Notwithstanding signs of reliance by both governments on traditional 'balance of power' concepts, at the end of the 1990s, at government and senior elite levels they have both made relatively calm assessments of each other's military posture. For example, a 1998 commentary in a Japanese magazine cited the view of a senior Chinese specialist in Japan studies: 'Japan, which does not possess offensive strategic weapons nor a large number of soldiers and reserves, cannot become a superpower for some time, and there is no possibility for a revival of Japanese militarism'.[8] A 1997 Japanese editorial on the twenty-fifth anniversary of normalisation suggested that the 'two countries have established in the past quarter of a century a relationship so deep that it is impossible to turn back now'.[9]

China constantly talks about strengthening cooperative security ties in a broad strategic sense. When its defence minister, Chi Haotian, visited Japan in February 1998, he invoked the principle that 'security should rely on mutual trust and the links of common interests'. He contrasted this with the Cold War security system based on

---

[7] Military planners in Japan and China told the authors of analyses of a military conflict over the Senkaku Islands. Other contingency plans for military operations against each other may exist, but neither country deploys, trains or plans for sustained military conflict with the other. See East Asia Analytical Unit, *Asia's Global Powers: China-Japan Relations in the 21st Century*, Canberra, Apr. 1996.

[8] Cited in Nobuo Miyamoto, 'Discord in the Quartet of Japan, the United States, China and Russia', *Chuo koron*, Feb. 1998, pp. 138–49 (FBIS-EAS-98-031).

[9] Editorial, *Mainichi shimbun*, 29 Sep. 1997, p. 5 (FBIS-EAS-97-274).

military alliance and military build–up and said such a system 'proved to be unable to build peace'.[10] China's base–line for trusting Japan has been frequently stated: it was laid out by Hu Jintao, in a visit to Japan in April 1998: a correct view of history; persistence in pursuing a path of peace; and correct handling of problems related to Taiwan.[11]

As we discuss below, mutual assessments have not always been so calm, and elite views within both countries range more widely. Some argue in a similar vein; others do not for reasons that reflect greater senses of insecurity or at times reflect support for a bureaucratic or ideological position.

US military presence in Japan

Patterns of cooperation and mutual predictability, and the confidence of each in the non–aggressive intent of the other continue to co-exist with calculations of balance of power. The US–Japan military alliance, even as it has transformed its outward political and military manifestations, has after five decades remained as central a foundation of peace between Japan and China as at any time.[12] China has lived with the alliance for this period. Although senior Chinese figures express at times their in principle opposition to foreign military bases, on balance they accept the stabilising effect of the alliance. The Chinese, however, are ambivalent about the longer term and are concerned about the changes being made in the alliance. Nevertheless, the US–Japan alliance continues to affect profoundly how the governments of Japan and China see each other from a military strategic perspective.

For the first two decades after 1949, Chinese leaders simply wanted US forces out of Japan. The basis of their policy was derived from deep geopolitical hostility. Chinese and US forces had fought each other in the Korean War, and the United States had provided military support to the rival Chinese government in Taiwan. Through the 1980s, Chinese leaders did not have such a unified view of the US

[10] Xinhua, 8 Feb. 1998 (FBIS-CHI-98-039).

[11] Hu Jintao, China's vice president is cited in He Chong, 'The Trend of Sino-Japanese Relations as Seen through Hu Jintao's Japan Visit', Zhongguo tongxun she, 28 Apr. 1998 (FBIS-CHI-98-118).

[12] Japan's close military relationship with the United States was founded in its wartime defeat and occupation by the USA but developed into a formal alliance after the North Korean attack against South Korea in 1950, and China's subsequent entry into the Korean War.

military presence in Japan. On the one hand, China was grateful for the US military presence in East Asia for its pressure on the Soviet Union. On the other hand, China's declared policy was, and remains, foreign military bases are not desirable. Most Chinese leaders remained instinctively opposed to the US military presence. Yet as Japanese military expenditure and capabilities grew in the 1980s, a realisation emerged in China that the US alliance, and its military presence in Japan, might actually constrain any urge by Japan to turn toward an independent and robust military posture that might destabilise China's own interests. Concurrently, Japan was developing a new confidence in its own military power,[13] and this served to confirm Chinese views that the US military presence constrained Japan's tendency toward a more active military posture.

After the end of the Cold War, Japan and China both saw opportunities to use the changed strategic order to create a new security relationship with each other and to redefine the influence of the United States in their bilateral security relationship. For Japan, the first instincts were to see that economics might replace military strength as a dominating currency of power, and to imagine that Japan could somehow increase its international leverage relative to the United States. Second instincts, associated with a change in government in Japan away from the LDP in 1993, imagined Japan might have more in common with countries of Asia than with its US ally, and that this could lead to an eventual weakening of the military relationship with the United States. At this stage, Japan did not see China as a potential long-term military problem – that many Japanese came to visualise subsequently toward the middle of the 1990s.[14]

For China, where *realpolitik* thinking and balance of power concepts were more dominant in the leadership, the end of the Cold War, and the surging economic relationship with Japan raised hopes that careful diplomacy toward Japan might help consummate the desires in that country to move away from its acceptance of US military bases and thereby dilute Japan's treaty arrangements with the United States. For Chinese leaders, this outcome was understood to mean some equalisation of power between China and Japan, and some

---

[13] This growing confidence through the 1980s culminated in Japan's despatch of minesweeping forces to the Persian Gulf in 1991 and of peacekeeping troops to Cambodia in 1992.

[14] China is not included in the discussion of 'Likely Military Dangers' in the 1994 report, 'The Modality of the Security and Defense Capability of Japan', p. 18. See discussion of Japanese security perceptions of China later in this chapter.

redirection of Japan's technological capacities in China's favour for both military and civil purposes. In late 1994, US naval forces had a confrontation with Chinese military forces in the Yellow Sea when aircraft from a US aircraft carrier had hostile contacts with a Chinese submarine and then with Chinese military aircraft. The US forces had deployed to this location in connection with developments on the Korean peninsula, and their activities were not directed at China, but the incident reawakened sentiment among Chinese leaders that US forces should withdraw from Japan.

Japan, already moving back from its thoughts of an independent position, had, by April 1996, abandoned any pretension to the goal of a security policy independent of the United States. This was reflected in its agreement on a package of measures to rejuvenate its alliance with the United States. Yet, at about the same time, China agreed that the US Navy could continue using Hong Kong after reversion to Chinese sovereignty on 1 July 1997. But China's moves toward acceptance of the US alliance with Japan did not occur without drama. By August 1997, Chinese leaders' anger at Japan's attitude to military operations in respect of Taiwan,[15] was reflected in a call by the Chinese foreign ministry spokesman for US forces to be withdrawn from Japan. By late 1998, however, the Chinese leadership shifted ground, reverting to its position that a US military withdrawal from Japan would not serve China's interests. Discussions in Beijing indicated that the leadership recognised that if US forces were withdrawn, Japan would almost certainly respond by adopting a more robust military posture, possibly including acquisition of nuclear weapons. Moreover, China's call for US withdrawal was raising suspicions in Japan and ASEAN that China wanted to take on a role as East Asia's pre-eminent strategic power. [16] China remains wary, however, of new forms of military cooperation between the United States and Japan, the revised defence cooperation guidelines, and the planned cooperation on theatre missile defence (discussed below) both with implications for China's position towards Taiwan.

Japan's view of China: wariness but not fear

Japan's security perceptions for most of the time between 1949 and 1989 were not coloured significantly by fear of China's military

[15] Discussed in Chapter 4.
[16] Interviews by the authors.

capacities. An early period of estrangement arose from the after-effects of the Japanese occupation of China, the success of the Communist revolution on the mainland and then the military intervention by China in the Korean war. But the estrangement had an additional dimension not related to China. Japan was gradually reemerging from the status of defeated and occupied power to that of an independent state, albeit one without military forces. The war in Korea helped Japan's re-emergence economically as well in its eventual re-establishment in 1955 of military forces as the Self Defense Force. The priorities of Japan's leaders at this time were domestic, restoring economic prosperity and political stability. Japan's security perceptions of China before 1989 were often more moderate than those of the United States but its responses were within the framework of the US relationship, and Japan's obligations to the Republic of China on Taiwan (ROC),[17] rather than being affected by any fear of military attack from China.

As we noted in Chapter 1, the Cultural Revolution beginning in 1966, like the Korean war before it, diffused pressure in Japan for restoration of normal contacts between Japan and China, but by 1970 most Japanese supported improved relations with China and Beijing's readmission to United Nations.[18] Japan's recognition of the Beijing government in 1972 preceded formal US recognition by six years but could only have occurred after the US rapprochement with China had been clearly signalled in 1971. The United States–China communique of February 1972 identified a common interest in opposing Soviet expansionism in Asia. Japan also came to share common ground with China on the Soviet Union, though this did not emerge so strongly until the second half of the 1970s. By this time, the Soviet Union had brushed off Japan's efforts to treat it even-handedly and while not specifically directed against Japan, had greatly expanded its military posture in Northeast Asia, including in Japanese claimed islands in the southern Kuriles.

Until the late 1980s, the Japanese government painted China's military posture in its annual White Papers largely but not exclusively in terms of the Sino-Soviet confrontation. On some occasions, China's military power was seen as working to Japan's advantage. For example, Japan's 1978 White Paper on defence noted that the

---

[17] Japan signed a Peace Treaty with the ROC government as the government of all of China and recognised it until 1972.

[18] Qingxin Ken Wang, 'Toward Political Partnership: Japan's China Policy', *Pacific Review*, vol. 7, no. 2, 1994, p. 172.

triangular relationship between the Soviet Union, the United States and China 'provides a certain equilibrium in Northeast Asia and reduces the probability of any conflict [there] progressing to a critical state'.[19] On other occasions, Japanese official assessments saw China's military capability as more than a little threatening. For example, the 1979 White Paper on defence, in commenting on the Chinese invasion of Vietnam, replayed China's justification that the invasion was a counter-attack in self-defence but observed that 'future moves of these nations [China, Vietnam, Cambodia] must be carefully watched'.[20] It warned that the possible effects of the conflict on China's military modernisation and strategic doctrine 'deserve close attention'.[21] By 1988, the official view of China was more confident, with the White Paper noting the constraints on China's military modernisation and the priority given to domestic economic reconstruction. It also noted the closer military cooperation between China and the United States.[22] The 1990 White Paper observed the damaging political effects of the Tiananmen Square incident but observed that while China was attempting to increase its military spending, the overall priority in China remained domestic economic construction.[23]

By the early 1990s, Japanese politicians and media commentators were less confident of China's intentions. Leading newspapers were carrying expressions of new concern, with views that China is now undertaking a 'military buildup' and 'territorial expansion', forming a new 'threat' in Asia.[24] Some Japanese commentators were seeing China's efforts to modernise its navy and air force and the 1992 publication of its 'territorial waters law' as evidence of efforts 'to fill the vacuum left by the military withdrawal from Asia of the United States and Soviet Russia'; and warned that 'China's twenty-first century naval hegemony strategy will threaten Japan's life-line for international trade'.[25]

Prime Minister Hosokawa, who came to power in 1993 as head

---

[19] Japan Defence Agency, *Defense of Japan 1978*, English edn, Tokyo, 1978, pp. 29–30.

[20] Japan Defence Agency, *Defense of Japan 1979*, English edn, Tokyo, 1979, p. 31.

[21] Ibid., p. 44.

[22] Japan Defence Agency, *Defense of Japan 1988*, English edn, Tokyo, 1988, pp. 48, 50–1.

[23] Japan Defence Agency, *Defense of Japan 1990*, English edn, Tokyo, 1990, pp. 57–8.

[24] *Yomiuri Shimbun*, 15 Apr. 1993, pp. 90–1.

[25] Ibid.

of Japan's first non–LDP government since 1955, took a more measured view of China's military spending and the prospects of its emerging as a threat. Hosokawa did not see China as becoming an immediate threat to Japan.[26] Foreign Minister Hata similarly noted that:'I do not believe China will go for a big power military status'.[27] Hosokawa argued, however, that it was 'important for China to disclose its military programs to the rest of the world. In this regard, I believe the Chinese leaders and I share the same understanding'. [28] More generally, Japan was falling in line with the US administration's views about China, which were to work constructively with China while keeping an eye on its strategic policy.

Japan's 1994 White Paper was somewhat more strident, but still reflected the lack of strong concern by the Hosokawa government. The White Paper highlighted an increase of 'more than 12% every year for five years in a row' in China's defence spending, with the last year's increase being 22%.[29] The paper noted that arms sales by China might be used to fund additional military spending not included in the officially announced figures. It also noted China's stepped up operations in the South China Sea referring again to its 1992 promulgation of its law on maritime jurisdiction. Otherwise, the 1994 White Paper reflected a low level of concern: China's future '. . . national defence modernisation is expected to gradually proceed at a moderate rate . . .'.[30]

A report commissioned by the Japanese government from a group of specialists and community leaders in 1994, assessed that a direct military confrontation between great powers (meaning China and the United States) like that of the Cold War, was unlikely.[31] It was more concerned about local wars, particularly in the Middle East, and lack of progress toward a global ban on nuclear testing and toward compliance with other non-proliferation regimes. The report warned, however, that the good will between the great powers in their mutual support for the existing international system could evaporate quickly.

---

[26] Reuters, 22 Mar. 1994.

[27] Xinhua News Agency, 7 Jan. 1994 (FBIS-CHI-94-006).

[28] Reuters, 22 Mar. 1994.

[29] Japan Defence Agency, *Defense of Japan 1994*, p. 51. These statements were highly misleading since in estimating the size of the increases the Japanese government took no account of inflation.

[30] Ibid.

[31] 'The Modality of the Defense Capability and Security of Japan', p. 4.

The Report noted the absence of a consolidated security architecture in the Asia Pacific, and the propensity of regional countries to spend more on military forces. The paper remarked on the potential for military conflict, particularly the danger that '. . . territorial claims to islands scattered off the coast of the Chinese mainland will develop into a military clash'.[32] (Japan's dispute with China over the Senkakus was clearly in mind.) The more direct security threat to Japan in the shorter term was seen as a possible massive outflow of illegal immigrants or refugees,[33] with China an obvious but unstated source.

By the mid-1990s, a consensus had formed among defence planners in Japan that China had become 'the most important security issue facing Asia' in the transition from the Cold War to undefined regional and global security orders.[34] In this view, if China's economy continued to grow, Japan would face a powerful China that could either be a responsible power supporting the status quo or a major military power seeking to challenge the status quo. Much would depend on how other countries regarded China and Japan in interaction, since Japan was determined to exert more political influence on the region and in doing this, Japan would be China's 'greatest rival'.[35] Although concerns were being expressed most strongly in the conservative media, the Japan Socialist Party, often more sympathetic to China than other political parties, was also critical of China's levels of military spending.[36]

By 1997, pessimistic views were being expressed more widely. The annual Defence White Paper noted the annual increases in military spending which it said had now been sustained at more than 10% for nine years in a row.[37] It also commented on China's military exercises against Taiwan in March 1996; China's inclusion of the Senkaku Islands in its 1992 Territorial Waters law; and China's crossing

[32] Ibid., pp. 5–6.

[33] Ibid., p. 18.

[34] Japan Forum on International Relations, 'The Policy Recommendations on the Future of China in the Context of Asian Security', The Forum, Tokyo, 1995, p. 2. This report was signed by 70 members of the Forum, which brings together most of Japan's prominent international relations specialists.

[35] Ibid., pp. 4–5.

[36] *Yomiuri shimbun*, 11 Mar. 1997, p. 2.

[37] The White Paper acknowledged that these figures did not take account of inflation, and cited the inflation figure in China for one year. The annual figure cited was one of the lower annual figures in the nine years.

of the median line in the East China Sea and intrusion into Japan's territorial waters for the purposes of oceanographic research. The White Paper noted, however, a number of positive developments involving China, including better relations between it and the United States toward the end of 1996, no repetition of the March military exercises, and China's hard work to establish stable relationships with its neighbours.[38] Yet former Prime Minister Hashimoto, in a speech on China in late 1997, asked: 'Do we see the same degree of political and military stability taking shape in Asia as in Europe, and is deepened economic cooperation being established as clearly? At this point, the answer is unfortunately no'.[39]

In the 1980s and early 1990s, Japan saw economic development in China as necessary to avoid instability in that country. There gradually emerged, however, an under-current of discomfort in Japan with the uncertainty of the future in the face of continuing expansion of China's economic power. Japan's assessments of China may have as much to do with Japan's particular vulnerabilities as with China's strategic posture. In the narrow military sense, Japan's sense of vulnerability related to its small size compared with China and its dependence on imports of raw materials. One observer also argued that Japan faced a great nuclear vulnerability because of its 50 or so nuclear power plants which if attacked by conventional weapons could devastate Japan as if it had been attacked by nuclear weapons.[40]

The 1995 report by the Forum on International Relations, however, saw the prospect of conflict as 'entirely unlikely' in the immediate future, the authors' concern being with China's 'size and potential'.[41] Whatever the concerns about the long-term future, Japanese assessments mostly do not consider that China has contemplated or is likely in the near future to contemplate preparing its military forces for conflict with Japan or for large-scale military operations against Japan.

[38] Japan Defence Agency, *Defense of Japan 1997*, English edn, Tokyo, 1997, pp. 47–9.

[39] Prime Minister Ryutaro Hashimoto, speech on Japan's foreign policy toward China, 28 Aug. 1997, Ministry of Foreign Affairs, Japan (provisional translation).

[40] Nobuo Miyamoto, 'Discord in the Quartet of Japan, the United States, China and Russia', *Chuo koron*, Feb. 1998, pp. 138–49 (FBIS-EAS-98-031).

[41] Japan Forum on International Relations, 'The Policy Recommendations on the Future of China in the Context of Asian Security', *The Forum*, Tokyo, 1995, p. 32.

China's view of Japan: quiet confidence

As with Japanese views of China after 1952, China has not seen Japan as a serious military threat. Prior to normalisation of relations in 1972, China's rhetoric toward Japan was ideology-oriented, attacking particularly Japan for its military ties with the United States. These propaganda attacks on Japan found accepting audiences at home because of Japan's war record. Yet, as we noted earlier, there was also pragmatism in China's policies toward Japan which often conflicted with the rhetoric, as the semi official agreements on fisheries and trade entered into over this period indicate. During the height of China's Cultural Revolution (1966–71), pragmatism largely disappeared from China's approach to Japan; Japan was once again a class-enemy of China, according to China's leaders of the time. By 1972, however, with normalisation of diplomatic relations with Japan, and diminishing Cultural Revolution radicalism in China, views of Japan once again relaxed.

The 1978 Peace and Friendship Treaty between Japan and China symbolised a determination by both Japan and China to reduce mutual fears. Foreign Minister Sonoda of Japan had told the Diet in October 1978 that Japan should not oppose China's military modernisation because both countries faced a common Soviet threat.[42] Yet as we noted earlier, in the decade or so after normalisation, China expressed displeasure on a number of occasions over Japan's failure to acknowledge its responsibilities for the war as China considered appropriate. Although China used the term 'militarism', few Chinese leaders identified this 'militarism' as representing a new turn back toward aggressive or expansionist intentions. It was as a code word for Japan's lack of contrition.

In the early to mid-1980s China was satisfied that Japan as part of the US alliance system contributed to countering the Soviet threat. Nevertheless, following the end of the Cold War, China watched Japan's military modernisation closely. With Japan's tentative moves towards a more independent foreign policy, views on its intentions differed. One Chinese analyst in 1990 noting increased US concern about Japan's longer-term ambitions, including its tendency to 'take the road of a military power', accepted that Japan's military capabilities remained limited and it still required security protection from the

---

[42] William R. Nester, *Japan and the Third World: Patterns, Power, Prospects*, New York: St Martin's Press, 1992, p. 157.

United States.[43] Few Chinese strategic thinkers saw Japan emerging as a threat in the near future. Their argument was that although Japan continued to strengthen its military capabilities, its primary goal was to enhance its political power. A PLA newspaper article argued in detail that Japan's military modernisation was mainly to strengthen its defence.[44] Not all Chinese analysts agreed. Japan's substantial conventional military capabilities led one Chinese analyst to conclude that Japan's military power had far exceeded that needed for territorial defence.[45]

China watched cautiously Japan's military modernisation. Analysts noted that Japan's Self Defense Force was now the best-equipped military force in Asia, and Japanese military expenditure, the second largest in the world, frequently exceeds Japan's stated limit of 1% of GNP. Japan was also seen as able to expand its armed forces rapidly if it wished. Chinese analysts acknowledge that although Japan lacks a strategic offensive capability, the SDF has long-range aircraft and naval combat capability to defend its northern approaches and to 'control 1,000 nautical miles of sea lanes', and its air force has an interception range of 800 km. around Japan.[46]

In the mid-1990s, Chinese analysts commented on what they saw as a lack of clarity in Japan's strategic directions.[47] A number of assessments were commenting on a sharp turn to the 'right' in Japanese politics, the rise of 'nationalism' in Japan and the resurfacing of maritime conflicts between Japan and China. Yet, attitudes remained basically relaxed. One noted analyst concluded that 'we cannot yet hold that Japan is experiencing a revival of militarism' because 'neither the Japanese government nor its citizens favour retaking the militarist path' and 'all countries, including the United States' would oppose such a development.[48] Again in 1998, it was concluded that

[43] Zi Jian, 'Two Problems in US-Japanese Relations', *Shijie zhishi* (World knowledge), no. 13, 1 July 1990, pp. 10–11 (FBIS-CHI-90-151).

[44] Xi Zhihao, *Jiefangjun bao*, 28 Jan. 1991, p. 4 (FBIS-CHI-91-028).

[45] Li Genan, op. cit., p. 26.

[46] Weixing Hu, 'Beijing's New Thinking on Security Strategy', *Journal of Contemporary China*, no. 3, summer 1993, p. 53.

[47] Lu Zhongwei, 'Post-War Japan at Fifty', *Contemporary International Relations*, vol. 5, no. 7, July 1995, pp. 2–3. Lu, as Vice President of the China Institute for contemporary International Relations, can be considered as one of a relatively large number of foreign policy advisers to the Chinese leadership.

[48] Liu Jiangyong, 'My Preview of Japan in 1997', *Shijie zhishi*, 16 Feb. 1997, no. 4, pp. 8–9 (FBIS-CHI-97-080).

while Japan had changed from 'passive defence' to 'active defence', this was merely a change from countering aggression once it arises to deterring aggression if it appears to be imminent.[49]

While overt signs of nationalist sentiment in China and Japan are evidenced mostly among the younger generation, Whiting has suggested that one can probably look to the younger generation of strategic analysts and Japan specialists in China to hold a more positive view of Japan. According to Whiting, this group appeared to see the world as increasingly interdependent in both economic and security terms, a disposition quite contrary to many older strategic thinkers in China. A Japan with greater political power, the younger analysts were arguing, would not necessarily result in a remilitarised Japan. Instead, it could be beneficial to China.

Chinese analysts usually look to external influences as most likely to cause any Japanese reorientation to a more robust military posture. Some warned that evolution of the regional and international situation, such as North Korea's alleged nuclear capability, could lead Japan to develop nuclear weapons. Other scholars, however, discounted this because of Japan's deep aversion to nuclear war and its vulnerability to nuclear retaliation.[50]

China has on occasion had concerns about what it sees as small shifts in Japanese strategic policy that over time may constitute a more substantial reorientation. It was especially concerned about Japan's 1992 Peace-Keeping Operations (PKO) legislation, which authorised deployment into foreign countries of Japanese military units for the first time since 1945. When Jiang Zemin visited Japan in April 1992, he repeated China's position that Japan should exercise caution about sending forces overseas.[51]

China's view of Japan's desire to become a more influential power was not necessarily totally negative in the early 1990s, the *Beijing Review* suggesting that Japan needed China's support and 'understanding' in achieving that new role.[52] Another believed it to be an inevitable trend in Japan's postwar historical development.[53] In April

[49] Zhang Taishan, 'Japan's Military Strategy for the New Era', *International Strategic Studies*, no. 3, 1998, p. 18.

[50] Zhou Jihua in *Shijie zhishi*, 16 Jan. 1991, p. 13.

[51] Xinhua News Agency, 11 June 1992,

[52] *Beijing Review*, no. 41, 12–18 Oct. 1992, p. 21.

[53] Du Gong, Director of the China Institute of International Studies and member of the 21st Century Committee for Chinese–Japanese Friendship in *Guoji wenti yanjiu*, no.3, 13 July 1992, pp. 1–4; carried in FBIS-CHI, 4 Aug. 1992, p. 11.

1992, when Jiang Zemin visited Japan, he signalled that China, for the first time, accepted Japan's regional political role, indicating support for Japan in playing a positive role in defence of peace in Asia and the world.[54] Then, in late 1993, China's foreign minister, Qian Qichen, deemed as 'constructive' Japan's participation in the UN peacekeeping operation in Cambodia.[55]

While content for Japan to play an expanded regional role, China was not keen to see Japan step on to the world stage as a strategic power. This was evident in China's position on Japan's quest for a permanent seat in the UN Security Council, noted earlier. There is some evidence that China was prepared, however, to act to assuage Japan's security concerns. China's foreign minister agreed to increase the transparency of his country's military efforts when raised with him by his Japanese counterpart.[56] China ultimately produced a Defence White Paper in 1998.[57]

Although concern emerged in Japan about China through the 1990s, strategic analysts and government leaders in China became more relaxed about Japan's strategic posture, aside from the growing level of defence cooperation with the United States. China's primary strategic assessments institutes with reporting responsibilities to government have long seen the United States, Russia, the Korean peninsula and the Middle East as presenting larger strategic problems for China than Japan in and of itself.[58] Chinese public comments about modest improvements in Japan's military capability or its military cooperation with the United States can be attributed to a significant degree to the concerns at US pressure on China and the increasing visibility of the Taiwan problem. Public protests by China represent not so much concern with the military forces at Japan's disposal, as with the longer-term implications of some of its more modest strat-

[54] As cited by Robert Delfs, 'Emperor, China-bound', *Far Eastern Economic Review*, 13 Aug. 1992, p. 11.

[55] Takagi, op. cit., p.109.

[56] Kyodo News Service, 8 Jan. 1994 (FBIS-CHI-94-006).

[57] *China's National Defense*, Beijing: Information Office of the State Council of the People's Republic of China, July 1998.

[58] This judgement is based on interviews by the authors in Beijing over a number of years but is borne out to some degree, though not conclusively, by the relative lack of attention to Japan in the publications on military issues by institutions such as the China Institute for International Strategic Studies and the China Institute for Contemporary International Relations.

egic initiatives. China is particularly wary about what some analysts see as a US security containment policy, with Japan as an integral component. China has also become irritated by Japan's more assertive language in its dealings with China and particularly regarding Japan's strategic pressure on China over nuclear testing and China's 'missile diplomacy' over Taiwan. Japan's pressure on China to change its strategic policies increased in the second half of the 1990s. China's irritation probably peaked in 1996 and 1997 in connection with the Taiwan issue and the revisions to the Japan-US treaty. Overall, however, the Chinese government has settled on a firm view that Japan does not pose a credible military threat to China on its own, and could only be one if there were a conflict with the United States, notably involving direct Japanese participation in some Taiwan-related combat operations.

Maritime disputes, naval power and common interests

Maritime power and security have been strategic preoccupations of successive Japanese governments beginning with the Meiji modernisation over a century ago. In recent decades, Japan's dependence on sea transport of its massive trade, including most of its raw materials, taken with the still substantial cultural reliance on fishing and seafood products, have ensured Japan's sensitivity to changes in China's naval capacities and activities. For China, maritime power and security became an important political issue only in recent decades. This turn to the sea by China at a time of its growing wealth and growing international prestige has provoked caution and some anxiety inside Japan over China's maritime intentions. Therefore, how Japan and China handle their maritime disputes, and their maritime strategic posture, should be a guide to the disposition of the two governments toward each other in military strategic affairs. In that respect, the record is that despite the bitter history and the potential for conflict, they have worked effectively to prevent serious escalation of disputes into military conflict. By 1997 Japan and China had achieved important symbolic breakthroughs on maritime disputes that will help to entrench this disposition toward conflict avoidance over maritime issues. Yet the Japanese government's concern about possible strategic pressure by China on shipping at some unspecified time in the future remains a point often raised by Japanese spokespersons. In practice, China's dependence on maritime trade, both in exports and imports of oil and other raw materials, points to a common interest in sea lane security.

Maritime security is one of the few areas where the security interests of Japan and China intersect on a day to day basis, a development of fairly recent origin. The two countries do not share a land border and their military forces have not come face to face in any hostile manner since 1945. The Chinese mainland coast is 350 km. from the nearest Japanese island in the south of the Ryukyu Islands (see Map 1). US administration of part of the Ryukyu island chain until 1972 meant that its powerful naval forces stood between the relatively weak naval forces of Japan and China. But as a result of a rush by coastal states after 1945 to claim expansive new rights to maritime resource jurisdiction, Japan and China now have overlapping claims to large areas of sea.[59] The exact limits of these overlapping claims have yet to be settled between the two countries even though a dispute has been evident since 1969.

In 1970, the two countries also discovered that they were in dispute over the territorial sovereignty of the Senkaku (Diaoyu) Islands.[60] Psychologically, Chinese leaders could not let Japan, the former aggressor and brutal occupier, have any edge in such a territorial dispute. The dispute is further complicated by its relationship to the status of Taiwan. One of the claims made by China is that these islands were territories associated with the island of Taiwan, and therefore were unambiguously (in their view) transferred back to China by Japan under the post-war settlements. Thus the dispute is simultaneously about two of the most sensitive issues in Chinese foreign policy: the international status of Taiwan and the war with Japan.

In 1978, the peace treaty negotiations led to discussion within China's leadership of the strategy for dealing with the Senkakus. In working toward a peace treaty, an obvious requirement for China would have been to convince Japan that China would not

[59] All of the East China Sea that separates Japan and China is subject to claim by Japan or China (or South Korea).

[60] Under the provisions of international law, the country which owns these islands has the hypothetical potential to increase its share of the East China Sea for economic exploitation by a substantial amount. In 1970, when China claimed the islands for the first time, it did so in reaction to a claim by the Republic of China government on Taiwan. China could not allow its rival for legitimacy make a claim to territorial sovereignty without matching that claim.

contemplate a military operation to seize the Senkaku Islands.Yet on 12 April 1978, during the negotiations, about 100 Chinese fishing boats, some armed, carrying placards saying that the islands were Chinese territory, entered the waters around the Senkaku Islands; although altercations occurred with Japanese government vessels, no shots were fired.[61] The vessels had come from different ports, obviously with approval from a high level of the Chinese government, and remained for one week.

One view is that it was an indicator of China's approaches to such disputes. According to this view, treaty talks between China and Japan had broken down in early April 1978, possibly as a result of strong Japanese statements that Japan saw no need to discuss ownership of the Senkaku Islands with any other government. China publicly described the incident as worth investigating and the defence minister, Geng Biao, asserted that 'we should not argue the island problem and we should resolve that problem in the future'.[62] China defused the incident by asserting that it 'intended to prevent conflicts caused by Chinese fishing boats around the Senkaku Islands'. The action might have been a signal to countries contesting China's claims to the islands in the South China Sea. But the interpretation was that China had been forced to accept Japan's position on the islands if it wanted the Peace Treaty.[63]

In October 1978, Deng Xiaoping said in Tokyo, of the Senkaku Islands, that the 'present generation is not wise enough to settle such a difficult issue. It would be an idea to count on the wisdom of the following generation to settle it'.[64] Deng was signalling China's intention to prevent the territorial dispute over the islands from becoming a major obstacle to relations.Also in 1979, when China's Vice-Premier Gu Mu visited Japan, he proposed that the two countries begin joint development of oil resources in the disputed areas around the Senkaku Islands, suggesting that any problems that arose

[61] Shigeo Hiramatsu, 'China's Naval Advance: Objectives and Capabilities', *Japan Review of International Affairs*, vol. 8, no. 2, spring 1994, p. 128; David G. Muller, *China as a Maritime Power*, Boulder, CO: Westview Press, 1983, p. 215.

[62] Daniel Tretiak, 'The Sino–Japanese Treaty of 1978: The Senkaku Incident Prelude', *Asian Survey*, vol. 18, no. 12, Dec. 1978, pp. 1242–3, citing AFP, 15 Apr. 1978.

[63] Ibid., p. 1245.

[64] *Sankei shimbun*, 26 Oct. 1978 (morning edn), p. 3, translated in Choon-ho Park, 'China and Maritime Jurisdiction: Some Boundary Issues', *German Yearbook of International Law*, vol. 22, 1979, p. 129n.

between the two countries in this undertaking could be solved by negotiations.[65]

The territorial dispute between Japan and China over the Senkakus has not been the cause of serious incident since 1978, although minor incidents have occurred from time to time – and then mainly between Japanese and Taiwanese authorities. Some of these incidents have provoked official protests by China to Japan. Both Japan and China reassert their sovereignty from time to time. Japan has controlled the disputed islands since they were returned to it as part of the Okinawa Reversion Treaty and China has not physically challenged that control, apart perhaps from the 1978 action. Similarly, Japan has not attempted to fortify the islands (which barely support human habitation anyway) or to deploy a regular deterrent naval force in the vicinity of the islands. A military campaign to control the islands would be predominantly a naval battle for control around the islands rather than an effort to capture and fortify the land for anti-air or anti-surface weapon emplacements. Both Japan and China have the military capabilities to mount a naval blockade around the islands and both sides have studied the prospects for and likely course of such an action. In May 1997, when some groups in Japan were pressing for the Japanese SDF to be mobilised to prevent incursions into Japan's claimed territorial waters around the Senkaku Islands, the head of the JDA drew public attention to the fact that the SDF could not be mobilised to deal with what was merely an 'illegal entry into Japan'.[66]

In 1997, China's foreign ministry marginally repackaged Deng's position of 1978 by saying that a solution 'should be sought when the time is ripe' on the basis of 'respecting facts'.[67] A 1996 commentary in China had described the disputes as 'small in scale and local in nature', a relatively strong statement that they were not a high strategic priority to China. [68] Both China and Japan have called for negotiations on joint development of the area around the islands[69]

[65] Paul C. Yuan, 'China's Offshore Oil Development: Legal and Geopolitical Perspectives', *Texas International Law Journal*, vol. 18, no. 1, winter 1983, p. 116.

[66] Kyodo News Service, 9 May 1997 (FBIS-EAS-97-129).

[67] Xinhua, 29 Apr. 1997 (FBIS-CHI-97-119).

[68] Xia Liping, 'Some Views on Multilateral Security Cooperation in Northeast Asia', *Xiandai guoji guanxi* (Contemporary International Relations), 20 Dec. 1996, no. 12, pp. 12-15 (FBIS-CHI-97-074).

[69] Paul C. Yuan, 'China's Offshore Oil Development: Legal and Geopolitical Perspectives', *Texas International Law Journal*, vol. 18, no. 1, winter 1983, p. 116,

but even if such joint development proceeded, the questions of sovereignty would simply be deferred.

That this territorial dispute was relegated to the status of minor irritant has not stopped some in Japan from becoming concerned about improvements in China's maritime reach. Through the 1980s, China had shown greater interest in projecting naval power; it expanded its fleet of major surface combatants by 50%; it began deploying a new nuclear missile submarine; its share of seaborne trade increased sharply; and its fish production rapidly began to outstrip Japan's declining fish production. Views in the conservative Japanese media repeatedly expressed concern that China had undertaken a qualitative buildup of its military capability and that its maritime expansion threatens Japan.[70] A retired SDF general told a conference in Washington that interference in the passage of ships in or around Taiwan waters would be 'serious threat to the survival of the Japanese people'.[71] Official assessments of China's maritime power reflect some concern, although expressed more moderately. The 1997 Defence White Paper, in expressing the official view, alluded in somewhat muted terms to China's destabilising actions in maritime affairs, including in the vicinity of the Senkaku Islands.[72]

Japan's low-key public position on the Senkaku Islands and incidents in maritime areas close to home actually belies a deeper concern among parts of the security community. This official concern was reflected in Japan's public position on the Spratly Islands. For example, in 1995, the Chairman of the Joint Staff of the Self Defence Forces observed in an interview that the dispute over the Spratly Islands in the South China Sea could affect Japan's sea-lanes.[73]

---

quoting *Far Eastern Economic Review*, 28 Sep. 1979; David G. Muller, *China as a Maritime Power*, Boulder, CO: Westview Press, 1983, p. 216. According to Muller, Japan's Prime Minister Ohira recorded in Apr. 1980 his country's willingness to discuss the seabed issues, including joint exploration around the Diaoyu. In Oct. 1980, Japan's Minister of International Trade and Industry undertook that Japan would not develop oil fields around the islands unless China took part. One of China's Vice-Premiers, Yao Yilin, responded by suggesting US involvement in tripartite development.

[70] See for example, *Sankei shimbum*, 1 Oct. 1997, p. 2 (FBIS–EAS–97–276).

[71] Toshiyuki Shikata, cited in *China, the United States and Japan: Implications for Future US Security Strategy in East Asia*, Center for Naval Analyses, Alexandria, VA, 1997, p. 25.

[72] *Defense of Japan 1997*, p. 51.

[73] *Sankei shimbun*, 9 Mar. 1995, p. 2 (FBIS–EAS–95–048).

In April 1997, Japan's foreign ministry expressed grave concern about yet another incident in the vicinity of the Spratly Islands, justifying its position on the basis that 'territorial claims in the South China Sea affect the peace and stability of the Asia–Pacific Region and have an impact on the security of stable maritime transport'.[74] In May 1997, Japan supported an attempt by the Philippines to raise the territorial dispute over the Spratly Islands at the ASEAN Regional Forum.[75]

Notwithstanding the impact in the past of all of these political considerations, reluctance by Japan and China to settle the dispute over the maritime resource boundaries is not simply the outcome of bilateral tensions or dispositions. China and Japan both try to position themselves on this dispute so as not to prejudice similar maritime resource disputes and associated island territory disputes with other countries. Japan has been forthcoming in considering options but not all countries in the region have been so accommodating. There are also narrow technical issues that have probably come further to the fore than previously as political sensitivities have subsided. For example, there is a requirement for Japan, South Korea and China to agree on a delimitation of overlapping claims in the south of the Yellow Sea and the northern part of the East China Sea. Negotiations on a similar delimitation problem involving France, Belgium and the Netherlands in the North Sea failed to deliver a resolution without international arbitration.[76] Thus the East China Sea issues involving Japan and China are likely to remain unsettled until the parties can resolve the technical aspects. Another obstacle is the need to settle the maritime boundaries between the island of Taiwan and Japanese territory at the southern end of the Ryukyu Islands.

From the perspective of international practice, disputes over maritime resource jurisdiction and territorial sovereignty of the islands can easily be separated. China's position of shelving the sovereignty dispute was probably not based on this consideration, but shelving it would be an appropriate step for both Japan and China in working toward a solution. Apparently, China would agree to a package with Japan that includes a definite boundary in the undisputed

---

[74] AFP, 30 Apr. 1997 (FBIS-EAS-97-120).

[75] Kyodo News Service, 16 May 1997 (FBIS-EAS-97-136).

[76] The dispute could only be resolved after the three countries agreed to accept a delimitation drawn by the International Court of Justice in 1969.

northern parts of the East China Sea while creating a joint development zone in the vicinity of the Senkaku Islands. Yet, obstacles remain here, since the way the boundaries of such a zone are drawn would be based in China's view, at least initially, on the assumption that the only possible area for joint development is east of the Senkaku Islands, and not as Japan might insist, an area west of the islands, and based on a median line between them and the mainland coast. Yet even were China to accede to Japan's position, any complete delimitation in the East China Sea would have to include some boundary between Taiwan and Japan.

As a first step, as a confidence building measure, the PRC and Japan agreed in September 1997 to a joint control zone in the central part of the East China Sea, with the zone stopping some distance to the north of the Senkaku Islands.[77] But the southern limit of this zone is well within 200 nm. of the disputed islands and therefore actually breaks the deadlock on what effect to give the islands in a future delimitation. There is some prospect that the joint control zone can in future be extended to include the Senkaku Islands. The two countries agreed to set up a joint fisheries committee to discuss, among other things, mechanisms for exercising joint control in the existing agreed zone. Successful implementation of such arrangements will be one test of the ability of the two countries to come to a workable solution for resource exploitation around the disputed islands. Japan and China continue to negotiate on an EEZ boundary, but this is unlikely to be resolved soon. Each agreed in principle to set fishing quotas within its future EEZ for the other side.

China and Japan have been more successful in working together on fisheries issues in the last part of the 1990s than Japan and the ROK. Cooperation in fisheries matters began as early as 1955, and has continued since. For most of that time it has been fairly rudimentary and confined largely to agreements on which areas of high seas should be fished. In recent years, prospects for closer cooperation have emerged. In April 1997, China's minister responsible for fisheries (the agriculture portfolio) met his Japanese counterpart (also the minister of agriculture) in Tokyo for talks, to meet with representatives of Japan's producer associations and to visit production facilities

---

[77] The joint control zone is located between 30° 4′N and 27°N and is bounded on the east and west by a line to be drawn 52 nm. from the coasts of Japan and China. See Kyodo News Service, 11 Nov. 1997 (FBIS-EAS-97-315).

in western Japan.[78] The joint fisheries committee, established in 1997, is an important vehicle for further cooperation.

Japanese commercial involvement in the development of Chinese offshore oil may prevent disputes in these areas from escalating. In late 1993, a consortium involving the two largest oil development companies in Japan (JAPEX and Teikoku) was awarded exploration rights in two blocks about 150–200 km. southeast of Wenzhou in Zhejiang province, with Japan's National Oil Corporation, a semi-governmental organisation, providing the bulk of the funds for the development. The two companies, with more than ten years of cooperation with China behind them, are already developing three fields in the Bohai Gulf and one in the mouth of the Pearl River near Guangdong. In late 1997, Japan's prime minister observed that Japan and China had already been cooperating in working toward common energy security and that this policy should be maintained.[79] But there are more pro-active strategic visions afoot, at least in Japan, which suggest that the spectre of energy shortages is something that Japan and China can cooperate on rather than fight about. The opening of an office of the New Energy Development Organisation in Beijing in February 1996 provides a vehicle for such cooperation.[80]

Weapons of mass destruction

As the only country attacked with nuclear weapons, Japan has pursued vigorously a no-nuclear weapons policy. By contrast, its neighbour China has developed a suite, if rudimentary, of nuclear weapons – strategic and tactical, land-based and sea-based. When the two countries started down their chosen, but opposite policy paths in respect of nuclear weapons, neither had the other particularly in mind. But the political management of the issue of weapons of mass destruction, including chemical and biological weapons as well as nuclear ones, has been an important issue in bilateral security interaction from almost that time.

Some reasons for that remain relevant as the two countries enter

[78] Kyodo News Service, 22 Apr. 1997 (FBIS-EAS-97-112).

[79] Prime Minister Ryutaro Hashimoto, Speech on Japan's foreign policy toward China, 28 Aug. 1997, Ministry of Foreign Affairs, Japan

[80] 'Ministry of International Trade and industry: Can it Take the Initiative in Establishing a Common Energy Policy for Asia?', *Ekonomisuto*, 26 Mar. 1996, p. 16 (FBIS-EAS-96-055).

the twenty-first century. We noted earlier that an enduring point of discomfort for China has been Japan's ambiguous policy of vigorous disavowal of nuclear weapons while relying on the US nuclear umbrella. At the strategic level, Japan's security treaty with the United States has implied that any threat to Japan either from nuclear or conventional forces would provoke use of force by the United States, possibly including nuclear attack. Throughout the Cold War, most observers and officials in Japan accepted that their country was shielded from nuclear attack by the Soviet Union or, after 1964, by China through this 'extended deterrence' of US military power. China's discomfort at the strategic level with Japan's reliance on the US nuclear umbrella was based less on fear of military attack by Japan than a recognition that as long as the US-Japan alliance held firm, China's possession of nuclear weapons gave it no military edge or strategic leverage over its non-nuclear, great power neighbour.

At the theatre level, Japan for many years allowed the United States to store nuclear weapons in an air force base on Okinawa, and for an even longer period allowed nuclear-armed US warships and submarines to be based in the Japanese port of Yokusuka and to visit other Japanese ports. Japan's tolerance of the US nuclear weapons basing policy ran contrary to an explicit public position adopted in 1967 by the Japanese government in its 'three non-nuclear principles': not to develop, possess or allow into Japan any nuclear weapons. Continued basing in Japan of nuclear weapons by the United States effectively undermined the credibility in China of Japan's three non-nuclear principles and it is unlikely that military leaders in China took Japan's three non-nuclear principles seriously in their military calculations. The commitment of US forces based in Japan to contingencies involving Taiwan or the Korean peninsula raised the possibility of US use of theatre nuclear weapons in the only two scenarios in which China could conceivably have engaged Japanese forces directly.

The decision by the United States in 1993 to withdraw all forward-deployed tactical nuclear weapons, including those on navy ships using Japanese ports, removed the most important basis of dispute over nuclear weapons in Japan-China relations. The decision by the United States to withdraw its strategic nuclear bombers from Okinawa in the 1980s had not had a similar effect because these forces had been superseded by longer-range ballistic missiles and cruise missiles. Thus by the late 1990s, China had little cause for complaint with Japan about its nuclear weapons policy. This change probably

allowed strategic advisers and planners in Japan and China a degree
of breathing space and confidence about the stability of the military
balance between them that they had not enjoyed for several decades.
Although China has retained its tactical nuclear weapons, Japanese
leaders have placed their trust completely in the extended deterrence
of the United States.

China's dissatisfaction in recent years with Japan's policies on
weapons of mass destruction has included Japan's failure to respond
appropriately to its wartime use of chemical and biological warfare
in China, which Japan's governments refused to disclose for several
decades after 1945. China does not see Japan's war-time record of use
of weapons of mass destruction as evidence of any renewed disposition to do so, but some Chinese leaders doubt that Japanese ruling
circles have the aversion to weapons of mass destruction that their
public disavowal of nuclear weapons suggests. China's leaders have
not seen a nuclear-armed Japan as likely. They have understood that
the main brake on the Japanese military buildup since 1955 has been
domestic opinion and particularly that supporting the Socialist Party
of Japan and other, smaller parties, and not the Liberal Democratic
Party. After a sharp loss of electoral support for the Socialist Party in
the second half of the 1990s, Chinese leaders now see the LDP disposition to an increased military capability as the dominant, almost
unchallenged, view in Japanese official circles. Contrary to some
other Chinese official thinking, Chinese military planners, in particular, probably remain convinced that if the US–Japan security alliance ceased to function Japan would almost certainly move to
acquire nuclear weapons.

Until the 1990s, while Chinese official propaganda railed against
Japan's association with the nuclear postures of the United States,
there were few points of direct interaction between the governments
of Japan and China on nuclear issues. Since 1978, China has had sufficiently urgent priorities with Japan in the economic sphere to avoid
arousing undue frictions over nuclear weapons. For the Japanese, it
has reacted to powerful and vocal anti-nuclear constituencies at
home with more circumspection and sensitivity than to any propaganda from China. A number of domestic and international developments pushed the Japanese government in the early 1990s to set
in train an intensifying policy of pressure on China over nuclear
testing and proliferation of weapons of mass destruction.

In Chapter 5 we discuss development in 1992 by Japan of its ODA principles, which purported to condition aid according to the military policies, especially for nuclear weapons, of recipient countries. This policy move was followed on the international stage by an intensification of pressure on the nuclear weapon states to suspend nuclear testing, moves to develop a comprehensive test ban treaty, and moves in the UN General Assembly and the International Court of Justice to have nuclear weapons classified as 'illegal' under international law. Public antipathy in Japan to China's nuclear testing was widespread and included most streams of political opinion. In opposition in October 1994, a senior LDP member and former finance minister, Yoshiro Hayashi, also the chairman of the 530-member all party Diet Members' League for Sino–Japanese relations, had called publicly on the Japanese government to do more than it had in registering the strong dissatisfaction of the Japanese people with China's continued nuclear tests.[81] Hayashi was opposed to curtailing ODA loans to China, but was adamant that China should not use the generosity of countries like Japan as a means of civil infrastructure development while spending considerable sums of its own on unnecessary military development.

After China conducted a nuclear test in May 1995, Sakigake, the junior coalition partner, called for suspension of grant aid as a bare minimum sanction.[82] In the week after the nuclear test on 17 August 1995, the New Frontier Party (Shinshinto) called for a full review of Japan's aid policy to China and a suspension of ODA loans pending the outcome of the review.[83] On 1 April 1996, the Sakigake party leader, Masayoshi Takemura, told China's foreign minister that Japan would stick to the one China policy but demanded an immediate end to nuclear testing.[84] In July 1996, Japan's Foreign Minister Ikeda called in China's ambassador to protest China's latest nuclear test, expressing Japan's view that the test was 'extremely regrettable' in the light of repeated calls by Japan and the international community to halt the tests. Ikeda acknowledged China's intention to suspend testing but called on China to stop them completely and sign a

[81] Hisane Masaki, 'Hayashi Urges Strong China Ties but Nuclear Tests, Military Buildup Cause for Concern', *Japan Times*, 27 Oct. 1994.

[82] Satoshi Isaka, 'China Faces Fallout of Less Aid from Tokyo after Nuke Test-Target – This time could be yen loans; Opposition Wants Full Review of Assistance', *Nikkei Weekly*, 21 Aug. 1995, p. 3.

[83] Ibid.

[84] Kyodo News Service, 1 Apr. 1996, BBC SWB and Reuters, 2 Apr. 1996.

comprehensive test ban treaty.[85] In August 1996, after China announced a plan to suspend testing, Sakigake was still insisting that the freeze on aid be maintained until China committed to a complete moratorium.[86]

China's eventual suspension of nuclear testing, and its signature of the CTBT in 1997, removed nuclear weapons from the agenda as a day to day issue but what, to the Japanese, seemed to be Chinese intransigence aggravated distrust of its military posture and heightened the sense of nuclear vulnerability to China among many Japanese opinion-makers and the population. Japan's pressure on China was at one level directed at nuclear testing, but at another was directed at China's right to develop nuclear weapons while receiving (even demanding) development aid from Japan and the international community. For Chinese leaders who knew their history, this strategic pressure from the country's principal aid donor of the 1990s evoked bitter memories of the Soviet Union's reneging on its promise to supply China with nuclear weapons and its subsequent withdrawal of all aid because of growing rifts with China on number of issues, one of which was China's determination to build its own nuclear weapons.

On balance, however, notwithstanding underlying sentiments, both governments handled the dispute over testing and aid with some sophistication and sought to quarantine its effect on the entire relationship. As noted in Chapter 4, the Japanese foreign ministry worked vigorously to shield ODA loans from any retrenchment. For its part, China gave Japan advance notice of the tests to try to register some more confidence in Japan about them.[87] Chinese officials tried to influence Japanese opinion to some degree by making it known in the Japanese press that continued pressure on China's testing policies would strengthen the hand of the Chinese armed forces leaders who supported continued testing.

Once the nuclear testing issue was put aside, Japan and China made progress on arrangements for disposing of more than 700,000 chemical artillery shells left in China by Japanese forces at the end of the war. The presence of these weapons of mass destruction had negative connotations for the public presentation of security issues,

[85] *Japan Times*, 30 July 1996.
[86] Hijiri Inose, 'Foreign Ministry Prepares to Resume Aid to China', *Nikkei Weekly*, 12 Aug. 1996, p. 4.
[87] Masahiko Sakajima, *Daily Yomiuri*, 3 July 1996, p. 6.

and in some respects undercut Japan's 'high moral ground' on nuclear testing. China ultimately agreed that Japan should build the chemical weapon disposal plants in China,[88] a proposition that Japan favoured given the high risk of transporting the shells to land-based factories in Japan and the political costs of locating disposal facilities in densely-populated Japan. One of the earlier sticking points had been China's insistence that Japan should indeed take them back home and dispose of them in Japan. Another sticking point had been the lack of disposal technology in Japan, and the US company Raytheon which operated a chemical weapons disposal facility on Johnson atoll in the western Pacific had been pressing to join the project. Other foreign corporations, such as Bechtel of the United States and Daimler-Benz of Germany, also expressed interest. China was reported to have changed its position, having been persuaded of the logic of not transporting the shells too far, because of the opportunity to create jobs at home and acquire new technologies for China. The project is likely to take at least 15 years, given the time required to build the plants, and the high disposal rate needed to destroy all of the shells (some 200 per day over ten years). The project is expected to get under way in the year 2000, and therefore will remain for at least a decade both a potential point of symbolic contention or a sign of a new spirit of cooperation.

Theatre Missile Defence

Japan and China have more recently come to disagree over Japan's agreement in 1998 to undertake joint research with the United States on Theatre Missile Defence systems (TMD). TMD is one element of a much wider US national missile defence program emerging out of President Reagan's Strategic Defense Initiative (Star Wars) program. It is designed to counter attacks by short to medium range (theatre) ballistic missiles as opposed to intercontinental ballistic missiles. Originally perceived as a protection for US forces and bases in Japan, the United States approached Japan in 1993 to participate in its extension to its Northeast Asian allies and share the large research and development costs.[89] Japan delayed a decision for several years for various reasons including questions of cost, reliability and regional

---

[88] *Sankei shimbun*, 10 Dec. 1996 (FBIS-TEN-97-001).

[89] A valuable history is given in *Theater Missile Defense (TMD) in Northeast Asia: an Annotated Chronology 1990-Present*, Monterey: East Asia Nonproliferation Project, Center for Nonproliferation Studies, 1999.

reactions. Eventually, the intensification of alliance politics was a significant factor in Japan's agreement to participate in a joint research program. Japan's agreement to participate was supported by some in Japan as confirming their view that Japan needed to do more to position itself defensively against China's growing military power and a growing disposition to use military force – even though they did not identify China as an immediate military threat to Japan. The launch in 1998 of a North Korean *Taepodong*-1 missile that passed over Japanese territory provided even further pressure in Japan (or perhaps just gave its TMD supporters more weight) on the government to agree to the US proposal.

As far as Japan's participation in joint research on TMD system is concerned, China's opposition is related more to what it sees as the underlying strategic meaning of the move, rather than a calculation of a the medium term military impacts on China of the move. China has argued that the joint Japan–US move, taken at a time when Japan and China have good political relations and when neither country poses a threat against the other, proves that some in the United States are looking to pursue a strategy of military containment of China, and that by joining the TMD research program, Japan would be aiding that process. China has argued that deployment of a TMD system would lead to a destabilising and expensive arms race in the region since a substantially enlarged missile arsenal would be sought to overwhelm any defensive system.

China's two principle concerns, however, are first that a US TMD system would conflict with the ABM treaty, a concern it shares with Russia. [90] China fears it would limit its defensive capability by undermining its ability to launch second strike nuclear retaliation against a US or Russian nuclear strike. Second, China opposes the Japan–US

---

[90] The Anti-Ballistic Missile (ABM) Treaty between the United States and the Soviet Union, which is still in force, was conceived to prevent either side in the Cold War from gaining the capability to protect itself from a nuclear missile strike by deploying a nationwide defence. The strategic purpose of this was to lock both parties into receiving an inevitable second strike (and nuclear devastation) in the event that either was foolish enough to launch a nuclear missile attack on the other. The US plans for National Missile Defence (NMD) are inconsistent with the ABM treaty and the United States has asked Russia to consider a revision of it, a move Russia has said it will consider even though its initial reaction to the proposal to revise the treaty has been hostile. China also claims that Japan's participation in TMD would conflict with US obligations under the Missile Technology Control Regime.

joint TMD research mainly in connection with Taiwan, as we discuss in the next chapter. China is using a variety of arguments to deter Japan from becoming party to an enhanced US regional defensive capacity that would come into play in a Sino-US military confrontation over Taiwan. China's military experts are sceptical about the viability of TMD against hundreds of offensive theatre missiles. They also recognise that even if it proves to be feasible in the field, a TMD system would take many years to develop and deploy, deployment coming only late in the first decade of the twenty-first century at best.

Japan's participation in the joint research can in many respects be seen as tokenism by Japan to satisfy a minimum requirement of support for its alliance partner. Government sources in Tokyo report that Japan is already looking for ways to dilute its commitment. In any event, Japan's contribution is unlikely to be a significant part of the overall project, and Japan's contribution in dollar cost is relatively small. China will continue to rail against Japanese participation in the project, and can be expected to oppose Japan's support for actual deployment of a TMD system even more vigorously than now if that occurs. But as long as Japan and China maintain cooperative relations, Japan is unlikely to deploy a TMD system on a sufficient scale to appear as directed against a Chinese offensive missile capability. This issue will probably remain a minor irritant in the larger scheme of Japan–China relations although, especially as it might affect or influence Taiwan, it is likely to remain on the bilateral security agenda for many years.

Bilateral security contacts

Neither Japan nor China have sought a military relationship but, as the initial euphoria at the end of the Cold War dissipated and the realisation set in that military factors were still important, interest in Japan in security discussions with China grew and efforts were made to develop a dialogue. The experience of such exchanges had been limited because of Japan's reluctance to get involved in the Cold War, continuing bilateral tensions, and domestic sensitivities in both countries. In China the main sensitivity is the history of Japan's aggression. In Japan, the involvement of the JDA raises questions about the military's role in Japan. Those wanting an enlarged role for the JDA are less inclined to favour close links with China. Those inclined to further links with China generally want the JDA's role tightly circumscribed. [91]

Japan and China exchanged military attaches in 1974, two years after normalisation of diplomatic relations. In 1982, the two sides agreed to exchange specialists in military affairs, a recognition of some common interests in strategic problems relating to the Soviet threat. The Chinese defence minister, Zhang Aiping, visited Japan unofficially in 1984 and the head of the JDA, a civilian official, visited China in 1986. Until 1989, bilateral military or security contacts continued through exchanges of senior civilian leaders and officials, but higher level military exchanges usually involved retired rather than serving personnel because of the difference in status of the JDA and the PLA. For both Japan and China, however, the failure to exchange senior military personnel was not significant given the limited interaction on security issues. Nevertheless, it underscored a continuing gulf between the two.

Gradually, interests changed. China saw value in a dialogue given its concerns at Japan's military build-up, its expanding military links with the US, and a security process that the Chinese saw as 'opaque . . . and unpredictable'.[92] The implications of China's military modernisation, the importance of the PLA in the Chinese political system, and the need to match growing US exchanges were important motives for Japan.

In December 1993, the two countries held their first postwar talks dedicated exclusively to mutual security concerns.[93] Japan used the talks to ask China to put pressure on North Korea to open its suspect nuclear facilities for inspections, to raise the question of regional anxiety over China's military modernisation, and to promote China's interest in a 'white paper' to increase the transparency of its defence planning. At this meeting, China was largely responding to Japan's concerns although it reiterated its 'no first use' and 'no use of nuclear weapons against non-nuclear countries' and that it did not intend to build an aircraft carrier.[94] The 1993 talks, led on both sides by foreign ministry officials, were to become annual events. Subsequently, in

[91] Benjamin Self, *Confidence-Building Measures and Japanese Security Policy*, Washington, DC: Henry Stimson Center, 1998, p. 44.

[92] Self, *Confidence–Building Measures . . .* , p. 46

[93] Kyodo News Service, 20 Dec. 1993 (FBIS-CHI-93-243).

[94] Ibid.

1994, officials of the defence ministries met in Beijing for the first military–military talks on security.

In 1994, Japan invited China's defence minister, Chi Haotian, for the first defence contacts at ministerial level since Japan's minister visited China in 1987. In 1995, China invited the chairman of the Joint Staff Council of the SDF to visit China, to be the first postwar visit to China by the most senior Japanese military officer.[95] Neither visit took place for almost four years, because of rising disagreements over political and security issues, including Taiwan, Korea and the Senkakus. The difficulties also led to the postponement of a planned visit to China to brief senior Chinese officials on the US–Japan guidelines.

Official security exchanges continued at more junior levels. In 1996 senior Japanese security officials went to China to provide briefings on the new guidelines and US–Japan agreements on the security treaty. In these meetings, Japan proposed more security exchanges, including officer exchanges between the PLA and the JDA at various levels. The annual talks for 1997 talks were held in Tokyo on 15 March (one day only) at director/director-general level, the major items being Japan's military links with the US and the defence cooperation guidelines.[96]

Prime Minister Hashimoto had strongly supported bilateral military contacts and, in 1997, suggested that to dispel China's doubts about Japan's security policies Chinese military officers should be invited to inspect units of Japan's armed forces.[97] In the following year, the ten-year pause in defence minister visits was broken when Chi Haotian visited Japan. Apart from meeting Prime Minister Hashimoto and Foreign Minister Obuchi, Chi held talks with his counterpart, the director-general of Japan's Self Defense Agency, Fumio Kyuma. The ministers agreed to promote security dialogue and military exchanges and reportedly foreshadowed reciprocal warship visits subject to subsequent discussion on modalities. Chi visited several military bases, including Japan's naval base at Yokosuka, where some 40% of Japan's naval forces are deployed.[98] In the same year, Kyuma reciprocated Chi's visit. These ministerial visits were to

[95] Jiji Press Newswire, 13 Jan. 1995 (Reuters).

[96] Xinhua, 16 Mar. 1997 (FBIS-CHI-97-075).

[97] Kyodo, 2 Sep. 1997 (FBIS-EAS-97-245).

[98] *China News Digest*, 5 Feb. 1998. Yokosuka harbour is also the site of the main base for US naval forces in Japan.

be followed by reciprocal visits at chief of general staff level. Japan and China also agreed to hold bilateral disarmament talks at middle foreign ministry level.[99] In January 2000, the two sides agreed after a bilateral security meeting to participate in region-wide talks on anti-piracy measures.[100]

The bilateral security contacts are likely to have had some impact, though probably not a profound one, on mutual suspicions. A journal with links to China's leadership had noted in 1996 that although considerable achievements had been registered in bilateral cooperation, 'frictions . . . are expanding', and that security cooperation lagged behind other sectors of the relationship.[101] One disagreement on security issues had been revealed in 1995 at a UN meeting in a sharp attack by the Chinese delegation on Japan's support of a comprehensive nuclear test ban treaty while relying on the nuclear umbrella of the United States.[102] While some progress was made in the immediate aftermath of the 1996 missile tests, this was confined largely to improved contact.

There is little evidence of harmonisation of views on a number of key bilateral issues, even though there was progress on some regional and global security issues. In 1998, the bilateral security talks were called off by China in reaction to the year of open controversy about the redefinition of the US-Japan guidelines. When the two sides met in October 1999 for consultations on security, a Chinese spokesperson reported that China still found Japan's explanation of US-Japan security cooperation unconvincing, a choice of words not often heard from China in earlier years in describing Japan's security policy.[103]

Nevertheless, the two sides continue to develop the institutional framework of security dialogue. Through 1999, there was discussion of how the level of the meetings might be upgraded in order to meet the intent of the joint declaration by President Jiang and Prime Minister Obuchi in November 1998 to do something to that effect.[104]

Japan and China are pursuing different objectives in their bilateral security contacts. On the one hand the contacts are regarded as

[99] Kyodo News Service, 8 Aug. 1998.
[100] *Nihon Keizai Shimbun*, 12 Jan 2000.
[101] Feng Zhaokui, *Liaowang*, 16 Sep. 1996, no. 38, pp. 41–2 (FBIS-CHI-96-187).
[102] Kyodo, 5 Sep. 1995 (FBIS-TAC-005).
[103] *Zhongguo xinwen she*, 12 Oct. 1999 (FBIS-CHI-1999-1012).
[104] *Japan Times*, 14 Sep. 1999.

important in contributing to transparency and providing some institutional foundations for confidence building. Japan and China, however, both see bilateral security contacts as enhancing their individual leverage relative to the United States.

In recent decades, neither Japan nor China has felt directly threatened by the other despite Japan's technological superiority in conventional arms and China's efforts at military modernisation (and its nuclear capacity). Their military postures owe much more to other factors, domestic and international, than to concern about each other. On the domestic front, these other factors have related mainly to economic or political constraints on structural reform of the armed forces and on technological modernisation. On the international front, these influences have included the continuing effect of previously powerful influences from Cold War security planning, especially the US–Japan security alliance and the Korean military stand-off. The military confrontation between China and Taiwan in 1996 has also been a powerful influence.

That said, Japan and China have in the last decade shaped their strategic policy with each other in mind more than at any other time since 1945. Each does have important concerns about the other, and while some points of contention have been removed or ameliorated, others remain or have become worse. At the same time, a pattern of limited cooperation between Japan and China on fishery resource jurisdictions appears to have become entrenched and looks set to expand to seabed resource jurisdiction, despite unresolved differences over ownership of the Senkaku Islands and lack of movement toward agreed maritime resource boundaries. Nevertheless, China's military pressure on Taiwan in 1996 fuelled Japanese concerns about China's potential in the longer term to threaten Japan's sea transport routes. In practice, the concern is qualified by, among other things, China's own growing reliance on the freedom of the seas. Its emotional and political salience in Japan however is high, given Japan's great dependence on imports of food and raw materials. Japan's objections to China's nuclear testing, which divided the two countries in the mid-1990s, ceased to be an issue after China signed the Comprehensive Test Ban Treaty; but because China remains a nuclear weapons power and Japan is not, many in Japan will not fully trust China.

There is also a long way to travel before China will fully trust Japan. In that case, the main causes of distrust are based on its historical experience. Security contacts are likely to intensify gradually but security dialogues will have limited impact in the shorter term. Although it seems that an increasing number of people in China regard the US as its most likely military adversary in the future, Chinese leaders still prefer the United States to keep a military presence in Japan as a restraint on moves by it toward any more robust military posture. If domestic political change in China throws up a more conservative government, some important differences might be expected in its foreign policies. In particular, if the PLA came to exercise more influence in the leadership, it would not be a surprise if China adopted a less accommodating approach to security issues involving Japan.

For its part, Japan has concerns about China's short- to medium-term domestic situation, and its longer-term strategic orientation. Japan is anxious to see greater transparency in military affairs on China's part, but there is otherwise a largely measured assessment of China's military modernisation. Although different views exist among officials and scholars, and competing interests push the arguments supporting those interests, the broad Japanese government view is that it will be a considerable time, possibly decades, before China has an effective blue-water naval capability about which Japan needs to be concerned.

As already observed, at an emotional or symbolic level, governments in Japan and China see each other in military terms more through lenses of history and imagined futures than through recent realities. The future security interactions between Japan and China will depend largely on the degree to which determination to avoid repetition of history overcomes residual prejudices left over from history. The record so far and the underlying political trends in both countries suggest that the principle of non-aggression will continue to have a powerful restraining effect on both countries.

4

TAIWAN BETWEEN JAPAN
AND CHINA

Of all the political issues in the relationship between Japan and China, the most important is Taiwan. The reunification of the components of Greater China has been the longer term Chinese political objective for at least five decades. With the return of Hong Kong and Macao to Chinese sovereignty in 1997 and 1999, Taiwan constitutes the unfinished element in the Greater China objective. China has declared the issue to be the fundamental determinant of its political relations with all states. Thus, while the overall Japan–China relationship has influenced attitudes to Taiwan, it is more the case that attitudes of each government towards Taiwan have shaped the overall relationship. In China's eyes, if Japan cannot accommodate China's interests on this issue, then the relationship must remain brittle since such a policy by Japan implies unfriendly motives.

China has long been suspicious of Japan's intentions, either on its own behalf or on that of the United States, towards Taiwan. In the aftermath of the communist victory in 1949, China was suspicious that Japan wanted to maintain a special relationship with Taiwan, based on ties established in the fifty years of Japanese rule from 1895 to 1945. These suspicions may have diminished but have not disappeared. Subsequently, China became anxious that Taiwan was becoming too dependent economically on Japan. These fears also seem to have diminished. China's leaders appear to have assessed that they can bind Taiwan to China with 'economic ropes'. They expect that in the longer term their country will be so powerful economically that existing strong economic ties with Taiwan will be enhanced. Consequently, they seem no longer to worry that Taiwan, with little more than 20 million people, will be more drawn to Japan than to China, despite it being physically as close to Japan as to China.[1] China has other strategic concerns, however, arising from its fears of foreign interests. Deng Xiaoping said in 1987 that if Taiwan was not returned to the motherland, 'it might be taken away by others'.[2]

For much of the quarter of a century or so of diplomatic relations with Japan, the question of Taiwan's international status was handled reasonably carefully by both sides within a 'one China' policy – notwithstanding quite frequent disputes. By 1996, China had again become suspicious of Japan's aims with respect to Taiwan. This followed some changes in Japan's policy on visits from senior Taiwan political leaders in the early 1990s, at the same time as the United States had undertaken a Cabinet-level review of relations with Taiwan, leading ultimately – if indirectly – to the controversial visit of Taiwan's president to the United States. China's response to that visit was sharp. It included missile launches and military exercises to intimidate Taiwan and demonstrate China's resolve to Japan and the USA. As a result, the Taiwan issue has again become difficult for Japan and China. Its management has been aggravated by a number of factors. These included Japan's responses to China's 'missile diplomacy' and to its military modernisation; and China's reactions to changes in US-Japan security arrangements. At a more fundamental level, Japan's long standing one-China policy has come under serious pressure as a result of the consolidation of Taiwan's democratic processes and its sustained economic prosperity. Moreover, US responses to many Taiwan issues have carried additional implications for China's relations with Japan.

Another change affecting Japan's position on Taiwan has been the rapid development over the past two decades of Japan's commercial engagement in Hong Kong. Concerns over the potential consequences of the reversion of Hong Kong to China in 1997, although diminished by the post reversion experience, have also provided a

---

[1] You Ji, 'Missile Diplomacy and PRC Domestic Politics' in Greg Austin (ed.), *Missile Diplomacy and Taiwan's Future: Innovations in Politics and Military Power*, Strategic and Defence Studies Centre, Canberra, 1997, p. 47.

[2] *Japan Times,* 17 Apr. 1987. Through the Taiwan Relations Act and in other ways, the US has maintained a firm commitment to the security of Taiwan in spite of the abrogation of it formal treaty with the Republic of China government in Taiwan as a precondition of normalisation of relations with China. The US maintained troops on Taiwan until it was agreed during the 1972 Nixon visit that they would be withdrawn.

new dimension to Japan's view of the 'one China' policy. At the same time, the intensity of China's interest in the reunification of Taiwan rose after it had resolved the issues of Hong Kong and Macau.

A further complexity is that although Japan has, in a substantive sense, been the centre of the economic development of the region and of economic regionalisation, China is now also becoming integral to the Pacific economy, as it had been before the Second World War. The possibilities for closer cooperation or intensified competition between Japan and China in the regional economic order have been strengthened by the closer economic integration of China, Hong Kong and Taiwan.

While Sino-Japanese relations tend to reflect internal factors in both countries, domestic political influences in both countries have affected how Taiwan issues have played in the bilateral relationship. When Hu Yaobang fell in 1987 under pressures from the hard liners, on grounds that included too close links with Japan,[3] it was also argued that Hu had not reacted sharply enough to Japanese tolerance of the activities of Taiwan groups in Japan.[4] In Japan's case, changes in political leadership, particularly at the prime ministerial level – a pro-China Yoshida or Ishibashi rather than a pro-Taiwan Kishi or Sato – have been important determinants. But Japan's leadership attitudes normally reflect shifts in the strengths of various factions or, more recently, of parties. In particular, substantial differences over Taiwan existed earlier within the LDP but these were largely invisible to public scrutiny. In the 1990s, Japan's China policy became more highly politicised publicly once the LDP's monopoly on government ceased to exist.

This chapter reviews how these various Taiwan and Hong Kong issues have played out in Japan-China relations in recent years and are playing out now. It reviews first the history of Japan's relations with Taiwan to 1996. It then discusses Japan's relations with the Greater China economy (Taiwan and Hong Kong) The chapter then looks briefly at the influences on Japan's one-China policy, and then

---

[3] Other factors were important, particularly opposition to the reform program but some effusive praise from, and statements in support of the reform program by, Japanese Prime Minister Nakasone in China did not help Hu. See Hidenori Ijiri, 'Sino-Japanese Controversy Since the 1972 Diplomatic Normalization' in Christopher Howe (ed.), *China and Japan: History Trends and Prospects,* Oxford: Clarendon Press, 1990, p. 76.

[4] Charles Chao, 'Peking-Tokyo Relations Over The Past Year', *Issues and Studies,* 14(4), Apr. 1980.

China's view of that policy, before analysing the two most important issues affecting Japan–China relations in respect of Taiwan at the end of the 1990s – China's military pressure on Taiwan in March 1996 and the subsequent changes in US-Japan defence arrangements.

Japan's role in a divided China to 1996

Since the PRC achieved victory on the mainland in 1949, and Chiang Kai-shek fled with his troops and followers to Taiwan, China has been a divided state. Although, as a result of the 1943 Cairo and 1945 Potsdam Declarations, it was agreed that Taiwan should be returned to China, for many years following 1949 there remained differences as to 'who' constituted the government of 'China', the PRC or the ROC. The rival Chinese governments each insisted that it was the only the legitimate government of all of China, and each maintained in formal terms a state of war or belligerency against the other.[5] The international community had no consensus on which of the rival governments constituted China. For example, in the negotiations for the 1951 San Francisco Peace Treaty with Japan, the issue of which China could not be resolved since the United States recognised only the ROC and its sovereignty over the mainland, while Britain and the Soviet Union supported the PRC that they had already recognised. In the early years after 1949, judgements on which China to recognise tended to reflect broader national policy stances, which were shaped by the responses to a succession of events: the outbreak of the Cold War in 1948, Communist China's intervention in the Korean War (1950–3), recurrent outbreaks of fighting between the two China's up until 1962, and the decolonisation of former empires and the rise of Asian nationalism.

In the early post-war years, Japan's leaders had been less concerned about Chinese communism than their US counterparts. Japan's main interest was economic – resources and markets. Although the mainland China market was smaller than in prewar days, Japan regarded it as important and had consequently wanted to return to it. Japan

[5] Just as in the early decades following its move to Taiwan, the ROC refused formal relations with any country that recognised the PRC, for the PRC, the policy of recognising only one China was, and remains, obligatory for any state wishing to have diplomatic relations with it. (The ROC claimed to be the rival government of the whole of China and maintained a state of war with the PRC until formally disavowed in 1991.)

had hoped and expected that the United States would recognise the PRC. It was reluctant to assign Taiwan formally to the ROC government led by Chiang Kai-shek in line with its end of war commitment that Taiwan and other Chinese territories taken by Japan in the five decades to 1945 should be returned to 'China'. Under strong US pressure, however, Japan signed a peace treaty with the ROC in 1952, a move which constituted recognition of the ROC and therefore continued non-recognition of the PRC.[6]

After 1952, Japanese businessmen, encouraged by their government, resumed contact with mainland China on an unofficial basis. This early enthusiasm came to be tempered, however, by the intensification of the Cold War, the PRC's aggressiveness toward the ROC and then by Japanese interest in the economic success of the ROC that, given its greater openness, became a larger market than the mainland. Although the ROC controlled capital imports, it depended substantially on Japanese technology and equipment for use in the manufacturing sector and Japan's economic influence remained strong. In the 1960s, some large Japanese companies transferred their assembly operations to the ROC. Such operations extended beyond the initial emphasis on textiles to encompass Japan's rapidly expanding manufacture of electronic equipment.

By 1964, Japan had become the leading trade partner of both the ROC (hereafter referred to as Taiwan) and the PRC (hereafter referred to as China). In practice, the economic relationships with both Taiwan and China then and subsequently were not as greatly affected by the presence or absence of diplomatic relationships as by other considerations such as China's level of receptiveness to foreign investment. From Japan's signing of the first unofficial trade agreement with China in 1952, Japan effectively pursued a 'two Chinas' policy.[7] This had economic advantages – with Japan developing a policy, known as *seikei bunri*, which involved differentiating economics and politics in its dealings with the 'two Chinas'. It also reflected the division of views between the pro-Taiwan and the pro-China lobbies, and the 'two Chinas' policy in commerce was able to offer something to both groups. China did not accept the *seikei bunri* policy, however,

---

[6] Akira Iriye, 'Chinese–Japanese Relations, 1945–1990' in Christopher Howe, op. cit., p. 48; Rajenda Jain, *China and Japan: 1949–1980,* Oxford: Martin Robertson, 1981 (2nd edn), p. 7. It interpreted the treaty at that time as applying only to areas then under Taipei's control.

[7] As did Canada, Australia and Britain.

and required assurances from those participating in the trade on Taiwan that they would adhere to the three political principles Zhou Enlai had laid down for Sino-Japanese relations.[8]

China and Taiwan were both sensitive to Japan's policies towards the other. Prior to the 1972 normalisation of relations, Taiwan was perhaps the more watchful of the Japanese position. For example, in the early 1960s there was an angry response by Taiwan to Japan's provision of official financial support for exports to China. This support was then discontinued, giving rise to considerable anger from Beijing. China responded angrily to incidents involving Japan and Taiwan, such as visits by Japanese Prime Ministers Kishi and Sato to Taiwan in the period before the change in Japan's recognition policy; and there were periodic disturbances in informal relations over other events that China saw as significant breaches of Zhou Enlai's three principles. Relations between Japan and China, in this context as in others, were especially difficult during the Cultural Revolution in China, a time of extreme radical dogmatism and isolation in foreign policy, when China's Communist Party even broke its links with the Communist Party of Japan. During the period, a particularly acrimonious issue arose, centred on the dispute between Taiwan and China over the control of the Kokaryo student dormitory in Japan. This proceeded in the Japanese courts over a period of some two decades.[9]

Meanwhile, constraints remained on Japan's trade with China before 1972 and many Japanese leaders were eager to cast off the constraints that Washington in particular had imposed on their relations with China. Fears held in Japan for some years that a US president would recognise China without advance warning to Japan were realised in 1972 with the Nixon visit to Beijing. Although there were inter-factional disputes about how to respond to the Nixon move and handle future relations with what was likely to be the rump state

---

[8] The three principles were that: Japan should not regard China as an enemy; participate in any plot to create 'two Chinas'; or obstruct the normalisation of relations with China. Quansheng Zhao, *Interpreting Chinese Foreign Policy: The Micro-Macro Linkage Approach*, Hong Kong: Oxford University Press, 1996, p. 136.

[9] Taiwan and China disputed ownership of this dormitory, occupied by mainland Chinese students during the Cultural Revolution. In 1967, Taiwan took the issue of ownership to the courts in Japan. Japan argued that it was purely a legal issue on which it could not intervene. China saw the issue as one of national sovereignty and a test of Japan's attitude towards Beijing's position on Taiwan.

of Taiwan, the 'scramble within and between Japan's political parties to win the race to Beijing was on'.[10] Consequently, when Japan normalised relations with China in 1972, expectations on both sides concerning the expansion of the economic relationship were high.

Yet, by the mid 1980s, Japanese investment in Taiwan was still about twice that in mainland China. At this time, however, as costs of labour rose in Taiwan and as political relations with the mainland eased, Japanese manufacturers started to move their production from Taiwan to the mainland. Nevertheless, they did so cautiously at this stage given the continuing deficiencies in China's investment climate.

For its part, during the 1980s in particular, China gradually became more flexible in respect of economic relations between countries that recognised the PRC but maintained commercial relations with Taiwan. In part this was an acceptance of the argument that the PRC could hardly be against anything that benefited economically a part of China. Among other things, China was prepared to give the ROC certain measures of international existence where it could not be seen as having compromised its sovereignty position; this meant denying Taiwan use of the name Republic of China. In the 1980s, China accepted Taiwan's membership, under appropriately qualified nomenclature, of the Pacific Economic Cooperation Council (PECC), the Asian Development Bank (ADB), the International Olympic Committee (IOC), and later in the early 1990s, the Asia Pacific Economic Cooperation forum (APEC) and the South Pacific Forum (SPF).[11]

Yet, often with domestic tensions reflecting instability in Chinese governing circles and factional competition, China reacted strongly to what it saw as Japan pushing the Japan–Taiwan relations envelope further than that flexibility permitted. Earlier, although subsequent to normalisation, several instances, while never allowed to breach the relationship, had generated particular bilateral tension. Among them were the substantial centennial celebrations in Japan of Chiang Kai-shek's birth in 1987; also in 1987, the visit of a Japanese official to Taiwan accompanying DPRK defectors, despite the normalisation

[10] Roger Buckley, *US-Japan Alliance Diplomacy 1945–1990,* Cambridge University Press, 1992, p. 131.

[11] The long negotiations were usually around such terms as Taipei, China (ADB), or Chinese Taipei (APEC).

understanding that specified that relations should be limited to non-governmental and local contacts; and Japan's moves to compensate Taiwanese who served in the Japanese army during the Second World War.

More recent political relations between Japan and Taiwan have not been confined exclusively to the issue of recognition and the one China policy. The war issue has also been important. After a long period of representations, in December 1994, Japan decided to settle claims from Taiwan citizens for wartime debts, such as postal savings and compensation for Taiwanese conscripted into Japanese military service.[12] The Japanese offer, however, was less than one-fiftieth of the level demanded by the Taiwan government. Taiwan takes a similar position to the PRC in the territorial dispute with Japan over the Senkaku islands and this is periodically the scene of incidents between Taiwanese citizens and Japanese officials. Japan and Taiwan are competitors in fisheries, although allies on some international fishing issues such as drift net fishing. Taiwan has also been critical (together with China) of Japan's lack of openness of its import markets. Yet the economic relationship has become a major influence.

Japan and the Greater China economy

Economic integration among the 'three China's', based on complementarities of labour costs, investment capital, technologies and marketing and other know-how, has been increasing rapidly.[13] Despite its full potential being limited by Chinese regulatory barriers and Taiwan's caution arising from its geopolitical concerns, it reflects in Naughton's words, 'the triumph of economics over politics'. While dependent initially upon the success of labour intensive manufacturing development in Hong Kong and then Taiwan in the 1960s and 1970s, China facilitated this development by opening up its economy from 1978 onwards and by establishing a number of economic zones in southern China.

[12] *Daily Yomiuri*, 16 Dec. 1994, p. 1.

[13] From 1985 to 1995, exports from Taiwan, Hong Kong and Guandong and Fujian provinces together rose from 2.8 to 6.6% of world exports. Although exports from the three economies together grew at some 14% a year over the ten-year period, exports among the three economies grew by 23% a year. Barry Naughton, 'The Emergence of the China Circle' in Barry Naughton (ed.), *The China Circle: Economics and Technology in the PRC, Taiwan and Hong Kong*, Washington: Brookings Institution Press, 1997, pp. 7–12.

China may have seen the close economic ties of trade, investment and technology transfer between Hong Kong, Taiwan and China's coastal regions as creating an economic bloc that would be effective against Japan and the United States in the economic warfare in which it saw itself engaged.[14] And for a while, Japan was sensitive to the apparent political as well as economic potential of this development, in part because of the strong cultural and ethnic relationships that had facilitated that integration. Initially there was also some fear of the three economies, together with the ethnic Chinese in the region, forming a cohesive and exclusive group.

This fear, however, had little substance. Not only have Japanese entrepreneurs linked up extensively with ethnic Chinese in the Asia-Pacific region, but the development of the greater China economy reflects above all the process of internationalisation of the three economies. While the internationalisation process contributes to the integration of the three economies, it limits the external political potential, even were the respective governing systems more compatible. It also limits how far the concept of an economic bloc could emerge in reality. Not only does Greater China look outside itself for its major markets but it also remains dependent upon Japan for capital goods and technology.

Greater China's economic integration does put China in a position of enhanced importance in the regional economy, and therefore something that Japan has to take more seriously than in the past.[15] The overall significance of the integration of greater China for the Japan-China relationship, however, is mixed. Japan gains from its access to the markets of greater China as well as through integrated processes of affiliated companies in Taiwan and Hong Kong. It continues to have some concerns about the emergence of a competing major economic power in the region. Nevertheless, Japan continues to expand its investment in China, in part because of its own domestic high costs and diminishing competitiveness and in part to gain access to a growing market. China for its part recognises the benefits for its modernisation program but also the vulnerabilities involved in increased economic interdependence. It is also aware of how globalisation affects its own political processes as well as those of Taiwan.

[14] Christopher Howe, 'China, Japan and Economic Interdependence in the Asia-Pacific Region' in Christopher Howe (ed.), *China and Japan*, pp. 98–126.

[15] It also adds to China's difficulties with the United States since much of the trade surpluses of Taiwan and Hong Kong now fall to China's account.

Japan's relationships with Greater China have been affected by the economic downturn that started in Thailand in 1997 and subsequently spread through the region. China, Hong Kong and Taiwan have each been affected although in many respects, the more critical influence on these economies has been the economic consequences of Japan's own recession with its reduced markets for imports from Greater China. Each of the Greater China economies has so far resisted pressures to lower (or lower further in Taiwan's case) their exchange rates. Given the reliance on inputs from Japan, exchange rate depreciation would not greatly help their competitiveness. Many of their export products, notably electronics, are not directly competitive with the bulk of exports from those East Asian countries whose exchange rates have fallen, and competitiveness improved, as a consequence of the crisis. While the full Japanese recovery is seen as a longer rather than shorter term phenomenon, despite the short run effects on Greater China and absent major political change, the integration process among the three economies is likely to continue or resume as a long-term trend and the dependence on Japan to remain.

Japan's concerns about Greater China's economic strength may have diminished given the limited overlap of traded items, a better appreciation of the impacts of internationalisation, and the recognition of its continued superiority in the field of technology. Nevertheless, although varying estimates of China's GDP raise uncertainties about just how large its economy is, China has already joined Japan as a major component of the Asia-Pacific economy, a fact recognised during the 1997 Asian economic crisis.

Taiwan

Japan's administration laid much of the foundation for Taiwan's social and, particularly, economic development. As already observed, China had therefore been concerned in the early postwar decades that Taiwan might become excessively dependent upon Japan in the economic realm. This concern has become less significant as Taiwan's economic links with China have grown, while proportionately the links with Japan have declined. Taiwan's exports to Japan have for some years constituted less than 10% of its total exports, substantially less than the quarter or so of its exports that go to each the United

States and China/Hong Kong. Taiwan has run a substantial trade deficit with Japan for many years, in part because of its continued dependence on Japan for inputs and capital equipment, a dependence it has been attempting to reduce. Taiwan's deficit with Japan is counterbalanced by substantial surpluses with the United States and China.

Taiwan's economic development process was also initially modeled substantially on that of Japan. Yet Taiwan has moved from an emphasis on large enterprises, now giving greater weight to private small to medium sized enterprises and away from the full extent of government intervention and involvement previously in place.

China's imports from Taiwan similarly consist largely of inputs to its manufacturing, especially its export processing enterprises. Taiwan, through its 'go South' and 'no haste, be patient' policies has tried to limit its economic dependence on China but, as one study has argued, Taiwan's economic future is inevitably tied to China.[16] Now, the magnitude of Taiwan's exports to China is substantially greater than to Japan but it represents a much more substantial proportion of Taiwan's total exports. Taiwan will therefore continue to have a significant dependency relationship with both China and Japan, if through investment as much as trade links.

Hong Kong

The economic integration of Hong Kong and China began ahead of, and still exceeds that of, Taiwan. In framing its policies on Taiwan and China in the last decade, Japan gave increased attention to the transition of Hong Kong to China's sovereignty. In China's trade disputes with the United States, Japan supported Hong Kong's efforts to maintain China's MFN status because of its importance to Hong Kong's trade. Through the transition period, China sought and obtained Japan's firm support for the return of sovereignty on the basis of the 1984 China and United Kingdom joint declaration.

Japan remained somewhat sceptical about the likely success of the 'one country, two systems' formula, but it did not raise objections to

---

[16] Heather Smith and Stuart Harris, 'Cross-Strait Economic Relations: Dependence or Interdependence?' in Greg Austin (ed.), *Missile Diplomacy and Taiwan's Future: Innovations in Politics and Military Power*, Canberra: Strategic and Defence Studies Centre, 1997, p. 188.

the Legislative Council that had been elected under a system approved by Beijing to undermine the changes put in place by Governor Patten in the final years of British rule. Nor did Japan follow the lead of the United States and the United Kingdom, which had refused to attend the swearing in of the Provisional Legislative Council on the occasion of the hand-over. Without taking a strong position on issues of democracy as such, Japan had on various occasions stressed to the Chinese leaders its view of the importance of maintaining Hong Kong's open system, the rule of law and efficient administration.[17]

A stable political balance between Japan and China on the question of Taiwan depends in some measure on the handling of Hong Kong (and to a limited degree Macao) and the relationship the Hong Kong SAR is able to maintain with Japan, its second biggest trade partner. While the hand-over of Hong Kong to China took place smoothly in 1997, the political loyalties of the population to China and the attitudes of foreign governments on aspects of China's rule cannot be taken for granted. The economic fallout from the region's crisis that was felt almost immediately following the hand-over did not help.

Although the early stages of Hong Kong's transition, other than the economic difficulties, have been unproblematic, given its interests Japan would wish it to remain that way. Japan's economic interests in Hong Kong are now substantial. These come in part from past investment, much of it being in enterprises linked with China. While it continues to invest in Hong Kong, Japan in recent years has been more prepared to invest directly in China. It retains however substantial financial interests in Hong Kong.

Japan's One-China policy

When Japan recognised China in 1972, the head of the Treaties Bureau of Japan's Foreign Ministry explained that the meaning of recognition was that Japan had no intention of supporting the independence of Taiwan.[18] Before normalisation of relations with the Beijing government in 1972, the parliament of Japan was split

[17] See, for example, Foreign Minister Ikeda's comments, *Bungei Shimbun*, Sep. 1997 (FBIS-EAS-97-234).

[18] Takakazu Kuriyama, 'Some Legal Aspects of the Japan–China Joint Communiqué', *Japanese Annual of International Law*, no. 17, 1973, p. 45.

between pro-China and pro-Taiwan members. The Socialist Party members had been among the strongest advocates of normalisation with China, and the Liberal Democratic Party (LDP) contained the largest number of staunch opponents of such normalisation. After the 1972 US moves to recognise Beijing, Japanese public opinion was overwhelmingly in favour of the Sino-Japanese rapprochement, though elements within the LDP were still opposed.[19]

Despite the internal divisions, for the two decades afterwards Japan was more faithful to its change of recognition from Taiwan to China than many other countries in the US-led alliance system.[20] In subsequent years, relations between Japan and Taiwan, while never smooth, became more routinised and, for a considerable period, less politically significant than they became in the 1990s. Japan's official policy on contacts during that time, and restated as late as 1994, was that Taiwanese heads of government and cabinet members should not come to Japan, but non-governmental relations, such as trade, investment or tourism should continue unhindered.[21]

For some years after normalisation, small groups of Diet members actively campaigned for recognition of Taiwan or for the upgrading of political relations.[22] By the 1990s, much of the emotion and ideology had gone out of the question of recognition of one Chinese government or the other. For example, when the LDP split in 1993, the new parties formed as a result set up their own Taiwan groups, but these did not conduct their affairs with anything like the passion that had characterised such groups in the 1970s. Economic interests had become much more important than the earlier debates about defining political allegiances.

Taiwan's democratisation and new assertive diplomacy under Lee Teng-hui, following China's increased flexibility in the 1980s towards Taiwan's participation in regional bodies, contributed to a

[19] As did the Japanese Communist party since such rapprochement was seen as an anti-Moscow move.

[20] Japan continued to address China's concerns on the Taiwan issue. After the long reign of the LDP ended this was reaffirmed by the head of a coalition government, Socialist Party Prime Minister Murayama, who assured the Chinese that Japan would 'never do anything to create two Chinas'. China Radio International, 29 Oct. 1994, carried in SWB (Reuters), 1 Nov. 1994.

[21] Press Conference, Ministry of Foreign Affairs, 9 Sep. 1994.

[22] Liu Jiangyong, 'Sino–Japanese Relations facing the 21st Century', paper to an International Workshop held at the Australian National University, 27 Aug. 1996, p. 9.

rethinking of the hitherto relatively uncontroversial 'one-China' framework of Japan–Taiwan relations. This rethinking was assisted by revulsion toward China around the world because of the 1989 Tiananmen Square killings, and by China's subsequent diplomatic weakness as it tried to restore economic and technology transfer links with the developed countries. In the eyes of some pro-Taiwan parliamentarians, however, the associated growth in sympathy for Taiwan in Japan did not translate into political support for Taiwan's diplomatic goals.[23] There were, however, changes in Japan's interpretation of the one-China policy. For example, in 1993, Japan allowed the first Taiwanese ministerial visit since 1972 when Taiwan's foreign minister, Frederick Chien, made a 'private' visit.[24] In September 1994, Japan allowed the visit of Taiwan's Vice Premier Hsu Li-teh in connection with the 1994 Asian games, having been forced by Beijing to abandon a tacitly approved invitation from the organising committee of the games, a Saudi Arabian official, to President Lee. While the refusal to allow Lee to visit Japan for the games was a concession to Beijing, Japan did not back down altogether and the vice premier's visit lifted the level of Taiwanese officials to have visited Japan since normalisation. Nevertheless, the Japanese government sought to dress the meeting up as successfully as it could in the one-China framework and as a non-official visit.[25]

In advance of the Asian games, 110 LDP members of parliament had signed a petition urging the government to allow President Lee to visit for the games.[26] PRC pressure on Japan over the invitations to Taiwanese leaders to attend the games included a threat to block Japan's bid for permanent membership of the Security Council.[27] The threat was made in advance of the visit by Vice Premier Hsu but was received coldly by Japanese officials.[28]

In October 1994, the first official visit by a government minister from Taiwan took place when the minister for economic affairs, Chiang Ping-kun, visited Tokyo on APEC business. Not only did Prime Minister Hashimoto chair the meeting but there were bilateral

[23] *Japan Times*, 3 Jan. 1996.
[24] Ralph Clough, 'Taiwan–PRC Relations' in Robert G. Sutter and William R. Johnson, *Taiwan in World Affairs*, Boulder, CO: Westview Press, 1994, p. 225.
[25] Press Conference, Ministry of Foreign Affairs, 16 Sep. 1994.
[26] *Japan Times,* 3 Jan. 1996.
[27] *Nikkei Weekly*, 3 Oct. 1994, p. 4.
[28] *Japan Times*, 27 Oct. 1994.

meetings between Mr. Hashimoto and Mr Chiang.[29] Japan ignored warnings from China that the meeting between Hashimoto and Chiang could seriously damage Japan–China relations,[30] portraying it as part of the preparations for the APEC meeting in Osaka in 1995 that Chiang was to attend.[31]

Subsequent to President Lee's 1995 visit to Cornell University, opposition politicians urged the Japanese government to invite Lee to visit Kyoto University. There was also pressure for him to participate in the Osaka APEC meeting. although China's President, Jiang Zemin indicated he would boycott the meeting if this were to happen.[32]

The Taiwan issue was complicated for Japan by the March 1996 missile crisis (discussed later in this chapter), and subsequently by the statement by President Clinton during his 1998 visit to China of the 'three NOs' policy.[33] In foreshadowing President Jiang's visit to Japan in November 1998, China sought a Japanese affirmation of the 'three NOs' policy.[34] Japan was unwilling to give this, but reiterated its understanding, as expressed in the 1972 Joint Communiqué, 'that there is one China'. Japan would continue, however, to maintain its exchanges of private or economic nature, including regional economic coordination, with Taiwan.[35] Prime Minister Obuchi had earlier been reported as saying that he accepts the first two noes but not the third on the grounds that Japan had supported Taiwan's participation in such international bodies as APEC.[36]

Obuchi reaffirmed his support for the one-China policy and Japan's unwillingness to support Taiwan's independence in his 1999 visit to Beijing.[37] Japan was also prompt to restate its support for the one-China policy after President Lee's statement in his interview

[29] Press Conference, Ministry of Foreign Affairs, 18 Oct. 1994.

[30] Reuters, 22 Oct. 1994.

[31] *Japan Times*, 24 Oct. 1994.

[32] *Kyodo News Agency*, 23 June 1995 (FBIS China, 26 June 1995).

[33] No independence for Taiwan, no 'one China, one Taiwan', and no support for membership in international organisations that consist of states.

[34] Seiichiro Tagagi, 'In Search of a Sustainable Equal Partnership: Japan–China Relations in the Post-Cold-War Era', *Japan Review of International Affairs*, 13 (1), spring 1999, p. 35.

[35] Ministry of Foreign Affairs of Japan, *Japan–China Joint Declaration on Building a Partnership of Friendship and Cooperation for Peace and Development*, 26 Nov. 1998.

[36] Taiwan Central News Agency, 20 Sep. 1998.

[37] *Xinhua*, Beijing, 9 July 1999 (FBIS-EAS-1999-0709).

with a German radio station asserting Taiwan's shift to a one-nation, two states policy in July 1999.[38] Some at least of China's leaders, and many international observers saw this statement as a further shift by President Lee towards a declaration of independence. Given the electoral context in which it was made, despite their hostility, China's response will depend on the action's of Lee's successor.

Japanese leaders are likely to prefer the maintenance of the status quo across the Taiwan Strait or even an independent Taiwan, provided it could be achieved peacefully. It has been argued that Taiwan is important strategically to Japan and that it lies within 'Japan's defence zone'.[39] It sits adjacent to Japan's sea-lines of communication to Hong Kong, Southeast Asia and its oil routes from the Middle East, and to many of its major air links. The area covered by the nominal Japanese policy of protecting its sea-lanes for 1000 nautical miles includes Taiwan and Taiwan's shipping routes to Japan. But the balance of opinion in Japan is very firmly in favour of the view that stable strategic relations with China are more important than any strategic advantages offered by an independent Taiwan. Occasional surfacing of views in Japan about the strategic value of an independent Taiwan is therefore unlikely to force Japan to shift from a 'one-China' policy.

China's view of Japan's One-China policy

For much of the period since normalisation, China could be reasonably reassured about Japan's position on the 'one China' policy but the adjustments in Japan's understanding of the policy beginning in 1994 ensured that some of China's old sensitivities about Japan's interests in Taiwan re-emerged. China's sensitivities on Taiwan affairs in general had been aggravated by Taiwan's 'pragmatic diplomacy', involving President Lee's 'golfing visits' to South East Asia, and then his visit to Cornell University in the United States in 1995. Taiwan's moves and the lean to Taiwan by US President Clinton in his first term brought Japan's response to these developments to the top of the Japan-China agenda for China's leaders.

China's concerns about Japan's policy toward Taiwan have three elements. First, China cannot tolerate growing support for Taiwan

---

[38] Reuters, Tokyo, 13 July 1999.

[39] Gary Klintworth, *New Taiwan, New China: Taiwan's Changing Role in the Asia-Pacific Region*, Melbourne: Longman/New York: St Martin's Press, 1995, pp. 41–3.

independence in any of the major powers, and in that respect Japan's position is especially important. If a major power like Japan moved to a 'two-China' policy and accorded Taiwan greater political recognition, this would start an avalanche of similar policy changes by lesser states. Japan's economic and political interests in Taiwan (though less substantial than those in China itself) do provide some incentive, though not a strong one, for Japan to change its recognition policy.

Second, many in China have been sensitive to the proposition that Japan may be more of a natural partner for Taiwan in economic and political terms than China itself. This sensitivity in China re-emerged as a result of actions by Lee Teng-hui, which hark back to the fifty-year period of rule by Japan of Taiwan between 1895 and 1945. Lee learned Japanese at school (he is understood to speak it better than Chinese), and studied at a Japanese university. He frequently received Japanese MPs, in marked contrast to the practice of President Jiang Zemin.[40] The sensitivity in Beijing is aggravated by the consideration that the government in power there has not effectively controlled Taiwan any time in the last 100 years. Although anti-Japanese sentiments in Taiwan have been powerful at times, they lacked the intensity that existed in Japan's other major ex-colony, Korea, or in mainland China. Older Taiwanese have held relatively comfortably to their Japanese links. By the 1990s, historical resentments in Taiwan tend to have settled more on the actions of the Nationalist Party mainlanders, such as a 1947 massacre, rather than on the Japanese colonialists.

The sensitivity in Beijing about the possible revival of Japan's links of governance with Taiwan was clearly aggravated by President Lee but whatever the substance for concerns in this direction might have had, it is diminishing. The strengthening Japan-China economic relationship, as demonstrated later in this study, provides strong incentives for Japan to maintain good political relations with China. Moreover, Taiwan's growing economic dependence on China itself helps discourage Taiwan from pursuing policies that risk a total breach with China. As importantly, strong sympathies for Japan in Taiwan are confined mainly to a section of the older generations. The strength of such connections may not last long after Lee and his generation pass from the scene.

[40] *Japan Times*, 3 Jan. 1996.

There are substantial personal and professional exchanges between Japan and Taiwan, but these do not provide a foundation for a political relationship that would justify fears in China of some reassertion of Japanese political domination of Taiwan.[41] If anything, most people in Taiwan feel either a rather strong sense of national independence, some close affinities with China, or some close affinities with the United States. Japan does not register for most Taiwanese as a source of cultural or spiritual identification. There is certainly little support in Japan for a closer political association with Taiwan of the sort that might draw upon historical memories of Japan's rule the island. For most of the time since 1972, Taiwan has been relatively invisible in the Japanese media since the main agencies had to choose between representation in Taiwan or on the mainland. This situation eased a little after 1988, but affairs in China are still covered far more extensively in the Japanese press than affairs in Taiwan. Overall, there has been little evidence in recent decades that any impact of Taiwan on the domestic life of Japanese people is perceived as operating to the exclusion or necessary disadvantage of China's image.[42]

Third, and regardless to some extent of Japan's history of possession of Taiwan from 1895 to 1945, there have been influential people in China who interpret Japan's interests in Taiwan from a strategic

[41] Many Taiwanese visit Japan. Of some two thirds of a million visitors to Japan each year from Taiwan, Hong Kong and China, Taiwan provides the large majority (see *Facts and Figures of Japan: 1998 edition,* Foreign Press Center, Japan, 1998, and earlier editions). There are more flights between Japan and Taiwan and Japan and Hong Kong than between Japan and China. Of the two Taiwan airlines involved (Eva Airways and China Airlines) China Airlines has no routes to Japan's three major international airports, Narita, Itami and Kansai (China Airlines is the only international airline to use Haneda, which although less prestigious is more convenient than Narita). Taiwan holds only a limited cultural appeal, and if anything, that is likely to decline in the future. While cultural interactions between China and Taiwan are much stronger than those between Japan and Taiwan, however, this is not to the total exclusion of Japanese influence through films, television programs and comic strips – there are also many karaoki bars in Taiwan, though it is being widely replaced by new orientations towards the United States, China and the world at large. Moreover, although the absorption of international popular culture generally needs an Asian cover, that cover is likely to be the Chinese characteristics provided by Taiwan and Hong Kong rather than Japan.

[42] In 1996 and 1997 polls, no Taiwanese city was included in the top ten cities that Japanese wanted to visit. Advertising Department of Mainichi Newspapers, Tokyo (Japan Information Network).

point of view,[43] somewhat analogous to former US security concerns about Cuba. The proposition is that as long as the Beijing government does not control Taiwan, it is still important to deny any strategic lodgement on the island to potential military adversaries, such as Japan.[44] Given the ever present concern about Japan's potential militarism and its strengthened military links with the United States, the continuing references by PLA sources to the support by 'foreign forces' of possible moves by Taiwan to independence undoubtedly encompass Japan.[45] A major concern is that the United States and Japan will in a crisis 'gang-up' on China.[46] Some believe that Taiwan would have strategic value to Japan were Japan's relations with China to worsen or should the US security link with Japan either become less secure,[47] or were the United States to seek to build up Japan's regional security role. Some PLA strategists are concerned at the potential for surprise attacks from the East and South China seas in the future. Their coastal strategy involves an objective of being able to operate effectively in the waters around the chain of islands that included Japan's home islands and Taiwan.[48] Obviously control of Taiwan by unfriendly hands would constrain this objective. The issue consequently remains central to the relationship and links up

[43] See, for example, *Beijing Review,* 26 Nov.–2 Dec. 1990, pp. 15–16, citing Yang Shangkun.

[44] Until normalisation with the United States, Taiwan was a US military base that was used, among other things, to service the war in Indochina against China's North Vietnamese allies. From China's perspective, it could be used in the future as a base for cooperation between adversaries of China and an independent government on Taiwan. See Robert Ross, *Negotiating Cooperation: The United States and China 1969–1989,* Stanford University Press, 1995, p. 11

[45] As, for example, Yang Shangkung, in Oct. 1991, cited in Allen Whiting 'Chinese Nationalism and Foreign Policy After Deng', *China Quarterly,* 142 (June 1995), pp. 295–316. There are still memories in China of Chiang Kai-shek's attempts to develop relations with the Soviet Union in the mid-1960s as a means of isolating mainland China. Those attempts were eventually unsuccessful. They were, however, an early cause of the Chinese statements that an alliance with China's enemies by Taiwan would lead to China using force against Taiwan. Simon Long, *Taiwan: China's Last Frontier,* London: Macmillan 1991, pp. 147–50.

[46] Mel Gurtov and Byong-Moo Hwang, *China's Security: The New Roles of the Military,* Boulder, CO: Lynne Rienner, 1998, p. 75.

[47] Andrew Nathan and Robert Ross, *The Great Wall and the Empty Fortress: China's Search for Security,* New York: W.W. Norton, 1997, p. 88.

[48] John Wilson Lewis and Xue Litai, *China's Strategic Seapower: The Politics of Force Modernization in the Nuclear Age,* Stanford University Press, 1994, pp. 229–30.

with, but goes beyond, China's concerns about resurgent Japanese militarism.

The March 1996 crisis

Whatever the underlying realities of the March missile crisis over Taiwan, and there are arguments that the firing of unarmed ballistic missiles into the waters not far off the coast of Taiwan had substantial elements of a shadow play,[49] the perceptions that were generally gained from it sensitised the international community to the problem of Taiwan. More specifically, it was widely believed in Japan that it offered the potential for a military conflict over Taiwan.

Japan had been uneasy over the earlier Chinese missile tests in the East China Sea in 1995, in part because it followed closely China's testing of nuclear devices to which Japan had taken particular exception. While the missile tests were designed as a warning to Taiwan, Japan continued to reaffirm its view to China that it expected the Taiwan issue to be settled peacefully. Nevertheless, by the time China announced in March 1996 that it was proposing missile exercises there had already been considerable discussion in Japanese conservative circles about the need to shore up its alliance with the United States against the prospect of a military confrontation over Taiwan, as well as concern over China's strategic policy generally. Although the initial Japanese response to the missile test announcement remained moderate, consisting of a call for restraint, subsequently Japan's reaction became stronger.

Various conflicting pressures exist within Japan with respect to China and Taiwan. We noted earlier that the pro-China lobby in Japan, many of whose members had been brought up in China, has diminished in size and influence. So, however, has the old pro-Taiwan lobby. Those who look at the issue afresh – whether anti-China or pro-China – have replaced them. That the Japanese position is now more influenced by public opinion, and less influenced by cultural memories or feelings of guilt towards China, was important in Japan's responses to the missile crisis.

Reflecting among other things a strong public reaction, Japan had frozen grant aid to China over its nuclear weapon testing in the previous year. There were calls from some Diet members to extend that action in 1996 to its provision of low interest loans to China under

<hr />

[49] See, for example, Chalmers Johnson, 'Containing China: US and Japan Drift Towards Disaster', *Japan Quarterly*, Oct.–Dec. 1996, p. 11.

its bilateral economic cooperation arrangements. Although the Japanese government did slow the processing of new loans it was reluctant to go further, given the impact it feared on the already strained nature of the bilateral relationship arising from its earlier response to China's nuclear testing. Moreover, Japanese experts were playing down any direct military consequences for Japan, recognising the limits of China's capabilities towards Taiwan.[50] Defence interests in Japan, however, expressed concerns about what might emerge as a consequence of the missile exercise and what that might mean for Japan's possible involvement.

Notwithstanding fairly measured assessments in Japan of the low likelihood of escalation by China, the missile tests provoked new expressions of concern on the part of the JDA about Japan's specific vulnerabilities in the event of military action by China. Japanese authorities were reported as unable to detect the M-9 ballistic missiles launched to land in waters near Taiwan in the first week of March 1996; Japan relied on US-supplied information to confirm China launches and their splashdown points. In particular, it was argued by security interests in Japan that Japan had no means of tracking a ballistic missile targeted on Taiwan if it veered off course and headed for Japanese territory – obviously a useful piece of information in itself.

Yet, from a Chinese viewpoint, the events of 1996 reflected 'the culminating failure of the moderate, peaceful approach' it had long been taking towards Taiwan.[51] In heading off what it saw as a Taiwanese move to independence, China judged the missile exercise a success. It had consequences that were unfavourable in Japan adverse to China. Apart from the generalities of increased US–Japan security cooperation, however, it strengthened support for a previously mooted plan to introduce a theatre missile defence (TMD) system in Japan, which is of considerable concern to China – among other reasons, because of its potential extension to Taiwan. It also led to talks on Japan–US cooperation in provision of early warning of ballistic missile launches on a real-time basis to the Japanese authorities.[52] Subsequently, US Defense Department pressures on Japan and concerns about reports of rocket development in the region,

[50] Reuters, 22 Mar. 1996.

[51] Richard Bernstein and Ross Munro, *The Coming Conflict With China*, New York, Alfred Knopf, 1997, p. 161.

[52] *Daily Yomiuri*, 10 Mar. 1996, p. 2. Japan has since launched its first 'intelligence satellite, the precise purpose of which remains somewhat ambiguous.

led to proposals for budget funds to be provided for Japan–US collaboration in TMD research.[53]

Although the missile crisis was not the major public issue in Japan at the time, it was an important item and public sentiments in Japan had 'swung largely in favour of Taiwan'.[54] It could also be argued, however, that the responses to the launches reflected a continuation of a shift in Japanese attitudes to China and Taiwan that had been taking place over the period since 1989. For example, new associations for closer relations with Taiwan were formed in the Diet in 1997. Yet, while Japanese public opinion had shifted, how far it had shifted is unclear, how long the heightened concern of the time will be sustained is similarly unclear. More generally, however, the crisis did contribute to a firmer stance on the part of Japan towards China over Taiwan. The formal protests it made to China in March 1996 constituted the first occasion since normalisation that Japan had made Taiwan the subject of such protests.

For Japan, the missile crisis taken with China's nuclear testing, raised more general concerns in the minds of the Japanese public over China's actions and behaviour. The immediate concern it raised in governing circles, however, concerned Japan's response to any US military involvement in the region in the light of Japan's constitutional and other constraints. This concern was the subject of discussions on the security guidelines within the US–Japan security arrangements which had coincided with China's pressure on Taiwan.

As the March missile crisis developed, an LDP commission had been asked to work out promptly guidelines for Japan in the event of a crisis in the Taiwan Strait (or on the Korean Peninsula). It was to make clear what steps Japan could take consistent with the Constitution and other laws.[55] At the same time, the commission was asked to look at ways to strengthen the US–Japan security treaty.

US–Japan defence arrangements and Taiwan

Although China might be seen as offering Japan its greatest long-term strategic uncertainty, the evidence is ambiguous as to whether

---

[53] *Tokyo Shimbun,* 21 Aug. 1998 (FBIS-EAS-98-238). TMD was discussed more fully in Chapter 3.

[54] *Japan Times,* 26 Mar. 1996.

[55] Hijiri Inose, 'China Missiles Wake-Up Call To Japan? Regional Friction Eases Security Issue Taboo', *Nikkei Weekly,* 18 Mar. 1996, p. 1.

Japan really sees it that way. It is not attempting to balance China's military modernisation,[56] nor is its economic relationship affected, directly at least, by any concern to limit China's economic growth. While Japan's military strategy remains tied to that of the United States, the strengthening of its security links with the United States in 1996 and 1997, although seen by many observers as substantial, has been portrayed by other analysts as much more limited.[57]

For Japan, other factors, such as the threats to the security of oil supplies raised by the Gulf War, the North Korean nuclear crisis, North Korea's rocket launch and China's nuclear testing were important influences. Given these other factors, precisely how influential were the Taiwan tensions in influencing those closer US links is difficult to assess precisely. It was also a time when memories of what the United States saw as Japanese policy failures over the Gulf War and Korean crisis involvement were still in mind and the Okinawa incident was still affecting domestic Japanese opinion. Nevertheless, while these other factors were probably more important, uncertainty over the Taiwan issue in 1995–6 helped to strengthen the support in Japan for the US-Japan security pact and for the revised guidelines.[58] It also raised the issue of what Japan would do, or was able to do, in the event of a conflict involving its US ally.

The reactions of the Japanese government to the missile launches can only be fully appreciated in the light of Japan's views on the US use of its bases in Japan in combat with China over Taiwan.[59] During

[56] Many security analysts believe that despite China's 'modernisation', it continues to fall further behind Japan's capability. See, for example, James Holt, 'The China-Taiwan Balance', World Policy Institute, New York, 7 Jan. 2000.

[57] For the view that it is insubstantial see Eric Heginbotham and Richard Samuels, 'Mercantile Realism and Japanese Foreign Policy', *International Security*, 22(4), spring 1998, pp. 171–203.

[58] A 1999 Kyodo public opinion poll showed 65.5% support for the new guidelines. *Kyodo News Agency*, Tokyo, 28 Apr. 1999 (FBIS-EAS-1999-0427). Other polls, however, were more equivocal raising questions about the level of understanding of the questions. See 'The United States and Japan in 1999: Coping with Crises', Washington DC: Edwin O. Reischauer Centre for Asian Studies, Johns Hopkins University, 1999, p. 32.

[59] There are five major US bases or base complexes in Japan – three on Honshu, one on Kyushu and one on Okinawa. Yokusuka is the home port of the US Seventh Fleet and US forces in Okinawa are just under 700 km. from Taipei. Details of the bases are given in Paul Giarra, 'U.S. Bases in Japan: Historical Background and Innovative Approaches to Maintaining Strategic Presence' in Michael Green and Patrick Cronin (eds), *The U.S. Alliance: Past, Present and Future*, New York: Council on Foreign Relations Press: 1999, 114–38.

the period of heightened tension between Japan and China in March 1996, Japan did not object to the US deployment of aircraft carriers, including the one home-ported in Japan. Japan's prime minister declined to comment on the US decision to deploy the naval forces normally based in Japanese ports, except to say that there was nothing to say since the US forces were operating in international waters.[60] Japan's position on closer support for US forces in the event of hostilities in the region created added tension in Japan-China relations shortly after China terminated its military exercises opposite Taiwan. During a visit by President Clinton to Tokyo in April 1996, which had been planned some considerable time earlier, he and Prime Minister Hashimoto signed a 'Japanese-US Security Assurance Joint Declaration'. The document, along with one on logistic support signed just prior to Clinton's arrival, reportedly repositioned the Japan-US alliance as a cornerstone of regional security, and reaffirmed the application of the treaty to include events in the Far East as well as direct military threats to Japan.[61]

Whether this was so in fact is unclear. Prime Minister Hashimoto seemed to move back from President Clinton's use of the term Asia-Pacific to describe the common defence perimeter, and Japan was concerned to assure China that the joint declaration was not aimed at expanding the coverage of the security treaty.[62] In practice, it is hard to see how it did not expand that coverage to some degree, although there is room for debate about how much expansion is involved. That will only be finally resolved when relevant situations arise and are responded to.

Certainly, in many respects, the agreements reached between Clinton and Hashimoto might be seen as little more than a clarification or reaffirmation of existing arrangements. They came after nearly a decade of fairly acrimonious disputes between the two countries on a range of economic issues. Added to these were the new pressures on US bases in Okinawa, differences on how to handle the Korean nuclear crisis of 1994, and continuing concerns over aspects of the

[60] Reuters, 12 Mar. 1996.

[61] On 15 Apr. 1996, just before President Clinton's visit to Tokyo from 16 to 18 April, the two countries had signed the 'Japanese-US Agreement on Mutual Supplies of Materials and Labour', a cross-servicing agreement which relates to peace-keeping or humanitarian missions, and which does not explicitly cover military emergencies not involving an attack on Japan.

[62] Heginbotham and Samuels, op. cit., p. 185.

long running issue of burden sharing.[63] China's military intimidation
of Taiwan during March 1996 was seen as demonstrating the need for
a new agreement between the United States and Japan on consultations during a regional crisis, since there had been no consultation
between them on the decision by the United States to deploy a Japan-
based carrier in connection with the crisis.[64] Moreover, Japan's foreign ministry had been conscious for several months before March
1996 of the need for the two countries to iron out any differences
on the use of Japanese forces or facilities in support of US military
operations in a Taiwan crisis if one occurred.[65]

   There were therefore pre-existing reasons for reaffirmation or
clarification of the Japan–US treaty commitments. Nevertheless, the
timing of this action, coming only one month after China's military
pressure against Taiwan, and after almost two years of cooling relations between China and Japan, carried substantial implications for
the future of the Taiwan issue in Japanese politics. At the very least,
China's military pressure reduced the domestic controversy that
might have surrounded the Japan–US military agreements as a result
of the sustained opposition in Okinawa to the US use of military
facilities there.[66] During March 1996, negotiations to reduce the US
military presence in Okinawa were underway. Foreign ministry
officials believed at the time that China's military pressure on Taiwan
would probably have a favourable effect in the longer term on the
US–Japan security alliance, even though it may not influence the
outcome of the specific negotiations over Okinawa.[67]

[63] Intensive negotiations between Japan and the United States on enhanced
security cooperation had been underway since 1994 in the wake of US disaffection
with Japan's response to US requests for support during the Korean nuclear crisis. The United States was seeking to clarify Japan's position on US use of military
facilities in case of a regional emergency, and Japan was seeking to satisfy its heightened interest in more effective participation in regional security affairs.

[64] Reuters, 12 Mar. 1996.

[65] *Japan Times*, 4 Jan. 1996.

[66] Okinawa hosts more than three-quarters of US bases in Japan and more than
half of the US military personnel and political opposition to the bases in Okinawa
became intense in the mid 1990s. Following the 1996 Clinton-Hashimoto summit,
it was agreed that a major air base would be relocated elsewhere in Okinawa, releas-
ing the key site to civilian control as part of a scaling down of the US presence. The
negotiations to locate an alternative site were proceeding slowly but with more
chance of success after the change in the provincial governor at election.

[67] *Nikkei Weekly*, 18 Mar. 1996, p. 1. This press report saw Japan's response, condi-
tioned by its desire to avoid serious offence to China, as consistent with that of many

Japan made considerable efforts to reassure China that the new arrangements were not directed at China. Even before Clinton arrived in Tokyo, Hashimoto had told China's visiting foreign minister, Qian Qichen, that the upcoming talks between Japan and the United States would not harm ties between Japan and China. Qian, in response, had called on Japan to ensure that the planned redefinition of the US–Japan alliance not affect China.[68] China was not convinced by a succession of such assurances.

Sharper exchanges between China and Japan took place in the lead-up to publication of the interim review on new guidelines for US–Japan security cooperation foreshadowed in the April agreements and discussed in Chapter 3. The publication in June 1997 of the interim report and then the subsequent publication of the agreed guidelines brought new controversy between Japan and China. The main point of contention was the adoption of a new terminology of 'areas surrounding Japan' instead of the term 'Far East', which figures in the 1978 guidelines and the 1960 US–Japan treaty.[69] Japan's Foreign Minister Ikeda suggested that the term 'surrounding areas' did not change the meaning of the 'Far East' but acknowledged that the two concepts were a 'little different'.[70] The new emphasis was on the 'situations themselves rather than on the areas in which they occur'.

Japanese officials remained firm in all discussions with Chinese officials that as long as China did not resort to force, then China could have no complaints about the guidelines. Japanese officials, including the prime minister, sought to address China's primary immediate concern by strongly denying any support for Taiwan's bid to join the UN or for greater official diplomatic recognition.

Immediately after the new guidelines were published, Japan briefed China (and South Korea) on their content and Ikeda responded to Chinese complaints about the outmoded nature of the guidelines by suggesting that China should be more active in a vigorous ARF process to assuage its concerns.[71] Hashimoto had sought to reassure

---

other occasions, although it did report Hashimoto's remarks that Japan and the United States were the only two at the time of his statement to have expressed concern directly to China through diplomatic channels.

[68] Ibid.

[69] The term 'Far East' was never defined by precise geographical coordinates or other means, though it was always conceived as being geographically determined.

[70] *Bungei Shunju*, Sep. 1997, pp. 370–7 (FBIS-EAS-97-234, 22 Aug. 1997).

[71] Ibid.

Chinese leaders in Beijing in September by invoking the transparency of the Japanese policy process on the question of military support of the United States and highlighting the lack of specificity of the sort of contingencies they covered. [72]

China again was not convinced. Assessing his visit to Japan in November 1997, Prime Minister Li Peng observed dryly that 'it would have been more satisfactory if Prime Minister Hashimoto had added that Japan-US security cooperation does not include Taiwan.'[73] In practice, the Chinese government has identified, quite reasonably, that the basic trend in the leadership circles of the LDP is towards redefining the security policy of Japan in order to maintain the alliance with the United States and to ensure the United States' continued provision of Japan's security. They point to a series of statements in August by leading officials, including Chief Cabinet Secretary Kajiyama and Foreign Minister Ikeda, in support of the view that the term 'surrounding areas' or the ambit of the US-Japan treaty unambiguously includes a threat to regional peace over Taiwan.[74] President Jiang Zemin commented that the remarks of the chief cabinet secretary that the guidelines covered the Taiwan Strait 'are indelibly imprinted on my mind'.[75]

When the guidelines were passed by the Diet in May 1999, they referred to 'situations in areas surrounding Japan'. They were limited to help in search and rescue operations, and undertaking minesweeping and to providing greater logistic support, including the use of Japanese hospitals, ports and airfields and the provision of fuel and equipment. In addition Japanese ships could be dispatched for the first time to evacuate endangered Japanese overseas.[76] The provisions of the bills specified that the situations in areas surrounding Japan are situations 'that could lead to the nation being the direct target of armed attacks if no action is taken'.

Japan has tried to avoid specifying under what circumstances it would provide rear-area support for US forces. The implication of

---

[72] See for example press conference with Hashimoto, HHK General Television, 6 Sep. 1997 (FBIS-EAS-97-251, 8 Sep. 1997).

[73] Interview with NHK, 13 Nov. 1997, Xinhua, 13 Nov. 1997 (FBIS-CHI-97-318), 14 Nov. 1997.

[74] See *Wen Wei Po*, 2 Aug. 1997, p. A2 (FBIS-CHI-97-234, 22 Aug. 1997); *Far Eastern Economic Review*, 4 Sep. 1997, p. 32.

[75] Nobumichi Izumi, 'Jiang Wants China-Japan Economic Plan', *Nikkei Weekly*, 15 Dec. 1997, p. 21.

[76] *Nikkei Weekly*, 31 May 1999.

this shift in terminology, however, is most probably that the guidelines now cover any threat to Japan's security, one of which would be
hostilities between China and Taiwan or perhaps even a threat by
China to use force against Taiwan, were such circumstances to arise.

At the same time, China has identified that key political groups in
Japan do not as readily accept the government's moves as being less
constraining on the SDF. The issue of the guidelines' coverage had
been caught up in LDP factional fights. Differences did arise within
the LDP at the time. Thus LDP Secretary General Kato argued publicly that the areas covered by the guidelines do not cover Taiwan.[77]
Kato also reprimanded the more conservative Kajiyama, a political
rival, for his statement that Taiwan was included in the guideline
coverage.[78] Kajiyama subsequently resigned. Others differing included the Socialist Party and the former Shinshinto Party.[79] The
Socialist Party, then a coalition partner in government with the LDP,
specifically advocated the exclusion of the Taiwan case from the
guidelines.[80]

China also probably appreciates that the moves by Japan on the
guidelines were pressed on it in part by the United States originally
for reasons other than China. It also probably accepts that Japan's
attitude on further cooperation with United States rests in part on
a desire not to alienate it as an ally rather than on any real desire to
become embroiled in military hostilities with China. Thus for
China, while the changes in the guidelines are not acceptable, their
long-term impact is probably assessed as manageable as long as trends
in Japanese opinion and in international diplomatic practice remain
sensitive to China's position on Taiwan.

Nevertheless, China does have continuing interests and concerns
over just what level of support Japan would provide to US forces
given the changed guidelines, and these remain to a degree still to be
resolved. Certainly, in the highly unlikely event of a conflict, Japan
would be in a difficult position. Japan's public position is that it
has ruled out direct participation in combat by its military forces,
but there remain questions whether the public position reflects the
likely reality in some future contingency. In a Chinese blockade of

[77] *Yomiuri Shimbun*, 24 July 1997, p. 2 (CND Daily Report, 23 July 1997).
[78] *Asahi Shimbun*, 3 Sep. 1997.
[79] See for example, *Xinhua News Agency*, 12 Nov. 1997 (FBIS-CHI-97-316).
[80] *Daily Yomiuri*, 24 Sep. 1997, p. 6 (NDB).

Taiwan, for example, Japanese minesweeping could involve Japan's forces in combat.[81]

In 1991, Paul Kreisberg assessed that there was little support in Asia generally for Taiwan's efforts to change its international status and that Japan's likely responses to military pressure by China on Taiwan would be shaped by the following considerations:

- Japan would want to see any hostilities end as quickly as possible;
- Japan would probably prefer to be presented with a *fait accompli* by the United States in respect of use of its military bases in Japan to intervene in a conflict over Taiwan, rather than be asked to make a decision;
- most Japanese are unlikely to see conflict with China over Taiwan as related to Japanese security;
- many Japanese would fear that involvement by Japan would revive Sino–Japanese antagonisms which would endure for decades;
- if compelled to choose between China and the United States, Japanese officials would choose the latter, but 'the domestic politics of this choice may not be so easy to resolve swiftly and decisively'.[82]

These considerations will at most have been changed only marginally by subsequent developments. In 1997 John Garver argued that were Japan forced to make a choice between the United States and China 'the result would be immense resentment in Japan'.[83]

The dilemma for Japan is even clearer today and would seem to have been reflected in the prompt Japanese response to Lee Teng-hui's special state to state relationship statement. Were Japan to be involved in military combat on the side of the United States over Taiwan, it would mean that it was engaged in a military conflict with China, an outcome that to many Japanese would be unthinkable; if it stayed out of such a conflict while US troops were engaged, this would almost

[81] Thomas Christensen, 'China, the US-Japan Alliance and the Security Dilemma in East Asia', *International Security*, 23 (4), 1999, pp. 69, 74.

[82] Paul Kreisberg, 'Asian Responses to Pressures on Taiwan' in Parris H. Chang and Martin L. Lasater (eds), *If China Crosses the Taiwan Strait – The International Response*, New York: University Press of America, 1993, pp. 82, 91, 93.

[83] John Garver, *Face off: China, the United States and Taiwan's Democratisation*, Seattle: University of Washington Press, 1997, p. 139.

certainly lead to the withdrawal of US domestic support for the security relationship.[84] The only way to save Japan from this dilemma would be to ensure that war over Taiwan does not arise.

For China's leaders, the need to re-establish China's sovereignty over Taiwan is symbolically and politically important. Their most pressing concern, however, is to prevent Taiwan from making a complete break from the principle that it is part of 'one China'. The century of Taiwan's separation from the Beijing government makes China especially sensitive to any suggestion that Taiwan might be drawn close enough to any other great power to be encouraged to make the final break with the 'one China' principle. After the United States, Japan would be the most significant. This sensitivity has been aggravated in recent years, and Japan-China relations have suffered some strain as a result. A determined move by Taiwan toward independence would, if supported by a significant number of important countries, provoke a serious crisis in Japan-China relations. China is also concerned about more gradual or evolutionary transitions whereby Japan, while holding to its 'one China' policy, might still encourage Taiwan in its moves to gain greater political recognition or strategic room for manoeuvre. The new US-Japan defence cooperation guidelines are seen in that light, as is the prospect for potential participation by Japan in a ship based regional theatre missile defence system that could easily be transferred to Taiwan.

Senior Chinese leaders balance these deeply felt concerns about Japan's direct influence on Taiwan against the consideration that Taiwan will inevitably grow closer to the mainland. While Taiwan was once a Japanese colony, it has over the decades since 1949 carved out an identity that owes much less to Japan than it does to China. Whether China's concerns about Japan's strategic relationship with Taiwan will decline over time will depend in part upon Japan but a bigger influence will be on US actions and China's perceptions of its relations with the United States.

For now, there are important domestic constituencies in Japan for supporting the status quo in Taiwan (as there are in Taiwan) and for

---

[84] The difficult security position of Japan (and Korea) is discussed in Edward Olsen, 'The role of Taiwan in Asian Multilateral Security: Towards the 21st Century' *Journal of East Asian Affairs*, XII (I), winter/spring, 1998, pp. 25–53.

preventing any military clash between China and the United States. Japan's interest in ensuring no such clash will have been heightened by its closer military links to the United States. In economic terms, there are also few incentives for Japan to abandon its support for the principle of 'one China'. Japan is considerably more important to Taiwan than the reverse. To Taiwan, Japan is one of only a few countries central to its economic prosperity. For Japan, Taiwan is just one of many partners, and is of considerably less economic significance to Japan in the longer term than China, especially when Japanese economic interests in Hong Kong are taken into account. More broadly, the history of benign or positive influences from Japan on Taiwan, often cited as the basis of closer relations, are likely to decline over time. Moreover, they do not compensate for the essentially unequal power relationship between Taiwan and Japan. Left to itself, Japan could be expected to continue to support the principle of 'one China' and to avoid any suggestion of support for Taiwan independence.

On the other hand, the political management of the Taiwan issue by Japan involves powerful interests beyond its economic, political and strategic interests in good relations with China. Japan remains influenced by the fundamental political and strategic circumstances of its alliance with the United States. This alliance is marked by a heavy Japanese dependence on the United States for military security and for access to natural resources. The Japanese government must also be responsive to a domestic public opinion that would be opposed to any significant reorientation of the country's strategic posture. The Japanese government may want to be seen as having a degree of independence from the United States by not following its policy too closely on the Taiwan issue, and not being involved in any possible military action that the United States might take in any conflict over Taiwan. It could not stay too far apart, however, without putting the security alliance at risk.

This chapter suggests that within Japan the greater sympathy for Taiwan as a result of democratisation and the growing discomfort over China's military posture have altered the dynamics of domestic politics on support for the US in any military confrontation with China over Taiwan. In such a confrontation, Japanese officials would be under pressure to side with the USA but the domestic politics of this choice would be difficult to assess ahead of some conception of the circumstances at the time. As well as the immediate China-Taiwan questions, they would also raise the basic and still unsettled question of Japan's military role.

The next decade will see more pressures on Japan–China relations, including growing pressure in Taiwan for greater international recognition; and increased sensitivity in both China and Japan to the greater influence of the other in regional security and economic affairs. China will continue to press Japan for assurances on the issue of guidelines for military cooperation with US forces in the event of military conflict. How important that will be will depend upon the atmospherics of regional relationships and upon the influence of particular interests within China. To China, anything that strengthens Taiwan's negotiating position will be seen as unhelpful. There will also be pressures from some domestic constituencies in China that favour a more confrontational posture towards Taiwan. As long as representatives of these groups remain in the minority in China's national decision-making bodies (either formal or informal), China is likely to work assiduously to prevent a Taiwan-related crisis from escalating to where it presents a major threat to regional security or to Japan. Yet the China-Taiwan relationship will remain not just uncertain but volatile and potentially destabilising.

As already mentioned, US-China relations will be an important determinant of the Japan-China relationship and how Taiwan affects it. Provided the US administration's policy of engagement with China is continued and the United States maintains the 'three NOs' line affirmed by President Clinton, the status quo is likely to be maintained across the Taiwan Strait. The US Congress, however, is more subject to Taiwanese pressure, and anti-China rhetoric is useful for domestic political purposes. In election periods, the China-Taiwan issue could, as in the past, became a campaign issue. Although, in those circumstances, the ability of Japan to stay neutral in the political and strategic debate may be tested, on present indications there is an increased likelihood that it will do so.

In the case of Hong Kong, the social contract between its population and Beijing is far from complete and the future of this relationship will have continuing implications for the question of Taiwan's future, even though Taiwan denies its relevance. Hong Kong's role as entrepot for China trade and as a regional financial centre may well decline somewhat under the integrationist course currently taking place between China and the rest of the world. Economic problems arose for Hong Kong from the Asian economic crisis and pressure came onto the political system in Hong Kong as a result of citizenship questions. Nevertheless, in the absence of political instability in Hong Kong, not at present seen as probable, Hong Kong is unlikely to constitute a major factor in Japan-China relations in the next decade.

The Hong Kong precedent of 'one country, two systems' created an opportunity for a policy within China of 'one country, many systems'. Debates in China before 1989, and at times since 1997 on Taiwan's future, have included the idea of a loose confederation of China's regions that could accommodate a continuing sociocultural commonality of China and Taiwan and a stronger, more formal, political link. Were Chinese domestic politics to evolve comfortably in the direction of support for this model, it is not inconceivable that within a decade or so, the Taiwan issue could be removed as a major potential source of serious rift in the Japan-China relationship. Given the way relations between China and Taiwan have developed since 1997, that now seems less assured, although Chinese statements have indicated a greater degree of flexibility in interpreting 'one country, two systems'.[85]

---

[85] Vice Premier Qian Qichen's speech on the Taiwan question in Beijing in Jan. 2000 referred to 'equal status' negotiations and 'recognising differences' in the two entities.

5

PRIORITIES AND OUTCOMES
FOR JAPAN AND CHINA IN
THE AID RELATIONSHIP

Japan's development assistance to China is in political terms the single
most important dimension of economic relations between the two
governments. Even though the aid relationship was conceived for
mutual benefit and has been useful to both governments, it is nevertheless one of dependence and is therefore characterised by many of
the tensions present in similar associations between a richer, more
technologically advanced state and a poorer, less developed state.[1]
Moreover, Japan and China have had to deal with four considerations
which are not present in most other aid relationships. First, Japan has
its war record to live down and its aid to China has been subject to
political pressure in both countries to be represented as war reparations.[2] Second, China is not the average less developed state. It was
a great power when the aid relationship began, and it has become
more powerful in the two decades since. China has resumed its own
relatively modest foreign aid programs to developing countries,
thereby raising the question of why others should provide it with aid.
Third, China is a nuclear weapons state and there are powerful anti-
nuclear constituencies in Japan who suggest that Japanese aid effectively subsidises the nuclear weapons program. Fourth, Japan's global

[1] To ease such sensitivities and to paper over the diversity of interests that engage
in foreign aid, the terms 'development assistance' and, to be even more egalitarian,
'development cooperation' have gained considerable currency as substitutes for the
term 'foreign aid'.

[2] This issue is present in Japan's aid relationships with a number of countries in
Southeast Asia and the Western Pacific.

foreign aid program has been characterised by an effort to compete for international leadership in strategic affairs where the country's economic power has had to substitute for both hard military power and cultural appeal. In pursuit of this goal, Japan has shown a distinct tendency to see aid as 'check book diplomacy' and has consistently devoted fewer resources to social development programs as a proportion of its total aid than most other aid donors.

In addition to these political considerations, the aid relationship is distinctly asymmetrical in its functionalist terms. For Japan, China may be an important target of its aid program, but it is one of several in similar categories. For China, Japan is the single most important source of development assistance. But the functionalist asymmetries extend more deeply. The aid program is administered in Japan in a bottom-up fashion typical for the Japanese civil service, a process which engages Japanese leaders mostly at the final stages. By contrast, China's leaders pay close attention to the specific projects selected at the initial stage. Simply put, China's leaders have much more riding on the economic impacts of Japanese aid than their counterparts in Tokyo. Notwithstanding this asymmetry in the intensity of interest in the aid relationship between the two governments, the chapter discusses the economic impacts for each country in turn. The first section reviews the effect of the aid program on the economic goals and priorities of the Japanese government. The second section of the chapter offers an assessment of the economic value to the Chinese government of the aid program. The third section of the chapter looks at the political and strategic impacts of the aid relationship where there is a more direct engagement between the leaders of the two governments. This section pays special attention to two sets of questions. First, what have the political goals of the Japanese aid program been, and has Japan achieved these? Second, how has China managed the political aspects of the aid relationship, especially attempts by Japan to put conditions on its aid?

The chapter suggests that the aid relationship has had quite positive stimulatory or flow-through effects on China's economy that are much more important than a simple comparison of aid money relative to the size of China's economy or to levels of domestic investment would indicate. These effects included contributions to long-term economic growth through infrastructure development, technology transfer, and stabilising macroeconomic impacts of capital inflows. Nevertheless, the value of Japanese aid, or other international aid, relative to domestic investment in an economy as large as China's has been low and this means that direct political and strategic benefits to the bilateral relationship have been equally insubstantial. The size of the aid program will not constrain China's attitude toward Japan where China's vital interests are at stake.

Indirect positive effects were important at the outset of the aid relationship, when it stood as a symbol of determination to develop good relations and as a symbol of China's new openness to international economic relations. In strategic terms, these symbolic aspects have remained an important positive influence on relations between the two governments but this positive influence has been increasingly counterbalanced by intensifying political pressures of a negative kind. Suspicions among some Chinese leaders about Japan's strategic motives in giving aid have been vindicated as the result of Japanese government attempts to use the aid program as a vehicle for direct political influence by placing conditions on it. Almost all Chinese leaders are now deeply resentful of such conditionality. This resentment, and the evidence in Chapter 2, would tend to confirm the view that after two decades of operation, the aid relationship has probably not delivered as much additional gain to either country in terms of positive images or increased sympathy by the end of the 1990s as might have been hoped or expected.

In spite of the emergence in the 1990s of these problems, there may be some structural impacts of Japan's aid to China that are quite conducive to stability in political relations between the two countries in the longer term. First, once the aid relationship was commenced, the cost of breaking it – even in the face of some political conditionality – probably became a major constraint on both governments. Second, the process of implementation of the large and diverse aid program creates processes and habits of dialogue, dispute settlement and cooperation between important sections of the two governments. A negative structural aspect of the aid program has been that when China breaches international standards in a way that runs counter to the interests of Japan's major international partners, Japan comes under pressure to place conditions on aid in a way that is seen by many in the Japanese government as undermining the very purposes for which the aid was given in the first place.

For all of the above reasons, the Japan–China aid relationship is highly complex and at times has placed considerable stress on the political relationship. This chapter provides an assessment of just how the aid relationship has affected the dispositions of the two governments toward each other at the end of the 1990s.

Japan's economic goals: outcomes and shifting priorities in the aid relationship

Japan has always regarded its aid programs as serving important domestic and international interests in economic, political and strategic domains. There are differing opinions on the balance between economic and strategic consideration in Japan's motivations for its aid program in China at particular points in time.[3] Any effort to establish for particular points in time the hierarchy of interest by Japan in providing aid to China is clouded by the bottom-up system of administration in Japan which allows commercial firms and middle level officials considerable say in aid implementation. Official explanations of why Japan pursues its aid program in general or with particular countries have varied over time or even between Japanese officials at a given time.[4] One scholarly study of the motivations of Japan's ODA in general identified its primary purposes as lying in industrial and trade policy, in foreign policy, in financial policy and in positioning Japan with an acceptable image in the international system.[5] That study gave a higher prominence to foreign economic policy as a motivation than to the non-economic strategic or diplomatic goals.[6] Other studies have painted the aid program as being more influenced by security considerations, the proposition that Japan's aid to China was serving common US and Japanese security interests and that Japan was therefore making an important contribution to US strategic policy through economic means where US law prohibited any US contributions.[7]

Japan has seen its aid to China as both strategic and commercial. The strategic goal was to cement political stability within China and to entrench some sort of friendly dependence of China on Japan. On

---

[3] For a summary of some of the main arguments, see Dennis T. Yasutomo, *The New Multilateralism in Japan's Foreign Policy*, London: Macmillan, 1995, pp. 16–30.

[4] Alan Rix, *Japan's Foreign Aid Challenge*, London: Routledge, 1993, p. 19.

[5] David Arase, *Buying Power: The Political Economy of Japan's Foreign Aid*, Lynne Rienner, Boulder, CO: 1995, p. 233.

[6] Arase, *Buying Power*, pp. 5–7.

[7] See for example, Yoshihide Soeya, 'Japan's Economic Security' in Stuart Harris and Andrew Mack (eds), *Asia Pacific Security: The Politics-Economics Nexus*, Sydney: Allen & Unwin, 1997, pp. 195–205.

the economic front, Japan initially saw long-term benefits to Japanese commercial interests in its aid program through the compulsory use of Japanese companies in feasibility studies, the tying of aid commitments to use of Japanese firms as project contractors, and the sourcing of equipment imports from Japanese suppliers. Suggestions that the goals of Japan's ODA program are weighted too heavily in favour of economic or commercial goals have been countered by Japanese offi-cials and commentators, who rightly point out that the aid programs of all of the major powers give commercial advantage to their firms.[8] The commercial benefit has been useful to the Japanese government as a domestic justification for aid programs against the voices of critics who are opposed for a number of reasons.

Since the main aim of this chapter is to address how the aid program affected government to government relations, it is not necessary to resolve the debate about the exact balance between economic and strategic motivations in Japan's aid to China (nor are they in fact separable). Both have been important to successive Japanese governments, and at few points has Japan been forced to choose between the two. When they have been forced to choose, after Tiananmen Square in 1989, or after continued Chinese nuclear testing in 1995, successive Japanese governments have given more weight to strategic or political considerations. (These events are discussed further in the final section of this chapter.)

In assessing the impact on Japan's economic interests in the China aid program, two levels of analysis stand out relating to two different motivations: the first motivation, to foster a friendly disposition in the recipient government toward Japanese economic and commercial interests in investment and trade; and the second, to provide contract opportunities within the aid program for Japanese firms. Of these two economic goals in the aid program to China, the first has probably been more important to successive Japanese governments, although much attention is often paid in scholarly analysis and public commentary to the value of contract opportunities within the aid program.

The economic motivations of Japanese ODA to China have

[8] Yutaka Kosai and Kenji Matsuyama, 'Japanese Economic Cooperation', *Annals of the American Academy of Political and Social Sciences*, no. 513, Jan. 1991, p. 66. While ODA loans, the larger share of Japanese ODA, have been directed to projects of economic interest to Japan, Japan's grant aid has been directed almost exclusively to humanitarian areas.

changed in two decades. For example, the oil shock of 1974 provided Japan with a strong incentive to diversify away from Arab sources of oil and to condition new and sustainable supply arrangements with whatever political sweeteners might work. This led to a massive expansion of Japanese ODA in the 1970s[9] and a promise by Japan in 1978 to its OECD partners that it would double the value of its global ODA. The decision by Japan to offer China ODA at several points in the 1970s can be seen in the light of its need for resource security. When Japan finally persuaded China to accept ODA in 1979, energy supply (notably coal) was an important focal point of cooperation. By the 1990s, the common interest in energy as a centre-piece of ODA had undergone a fundamental change. As China became a net importer of oil and was likely to be importing as much as 25% of a growing consumption, the prospect that Japan could use its ODA to guarantee energy supplies from China began to diminish. Japan developed an urgent interest in re-orienting its ODA in China to projects that would enhance China's own energy efficiency so that pressures on China to become a competitor for energy resources would be reduced.

As the following two chapters suggest, Japan has been able to maintain a beneficial working relationship with China in trade and investment, and the relationships developed with China in the aid program have contributed directly to that outcome. The degree to which the aid relationship influenced Chinese government decisions relative to other factors, such as Chinese demand for foreign investment, or the acceptability to Japanese investors of the domestic investment regime in China, is however a different question. As the next chapter suggests, these factors may have been more influential than the provision of aid. After all, the United States has not provided ODA to China, but it has managed to develop an equally vigorous trade and investment relationship. On the other hand, Japan may have needed to provide the aid if its firms were to be accepted by Chinese people still hostile toward Japan because of the war history.

If the aid relationship did contribute, however marginally, to the development of the trade and investment relationship, then the corollary is probably also true. To the extent that the aid relationship becomes a point of contention, then it would be reasonable to expect that the Japan-China investment and trade relationship might also

[9] Arase, *Buying Power*, pp. 73–6, 214.

suffer. Goodwill earned in the early days of the aid program has not in the estimation of Japanese specialists been maintained since. A 1995 Japanese report concluded that 'it is uncertain whether yen credits have fostered understanding and friendship between the two countries'.[10] One reason is that in spite of the high cost of the aid, its visibility in China is small. This is in part because the ODA program has concentrated on building things (railways, bridges, airports and dams) and not on institutional enhancement or personal training. Most people who use the railways supported by Japanese ODA would have no idea that Japan had provide concessional loans to China for the purpose. The impact of even a large aid program like Japan's is further diluted by the very large population in China. Over the twenty year program of ODA loans, Japan has loaned about 2 yen per person.

Contract opportunities for Japanese firms in the aid program in China have been substantial, and the aid program remains an important target of lobbying efforts by them. Nevertheless, this income stream represent a small and decreasing fraction of the business of most firms. In the 1960s and 1970s, much of Japan's aid was delivered in tied commitments, but by the 1990s the global average for the tied proportion of Japanese ODA loans had fallen to just under 20%.[11] For China, the tied portion had fallen to zero by 1989 and the partially tied portion had fallen almost to between one and 4% by 1993.[12]

While the officially tied portion of ODA may be negligible, Japanese firms can and do still win substantial shares of the contracts. A 1992 study of Japan's ODA program concluded that the bulk of ODA loan contracts were still being awarded to Japanese firms despite historically low levels in the formally tied component.[13] According to official Japanese information, there have been considerable inroads by non-Japanese firms since 1992, but estimates from non-Japanese specialists estimate the Japanese commercial share of ODA contracts to be at least 30% of the total value of ODA loans. For China, figures are not available but Japanese firms have probably

[10] *The Policy Recommendations on the Future of China in the Context of Asian Security*, p. 24.

[11] This information is drawn from the OECD DAC on-line databases. The low proportion of tied aid in Japan's program has been has been the source of some aggravation among Japanese commercial interests. See Kee, Nakade and Take, *Japan's Aid Program*, pp. 29–32.

[12] OECD DAC On-line Statistics.

[13] Ensign, *Doing Good or Doing Well?*, p. 61.

won the greater share of ODA contract values, largely through the device of creating firms of non-Japanese nationality in China or other countries with equity from the Japanese firms.

On the other hand, commercial aspirations of the Japanese aid program in China may not have been met to the extent that most observers believe. Japanese specialists inside and outside the government have been critical of the lack of a Japanese face on its ODA to China. They attribute this in part to the increasing proportion of non-tied aid. The 'tied' proportion of Japanese aid is smaller than for many other countries, and the government has been forced to respond to a requirement expressed by Keidanren in a 1992 report to re-establish a more prominent place for Japanese commercial interests in the aid program: 'ODA and private sector activities are two wheels on a cart in the economic development of developing countries, and a system for creating better relations between government activities and private sector activities needs to be prepared'.[14] One government response was to merge the OECF and Eximbank, a move completed in 1999. But according to a report issued by Keidanren in January 1998, structural arrangements were not the main problem.[15] A number of Keidanren proposals, such as simplifying the feasibility study and approval stages, and providing for loans in currencies other than yen, would satisfy a number of second-order problems identified by Chinese officials in Japan's administration of its aid program. Other critiques included the need to strengthen technical assistance through the provision of expert advisers or the training of personnel.[16] OECF had already moved in its FY1997 to achieve better coordination with JICA in supplying technical assistance.[17] By 1999, China was reportedly insisting on large shares of aid projects to be supplied by Chinese firms, up to 70% in some cases.[18]

[14] Cited in Arase, *Buying Power*, p. 124.

[15] Keidanren, 'Promotion of Privately Funded Infrastructure Projects in Developing Countries', 27 Jan. 1998. Keidanren had issued a more detailed study in Apr. 1997 entitled *Reforming Official Development Assistance (ODA) in Japan*.

[16] OECF Press Release, 'Report on the OECF's Survey of Japanese ODA Loans and OECF of Developing Countries', 3 Feb. 1998. These critiques were not recorded in this document as coming specifically from China, but these views are held by some senior officials in China.

[17] OECF Press Release, 'OECF Operations in FY 1997', 28 Apr. 1997.

[18] David Murphy, 'Competing to Build China's Railroad', *Japan Times*, 3 July 1999.

Goals, outcomes and shifting priorities for China in 'economic cooperation' with Japan

For communist China, acceptance of 'development assistance' has always been a highly sensitive political issue because of strong tendencies in the leadership toward autarky, a disposition based in part on precedents from the imperial period when foreign countries had demanded territorial concessions from China to conduct trade and then used these agreements as an excuse for intervention in Chinese domestic affairs. But the disposition of China's revolutionaries toward maximum independence in economic development and international affairs when they gained power was not that different from values held by governments around the world at that time, and in China, as in many other countries, a desire for maximum national economic self-reliance remains a powerful political consideration. Yet governments of less developed countries have felt obliged to subordinate such sentiments to the goal of national economic development, and in this China has proven to be little different.

In 1972, when Japan recognised the People's Republic of China, China rejected a Japanese offer to provide it with development assistance through concessional loans. It rejected a similar offer several times in subsequent years as late as 1977. China's domestic politics were still giving priority to doctrines of autarky, partly in response to the Soviet Union's abrupt halt in 1960 to its massive economic assistance. China was also conducting a virulent anti-capitalist propaganda campaign through much of the 1970s and certainly did not want any contamination of its socialist society by foreign money, foreign officials or foreign entrepreneurs.

Through 1978 China's attitude on accepting official development assistance from capitalist countries began to change after the return to power of Deng Xiaoping led to shifts in the domestic consensus on what sort of modernisation was needed and how it was to be achieved. Chinese officials began talks with Japanese counterparts on a possible aid relationship.[19] The new policy directions for the economy and relations with capitalist countries were endorsed at a CCP Central Committee meeting in December 1978. The signing of the

---

[19] Zhao Quansheng, *Interpreting Chinese Foreign Policy: The Micro-Macro Linkage Approach*, New York: Oxford University Press, 1996, p. 155.

Treaty of Peace and Friendship with Japan in that year also was an important milestone which helped create the necessary conditions for China to accept aid from Japan.[20]

In 1979, China agreed publicly to accept Japanese foreign aid as part of a general policy position that it would accept aid from foreign countries 'as long as China's sovereignty is not impaired and the conditions are appropriate'.[21] But Japan was not the only non-communist country from which China had accepted aid. In the same year, China received small amounts of bilateral aid from Austria, Germany, Italy, Sweden, Switzerland, and Australia; and some multilateral aid from UN agencies.[22] The total value of ODA received by China in 1979 from all sources was US$17 million (1979 prices), of which Japan's share was US$2.6 million in bilateral aid and US$1.26 million in imputed multilateral aid,[23] although Japan had pledged a much larger amount for delivery in the subsequent years.

Economic impacts in China of Japan's aid program

What aid has China received from Japan? In accepting aid from Japan, China was obliged to accept the Japanese system of aid giving which relied heavily on loans with concessional interests rates and terms, and in which grant aid played only a small role.[24] China must repay each loan within thirty years. China received some special treatment in being one of the first countries to receive the concessionary rates[25]

[20] The aid program was not announced until 1979 and both sides took some steps to distance the aid program from the treaty. Japan had signed a Peace Treaty with the Republic of China in 1952 after the conclusion of the San Francisco Peace Treaty of 1951 with other victorious allies in the Pacific War, such as the United States, Britain, and Australia. Neither the Republic of China nor the People's Republic of China were represented at the San Francisco conference because of a dispute among the allies over which government should represent China.

[21] Vice Premier Gu Mu, during a visit to Japan in 1979, cited in Zhao Quansheng, p. 156.

[22] These included such as UNDP, UNTA, WFP, and UNHCR.

[23] OECD Development Assistance Committee, On-line Statistical Databases.

[24] Kee Pookong, Yayoi Nakada, and Hironbu Take, *Japan's Aid Program: Trends, Issues and Prospects*, A Report Prepared for the Australian Agency for International Development, Feb. 1996, pp. 43–4.

[25] Zhao Quansheng, 'Japan's Aid Diplomacy with China' in Bruce M. Koppel and Robert M. Orr, *Japan's Foreign Aid – Power and Policy in a New Era*, Boulder, CO: Westview Press, 1993, p. 166.

and being the only country to receive loans from Japan as part of a package approved for disbursal over periods longer than one year. Until 1996, China's ODA loans from Japan were approved in five year packages, and after 1996, in a three plus two year package. This change is discussed later in this chapter.

Japan has justified its preference for loans as opposed to grant aid on the grounds that the loan system provides the recipient with larger amounts of money to invest than would be the case if an equivalent amount of 'grant' were simply transferred for specific projects.[26] The grant element in Japan's 'soft' loans can be calculated according to the difference between the net estimated cost to China of loans to the same value on notional market terms and this grant element has varied over time.[27] Japan has also used the argument that provision of ODA loans is preferable to direct grant aid because the former tends to foster self-reliance in the recipient more than gifts of money. According to the Japanese government, the grant element in the loans has been rising steadily since they were introduced. At a global level, the highest grant element reached in Japanese ODA loans has been 62.1%.[28] If this figure is applied to the amount of Japan's loans to China committed for 1996 to 1998, then the effective grant element in the loans would still be quite high – US$500 million per year on average for the three years. Japan's foreign aid statistics, like those of the Development Assistance Committee (DAC) of the OECD, classify the full value of such loans by any country as official development assistance (ODA) regardless of the size of the grant element in them.

Apart from the concessional loans, China has also accepted grant aid, technical assistance for projects approved for the loans, and

[26] The interest rate has consistently been around 3%. The 1994 the average rate was 2.6%. This compared with rates for loans from Japanese banks in 1979 of 6.25% and higher. See Zhao 'Japan's Aid Diplomacy with China', p. 183, n.8. By 1997, the average interest rate on ODA loans disbursed in that year by Japan to all countries was down to 2.34%. See 'OECF Operations in FY 1997', 28 Apr. 1997 (OECF home page, accessed 6 July 1997). The rate for ODA loans for China disbursed in 1997 was 2.3%. Loans for environmental projects were disbursed at a preferential rate of 2.1%. OECF Press Release, 12 Sep. 1997. Japan sets the rate in a range from 1–3% according to the per head income levels in the recipient country.

[27] 'OECF Operations in FY1997', OECF Press Release, 28 Apr. 1997. Between 1993 and 1997, the grant element in all of Japan's ODA loans disbursed in each year rose from 58.8% to 62.1%, a record high.

[28] This figure has been provided by OECF.

personnel exchange programs for specialists, trainees and students. Under the loans program, China receives designated funds for technical assistance which covers the costs of specialist advisers and trainees. Since Japan was one of the first countries to provide ODA loans to China, by 1986, according to one estimate, about 40% of foreign specialists in China were Japanese.[29] Since 1982, the number of specialists involved in the designated technical cooperation program has varied between 599 in 1982 (the lowest) and 2,152 in 1994 (the highest to 1996).[30] Under Japan's aid program, China also receives support for trainees and student exchanges. In 1996, the trainee program involved some 6,000 people (its highest level)[31] and the official student support program involved some 14,000 people, a massive increase from the previous year of just over 2,000. China is among the top recipients of personnel training under Japan's aid program, although it is not the leader.[32] But the high value of the expenditure alone does not offer any insight into whether the training may have been conducive to transmission of knowledge or expertise.[33] In fact, the numbers of trainees from China is very low relative to the huge population of that country. Even so, Japan's aid program introduced higher technology levels and more advanced specialised training than would have been available to China without these projects.

China also receives indirect aid from Japan through its contributions to the assistance programs for China of multi-lateral agencies, such as the International Monetary Fund (IMF), the World Bank, the Asian Development Bank (ADB), and the UN agencies, such as the UN Development Program (UNDP) and the UN Food and Population Program.[34] Through a series of concessional loans, the World Bank has provided about 25% of China's total ODA in the 1990s, and

[29] Zhao, 'Japan's Aid Diplomacy with China', p. 168.

[30] OECF Home Page, Geographical Distribution of Technical Cooperation Human Resources, 1982–92.

[31] Prior to 1998, Malaysia and Thailand actually sent many more trainees to Japan under official technical assistance programs than China.

[32] Indonesia, a country with one fifth of China's population, has received slightly more specialist visits than China under the technical cooperation program.

[33] Leslie S. Hiraoka, 'Japan's Coordinated Technology Transfer and Direct Investments in Asia', *International Journal of Technology Management*, 1995, vol. 10, nos 7/8, p. 720.

[34] Kwang W. Jun and Saori N. Katada, 'Official Flows to China: Recent Trends and Major Characteristics' in Kui-Wai Li (ed.), *Financing China Trade and Investment*, Westport, CT: Praeger, 1997, p. 171. China joined the International Monetary Fund and the World Bank in 1980 and the Asian Development Bank in 1986.

about 70–80% of all multilateral ODA China. By 1994, China was drawing more than twice as much from World Bank loans each year as it was receiving from Japan through ODA.[35] China began drawing UNDP grants in 1982, and by the 1990s, the UNDP was contributing about 5% of multilateral ODA going to China. The ADB is a major source of non-concessional loans for China.

Table 5.1 shows China's receipts of ODA from Japan between 1979 to 1998 as registered by the OECD.

China has also benefited from a variety of other loans from Japan

Table 5.1. CHINA'S ODA RECEIPTS FROM
JAPAN 1979–98[36]
(US$ million current prices)

	ODA loans	Grants	Net bilateral ODA[37]	Of which, technical cooperation	Imputer multilateral ODA
1979	0	2.59	2.59	2.59	1.26
1980	0.93	3.35	4.28	3.35	8.31
1981	12.05	15.62	27.67	9.56	10.53
1982	330.18	38.61	368.79	13.52	9.69
1983	299.07	51.08	350.15	20.46	26.78
1984	347.86	41.49	389.35	27.33	63.57
1985	345.2	42.72	387.89	31.16	51.33
1986	410.08	86.87	496.95	61.19	84.59
1987	422.81	130.31	553.12	76.00	139.94
1988	519.88	154.71	673.70	102.67	0.55
1989	669.23	164.11	832.17	106.16	129.92
1990	538.47	201.31	732.02	163.49	139.98
1991	423.67	194.09	585.30	137.48	164.11
1992	871.27	259.53	1,050.76	187.48	199.35
1993	1,189.06	299.49	1,350.67	245.06	274.88
1994	1,298.46	346.34	1,479.42	246.91	186.63
1995	1,216.08	387.87	1,380.15	304.75	296.22
1996	774.08	328.72	861.72	303.73	12.84
1997	556.75	267.19	576.86	251.77	168.98
1998	1,083.6	339.83	1,158.15	301.62	80.43

[35] In 1994, China drew US$2.9 billion, the single largest annual amount drawn from the IBRD and US$1.1 billion from the IDA. See Jun and Katada, 'Official Flows to China: Recent Trends and Major Characteristics', pp. 174–5.

[36] OECD Development Assistance Committee, On-line Statistical Databases, accessed 18 Oct. 1998 and 6 Feb. 2000. In cases of conflict between the data at these two occasions of access, the later data has been used. These prices have not been adjusted for inflation. Moreover, since the yen-dollar exchange rate has changed so dramatically in the 18 years represented in the table, the changes from year to year should not be read as increases or decreases.

[37] Net bilateral ODA for each year is the sum of ODA disbursed minus

on a non-concessional basis, and is one of the few governments to do so.[38] Japan made a large loan to China, some ¥420 billion, for joint exploitation of natural resources and energy, some seven months in advance of its first ODA loan package of December 1979.[39] In 1981, the Japanese government agreed to rescue the Chinese government's participation in the Baoshan steel mill project, with ¥300 billion in commodity loans, ¥100 billion in suppliers credit by its Eximbank, and ¥70 billion of government encouraged commercial loans.[40] Japan has assisted China through provision of loans by the Export-Import Bank of Japan and through export insurance coverage from the Ministry of International Trade and Industry. By 1994, the Eximbank had committed more than ¥1,700 billion in non-concessional loans for energy development in China – ¥420 billion in 1979, ¥580 billion in 1985 and ¥700 billion in 1992.[41] Each of these loans was committed when Japan–China political relations were at high points. In 1996, the two agencies were considering support for Japanese sale of generators worth ¥50–70 billion to the Three Gorges Dam project.[42] Japan has also made two special loans by way of trade surplus compensation – in 1987 and in 1994. In 1998, Japan offered China official loans of more than ¥100 billion to support a bid by Japanese companies competing with French and German companies to win contracts on China's proposed Beijing-Shanghai bullet train.[43]

To make quantitative assessments of the direct contribution of Japan's aid to China's total growth or average productivity levels, or

repayments on the principal of ODA loans. These repayments of principal commenced in 1988.

[38] Kwang W. Jun and Saori N. Katada, 'Official Flows to China: Recent Trends and Major Characteristics' in Kui-Wai Li (ed.), *Financing China Trade and Investment*, Westport, CT: Praeger, p. 172.

[39] Yong, 'Chinese Relations with Japan', p. 374. The Ministry of Finance urged private banks to participate in this loan, for which no fees were charged, in order to position themselves well for future business in China. See William R. Nester, *Japan and the Third World – Patterns, Power, Prospects*, New York: St Martin's Press, 1992, p. 82.

[40] Nester, *Japan and the Third World*, p. 153. This move by Japan was made in part to rescue its own substantial private sector interests whose contracts had been breached by China.

[41] Kwang W. Jun and Saori N. Katada, 'Official Flows to China: Recent Trends and Major Characteristics' in Kui-Wai Li (ed.), *Financing China Trade and Investment*, Westport, CT: Praeger, p. 172.

[42] *Nikkei Weekly*, 23 Dec. 1996, p. 6 (NDB).

[43] *Kyodo*, 20 Aug. 1998.

other macroeconomic indicators, is a complex if not impossible problem. Numerous studies which have been undertaken on the impact of foreign aid on the economies of developing countries demonstrate a large diversity of causal relationships and a large diversity of interactive factors, including the size of the recipient economy, the level of development, political stability, the balance between primary and secondary industry, education levels, or the volume of direct foreign investment and foreign exchange earnings relative to foreign aid.[44] These methodological problems are exacerbated in China's case by the consideration that foreign aid in total, and Japanese aid in particular, have been small, almost negligible, in dollar value compared with the total size of the Chinese economy. For most of the 1990s, Japan's annual ODA flows to China represented less than one half of 1% of gross annual domestic investment.[45] Thus the size of the Japanese aid program was not in and of itself ever going to be big enough to affect more than a few sectors of the economy. (Sectoral impacts are discussed below.)

These considerations may account for the fact that few quantitative studies have been undertaken either on the direct effects on China's macro-economic development of foreign aid in general or on the direct effects of Japan's aid specifically.[46] Nevertheless some general observations at the macro-level are possible, although these are qualitative assessments.

Aid projects which provide new employment, build durable and more efficient infrastructure, support exports, aid technology transfer and link up with domestically-sourced investment will have maximum stimulatory effect. These effects will be felt in levels of economic activity, in growth rates, and in new domestic investment. Since up to 60% of the total project costs are funded from domestic sources, the value of projects helped in this way is considerably larger than the foreign aid component might suggest. Moreover the project appraisal and technical assistance process has helped build up Beijing's

[44] See for example, Robert Cassen and associates, *Does Aid Work?* 2nd edn, Oxford: Clarendon Press, 1994, pp. 29–31.

[45] For example, in 1996, Japanese net ODA to China was US$850 million compared gross domestic investment of the order of US$275 billion. The domestic investment figure is taken from APEG, *Asia Pacific Profiles 1998: Northeast Asia*, p. 127.

[46] For the case of direct foreign investment in China, these stimulatory effects have been estimated to be significant, as discussed in the next chapter, but in the case of foreign loans, the stimulatory effect is positive but probably not as significant. Haishun Sun, *Foreign Investment and Economic Development in China: 1979–1996*, Aldershot: Ashgate, 1998, p. 70.

technical capabilities in project evaluation and management of large projects to a relatively high level.[47]

During much of the reform period from 1978, China's government was unable to fund all of its normal government expenditures from the budget. Tax revenues did not rise as fast as the economy and so were a declining share of GDP. A large public sector deficit was the consequence. Apart from the many other problems this created, this would have greatly limited government investment programs, and hence economic development, had it not been for overseas financial assistance – grants or low interest concessional, usually long term, loans. Even with the very high levels of domestic (particularly household) savings, given the constraints that came from the inflationary impacts of government spending, foreign financial aid was often crucial for investment programs. At the macroeconomic level, imports of capital have helped, however, along with foreign private investment to stabilise the Chinese economy with a tendency to instability by limiting the extent of policy reversals that would otherwise have been needed at times of overheating.[48]

In government budgets in most countries, the amount available for discretionary expenditure is normally small. Where, as in China, budgetary constraints are large, foreign financial aid provides a disproportionate benefit by enabling a government to fund its priority programs, commonly for infrastructure investments. State infrastructure investment ranged from 5–7% of GDP in China in the 1990s and even half of a percent of GDP added significantly to the level of public investment in this sphere.

While China has gradually raised its central government revenue raising capacity, and the potential for inflationary pressures has diminished, its infrastructure investment needs in agriculture, the environment and transport in particular are very substantial and the need for investment capital will not diminish. Although China has been able to depend heavily on domestic savings to finance development, there are now reasons for questioning whether the Chinese propensity to save could decline in the future.[49] Consequently, the need for

[47] Gang Zhang, 'Rail Aid to China' in Marie Soderberg (ed.), *The Business of Japanese Foreign Aid*, London: Routledge, 1996, pp. 245–76.

[48] Barry Naughton, 'China's Economic Reform Strategy' in Thomas Robinson and David Shambaugh (eds), *China's Foreign Policy: Theory and Practice*, Oxford: Clarendon Press, 1944, pp. 47–69.

[49] Nicholas Lardy, *China's Unfinished Revolution*, Washington, DC: Brookings Institution Press, 1998, pp. 9–11.

Japanese financial aid will remain important in maintaining infrastructure investment levels.

The impact of Japan's aid projects in China's economy has been localised. Table 5.2 shows information compiled from Japan's Organisation for Economic Cooperation and Development (OECF) on the loan values allocated to each sector and the small number of specific projects[50] funded by Japan – which has been China's biggest single bilateral donor after 1979. Table 5.3 presents the share of the total multi-year packages allocated to each sector. The number of aid projects approved in the first ten years of Japan's aid program was small

Table 5.2. JAPAN'S ODA LOANS TO CHINA 1979–98
BY VALUE AND BY PROJECT APPROVALS[51]
(¥ *million, current prices*)

	1979–83		1984–9		1990–5		1996–8	
Rail	130,030	3	170,285	3	207,457	9	50,173	3
Ports	70,730	3	116,000	3	58,195	9	15,400	1
Power	140	1	112,635	3	151,289	9	65,000	2
Commodities	99,100	–	30,900	–	–	–	–	–
Telecoms	–	–	35,000	1	81,949	7	–	–
Social services	–	–	34,470	4	105,416	13	29,541	6
Manufactures[52]	–	–	70,000	1	30,999	1	–	–
Other transport	–	–	2,510	1	128,540	13	40,000	1
Agriculture	–	–	–	–	127,747	7	2,792	1
Irrigation and flood	–	–	–	–	22,535	3	–	–
Total	300,000	7	571,800	16	912,1 27	71	202,906	14

[50] The number of projects is not always easy to define, since what is identified as one project in certain OECF master-lists can often comprise a number of sub-projects. But for the period 1979 to 1998, it is possible to identify the geographic limits of all of the 108 projects on the OECF master list.

[51] This table is based on figures for annual approvals in the OECF On-Line Data Base, accessed through OECF Home Page, 16 July 1998. Since not all approvals were completed in the fiscal years for which the money was pledged, Table 5.3 shows different levels of aid delivery for certain multi-year periods compared with most sources which list the aid pledged according to the time periods for which it was pledged. The year groupings in Table 5.3 match as closely as possible the complete batch of projects for each multi-year grouping as announced at the start of the period. The last project approvals included in this list were those approved on 12 Sep. 1997. The figures for the numbers of projects included in the approvals list for FY 1990–5 is larger than the figure announced by the Japanese government. The discrepancy arises because the approvals list for those years shows a number of projects as individual approvals even though they were associated with other projects.

[52] The manufacturing project in the second loan period was for export

Table 5.3. JAPAN'S ODA LOANS TO CHINA 1979–98

(*sector % share by value*)

	1793-83	1984-9	1990-5	1996-8
Rail	43	30	23	25
Ports	24	20	6	8
Power	–	20	17	32
Commodities	33	5	–	–
Telecoms	–	6	9	–
Social services	–	6	12	15
Manufactures	–	12	3	–
Other transport	–	<1	14	20
Agriculture	–	–	14	1
Irrigation and flood	–	–	2	–
Total	100	100	100	100

(23) and they were confined to a few sectors of the economy. In the 1990s, the project list grew in size and value and expanded to other sectors of the economy, but the number of projects was still not large relative to the size of China's economy and population.

As the data in Tables 5.2 and 5.3 suggest, Japan's biggest and most widespread interventions in China's economy through its aid program came in the first half of the 1990s, more than a decade after the aid program started. Thus, ironically, Japan's biggest contributions to China's development came when China needed them least. By the early 1990s, China's foreign exchange reserves had already become quite substantial, its creditworthiness for international loans was high, and other countries and multilateral institutions were also providing substantial amounts of aid. Importantly for China though, some of the soft loans came to it from Japan well in advance of substantial direct investment by the Japanese private sector and in some respects the Japanese loans husbanded the development of a positive relationship between the Chinese government and Japanese investors. The size of the loans was consistently much larger than direct foreign investment by Japan's private sector for most of the time since 1979, although by the late 1990s this gap had been closed and the average annual value of Japan's direct investment (about US$2 billion per year) was roughly double the annual value of its loans (about US$1 billion). (Annual levels of new Japanese investment fell

---

promotion, and the one in the third loan period was mining-related (Baoshan infra-structure development).

between 1995 and 1999 from US$4 billion to less than US$1 billion. For more exact dollar values of Japanese direct investment in China each year see Chapter 6.)

Japan can claim impressive contributions to particular sectors of development in China. For example, by 1995, according to the OECF, its loans had financed the electrification of 25% of all rail lines electrified after 1981 – some 2,700 km. out of a total 10,900.[53] However, Japan cannot claim in respect of China such a staggering dominance in infrastructure development as it can in respect of some countries as Indonesia, where by 1991 it could claim credit for 31% of all electric power facilities, 14% of all railways, or 76% of power lines in the national capital.[54] Seen in this light, and in the light of the small size of Japan's aid program relative to total domestic investment, the direct positive impact on China's economy, while important, should not be overstated.

The export of coal from some parts of China, and the export capacities of several of China's major ports have been enhanced as a result of the twenty years of Japan's aid. By the fourth loan offer (¥580 billion approved for the three years FY1996–8 for forty projects extending over five years), there had been a marked shift away from support for commodities trade toward urban transport and urban social services. This supported the common interest of Japan and China in both the economic development and social stability of the cities. The sharp increase in the share going to power by the fourth loan period represented an intensification of China's need to improve energy supplies to its industrial centres and Japan's interests in promoting clean power technologies to reduce pollution.

In marked contrast to its ODA loans, Japan's grant aid to China (more than ¥100 billion in two decades) has been directed to projects in education, medical services, agriculture and the environment. For example, in the province of Hainan by February 1998 Japan had contributed 'free aid' directed to poverty alleviation for the purchase of medical equipment, improvement of facilities in the province's school for the hearing-impaired and speech-impaired, clean water projects, and the construction of small bridges in two counties.[55]

[53] Gang Zhang, 'Rail Aid to China' in Marie Söderberg (ed.), *The Business of Japanese Foreign Aid: Five Case Studies from Asia*, London: Routledge, 1996, p. 248.

[54] These figures are cited in Alan Rix, *Japan's Foreign Aid Challenge: Policy Reform and Aid Leadership*, London: Routledge, 1993, p. 151.

[55] Xinhua, 16 Feb. 1998 (FBIS-CHI-98-046, 15 Feb. 1998): 'China: Sources Say Hainan to Receive Free Aid Program'. Other projects include the China-Japan

Between 1992 and 1996, grant aid accounted for about one quarter of Japan's total net bilateral ODA to China.

What are the negative effects on China's economy of Japan's ODA? In the absence of detailed studies, one can only point to such effects in aid programs to other developing countries from a range of donors. Possible disadvantages for China include acceptance of higher than market prices for the goods and services imported from Japan; higher than usual costs associated with maintenance of imported Japanese equipment; prioritising aid projects in favour of lower quality sectors of commercial interest in preference to higher quality non-commercial sectors, such as education and health.[56] It cannot be assumed that all of these negatives are at play in Japan's aid program in China, but there must be a reasonable probability that China has not benefited as greatly from Japan's aid as it might have if a greater proportion of it been spent in education and social areas and if less of it had been spent on importing very expensive Japanese goods and services.

Chinese perceptions of political and economic impacts of Japan's ODA

How then have Chinese leaders and the citizenry judged the impact in China of Japan's aid? Positive sentiments about it certainly mix with some quite entrenched views that detract from feelings of gratitude on the economic front. The dominant view appears to be that the aid clearly benefits China's economy; that it also benefits the Japanese economy; that Japan owes it to China; and that the aid has been an important symbolic gesture of contrition and international friendship. There appears to have been relatively little controversy between Japan and China since the aid began in 1979 over the sector

---

Friendship Hospital in Beijing which accounted for 57% of all grant aid between 1980 and 1985; a rehabilitation centre in Beijing for the physically handicapped; water purification in Changchun; forest restoration; a fishery station in Hebei province; and preservation of an historically important cave on the Silk Road at Dunhuang. See Zhao, 'Japan's Aid Diplomacy with China', p. 168. The 'free aid' money is disbursed in small amounts through the Japanese Embassy and consulates in China, and is administered by the Japan International Cooperation Agency (JICA), under the Foreign Ministry. The projects for grant aid are proposed by the Chinese side and evaluated by the Japanese government through despatch of review teams.

[56] Margee M. Ensign, *Doing Good or Doing Well? Japan's Foreign Aid Program*, New York: Columbia University Press, 1992, pp. 86–92.

allocation of aid or specific projects, with the interests of the two countries served quite comfortably in sector and project choices. Through the 1990s, the priorities of the two countries in the aid program shifted, but without a visibly negative impact on bilateral relations. These issues are elaborated below in this section. (The political impact of Japan's efforts to impose conditionality are discussed in the last section of the chapter after a more detailed discussion of Japan's motivations and shifting priorities.)

Some in China's government will remember Japan fondly as the country which took a lead among the wealthy industrialised countries in establishing development assistance to China and that it did so on a large scale. There are no shortage of statements by Chinese leaders emphasising Japan's special place in China's overall development. One veteran Minister noted in 1997 that by then Japan had been the source of 40% of total foreign loans provided to China as ODA.[57] For China, Japan has consistently been one of its two or three

Table 5.4. COMPARISON OF AID DONORS
FOR CHINA 1979–98[58]

(*US$ million current prices*)

	All donors (bilateral multilateral)	Japan	EU	Multilateral total	USA imputed multilateral	Japan imputed multilateral	Japan's share of OECD ODA to China
1979	16.94	2.59	1.65	12.63	2.04	1.26	23
1980	66.12	4.28	17.36	43.88	15.21	8.31	19
1981	476.96	27.67	21.76	424.74	18.85	10.53	8
1982	523.98	368.79	81.25	65.45	19.27	9.69	72
1983	669.61	350.15	124.99	141.43	50.48	26.78	56
1984	798.21	389.35	83.51	246.53	75.22	63.57	57
1985	939.97	387.89	149.34	344.32	33.98	51.33	47
1986	1097.48	496.95	126.67	414.08	98.27	84.59	53
1987	1381.63	553.12	248.92	508.24	121.9	139.94	50
1988	1924.44	673.70	463.38	700.75	2.91	0.55	35
1989	2076.65	832.17	588.62	576.94	16.38	129.92	46
1990	2092.54	732.02	674.22	586.07	137.01	139.98	42

[57] Wu Yi, 'Finally Push Good Sino-Japanese Economic and Trade Cooperative Relations to 21st Century', *Renmin ribao* (overseas edn), 11 Nov. 1997, p. 2 (FBIS-CHI-97-317, 13 Nov. 1997): 'China: Wu Yi on Sino-Japanese Trade, Economy'. This observation applies only to the developed countries after 1978 and does not take account of loans by the Soviet Union before 1960.

[58] Net bilateral ODA for each year is the sum of ODA disbursed minus repayments on the principal of ODA loans. This information has been obtained from DAC on-line databases.

1991	1998.74	585.30	556.28	740.53	152.79	164.11	37
1992	3055.09	1050.76	901.79	966.19	327.69	199.35	41
1993	3271.22	1350.67	750.87	1030.01	0	274.88	50
1994	3238.39	1479.42	739.37	820.02	95.63	183.45	51
1995	3534.43	1380.15	1020.07	967.49	97.05	291.01	47
1996	2617.57	861.72	728.71	928.34	105.51	8.98	33
1997	2041.87	576.86	559.87	803.72	117.13	168.98	36
1998	2371.02	1158.15	477.83	639.47	130.54	80.43	53

most important sources of ODA by value along with multilateral agencies and EU members, as indicated in Table 5.4.

This comparison of Japan's importance relative to other sources of ODA revealed in Table 5.4 does not offer a qualitative measure of Japan's aid relative to that of other countries. Nevertheless, the size of the Japanese program is so substantially greater than all other single donors that Chinese leaders almost certainly appreciate Japan's support in a class above that of other donor.

Moving beyond considerable satisfaction within China at Japan's special place as an aid donor, the economic impacts outlined above have vindicated the original decision of the Chinese government in 1979 to accept Japanese aid. The positive benefits to the economy from the loans have been assessed by Chinese sources both in sector specific terms (infrastructure for energy development and transport) and in overall national development terms as an important contribution.[59] Chinese sources have included among the national impacts such outcomes as easing of transport bottle-necks, growth in foreign trade, increased technology imports and introduction of more efficient management practices from overseas. There is an awareness in China though that as time has gone on, the relative impact of Japan's aid has diminished. This declining relative impact has been exacerbated by the change in Japan's priorities away from infrastructure to environment and agriculture, which some Chinese sources see as making less of a contribution to the country's economic development and comprehensive strength.[60]

[59] See for example, Liu Jiangyong, 'Facing the Challenges: China-Japan Relations Crossing the Century' in Yuan Chengzhang and Cheng Feng (eds), *The International Environment of China's Modernisation Development Crossing the Century* [in Chinese], Beijing: Chinese Communist Party University Press, 1998, p. 248; and Lu Huiru, 'An Analysis of Japan's ODA Loans to China', *Riben wenti yanjiu* [Studies in Japanese Affairs], 1998, no. 1, pp. 18–22.

[60] See for example Li Genan, 'The Reorientation of Japan-US Security Assurance Mechanism', *Waiguo wenti yanjiu* [Foreign Affairs Studies], [Changchun], 1996, no. 2, pp. 1–3.

In the next decade or so, only a small percentage of China's population outside the government will remember the Japanese aid program. While major cities in most provinces of China will continue to benefit from Japanese aid programs, the visibility of these programs to the vast majority of the Chinese people (who live outside the major cities) has been insubstantial.[61] Few will be able to name a single aid project supported by Japan. Statistics of the sort often cited by Chinese leaders to suggest that Japan was the primary source of China's ODA will have increasingly less impact. And such estimates are not an accurate reflection of Japan's share of net ODA flows to China from all sources in more recent times. According to the data maintained by the Development Assistance Committee of the OECD, Japan's share of net ODA flows to China accounted for 10–15% for most of the 1990s,[62] although in 1998 it was as high as 30% share.[63] (Net ODA reflects the balance of payments between the donor and China after repayments have been taken into account.) Many Chinese officials see the Japanese aid program as benefiting Japan at least as much as it benefits China.[64] One fairly balanced commentary identified the benefits for Japan as ensuring long-term supply of energy resources; an opportunity to occupy the China market; and greatly increased trade that revitalised Japan's economy.[65] (The

---

[61] Rail lines were built or upgraded in a number of parts of the country, including the south and the interior. Port development focussed mainly in the north (Qingdao, Qinhuangdao, Dalian), but southern ports, such as Haikou in Hainan or Yantian for Shenzhen, have also been supported. Most of the 'other transport' projects have been for bridges or airport upgrades (Wuhan, Beijing, Urumqi, Lanzhou, Shanghai). Two of the other transport projects have involved support for China's air traffic control system. Telecommunications projects have a wide geographic spread, taking in many of the major cities of China, including Lhasa and Lanzhou, and some of the poorer provinces. Most of the social services projects have been related to urban water or sewage, but some have been involved with national administrative systems.

[62] DAC On-line database, DAC Home page, accessed 16 July 1998. For example, in 1996, total ODA flows to China from all sources reached US$2,617 million, while those from Japan to China reached US$387 million, but in 1993 Japan provided US$299 million out of a total US$ 3,271 million.

[63] DAC online database.

[64] See for example, Liu Jiangyong, 'Japan's Diplomacy after the Disintegration of the Soviet Union', *Xiandai guoji guanxi* [Contemporary International Relations], 1992, no. 2, pp. 25–30; and Zhang Guang, 'The Trend of China's Post-Cold War Foreign Aid Policy', *Riben xuekan* [Journal of Japanese Studies], 1993, no. 4, pp. 35–54.

[65] Lu Huiru, 'An Analysis of Japan's ODA Loans to China', *Riben wenti yanjiu* [Studies in Japanese Affairs], 1998, no. 1, pp. 18–22.

economic benefits to Japan are discussed in the next section of this chapter.)

The view that Japan owes the aid to China is deeply entrenched and has two main foundations. The first is that many in China also see the aid as reparations for war damages, even though these were foresworn by China in the 1950s.[66] The public record does not register any direct evidence that Japan and China explicitly agreed in 1978 or 1979 that the aid package would substitute for China holding to the line of surrendering any claim to reparations. Many senior officials in Japan and China deny that any such agreement was made, or that any sort of tacit understanding was reached. However, many in China continue to believe that such an agreement was made and a senior Japanese source told the authors that in 1972 Japan explicitly sought a written reaffirmation of China's oral pledge in the 1950s not to seek reparations. In May 1989, Deng Xiaoping made a very strong statement in this connection: 'In terms of death toll alone, tens of millions of Chinese people were killed by the Japanese. If we want to settle the historical debt, Japan owes China the large debt'.[67] Such an understanding seems credible given the high domestic political cost within China of 'forgiving' Japan for its massive plunder and devastation of China over more than a decade up to 1945.

The second foundation of the view is that it is the obligation of richer countries to provide such assistance to all developing countries.[68] In this context, the importance to Japan-China political relations of Japan's decision to provide official development assistance (ODA) was substantial. Japan was the first non-communist country to offer substantial development assistance to the People's Republic of China[69] and Japan fought for and secured the agreement of its

[66] See for example Lu Huiru, 'An Analysis of Japan's ODA Loans to China', *Riben wenti yanjiu* [Studies in Japanese Affairs], 1998, no. 1, pp. 18–22. Japan's peace settlements with a number of other Asian countries did include reparations and these were paid between 1954 and 1976, separately from ODA loans, which were first made to India in 1954. See Kee, Nakada and Take, *Japan's Aid Program*, p. 10.

[67] Cited by Yong, 'Chinese Relations with Japan', p. 377, from a speech published in the early 1990s.

[68] It is the premise of the Development Assistance of the OECD, which has agreed on 'guidance' for its members that should aspire to spend about 0.7% of GDP each year on foreign aid. For a Chinese view on Japan's obligation as a developed economic power, see Song Shaoying, 'Establishment of a New Economic Order in East Asia and Sino-Japanese Economic Relations', Chinese Economic Studies, 1994 (July–Aug.), vol. 27 (4), p. 50, translated from *Shijie jingji* [World Economy], 1993 (Mar.).

[69] Zhao, 'Japan's Aid Diplomacy with China', p. 178.

OECD partners to admit China to the organisation's Development Assistance Committee as a 'developing country'.[70] Yet the agreement on aid underscored then, as now, the huge disparities in the levels of development of the two countries. The aid almost certainly carries with it the tendency for people in China to react to it with an insecurity founded in inadequacy or jealousy, and for people in Japan to treat the aid with condescension founded in the luxury of far more comfortable circumstances.

In spite of consistent official rhetoric to the contrary, China's leaders do not see the Japanese loans as 'charity' or as a particularly strong offering of friendship. China must repay Japan's ODA loans in full, even though at concessional rates of interests.[71]

As mentioned above, China has not had much difficulty agreeing with Japan on the types of projects targeted by the aid program. For much of the time, the two countries appear to have a mutual interest in infrastructure projects. Table 5.5 shows the asymmetries between

Table 5.5. SECTOR ALLOCATION OF JAPANESE AND EU AID FOR INVESTMENT PROJECTS[72]

	Social infrastructure		Economic infrastructure		Production		Multi-sector	
	EU	Japan	EU	Japan	EU	Japan	EU	Japan
1984	17	36	57	42	24	22	2	0
1985	16	24	50	51	28	25	5	0
1986	21	20	44	56	29	22	5	2
1987	21	13	45	71	29	16	6	0
1988	21	19	51	57	25	24	3	0
1989	22	19	52	56	21	24	5	1
1990	18	26	50	50	20	24	12	0
1991	24	11	56	73	17	16	4	0
1992	24	20	41	46	30	34	5	0
1993	27	28	47	57	17	15	9	0
1994	34	23	44	59	13	13	9	8
1995	35	23	42	61	14	11	9	7
1996	35	19	44	55	15	19	7	8

[70] Yong Deng, 'Chinese Relations with Japan: Implications for Asia Pacific Regionalism', *Pacific Affairs*, vol. 70, no. 3, fall 1997, p. 375.

[71] Japan's use of loans as opposed to grants does impose a bigger repayment burden, although China has not seen foreign debt repayment as something to be avoided. But interest in self-reliance has not stopped the Chinese government from accepting large volumes of grant aid from a number of countries, including Japan. The self-reliant aspect of Japanese loan aid must have been useful in internal debates in China as a counter to those who opposed acceptance of gifts from capitalist countries.

[72] OECD DAC Online Databases, 1998. Social infrastructure includes educa-

the sector distribution of Japan's aid to China and that of the EU, with Japan consistently delivering a large share of its aid program to economic infrastructure and the EU in a large number of years delivering much bigger shares than Japan to social infrastructure.

By the time of the fourth package of loans, Japan and China began to move away from the prior concentration on China's coastal areas in favour of more funds for poorer inland areas. By 1997, only one of the 14 major projects programmed for disbursement in that year was in the coastal regions.[73] This project, an international airport in Shanghai, was allocated ¥40 billion out of a total ¥202.9 billion for the year. The fourth package also marked a move away from infrastructure funding to environmental alleviation projects in the wake of Japan's commitments at the 1992 earth summit in Rio de Janeiro.[74] In 1997, Prime Minister Hashimoto announced that Japan would provide even easier terms for ODA loans supporting environmental projects – an interest rate of 0.75% and a repayment term of 40 years.[75] This has a direct benefit for Japan in promoting Chinese awareness of and actions to reduce atmospheric pollution, especially acid rain, that originates in China but which affects Japan. Japan has sought to justify small reductions in its aid program in 1998 and 1999 by telling China that the loans, though reduced, will be higher quality aid because more of them will be spent on environmental work.[76]

---

tion, population programs, health, water supply, civil society, employment and housing. Economic Infrastructure and services includes transport, communications, energy, banking and business. Production includes agriculture, forestry, fishing, mining, industry, construction, trade and tourism. Multi-sector includes environment and women in development programs.

[73] Kyodo, 11 Feb. 1998, FBIS-EAS, 98-042, 11 Feb. 1998: 'Japan: Tokyo To Halt Loans for China's Coastal Infrastructure'.

[74] One of the reasons cited by Japanese officials for the move away from the coastal areas is that high levels of private sector investment there have obviated the need for government development loans on soft terms. Since the shift occurred at a time when Japanese commentators were becoming concerned about China's military power, a less visible strategic consideration may have been that Japan should not continue to support the development of infrastructure that could easily be turned to military uses in a confrontation with Japan. Another strategic reason for shifting development assistance to the inner provinces may have been a desire to enhance their power politically relative to the coastal provinces of China. Japan has also been sensitive to international perceptions that its aid program may be too self-interested. These issues are discussed later in the chapter.

[75] *Nikkei Weekly*, 22 Sep. 1997, p. 27 (NDB).

[76] *Sankei shimbun*, 2 June 1998 (morning edn), p. 1, FBIS-EAS-98-160, 10 June 1998: 'Japan: Tokyo to Cut Yen Loans to China'.

But the shift to environmental projects in Japan's ODA has not been confined to China, with OECF recording a sixfold increase in its total loans to developing countries for such purposes between 1989 and 1996.[77]

From its acceptance of the first foreign aid, China has sought to establish firm control over the most important decisions.[78] Yet there is evidence that China has been willing to go along with some of the sector preferences of Japanese governments. At the operational level, for each set of loans, China has formally proposed a series of projects to Japan with a request for a certain value of loans, which Japan has then considered. This is normal practice for Japan's ODA program globally. All projects considered by Japan for development assistance funding are made by the recipient country to the Japanese embassy.[79] But there is room to consider how much discussion goes on between Japan and its aid recipients before a formal request is made to Japan. China's central planning mechanisms, through five year plans, have enabled it to easily identify projects for Japanese development assistance. Moreover, since China's decision to accept foreign aid did not mean the end of the strong self-reliant dispositions among its political leaders, its government officials have been forced to work hard to control the allocation of foreign aid funds. Yet, even for China, the selection of projects by it for presentation to the Japanese embassy have clearly been based on a judicious estimation of where common interests could best be served without undue political controversy. The types of projects, if not the specific ones, have been discussed in high level meetings between the Japanese and Chinese governments prior to formal requests being made by China.

There is not a substantial body of evidence on how often or in what manner Japan turns around a strong set of preferences by recipient countries, but there is clear evidence that it can happen, and that even in China's case it has happened. After China nominates selected projects to the Japanese Embassy, the formal selection process involves protracted negotiations with Japan's Overseas Economic Cooperation Fund (OECF), which is supervised by

[77] Tsutomu Wada, 'Japan Lays Out Leaner, Greener Aid Plan', *Nikkei Weekly*, 15 Dec. 1997, p. 1.

[78] Zhao, *Interpreting Chinese Foreign Policy*, p. 156.

[79] See Sandra Tarte, *Japan's Aid Diplomacy and the Pacific Islands*, Canberra: Asia Pacific Press, National Centre for Development Studies, 1998, p. 39.

an inter-agency group including the Foreign Ministry, Ministry of Finance, Ministry of International Trade and Industry, and the Economic Planning Agency.[80] Evaluation by these Japanese agencies is very intense and Japan reserves the right for all initial feasibility studies to be undertaken by Japanese consultants.[81]

Japan has not always approved China's choices, either for organisational or political reasons. In preparing for the first batch of loans, Japan rejected two out of eight projects put up by China[82] and China experienced considerable delays in achieving approvals of the other six. For this reason, disbursements of aid fell short of announced commitments for loan packages in the first multi-year period.[83] Japan originally promised some ¥510 billion for FY 1979–83 but only ¥330 billion was committed for seven projects which, according to the OECF, were completed on an 'almost satisfactory' basis, a euphemistic way of saying less than satisfactory.[84] This lag carried over through the second loan period (a promised ¥470 billion covering sixteen projects for Japan's FY 1984–9). After the second loan period, there was an eighteen month gap (May 1989 to November 1990) in approvals by Japan because of its freeze on relations in response to the Tiananmen Square repressions. This meant that for much of two years, there were no new project approvals, although previously approved money continued to flow and planning continued. By the end of the third loan period (¥810 billion for fifty-two projects in

[80] Leslie S. Hiraoka, 'Japan's Coordinated Technology Transfer and Direct Investments in Asia', *International Journal of Technology Management*, 1995, vol. 10, nos 7/8, p. 717. OECF has been superseded by the Japan Bank for International Cooperation.

[81] By 1988, Japan had sent over 3,000 inspection or survey missions to China to evaluate projects under the loan program from initial feasibility stages to final completion, an average of 150 visits for evaluation for each project. Leslie S. Hiraoka, 'Japan's Coordinated Technology Transfer and Direct Investments in Asia', *International Journal of Technology Management*, 1995, vol. 10, nos 7/8, p. 721.

[82] William R. Nester, *Japan and the Third World – Patterns, Power, Prospects*, New York: St Martin's Press, 1992, p. 152.

[83] Between 1979 and 1997, China received around ¥2,000 billion in such loans from Japan. Wu Yi, 'Finally Push Good Sino-Japanese Economic and Trade Cooperative Relations to 21st Century', *Renmin ribao* (Overseas edn), 11 Nov. 1997, p. 2, FBIS-CHI-97-317, 13 Nov. 1997:'China: Wu Yi on Sino-Japanese Trade, Economy'. The total figure is the sum of four amounts, each of which were in current prices for the separate occasions on which the loan packages were agreed.

[84] OECF Press Release.

FY 1990–5), Japan had delivered all of the aid promised in the three packages.

For its part, OECF has consistently sought to influence the selection of projects according to its own policy interests. In the first decade, projects favouring transport to Japan of energy resources and transport from Japan of traded goods received high priority.[85] Zhao has suggested that since most of the loans have been spent on large-scale construction projects, with almost one third going to rail construction in the first three loan periods, this may reflect the fact that the construction industry is one of the most powerful political lobby groups in Japan.[86] But development of this infrastructure was also one of China's highest priorities for such loans, since private investors were not likely to be interested in developing infrastructure because of the lack of a mechanism in 'socialist' China that provided for returns on such investment.[87] China sought Japanese support for power projects because of the multiplier effect on China's development goals of greater efficiencies in that sector and for transportation projects because of their contribution to trade in energy resources, one of the few areas where China enjoyed a comparative advantage. China also reaped some benefits in terms of energy availability for some of its major cities closer to the coast.

Thus, marked shifts in the targets of the ODA loans have occurred on several occasions. In 1988, rail development began to take a noticeably lower share, and in 1990, projects in the interior of China began to receive a much larger share. Greater attention to environmental alleviation, particularly in respect of water quality, occurred as early as 1988.[88]

China's strong influence on the project choices to be assisted under Japan's aid program, and the personal intervention of China's senior leaders in these choices, can be inferred indirectly from the sharp changes that occurred in some sector allocations between the third and fourth loan periods. The choices for the fourth loan period were made around 1994, when the power of the post-1989 CCP

[85] Zhao, 'Japan's Aid Diplomacy with China', p. 167 (citing Greg Story, 'Japan's Official Development Assistance to China', Canberra: Research School of Pacific and Asian Studies, 1987, p. 35).

[86] Ibid., p. 166.

[87] Robert Taylor, *Greater China and Japan: Prospects for an Economic Partnership in East Asia*, London: Routledge, 1996, p. 60.

[88] These changes in priority can be seen more readily in OECF's annual approval data used to compile Table 5.3, rather than in the five year composite data in the table.

leadership (Jiang Zemin and Li Peng) had been quite firmly consolidated, while the choices for the third loan period were made or
at least set fairly firmly in train prior to June 1989. The sharp drop
off in interest in support for agricultural development in the fourth
loan period is somewhat curious given that this sector took a 14%
share in the third loan period and went to 1% in the fourth. (The
agriculture projects have mostly been in the construction or refur-
bishment of fertiliser plants.) There is room to believe that the
leadership became seized with urban stability but it is equally likely
that the Prime Minister, Li Peng, who had very strong connections
in the power industry, saw this sector as even more urgently in need
of support, because of its multiplier effect on economic performance, than it had been regarded in previous periods. Even so, in a
situation where China has massive development needs, and where
substantial development funds are available elsewhere, there has probably been little political cost to China in accommodating donor
preferences.

At times, China's leaders have regarded repayments on the Japanese loans as something of a burden. When the yen began to appreciate in value against both the US dollar and the Chinese currency
after 1990, one effect was to drive up the amount of those currencies
China had to find to repay the loans.[89] What had been low-interest
loans therefore lost their appeal as aid, with the appreciation of the
yen exceeding the size of the concession offered by Japan on interest
rates. This issue was a sensitive topic in bilateral relations for much
of the 1990s. Japan has been unsympathetic, however, to a call by
China for a further easing of the terms of Japanese loans to compensate for the effects of yen appreciation. Japan's response was that
China should 'cope' with the situation according to the principles of
the market.[90] By 1998, the exchange rate problem was alleviated
somewhat as the yen depreciated to its lowest value against the US
dollar in eight years. Exchange rate variations are not the only concerns, with China's annual repayments at the beginning of fiscal 1996
being as large as ¥40 billion.[91]

Japan's position in multilateral development agencies, especially

---

[89] At the end of 1995, China had an outstanding debt of ¥1,214 billion, which
suggests that it had repaid about one third of what it had borrowed: some ¥600
billion out of a total of ¥1,790 billion. OECF Press Release, 7 June 1998.
[90] Kyodo News Service, 9 Jan. 1995, carried in SWB (Reuters), 11 Jan. 1995.
[91] Ibid.

the Asian Development Bank but also the World Bank, is probably as important to China in political terms as bilateral aid from Japan has been. As Breslin has observed, 'China is the main recipient of Asian Development bank loans, which Japan now clearly dominates'.[92] China has also borrowed more from the World Bank than any other country, and World Bank loans have surpassed the volume of Japanese ODA loans, though the Japanese loans have more favorable terms. The Chinese government certainly courts the Japanese officials from the Asian Development Bank as assiduously as it courts most foreign donors, but it is doubtful that Chinese officials see a Japanese face to the ADB in any way that impacts positively on bilateral relations. On the other hand, any effort by Japan to use the ADB to impose specifically Japanese policy interests on China's programs or loan schedules would be met with considerable resistance from other ADB members and would arouse a sharp reaction from China. In fact, as mentioned above, one of the critiques made in Japan of its development assistance is that it doesn't have a Japanese face and the government has moved to reduce multilateral aid more than bilateral aid.

As mentioned above, the volume of training of Chinese personnel by Japanese agencies or firms associated with the aid program has been regarded in China as important, but the most important effect of this on the Chinese economy has been indirect given the small numbers of Chinese people involved relative to the size of the country. Japan through its aid program has played an important part in breaking down barriers between China and the outside world. The aid program provided many more opportunities for interaction between Japanese people and a number of Chinese people in privileged positions in the government and Communist Party. This has certainly fostered a gradual acceptance by them that they had little to fear and much to gain from such interaction with foreigners, outcomes that have in turn fostered the process of further opening and liberalisation of China. While such opening and liberalisation has not conformed to the wishes and desires of all of China's leaders and has contributed to the undermining of communism as an ideology that some had warned about in opposing foreign aid, most in the Chinese

---

[92] Shaun Breslin, 'China's Integration into the Regional Economy' in Sam Dzever and Jacques Jaussaud (eds), *Perspectives on Economic Integration and Business Strategy in the Asia-Pacific Region*, London: Macmillan, 1997, p. 98.

government regard with pride and satisfaction the process of opening up and modernisation, and most regard foreign aid programs and foreign governments as having played a positive part in that. (But they probably lump Japan into a group in making such assessments.)

Thus Japan's aid program probably made its biggest contribution to China's development in the 1980s by providing international confidence to China's open door and economic modernisation policies. The improvement of some of China's rail links and ports using Japanese loans, and the Japanese engineering and planning expertise associated with them through the tied portion of these loans, provided important boosts to the perception at home and abroad that China was serious about modernisation and that it was prepared to take the political risk of at least some penetration of its society by the outside world to achieve the goal. But by providing loans with a tied portion, Japan provided China with an important draw card for private investment from Japan and, as a consequence, from private sector firms from other countries who were anxious to compete with Japanese firms in China.[93] The commitment by Japan in 1979 to ODA loans to China may have served as something of a wake-up call to business interests in other major economic powers that if they too did not find ways to engage with the Chinese economy, then Japanese commercial interests would get some advantages. For China, this competitive element was useful because as much as it valued the move by Japan to provide aid, it did not see Japan as an exclusive source and was very keen to attract other countries into the development of the Chinese economy. Over the twenty years of Japan's ODA program, direct foreign investment from Hong Kong and Taiwan has been more substantial than total ODA from all sources, so this has been more significant as an engine of economic growth than ODA.

Political and strategic impacts

This section addresses two sets of questions. First, what have the political goals of the Japanese aid program been in the last decade, and has Japan achieved these? That is, what influence falls to Japan from

[93] Yutaka Kosai and Kenji Matsuyama, 'Japanese Economic Cooperation', *Annals of the American Academy of Political and Social Sciences*, no. 513, Jan. 1991, p. 74.

the aid? Second, how has China managed the political aspects of aid relationship, especially attempts by Japan to put conditions on its aid?

Japan's political goals and influence. It is possible to identify a number of political or security considerations that underpinned Japan's offers of ODA to China. Some relate specifically to China, while others relate more to Japan's global posture. For the first decade, the two sets of goals were not for the most part in conflict. By the 1990s, it became apparent that the China aid program – as important as it had seemed in political and security terms as a means of enhancing Japan's relations with China – was less important to Japan than other security considerations, such as maintaining alliance solidarity with the United States and appeasing domestic sentiment about China's behaviour on human rights, nuclear testing and military posture.

There were four China-specific political goals of Japan's aid to China that had emerged either by 1979 or not long after: to foster a friendly disposition in China toward Japan to overcome suspicions and animosities created by the Fifteen Year War, the Korean War, and the Cold War; to prop up China's continued tilt to the United States and its allies in their global confrontation with the Soviet Union and the Soviet bloc;[94] to help maintain political stability in China;[95] and to support China's policy of opening up and reform, launched in 1978. There was little expectation in Japan that the aid program would deliver any more specific forms of political influence over Chinese leaders of the sort that the United States and Soviet Union were vigorously pursuing in the Third World through their military and economic aid packages. Japan's aid program to China supported Japan's global ambitions in several ways: as an indicator of its willingness to meet its responsibilities as a wealthy, developed state to contribute foreign aid to poorer countries; as an indicator that in taking a lead among the developed countries in aid to China, Japan could

---

[94] In doing so, Japan was probably acting in accordance with the desires of the United States, which wanted to keep friendly relations with China for the same reason, but which was forbidden by entrenched domestic legislation from supplying aid to communist countries.

[95] Kimio Fujita, 'China and Its Asian Neighbours' in Michael Ying-Mao Kau and Susan H. Marsh (eds), *China in the Era of Deng Xiaoping*, Armonk, NY: M.E. Sharpe, 1993, p. 452. The premise was that serious political disturbances within China would threaten Japan's international interests. Many in Japan had been concerned by the severe turmoil in China during the worst years of the Cultural Revolution and by the bellicose international posture taken by China at the same time.

exercise both regional and global leadership; and as an indicator that Japan's role as a 'civilian' great power, which lacked the political will to engage in military diplomacy, could be a credible one.

From the outset, the aid program has also been subject to pressures arising outside the Japan–China relationship. For example, in 1979 the United States complained that Japan was using its aid in an attempt to monopolise the China market; and the Soviet Union, Vietnam and South Korea complained that Japan's aid would contribute to China's strategic capacities. The Japanese government responded with a statement of principles to assuage these suspicions: first, to cooperate with the United States and other friendly countries in development assistance to China; second, to balance aid to China with aid to other Asian countries, particularly in ASEAN; and third, to avoid loans to defence-related sectors. [96]

China has remained a high priority for Japan in its bilateral aid program, but ASEAN as group is more important to Japan than China. China received some 8.9% of the value of all Japanese bilateral ODA, including grant aid, in the two years 1995 and 1996[97] and some 11.7% of the value of all Japanese ODA loans between 1966 and 1997.[98] But Northeast Asia has not been the primary focus of attention for Japan's development assistance in this thirty-one year period. Both Southeast Asia and Southwest Asia – the major source of Japan's oil – have received more ODA loan assistance than Northeast Asia in that 31 year period.[99] In FY1996 and 1997, Japan committed more ODA loans to Indonesia than to China.[100] In FY1991, Indonesia, Egypt and India received more ODA from Japan than China did, and the Philippines, Jordan, Turkey and Thailand each received more than 80% of the ODA China did. Thus while in some years China has figured more prominently than any other single country, in other years it has not. The higher per head level of aid to a variety of Southeast Asian, Middle Eastern and South Asian countries probably provides a better indication of how Japan views the balance of its

---

[96] See Zhao, 'Japan's Aid Diplomacy with China', p. 169.

[97] DAC on-line data base, DAC Home Page.

[98] OECF Press Release, 'The 25th Anniversary of the Normalization of the Diplomatic Relations between Japan and China', 12 Sep. 1997.

[99] 44% of all loans for Southeast Asia and some 20% for Southwest Asia, compared with some 16%. OECF press release, 'OECF Operations in FY 1997', 28 Apr. 1997.

[100] Twenty projects involving ¥215 billion for Indonesia as against 14 projects involving ¥202 billion for China.

strategic interests in China compared with the value of development of strong ties with a large number of other countries. It is possible to see the per head level of Japanese aid to China as rather dismal. One scholar writing in 1993 has seen Japan's aid relationship with ASEAN countries as far more important to Japan than the aid relationship with China: 'no other recipient, even China, has the same status', 'no other set of aid relationships has so vividly vindicated to Japan its particular brand of aid policy'.[101]

In the twenty years of the aid program, Japan's strategic goals have been modified as the international strategic environment and domestic political sentiment in Japan have changed. The shifting ground of Japan's motivations for providing ODA to China have been revealed in a series of political shocks in the past decade, and these have intensified over time to the point where some in the Japanese parliament no longer support the ODA program to China and want it to end. The first serious threat to continued Japanese aid to China came after the Tiananmen Square incident on 4 June 1989. After some initial reluctance to join its G-7 partners in applying sanctions on China, Japan did so to show solidarity with its partners in common opposition to the actions of the Chinese government (or to avoid being isolated from its alliance partners). Japan's actions included a suspension of the current aid program and a freeze on an already agreed ODA loan of ¥810 billion due to be offered in 1990.[102] In August 1989, Japan lifted the suspension applying to existing ODA loans, and in December 1989 released new grant aid for a television broadcasting project and a hospital project. By May 1990, Japan announced that it would honour its promise for the next ODA loan of ¥810 billion but that the time was not yet right to let the money flow.[103] This was very well received by China's leaders.

Opinions differ as to whether or how soon Japan broke ranks with its G-7 partners,[104] but the Japanese government had to juggle

---

[101] Alan Rix, *Japan's Foreign Aid Challenge: Policy Reform and Aid Leadership*, London: Routledge, 1993, pp. 151–2.

[102] Zhao, 'Japan's Aid Diplomacy with China', p. 170. Other measures included a suspension of high level contacts, military links, and a variety of economic and cultural exchange activities.

[103] Zhao, 'Japan's Aid Diplomacy with China', p. 174.

[104] It has commonly been argued that Japan moved earlier than its G-7 partners in easing sanction on China but in Dec. 1989, one of China's Vice Premiers, Wu Xueqian, criticised Japan for being behind the United States in restoring relations with China after the visit to Beijing of US National Security Adviser, Brent Scowcroft. See Zhao, 'Japan's Aid Diplomacy with China', p. 179.

competing domestic and international pressures, as well as its emerging aspirations for greater global leadership. As discussed in Chapter 1, there was widespread hostility in Japan to the actions of the Chinese leaders against demonstrators, so the Japanese government had no difficulty in making some gesture to demonstrate its hostility to the use of force. Differences soon emerged within Japan about how long such punitive measures should remain in place. Business interests were arguing for an early end, as were a number of foreign policy analysts who saw Japan as having a special requirement to maintain friendly relations with China, even it that meant that Japan would be ahead of its major allies in resumption of ties. Japan came under immense international pressure, including from the United States, not to break ranks. Even as Japan seemed to be breaking ranks by sending a semi-official delegation of scholars in August for meetings with senior Chinese officials (Vice Foreign Minister level), the delegation stipulated that any improvement in ties with Japan would depend on signs of improvement in relations between the United States and China.[105] But behind the scenes, Japan was also trying to stake out a position of leadership in the international community, and in the case of the sanctions on China, it sought to portray itself as the bridge-builder between the G-7 and China. Whatever the historical record, the conventional wisdom among Chinese specialists in subsequent years has been that Japan was significantly less demanding of China as a result of the Tiananmen incident than the United States and other G-7 members.

Having restored full ODA ties with China only in late 1990, the Japanese government in 1992 imposed a new set of conditions on its pro-vision of ODA, a move partly in response to domestic pressures, and partly in response to pressure from the United States which had been dissatisfied with Japan's underlying attitudes to the Tiananmen incident in 1989. The ODA principles declared that Japan would henceforth condition its aid to countries which were developing weapons of mass destruction, spending excessively on their armed forces, exporting arms to conflict areas, or abusing human rights.[106] There is a view that the ODA principles may be sufficiently vague to allow flexibility or that the Japanese government was not committed at all to them, that they represented statements the government had to make to placate domestic constituencies. But the actions of

[105] Zhao, 'Japan's Aid Diplomacy with China', p. 176.
[106] The government does not impose these political conditions associated with ODA onto Japanese banks making commercial loans to China.

the Japanese government in its China policy have been shaped substantially by these principles even if important ministries have been reluctant to apply them in the case of China.

Japan expressed these principles in universal terms, but it is likely that trends in China were an important stimulus for development of the new policies. China was the only developing country at that time which Japan acknowledged as producing nuclear weapons, but Japan may have also had an eye on India and Pakistan, both of which were recipients of Japanese ODA. According to one scholar, the decision to link military spending to receipt of ODA funds was made by Japan in order to exert more influence on regional affairs after the US government announced in 1990 a phased drawdown of US forces based there and a more modest US role as a security balancer in Asia.[107] But it was precisely at about this time that governments and international relations experts around the world were beginning to take stock of China's new wealth accumulated through almost fifteen years of high economic growth. The talk of a 'rising China' as a challenger state to Japan, to the United States or to international order became commonplace. The implementation of the ODA principles would have posed a threat to the future of the aid program in China but Japan took no immediate public action.

A number of political incidents after 1992 intensified domestic pressure on the Japanese government to curtail or suspend aid to China in accord with the ODA principles. In October 1994, Japan's Deputy Foreign Minister had reacted to a second Chinese nuclear test after the introduction of a moratorium by three other nuclear weapon states by saying that China's tests could influence Japan's aid policy toward China.[108] In the event, Japan decided to lend only one third of the amount requested by China and announced in late December 1994 the new loan of only ¥580 billion.[109] In August 1995, in response to China's second nuclear test in that year, Japan suspended grant aid to China, exempting humanitarian aid. This move by Japan was relatively mild compared with the measures demanded by important political groups in the country, including the LDP's coalition partner, Sakigake, which had demanded

---

[107] Arase, *Buying Power*, p. 230.

[108] Reuters, 20 Oct. 1994.

[109] Charles Smith, 'Eager to Please', *Far Eastern Economic Review*, 26 Jan. 1995, p. 25.

suspension of the soft loans.[110] The Foreign Ministry is reported to have argued against the suspension. Some indication of the seriousness with which Japanese agencies involved in ODA policy viewed nuclear proliferation can be found in the initiation of an ODA-funded global project to train people from developing countries in seismological techniques to detect nuclear weapon detonations.[111] In March 1996, when China used military exercises and the 'test' launch of ballistic missiles close to Taiwan to intimidate its voters in the Presidential election and its political parties, calls for suspension of ODA loans became even more strident. By late 1996, as mentioned in the introduction to this chapter, an LDP policy committee called for a more consistent conditioning of development aid to China that would be responsive to its poor international behaviour. The suspension of grant aid put in place in August 1995 was not lifted until March 1997. As of June 1998, according to one source, Japan's Foreign Ministry was still being forced to counter calls from within the LDP for cuts in ODA as a means of applying sanctions on China in line with the ODA principles.[112]

At the same time as Japan was expressing disquiet with China's nuclear policies, the Japanese government was looking to change the method of disbursement for ODA loans to China to bring it into line with the practice in Japan's ODA to other countries. In announcing the fourth loan package in 1994, Japan made minor adjustments in the disbursement conditions both in terms of the duration of the period and value.[113] The new approach probably resulted from a

[110] Hijiri Inose, 'Foreign Ministry Prepares to Resume Aid to China', *Nikkei Weekly*, 12 Aug. 1996, p. 4 (NDB).

[111] This low-cost project is described in Ministry of Foreign Affairs, *Japan's Official Development Assistance, Annual Report, 1997*, Association for the Promotion of International Cooperation, Tokyo, Feb. 1998, p. 14.

[112] *Sankei shimbun*, 2 June 1998 (morning edn), p. 1, FBIS-EAS-98-160, 10 June 1998: 'Japan: Tokyo to Cut Yen Loans to China'.

[113] Economist Intelligence Unit (Reuters), 14 Nov. 1994, 'China: EIU News Analysis – Japan Slashes Aid Package – Tensions Heighten'. The total amount pledged in 1994 was divided into two sequential loans, the first to be taken up over three years and the second over the subsequent two years. The value of the first batch of new loans was ¥580 billion over three years (1996–8) compared with the previous five-year round (1991–5) of ¥810 billion. China reportedly had sought ¥1.5 trillion, nearly the equivalent of the total amount loaned to China since 1979 and double the previous five-year amount. Because the new loan package was pledged for a three-year time frame rather than five, the overall amount was actually lower than

variety of factors, some political and some simply bureaucratic. There were important political considerations. Since the five-year period was a special concession unique to China, it may have been, like the loans themselves, a partial offset for China's willingness to forgo war reparations.[114] The move in 1994 to normalise the period was probably a sign that Japan felt it had paid its dues for the war. Japan may also have wanted to put China on notice that the leverage inherent in not having made a pledge for five years could be exercised at the three-year mark. But Japan's desire to change the manner and volume of aid disbursement in China is not necessarily attributable completely to changes in political attitudes to China. Other developing countries are making claims on Japan's soft loans and are critical of the special attention China has received. Moreover, the richer provinces of China are now in a position to apply for normal commercial loans from Japan's Export–Import Bank rather than at the concessional rates. Beginning in 1995, Japan set in place new policies, such as trade insurance and more flexibility in Exim Bank loans, to encourage its private sector to take up some of the demand for infrastructure investment that its ODA could not meet or that it did not want to continue to meet.[115]

Budget pressures on the Japanese government are also important. In Japan's FY1997, commitments of new ODA loans fell by 19.1% compared with previous year.[116] By 1998, as mentioned in Chapter 2, Japan announced a 10% cutback in global ODA, including grant aid. In the case of China, this was likely to result in a reduction of about ¥17–18 billion for each of FY 1998 and FY 1999.[117] This will be the first cut in the amount of ODA loans to China (calculated on an annual basis). The global cuts were to be made in projects that were being poorly managed, and the cuts were supposed to fall more heavily on Japan's aid to UN agencies (a projected decrease of 14.7%) rather than Japan's aid to developing countries (a projected 9.4% cut),

---

that pledged for the previous five-year period, even though the new amount was greater on a 5-year pro rata basis.

[114] Charles Smith, 'Eager to Please', *Far Eastern Economic Review*, 26 Jan. 1995, p. 25.

[115] Mashato Ishizawa, 'Aid Cuts Hurt Regional Buildup', *Nikkei Weekly*, 26 Jan. 1998, p. 1.

[116] OECF Press Release, 'OECF Operations in FY 1997', 28 Apr. 1997.

[117] *Sankei shimbun*, 2 June 1998 (morning edn), p. 1, FBIS-EAS-98-160, 10 June 1998: 'Japan: Tokyo to Cut Yen Loans to China'.

and China took just under a 9.4% cut.[118] The cuts were forced by the Finance Ministry, against the wishes of the Foreign Ministry, but there have been complaints in Japan that there is no unifying political purpose behind Japan's ODA. A group of LDP politicians, some of whom are reported to be quite suspicious of China, have led the push for smarter, higher quality aid policies which show a clearly Japanese face.[119] The budget pressure may have prompted Japan to seek more flexibility from year to year, as it had with its ODA loans to other countries. The reduction to three years was a compromise position with China which had opposed Japan's efforts to reduce the period from five years to one to bring the China case into line with Japan's normal practice.

The low point in the Japan–China aid relationship came in 1997 when the Policy Research Committee of the government party in Japan, the LDP, recommended suspension of the aid if China did not act more responsibly – according to the Japanese definition. By then, even the Ministry of Foreign Affairs, one of the key supporters in the government of the aid program, had come to accept that Japan had not been able to purchase much political influence with its aid program. In particular, the burst of check-book diplomacy pursued by Japan through its global program after 1994 to win support for its permanent membership of the UN Security Council was seen as having failed. Even commercial interests in Japan, represented by Keidanren, were expressing misgivings about the aid program because the initial commercial opportunities that had fallen to Japanese companies from the aid projects had been drying up. By 1998, a report by the Japan International Cooperation Agency (JICA) was recommending that aid programs to China should give more attention to health, education and social welfare than economic development. The goal of helping China advance its market economy remained in place, but the report suggested this could be better achieved through a focus on eliminating poverty, reducing regional

[118] Tsutomu Wada, 'Japan :Lays Out Leaner, Greener Aid Plan', *Nikkei Weekly*, 15 Dec. 1997, p. 1. Japan cut its contribution to the UN High Commission for Refugees, provoking a sharp rebuke from its Japanese head, Sadako Ogata. UN Secretary General Kofi Annan and World Bank President James Wolfenson asked Japan to reconsider the cuts to ODA.

[119] 'New Breed Seeks Quality in Foreign Aid, Not Quantity', *Nikkei Weekly*, 9 June 1997, p. 2. Three of the politicians named in this article as being suspicious of China were Keizo Obuchi (appointed Prime Minister in 1998), Koichi Kato, and Taku Yamasaki.

differences, and protecting China's environment and food supply. Some support for the reforms of the financial system were also identified as useful goals.[120]

Assessing the degree of influence that arises from a foreign aid program is a notoriously difficult problem. There are differing views on this aspect of Japan's foreign aid relationships. Some suggest that Japan's aid program creates considerable leverage over recipient governments.[121] In the case of the aid program in China, one study concluded that by tying its aid to purchase of Japanese goods and services, Japan uses its aid to China as a 'Trojan horse' which has enabled Japan to entangle China in a 'vicious cycle of dependence' that gives Tokyo leverage with which to extract economic concessions.[122] Others argue that Japan has not sought strategic leverage with its aid program, or has not in general been able to transfer its aid policies into political influence.[123]

For most of the time since 1979, Japan's ODA to China has continued to serve the strategic needs of Japan with respect to diversification of resource supply and the opening of markets, and in contributing to an advance in China's prosperity. The picture with respect to the internal stability and strategic orientation of China is more mixed. The general economic advance of China, to which Japan contributed, has promoted rapid change. While Japan had been relatively comfortable with China's new prosperity for the most part, the brutality of the Tiananmen incident gave many in Japan considerable pause for thought. China's continued military spending and nuclear testing, and its military intimidation of Taiwan in 1995 and 1996 led to a belief that while Japan's aid may have fostered prosperity in China, it had not fostered a more accommodating international posture. By the mid-1990s, few in Tokyo believed that its ODA to China was contributing to Japan's security. Many felt that by providing ODA to China while it continued its military programs, Japan was actually subsidising China's military posture. A 1995 report to the government by a large group of experts concluded that the 'wisdom of continuing yen credits in their present form can be questioned for a variety of reasons'.[124]

[120] Kyodo, 3 Oct. 1998.

[121] Arase, *Buying Power*, p. 252.

[122] Nester, *Japan and the Third World*, pp. 155, 159.

[123] Bruce Koppel and Michael Plummer, 'Japan's Ascendancy as a Foreign Aid Power: Asian Perspectives', *Asian Survey*, Nov. 1989, vol. 29, no. 11, p. 1055.

[124] Japan Forum on International Relations, *The Policy Recommendations on the*

Japan may have succeeded in some respects for a while in meeting one of the prime motivations of development assistance, that is to foster friendly attitudes in China toward Japan, but as discussed above, this achievement was as short lived as it was thinly-based in terms of its visible social impact in a country of one billion people.

Japan appears to have judged that access in China is not influence and that it has not been able to acquire any consistent political leverage there through its aid programs. In very small countries, such as those in the South Pacific, Japan has clearly been able to buy support for certain of its international gambits through provision of aid since these countries are excessively dependent on foreign aid, Japanese aid in particular, and many of the leaders respond quite readily to Japan's check-book diplomacy. However, there is room to doubt Japan's ability to use aid to obtain influence over larger countries, such as China, for which Japan is just one source of development funds and for which development assistance is a small percentage of total fixed asset investment.

It would appear that Japan failed to 'win' China's support for its bid for permanent membership of the UN Security Council in spite of the high levels of aid. Japan may not have been seeking such direct influence from the aid program to China, but it has certainly used its aid program to buy votes among small South Pacific states on fisheries issues. What the aid program did probably influence was the way in which China expressed its opposition, which was not outright rejection, but a politely expressed deferral. For China, finding polite ways to reject Japan's political overtures is a low-cost way of coping with such pressures, but there is probably a limit to Japanese tolerance of lack of responsiveness by China to Japan's diplomatic gambits. The refusal by China to support unreservedly Japan's UN bid may explain in part the more questioning approach to Japan's ODA relationship with China that has been revealed in several prominent advisory reports for the government and in more negative public commentary about the aid program. By 1997, according to a Japanese official working in Japan's UN mission, recognition within Japan that the bid for a permanent seat on the security Council was probably doomed did contribute to the push to cut back on ODA, though this was not necessarily directed at China.[125]

Future of China in the Context of Asian Security, Tokyo, Jan. 1995, p. 23. The report was signed by 69 members of the Policy Council of the Forum.

[125] Interview, Tokyo, July 1998.

China's management of political dimensions of Japan's aid, especially conditionality

While Japan's ODA has been an important, if far from indispensable bulwark of China's economic policy, the aid program has been a mixed blessing for China in strategic terms. As opponents of such aid would have argued in the 1970s, China's acceptance of the aid from Japan has made it subject to pressures to modify both domestic and international policies, some of which go to the very heart of the leadership's conception of what gives China its identity or cohesiveness – in domestic policy, the authoritarian rule of the communist party, and in international policy, a robust military posture as a nuclear weapons state. China's leaders in the 1990s have shown themselves to be somewhat resistant to such pressures, and have been able to accept the aid while deflecting the pressure or conditionality from Japan. This politicisation of the aid program beginning in 1989, and then intensifying through the 1990s, became all the more apparent when in 1996 Japan began a very small ODA program to Taiwan for the first time since Japan had changed its recognition policies.[126]

In 1997, China published six principles of foreign aid which were a reiteration of previously known Chinese government views but which firmly registered its opposition to the politics of conditionality of the sort Japan had been engaging in. One of these principles was that: 'Such practices as bullying the weaker or less fortunate by dint of one's power or wealth should not go unchecked, still less should countries be allowed to impose sanctions'.[127] One of China's leading government advisers on relations with Japan painted Japan's attempts to shift to one-year disbursement as 'great power diplomacy', an attempt to 'play against China the loan card with political strings attached from one year to the next, in order to contain China'.[128] The government analyst warned that such policies would 'make it impossible even for the material achievements built on the

[126] DAC Online Database, accessed 16 July 1998.

[127] Xinhua, 23 Sep. 1997, FBIS-CHI-97-226, 23 Sep. 1997: 'China: Li Peng on Aid for Developing Countries'. China's Prime Minister outlined the six principles for foreign aid at the 1997 annual meeting of the World Bank and IMF in Hong Kong.

[128] Liu Jiangyong, 'Prospects of Sino-Japanese Relations', *Liaowang*, 23 Dec. 1996, no. 52, pp. 17–18, FBIS-CHI-97-019, 30 Jan. 1997: 'China: Outlook for Sino-Japanese Relations Viewed'.

yen loans to be transformed into spiritual achievements that bond the Chinese and Japanese people together'. But this same analyst also appreciates the difficult financial circumstances of the Japanese government, as he noted in another report that in 1996, Japan's budget deficit was 7.4% of GDP, the highest of the G-7 countries for that year.[129] While this balanced appreciation of Japan's tight circumstances might seem to suggest that talk of a 'loan card' is just diplomatic strategy by China, the discussion of the budget constraints was accompanied by analysis of the turn to more 'conservative' politics in Japan, and the rise of 'right wing forces'.

China would be hostile to any move by Japan to reduce or modify its high levels of development assistance in response to failure by China to respond to Japanese pressure. In the first place, China would not want to see any cut in the aid for its own sake. More importantly though, it would see it as necessary to avoid at almost all costs the appearance that Japan could throw its political and economic weight around and China would have to submit. Yet, in China's view, this is exactly the dynamic that Japan has attempted to set in place, by putting conditions on provision of ODA which relate to the recipient government's policies on military spending and weapons of mass destruction. For its part, the Japanese government can point readily to domestic political reasons to do so, and from Japan's viewpoint there is an inescapable logic that a developed country like Japan should not give as much assistance to a large, adjacent developing country that is prepared to spend large amounts of money on military forces and weapons of mass destruction when, as Japan sees it, the military threats facing China are the most insubstantial for more than 150 years.

On the other hand, there are specialists in Japan who now see the social situation within China as sufficiently unstable that Japan should not undermine it further through major reductions in infrastructure investment. This view does not take account of any assessment of whether Japan's ODA has a significant effect on China's economy. The 1995 study group report mentioned above suggested that the Japanese government should balance application of the four ODA principles against China's persistent poverty and the critical

[129] Liu Jiangyong, 'My Preview of Japan in 1997', *Shijie zhishi*, 16 Feb. 1997, no. 4, pp. 8–9, FBIS-CHI-97-080, 28 Apr. 1997: 'China: Scholar Previews Japan in 1997'.

underdevelopment in most of the country.[130] One way out, according to this report, would be to direct funding more to the priorities
of regional authorities in China rather than to the central government, since it 'is doubtful that the credits granted will indeed help
make up for the capital shortages in China's development strategy'.
This probably meant that Japan should surrender in the fight for
political influence at the central government level.

At one level of analysis, it is possible to identify a concrete 'aid
relationship' between the governments of Japan and China: this is the
delivery of Japanese money and specialist advice to specific development projects or activities in China. At this level of analysis, there is
little doubt that particular communities, economic sectors and
administrative networks in China have benefited substantially. The
central government, like many regional governments, has also been
able to benefit politically from the aid program through community awareness of the delivery of services that otherwise would have
had to be funded by them. (This awareness of new services does not
depend on the public knowledge that they have been provided in
whole or in part by foreign ODA.) These governments have been
able to use the aid relationship with Japan as one legitimating symbol
of their capacity to oversee a gradual improvement in the standards
of living in the country. For the national government in particular,
the acceptance of foreign aid, including from Japan, has been an important and consistent component of the economic strategy of reform and opening up set in place in 1978. The aid served as a conduit
of expertise and scarce investment capital, particularly in foreign
currency. The aid program also stimulated the growth of business
relations between the Chinese government and the Japanese commercial sector, and this in turn contributed to a growth in two-way
trade and in Japanese investment in China. Thus, it is also possible to
identify commercial and government interests in Japan which benefited from the aid program to China. In fact, Japan's initial success in
exploiting its China aid program for commercial gain aroused powerful competitive instincts in other countries, especially from their
commercial sectors, in a way that rebounded to China's net gain in
terms both of investor interest and government interest in providing
aid.

[130] Japan Forum on International Relations, *The Policy Recommendations on the
Future of China in the Context of Asian Security*, Tokyo, 1995, p. 24.

It will be for these indirect economic effects – aid as stimulus for private sector development – that the aid program will be remembered by Chinese economic planners and experts in the longer term. The net effect of the Japanese aid program on China's economic development if measured in terms of direct effects would probably be relatively small. While the absolute value of the funds delivered was substantial by international aid comparisons, the direct effects on national gross indicators of economic performance were dampened for two reasons. First, China is such a populous country with so many pockets of underdevelopment that the per capita amounts of aid have been very low. Second, because of China's size and the absolute value or resources in its economy, the share of total domestic investment in China taken by Japanese aid is quite small.

At a less tangible level, Japan's decision in 1979 to provide aid, and China's decision to accept, were powerful symbols of new strategic directions in China's politics, in bilateral relations and in global affairs. For China's domestic politics, the aid program with Japan signalled abandonment of xenophobic and autarkic policies which had closed off the society from foreign ideas and specialist expertise. For bilateral relations, the aid program offered some opportunity for dealing an end to the bitter memories of the war and opening up the prospect in the longer term of a new mutually respectful relationship. At the global level, the largest communist great power and the second richest capitalist power were signalling acceptance of the possibility of mutual benefit from economic development and interaction between capitalist and communist powers, and abandonment of the concept of a hostile and permanent division of the world based on ideology. At all three levels, Japan earned considerable good will from Chinese leaders by its decision to offer aid, and by accepting China had earned equal good will in Japan.

These symbolic referent points have remained firmly visible in the two decades since 1979, although with varying impacts and meanings during that time. For example, in domestic politics, China was at first seeking aid for a very small number of projects in very narrow areas of the economy, mainly in construction of infrastructure. As China prospered and its modernisation goals became more ambitious, its government was prepared to countenance a more open society and the two governments have been able to agree on a greater variety of types of assistance. The two governments worked well together during the 1980s to form mutually productive ties through the aid program. Ironically, as the institutional foundations of the aid program become more finely tuned and Japan was winning considerable praise for its efforts in China, politics intervened. The aid relationship, like economic ties in general, was subjected to political pressures arising from domestic reform and political crisis in China as well as Japan's efforts to exploit the aid relationship for political purposes. The period of the largest and most extensive Japanese ODA to China began after 1990, but it was precisely in these years that important constituencies in the two countries began to feel most uncomfortable with the conduct of the aid relationship, although this was far more pronounced in Japan than in China and the negative views in China developed largely in reaction to developments in Japanese views.

It is Japan's commercial sector that remains one of the more substantial constituencies for continuing the aid program. As Japan's trade and investment interests in China grew, the aid program became a substantial government-supplied good-will offering that oiled the wheels of business for Japanese firms. As the Japanese face of the aid began to be less prominent, as Japanese businesses report, this has been less useful. But the reverse consideration is now also in play. If any move were made to cut the aid substantially, Japanese firms might expect to be disadvantaged while US firms would not be, even though the US government has not supplied bilateral development assistance to communist China.

Thus, while important constituencies in Japan have seriously questioned the value of the aid program Japan is not prepared to bear the political cost of China's hostility to any sharp reductions, which would damage Japan's strategic and economic interests. But Japan has already reduced the aid program in China, taking advantage of general budget pressures to do so. The next decade will see considerable turbulence in Japanese aid policy councils as different constituencies struggle to protect or advance their interests. The Ministry of Foreign Affairs will have considerable sway, and the aid program will probably be largely protected, but the political battles in Japan on this issue will undermine the positive aspects in having such an aid program from the point of view of Japan's efforts to foster good will in China. From here on, Japan faces the difficult prospect of maintaining China as one of its most important bilateral aid recipients in part from choice arising out of economic considerations but also in part by compulsion arising out of the need to avoid a major breach in relations with this large and increasingly unstable neighbour.

For its part, China will resist Japan's efforts to place conditions on aid. But in the interests of the broader bilateral relationship, and in the interests of maintaining international confidence in China's capacity to deal with foreign aid and foreign investment, Chinese leaders will go to considerable lengths to avoid any major confrontation over the aid that might threaten it.

6

JAPANESE DIRECT INVESTMENT IN CHINA: POLITICAL AND ECONOMIC IMPACTS

As with the aid relationship, the direct investment by Japanese firms in China is regularly held up by both governments as an important indicator of the health of bilateral relations. In contrast to the periodic tensions in the aid relationship through the 1990s, relations between the two governments on matters of Japanese investment in China improved steadily in the same period. Foreign direct investment (FDI) by Japan's private sector in China has grown rapidly, to a cumulative value of about US$20 billion.[1] Some 1500 Japanese firms have equity investments in China while a much greater number have a variety of business arrangements in China not involving equity.[2] At the end of 1997, there were some 716 Japanese-invested enterprises in China.[3]

Despite the good atmosphere of the investment relationship in the

---

[1] The broad estimate reflects inaccuracies in measuring actual investment flows from Japanese companies, reinvestment by Japanese companies in China, and difficulties in estimating withdrawals of investments from China. There is an added difficulty of taking account of inflation and exchange rate movements over the twenty years of Japan's investment in China.

[2] The estimate of firms with equity investments is in Toshihiko Kinoshita, 'Japan's Direct Investment in China: Current Situation, Prospects, Problems' in Kui-Wai Li (ed.), *Financing China Trade and Investment*, Westport, CT: Praeger, 1997, p. 107; Ryusuke Ikegami of the Japan-China Investment Promotion Organisation (JIPO) says that approximately 10,000 Japanese firms are operating in China (FBIS-EAS-1999-0612, 14 June 1999).

[3] Export-Import Bank of Japan, 'The Outlook of Japanese Foreign Direct Investment', 5 Nov. 1998, p. 17.

1990s, compared with the more fractious aid relationship, there are many political and economic complexities in the bilateral investment ties. For various reasons, FDI in China is still a relatively small item for Japan. Moreover, there have been changes in motivations for both governments and in the strategies of the investors. The complement-arities of the two economies have also changed and in some areas competitive situations could emerge in due course. Consequently, the political and economic complexities, while unlikely to be a major factor in the future, will remain important in the relationship.

The interests of the two governments in Japan's FDI are different and those interests have changed in the two decades or so since the start of China's reform period. Above all, the investment relationship is not one of equals. This chapter therefore deals almost entirely with Japan's FDI in China, reflecting an investment relationship between the two governments of even greater asymmetry than the aid rela-tionship. China has invested internationally, but largely in resource projects. Around 5,600 Chinese enterprises operate outside China.[4] Chinese enterprises, however, have made only small investments in Japan: around US$40 million between 1994 and 1998,[5] with the first Chinese firm seeking listing on the Tokyo stock exchange in 1998.[6] Even so, this was significant as a measure of China's changed attitude to economic policies since 1978. China's investment in Japan could become a factor in government to government relations in coming years as China seeks to gain for its own firms more access to invest-ment opportunities in Japan. But in so far as FDI has been an active issue of bilateral diplomacy between Japan and China since China's reform program made foreign investment in China possible, this has related to Japanese private sector FDI in China.

The 1980s was a period of low commitment by Japanese investors, the turning point in the framework for FDI coming in a bilateral investment agreement in 1988, followed by a surge in manufactur-ing commitment from 1991 to 1995, after a hiatus associated with the 1989 Tiananmen Square repression. This surge was also partly

---

[4] Sun Zhenya (vice minister in MOFTEC), *Beijing Xinhua* (FBIS-CHI-1999-0630, 1 July 1999).

[5] Ministry of International Trade and Industry (MITI), 'Charts and Tables Related to Foreign Direct Investment in Japan', Tokyo, Jan. 1997, and 'Charts and Tables Re-lated to Japanese Direct Investment Abroad', Tokyo, Jan. 1998; Ministry of Finance, 'Inward Direct Investment by Country and Region', 9 Dec. 1999.

[6] CIEC, 21 July 1998.

attributable to the improved performance of existing FIEs (foreign-invested enterprises) after a marked downturn in the period 1987–91.[7] The picture for new FDI flows in the last years of the 1990s was also one of a downturn, for a variety of economic reasons. Even though medium term investor interest in China has remained high in Japan, there has been some decline in interest, reflected more strongly for the longer term (10-year prospects).[8] However, several Japanese firms involved in telecommunications, information technology, and automobile manufacture reported high levels of interest in late 1999 and early 2000, accompanied by concrete plans for new investment.

Japan and China have interacted at the government to government level in at least three ways: over China's investment regime; through their bilateral political relations; and over the economic and strategic objectives of the two governments.

First, China's government has been prepared to accommodate foreign investment in some form in order to advance its modernisation program. Its understanding of how this could best be achieved has varied over the past two decades and at times it has struggled to shape a domestic consensus in favour of aspects of the FDI regime or even of FDI itself. The Japanese government has also had changing interests in the broad thrust of Japanese private sector investment in China. It sought to provide incentives to Japanese investors and has an interest in ensuring that Japanese investors are not disadvantaged in comparison with domestic Chinese enterprises or with other foreign investors.

Second, political relations between the two countries have affected significantly the interest of Japanese companies in investing in China; it is less clear that disputes over foreign investment have been a major influence on the bilateral relationship. Investment-related policies have been the basis of substantive and extensive engagement between the two governments for twenty years. At times, these have been the subject of considerable controversy, mainly as the result of conflicting perceptions and disappointed expectations. But much of the discussion has been about more mechanical aspects of FDI,

[7] See Yanrui Wu, 'The Performance of Foreign Direct Investment in China: A Preliminary Analysis', discussion paper, Dept of Economics, University of Western Australia, 1998, p. 12.

[8] Ministry of Finance information citing comparisons between 1994, 1995 and 1996 Eximbank surveys which show a declining number of countries expressing interest in long term investment in China.

such as the desired level, the sector direction, and the legal regime. Through the 1990s, greater mutuality of purpose, and hence greater compatibility of method, has been achieved, but differences of purpose and approach remain.

Third, as well as seeing investment as an important element of their bilateral relations, both governments have broad objectives for the investment relationship. Japan in particular has viewed it strategically in terms of its comprehensive security concerns, although that strategic focus has changed over time. In addition, FDI increases the mutual interdependence of the two economies. A question is how important are the concomitant vulnerabilities.

In addressing these three issues in this chapter, we start by considering the investment relationship between the two governments and what FDI has achieved in terms of the objectives of the two countries.

Japan and FDI in China

In the 1950s and 1960s, Japan's government limited outward investment by its private sector because of foreign exchange problems. It permitted FDI mainly for the development of natural resources, providing preferential tax treatment, low interest loans and national interest investment insurance for the purpose. Restrictions on FDI were formally lifted in 1971 after large export surpluses emerged in the late 1960s. FDI in general was seen as limiting the impact of rising domestic costs and the yen appreciation, and as reducing Japan's large and politically difficult trade surpluses. In this liberalisation, government incentives for resource-related outward investment of the previous two decades were extended to FDI in general.[9] As we saw in Chapter 5, the Japanese government also used its expanding development aid in developing countries to promote economic openings for its firms, mostly for trade in manufactures or services. The Japanese government gradually reduced or removed incentives to FDI in reaction to the freeing of the yen exchange rate in the 1970s and its subsequent sharp rise.[10] Formal support programs are less vigorous

[9] Ryuhei Wakasugi, 'Japan's Trade and Investment Policies towards Asian Countries', Paper to an international workshop on 'Japan and China in the Asia-Pacific Region: The Southeast Asia Dimension', Australian National University, Canberra, Aug. 1996.

[10] Wakasugi notes that preferential tax treatment and low interest loans still apply to small and medium size enterprises (SME) investing overseas as part of the general

than they once were, but connections remain between Japanese government aid and investment, notably in the provision of infrastructure.[11] Market forces, however, have become a greater determinant of the FDI practices of Japanese firms than government intervention.

Japanese government policies on FDI in China after 1978 had, for the most part, limited objectives. The government wished to support Japanese firms in a growing but new and, compared with established investment outlets elsewhere in Asia, uncertain market. Overall, however, Japan's general objectives in China initially differed little from those for its aid provision: contributing to China's economic development to ensure China's political and social stability, developing the potential of China as a major market for Japan, securing supplies of raw materials and generally developing closer economic relations to help its bilateral relations. In practice, studies indicate little support for the view that the roles of Japanese FDI differed from those of 'Western' FDI or that Japanese FDI was 'ominously strategic'.[12]

By the 1990s, Japan's motivations had changed as Japan's circumstances changed. Japan still supported the interests of its firms in China. Their main goals were access to China's domestic market and use of lower production costs in China for export to third countries but with the pattern of investment by Japanese manufacturing firms moving in the 1990s, belatedly, from export platform production to regional production strategies.[13] The growth of regional economic integration through the spread of company-based production networks has therefore provided some further impulse to the expansion of FDI flows.

SME policy. Wakasugi, 'Japan's Trade and Investment Policies towards Asian Countries', p.3. Investment insurance is still provided for national interest projects.

[11] Jean Francis Huchet, 'The China Circle and Technological Development in the Chinese Electronic Industry' in Barry Naughton (ed.), *The China Circle: Economics and Electronics in the PRC, Taiwan and Hong Kong*, Washington DC: Brookings Institution Press, 1997; see also Walter Hatch and Yozo Yamamura, *Asia in Japan's Embrace: Building a Regional Production Alliance*, Hong Kong: Cambridge University Press, 1996, pp.123–4. Japan's OECF has funded several industrial parks in China in association with provincial authorities, as in Dalian and Hangzhou, which provide an operating base mainly for small and medium enterprises from Japan.

[12] See, for example, Sun Haishun, *Foreign Investment and Economic Development in China, 1979–1996*, Aldershot: Ashgate, 1998, p. 41.

[13] See Dieter Ernst, 'Partners for the China Circle' in Naughton (ed.), *The China Circle*, pp. 210–57.

Although Japan remained concerned to support China's economic modernisation to counter potential economic or political instability there, it subsequently saw FDI as its contribution to the objective of integrating China more fully into the regional community. The interest in resources has also changed. In the early post-reform period, coal and oil development for export to Japan were substantial interests. Those interests have diminished, with more concern now on the availability to China of oil and gas resources to meet China's rapidly growing energy demand and so to avoid undue market pressure that would raise Japan's energy costs.

Japanese firms were late in investing in China apart from a limited number of national projects on the basis of government to government agreements, and Japan's FDI is still smaller than might have been expected from the complementary nature of the two economies. Factors that might explain this reflect in part at least the early history.

The early experience of Japanese investors in China

One inhibiting factor was no doubt China's lack of political stability and transparency, but that did not inhibit US, European or overseas Chinese investors from Hong Kong and Taiwan to the same degree. Japanese investors' confidence in China was badly damaged by China's suspension in 1979 of some thirty-two contracts with Japanese companies, worth more than US$2 billion, as part of an austerity program to combat high inflation and a large budget deficit. Further suspensions two years later of contracts worth around US$1.5 billion included construction of the second stage of the Baoshan steelworks in Shanghai, a high profile Sino-Japanese project. Compared with these suspensions, those for other investors were relatively small: only a few hundred million dollars.[14]

The Japanese government was concerned, not only at the immediate impact on Japanese companies but over the longer term ramifications and, as noted earlier, it moved quickly to help fill the Chinese government's budgetary gap.[15] Although many of the contracts with Japanese firms were restored and compensation paid after the

---

[14] Allen Whiting, *China Eyes Japan*, Berkeley: University of California Press, 1989, p. 97.

[15] Saburo Okita, *A Life in Economic Diplomacy*, Canberra: Australia-Japan Research Centre, 1993, p.120.

Japanese Direct Investment in China

provision of concessional financing from Japan,[16] the confidence of many potential Japanese investors remained shaken. From hindsight these events clearly resulted from undue optimism on both sides. China overestimated what foreign exchange and government revenue they could earn; Japan overestimated the absorptive capacity of

Table 6.1. JAPANESE COMMERCIAL INVESTMENT
IN CHINA BY SECTOR:
VALUE (US$ million) AND SHARE (%), 1981–8[17]

	1981	1982	1983	1984	1985	1986	1987	1988
Total	26	18	3	114	100	226	1226ᵃ	296
share	100	100	100	100	100	100	100	100
Resource development	5	–	–	–	4	3		18
share	19.2				4.0	1.3	1.4	6.1
Fisheries	–	–	–	–	3	1	16	15
share					3.0	0.4	1.3	5.1
Mining	5	–	–	–	–	1	–	–
share	19.2					0.4		
Services	17	15	1	94	74	146	1138	74
share	65.4	83.3	33.3	82.5	74.0	64.6	92.8	25.0
Real estate	–	–	–	1	11	14	61	2
share				0.9	11.0	6.2	5	0.7
Manufacturing	4	3	2	21	22	23	70	203
share	15.4	16.7	66.7	18.4	22.0	10.2	5.7	68.6
Electric/electronic	–	–	–	1	3	5	43	101
share				0.9	3.0	2.2	3.5	34.1
Textiles	–	–	–	1	1	1	4	16
share				0.9	1.0	0.4	0.3	5.4
Machinery	–	–	–	1	2	3	2	3
share				0.9	2.0	1.3	0.2	1.3

ᵃThis annual figure includes a special loan of US$1 billion for an oil-related project.

[16] This consisted of a mix of ODA, Export Import Bank credits and commercial credits. Whiting, op. cit.

[17] See Dong Dong Zhang, 'The Political Economy of the Japan-China Relationship in an Era of Reform and Liberalisation', Ph.D. Thesis, Australian National University, 1997. The figures for foreign direct investment are provided by the Japanese Ministry of Finance (MOF) in current year prices. China's Ministry of Foreign Trade and Economic Cooperation (MOFTEC) has a different data set that puts levels of FDI from Japanese companies at higher levels. For example, for the period 1979–89, Japan's data shows total FDI by Japanese companies in China of US$2,447 million. China's MOFTEC records US$2,855 million for the same period. By 1993, the difference in the two sets of data was larger, with Japan recording US$1,691 million and China recording US$2,960 million. China's data is for contracted new foreign investment. Japan's data may be for delivered investment.

China and the management ability of Chinese economic managers. At the time, however, the contract breaches created a difficult relationship between the two countries that included accusations on both sides of deliberate exploitative approaches or at least of a lack of good faith.

Consequently in the early reform years, for most Japanese investors China lost much of its attraction. Moreover, divisions within the Chinese leadership about economic reform, and the possibility that reforms made could be unmade, putting foreign investment at risk, provided added disincentives. Geographic proximity also led Japanese firms to prefer agency arrangements that they could manage from Tokyo, rather than direct investment. Consequently, through the early 1980s interest by Japanese companies developed slowly, as is shown in Table 6.1.

Investment started to increase between 1984–7, years of the closest Japan–China political relations in the five post-war decades. Even then, investment in China by Japanese firms constituted only a small share of total Japanese FDI. Even though, by the end of the 1970s, Japan had become an important source of FDI globally, China accounted for less than 1% of that investment each year until 1991.[18]

Driving the growth in Japanese investment between 1984 and 1987 in particular was a desire by Japanese companies, particularly in manufacturing, for access to China's expanding consumer market. Japanese companies were also concerned that foreign competitors were gaining a better foothold in China; US investment in these years, for example, outstripped that from Japan. Yet, Japanese firms

---

Japanese MOF statistics report only the money sent directly from Japan and not local re-investment, thereby understating FDI. See Kiyohiko Fukushima and C.H. Kwan, 'Foreign Investment and Regional Industrial Restructuring in Asia' in *The New Wave of Foreign Direct Investment in Asia*, Nomura Research Institute and the Institute of Southeast Asian Studies, Singapore, 1995, p. 16. The MOF data classifies direct investment (as opposed to portfolio investment) according to the proportion of the target firms stock or equity acquired by the Japanese investor. Thus, an acquisition of shares (portfolio investment) greater than 10% is treated in the MOF data as direct investment.

[18] See Roger Farrell, 'The Political Economy of Japanese Foreign Direct Investment, 1951–95', Pacific Economic Papers, no. 295, Australia-Japan Research Centre, Canberra, Dec. 1998, Tables 2 and 7. The statistics cited by Farrell from Japan's Ministry of Finance (MOF) show that in 1987 Japanese FDI in China was more than 1% of global Japanese FDI, but the figure for China in that year is inflated by a loan for an energy project that would not in most estimations count as direct investment.

had a high profile in China in the mid-1980s compared with those of other countries. Japanese banks accounted for 45% of the total exposure of commercial banks and Japanese firms had the largest number of representative offices of foreign companies there.[19]

It was possible, therefore, for Japanese entrepreneurs to do business in China in ways that may ultimately have disadvantaged them in the longer term. Their trading houses and organisations, as well as their closer geographic proximity, provided greater knowledge of Chinese conditions than other foreign investors. Japanese businesses were also more prepared than investors from other developed countries to accept the Chinese position that foreign firms could not hold a majority stake in a joint venture.[20] Consequently, for a considerable time, Japanese investor interest was substantially in trading house business (agency and consignee arrangements with Chinese partners). Even where joint production arrangements were in place, they were commonly simple assembly based plants based on inputs from Japan. Compared with other foreign investors in China, the centralised control exercised by Japanese companies from company headquarters in Japan ultimately meant a decline in the relative attractiveness of Japanese firms as investment partners, a decline that these firms sought to rectify only much later.

In the 1980s, Japan and China had some difficult exchanges of opinion over FDI and particularly over technology transfer issues. On both sides expectations were excessive. In Japan, 'China fever' reflected expectations of large profit opportunities that were not met. Moreover, for much of the 1980s, China insisted that almost all production of joint ventures be exported, so firms whose interest was in capturing the China market were less interested in investment in China.

For China, not only were there optimistic views of the ease of reform but also continuing conflicts between reformist Chinese economic managers and resistant party officials and bureaucrats.[21]

---

[19] Zhang, *The Political Economy of the Japan-China Relationship*, p. 135, citing statistics of the Bank of International Settlements (BIS) on bank exposure and citing *Nikkei Sangyo Shinbum* on representative offices; Tasuko Okubo, 'China and Japan–Financial Aspects', Sophia University, Tokyo, 1986, p. 7

[20] Leslie S. Hiraoka, 'Japan's Coordinated Technology Transfer and Direct Investments in Asia', *International Journal of Technology Management*, 1995, vol. 10, nos 7/8, p. 724.

[21] See Susan Shirk, *The Political Logic of Economic Reform in China*, Berkeley: University of California Press, 1993, esp. Chapter 8.

The learning process for China's officials on how markets worked and what affected business confidence was slow. Further uncertainty had been created by volatility in the pattern of Chinese economic growth, inflexibility of the economic management regime, and inconsistencies and changes in investment laws and regulations (in some years, at times of foreign exchange shortage, foreign-invested enterprises had their access to foreign exchange restricted). General political factors were also important. Persistent anti-Japanese sentiment, which manifested itself in demonstrations and violent incidents directed at Japanese tourists and corporate representatives in 1985, provided a further disincentive to Japanese investors.[22]

Specific efforts by the governments of Japan and China played only a small part in encouraging investment in these years and in overcoming the negative features of China's investment climate from a Japanese corporate executive's perspective. Both governments, however, pursued a rhetoric that promoted investment in China, with leaders in Beijing gradually committing themselves in public to reform of the investment regime.

Bilateral investment agreement in 1988: foundations for take-off

A substantial governmental boost to investment by Japanese firms came in August 1988, when, after years of negotiation and following a visit by Japan's Prime Minister Takeshita, the two governments signed an investment protection agreement. For joint ventures with Japanese investment the agreement provided the same legal status as domestic Chinese enterprises – in effect, national treatment. This broke with the previous discriminatory treatment of foreign investment. Although this concession was ultimately extended to other investors, Japan was the first country to negotiate such a status in China.[23] Major Japanese firms responded almost immediately to this agreement (see Table 6.2).[24] Most of the 1989 investment was delivered in the first half of the year – before the June 1989 crackdown.

[22] Zhang, *The Political Economy of the China-Japan Relationship*, pp. 132–4.

[23] The levelling was confined to only some aspects of the investment regime, and as of 1998, many restrictions remained. Bijit Bora and Chen Chunlai, 'The Internationalisation of China and its Implications for Australia', Chinese Economies Research Centre, University of Adelaide, working paper, 97/5, 1997, p. 16.

[24] Zhang, *The Political Economy of the Japan-China Relationship*, pp. 137–8, observes that by 1988 China had signed some 20 investment protection agreements with

The pre-1989 trends suggest that without the reaction to the Tiananmen Square events Japanese investment would have surged in 1989. As Table 6.1 shows, Japanese manufacturing companies had already increased their investment in China as early as 1987.

Table 6.2. JAPANESE COMMERCIAL INVESTMENT
IN CHINA BY SECTOR:
VALUE (*US$ million*) AND SHARE (%), 1988–92[25]

	1988	1989	1990	1991	1992
Total	296	438	349	579	1070
share	100	100	100	100	100
Resource	18	10	26	6	19
development					
share	6.1	2.3	7.4	1.0	1.8
Fisheries	15	6	5	3	12
share	5.1	1.4	1.4	0.5	1.1
mining	–	4	20	1	2
share		0.9	5.7	0.2	0.2
Services	74	220	160	223	341
share	25.0	50.2	45.8	38.5	31.9
Real estate	2	8	9	16	65
share	0.7	1.8	2.6	2.8	6.1
Manufacturing	203	206	161	309	650
share	68.6	47	46.1	53.4	60.7
Electric/electronic	101	80	22	123	189
share	34.1	18.3	6.3	21.2	17.7
Textiles	16	11	21	70	120
share	5.4	2.5	6	12.1	11.2
Machinery	3	2	12	29	50
share	1.3	0.2	4.1	5.0	4.7

Japan's government and business organisations were reluctant partners in the policy of sanctions of its major allies, such as the USA, in response to China's 1989 suppression of the democracy movement. They argued the need to keep China's door fully open.[26] The Chinese government, in its isolation, sensed an opportunity to engage Japan and its private sector while other G-7 governments were applying sanctions.[27] Nevertheless, as Table 6.2 shows, 1990 was not

other countries, but none provided for 'national treatment' as the agreement with Japan did. This treatment was eventually extended to all foreign-invested enterprises. See Taylor, *Greater China and Japan*, p. 58.

[25] The data for 1994–6 has been provided by Zhang. See Zhang, *The Political Economy of the Japan-China Relationship*, p. 130, for sector data from 1981–93.

[26] Ryosei Kokubun, 'Patterns of Cooperation in Chinese Foreign Policy towards Japan since 1972', unpublished paper, p. 46.

[27] Ibid., p. 139.

a good year for Japanese private sector commitments to new investments in China. Japan's private sector organisations were keen to keep open its channels of communication, especially given what they saw as a rush back to China by US corporations,[28] but individual Japanese firms remained cautious. China continued reform of the investment regime at this time and the commercial interests of Japan in investment in China led to the establishment in Japan in March 1990 of a Japan–China Investment Promotion Organisation (JCIPO).[29] The organisation, nominally an association of private sector Japanese firms, had a Chinese counterpart, the two providing a joint governmental commission to promote Japanese FDI. This measure signified a long-term mutual interest by the Chinese and Japanese governments in promoting the investment relationship.

Take-off in new investment: 1992

Immediately after 1989, the Chinese government allowed greater intrusion of market influences into the economy and consolidated a more open investment regime. Many Japanese firms were looking beyond the use of China as a manufacturing-for-export base to tapping China's large internal market in the face of slow growth and trade protection in their western export markets. Consequently, the liberalisation of China's domestic economy was a major stimulus to investment, the importance of which was demonstrated after 1992, as Table 6.3 (overleaf) shows.

Japanese companies responded to the reform measures undertaken by China after 1992. For example, Japan's Daiwa Security Company in December 1993 backed the first (one of many) overseas bond issue of the Industrial and Commercial Bank of China for ¥15 billion, one purpose of which was to fund the development of South China Sea oilfields.[30] Within China, controls on internal movement were relaxed and then collapsed, and restrictions on onshore oil development and then mining were opened up. The Chinese government began to identify sectors of the economy where it wanted

[28] By the end of 1989, US firms had invested about a third as much again as Japanese firm. See Table 6.8.

[29] Zhang, *The Political Economy of the China-Japan Relationship*, pp. 141–3. Japan provides technical assistance to China as part of this arrangement. The JCIPO is staffed and funded by Japan's Ministry of International Trade and Industry (MITI).

[30] Xinhua News Agency, 2 Dec. 1993, translated in FBIS-CHI-93-243, 21 Dec. 1993, pp. 7–8. In Aug. 1994, the Fuji Bank announced a loan of US$50 million to the China National Offshore Oil Corporation for development of fields in the

Table 6.3. JAPANESE COMMERCIAL INVESTMENT
IN CHINA BY SECTOR:
VALUE (*US$ million*) AND SHARE (%), 1992–5[31]

	1992	1993	1994	1995
Total	1070	1691	2565	4319
share	100	100	100	100
Resource development	19	10	10	34
share	1.8	0.6	neg.	0.01
Fisheries	12	6	10	27
share	1.1	0.4	0.004	0.01
Mining	2	–	–	7
share	0.2	–	–	neg.
Services	341	259	519	730
share	31.9	15.3	20.2	16.9
Real estate	65	43	141	261
share	6.1	2.5	5.4	6.0
Manufacturing	650	1377	1853	3368
share	60.7	81.4	72.2	78.0
Electric/electronic	189	332	492	904
share	17.7	19.6	19.2	20.9
Textiles	120	232	332	455
share	11.2	13.7	12.9	10.5
Machinery	50	229	131	463
share	4.7	13.5	5.1	10.7

more rapid foreign direct investment, such as energy, transportation, petrochemicals, machinery and automobiles.[32]

Japanese firms could see new opportunities in value-added manufacture, rather than light-scale assembly operations. China sought to shift new investments in labour-intensive industries into the poorer inland provinces. In 1993, China allowed large foreign corporations with selected specialisations to open up branches in China to exploit the China market, and eased controls on currency handling from foreign-invested ventures.[33] Overall, there was a substantial increase in Japanese FDI to China in the 1990s, peaking at 8% of total new Japanese FDI in 1995. In that year, a surge in investor interest in

South China Sea. Japanese bank lending often came in behind projects in which Japanese corporations were not partners.

[31] See Farrell, 'The Political Economy of Japanese Foreign Direct Investment, 1951–95'.

[32] Zhang, *The Political Economy of the Japan-China Relationship*, pp. 144–5.

[33] Taylor, *Greater China and Japan*, p. 73.

electrical/electronics manufactures in China – some 20% of total Japanese FDI globally in that sector – reflecting increased investor access to the domestic market.[34]

Investment prospects were now so good that China's government was able to insist on terms for high domestic content, larger scale investments and greater effort at technology transfer,[35] (which we discuss in Chapter 7).While most Japanese FIEs in China are small, larger enterprises were showing increased interest in investing substantially in China.[36] According to Chinese statistics, by June 1996, Japanese companies had contracted almost US$25 billion of direct investment. Most of the large investments in these years came from Japan's major industrial corporations. Mitsubishi, Sony, and New Nippon Steel began to invest substantially in China in the early 1990s, and China succeeded in attracting investment in key sectors of interest to it, such as telecommunications and automobiles where Toyota joined other Japanese auto companies such as Suzuki, Daihatsu and Nissan in China. Nevertheless, the absolute numbers of large Japanese multinational corporations investing in China, although growing, remains small.

Fall-off after 1995

Defaults on Japanese commercial loans by state-owned enterprises in China in late 1994 and early 1995, and rising levels of indebtedness due to higher yen rates on international currency markets soured the bilateral economic relationship somewhat. Japanese business groups became concerned about declining profitability in China compared with investments in the US and EU.The problems they saw included continuing changes in the investment regime in China, even though mostly liberalising, and the withdrawal of certain tariff and tax concessions for foreign-funded joint ventures that brought them into line with Chinese-funded enterprises.[37] Reflecting this, and the deteriorating atmosphere in Japan–China relations prompted by the

[34] See Shaun Breslin, 'China's Integration into the Regional Economy', Sam Dzever and Jacques Jaussaud (eds), *Perspectives on Economic Integration and Business Strategy in the Asia-Pacific Region*, London: Macmillan.

[35] Zhang, *The Political Economy of the Japan-China Relationship*, pp. 144–5.

[36] Daniel Rosen, *Behind the Open Door: Foreign Enterprises in the Chinese Marketplace*, Washington, DC: Institute for International Economics, 1999, pp. 57–8.

[37] Zhang, *The Political Economy of the China-Japan Relationship*, p. 147.

latter's nuclear tests in 1995 and military intimidation of Taiwan in 1996, the Japanese Federation of Economic Associations (Keidanren) sent the largest delegation to China for 19 years in September 1996.[38]

In 1998, Japanese firms with overseas production were reporting that, despite the views of other countries, support for China as a favoured destination for investment among Japanese investors had dropped in their medium and long term plans.[39] This trend, further consolidated in 1999, is mostly due to China's investment policy and worsening investment climate, although Japanese corporate restructuring was also a factor.[40] The collapse of the Guangdong International Trust and Investment Corporation (GITIC) and the lack of the expected priority to its overseas creditors also adversely affected Japan's confidence.

The Chinese government presented the fall in Japan's foreign direct investment in China in 1997, and again in 1998, as 'evidence of an adverse impact of the financial crisis and substantial slide of the yen'.[41] China's White Paper on foreign trade and economic cooperation had predicted earlier that foreign investment to China overall would fall in line with a global downturn after the Asian financial crisis.[42] Yet even through 1999 there was no pick-up, although the decline in the value of new investments was on preliminary figures almost negligible. Table 6.4 shows the declining growth rates in new Japanese investment in China from 1995 to 1998, and compares this with changes in Japanese investment globally.

The downturns in 1997, 1998 and 1999 in the value of new contracted commitments demonstrated problems for the Chinese government after two decades of reform, one decade after the signing of a bilateral semi-official investment agreement, and following the creation of standing bilateral governmental investment mechanisms. China has often failed to get the balance of requirements and

---

[38] Liu Jiangyong, 'Prospects for Sino-Japanese Relations', *Liaowang*, 23 Dec. 1996, no. 52, pp. 17–18 (FBIS-CHI-97-019, 30 Jan. 1997): 'China: Outlook for Sino-Japanese Relations Viewed'.

[39] Export-Import Bank of Japan, 'The Outlook of Japanese Foreign Direct Investment', 5 Nov. 1998, pp. 1, 7–8. The survey was conducted in 1998, after the financial crisis had already struck Indonesia, South Korea and Thailand.

[40] Japan-China Investment Promotion Organisation (JCIP), cited in FBIS-EAS-1999-0612, 12 June 1999.

[41] 'Q&A on China's Foreign Trade and Economic Cooperation', MOFTEC Home Page, www.moftec.gov.cn/moftec, accessed 15 Jan. 1999.

[42] Cited in Xinhua, 3 July 1998 (FBIS-CHI-98-184, 3 July 1998).

Table 6.4. JAPANESE COMMERCIAL INVESTMENT IN
CHINA AND THE WORLD 1995–8: VALUE
(*US$ million*)

	1995	1996	1997	1998
China: Value	4.473	2.510	1.987	1.065
% change previous year	74.4	−43.9	−20.8	−46.4
World: Value	50.694	48.019	53.972	40.747
% change previous year	23.5	−5.3	12.4	−24.5

incentives right and still has not satisfied concerns of private sector Japanese investors about its regulatory framework, including concerns about protection of intellectual property, poor infrastructure and the taxation system.[43] But commercial considerations also played a big part in the change of Japanese investments, with new opportunities for cheap investments in Indonesia, where Japanese FDI showed positive growth in 1996 and 1997 (51% and 4%).

Importance of China to Japanese investors in the 1990s

In the 1980s and early 1990s, the original Chinese emphasis on export led growth was reflected by Japanese FIEs, and to a greater extent than FIEs from the US and elsewhere. In the 1990s, Japanese investors increasingly focused on China's domestic market. From less than 20% in the early 1990s, by 1997 some 60% of production from Japanese manufacturing FIEs was sold within China.[44] In some sectors, production was hardly oriented to the domestic market at all. For example, in electronics, the share of production going for export was 95%.[45]

The search by Japanese investors for more competitive external production sites remains a factor but its relative importance continues to decline. The interest in a strong regional market, however, has grown in importance.[46] Nevertheless, although some specialists saw Japanese investment decisions as being motivated by well developed

[43] Export-Import Bank of Japan, 'The Outlook of Japanese Foreign Direct Investment', 5 Nov. 1998, p. 9.

[44] Eximbank Surveys 1993, 1997.

[45] Australian Pacific Economic Cooperation Committee, 'Switching On – The Effects of Liberalisation in Asia's Electronics Industry', *Studies in APEC Liberalisation*, Canberra, 1998, p. 11.

[46] See Kiyohiko Fukushima and C. H. Kwan, 'Foreign Investment and Regional Industrial Restructuring in Asia', p. 17.

plans for regional networks, a little under one in ten of the respondents in a 1996 survey identified participation in regional production networks as a motivation for their investment.[47] Intra-regional trade, although given increasing weight, is not yet a major motivation for Japanese investment in China.[48]

Again, while China has provided opportunities to a relatively small number of firms to maintain or strengthen their competitiveness, the share of total business activity of parent companies taken by the production from Japanese FIEs in China will remain small for some time. For example, Matsushita, which by 1997 employed 20,000 workers in China in 38 wholly or partially owned enterprises, had 265,000 employees worldwide, and some 200 affiliated firms or subsidiaries in 46 foreign countries.[49]

From 1996 on, China's attractiveness for new Japanese investment relative to other destinations appeared to decline. Japanese business groups told China's premier Li Peng in November 1997 that they were still looking for a secure investment environment in China with consistent and transparent economic policies.[50] This concern is reflected in trends in Japanese direct investment (Table 6.5) which suggest that within the Asia Pacific region, ASEAN as a group was more attractive to Japanese investors than China, with Indonesia then at least as attractive.[51] Chinese specialists acknowledge that Japan 'relegates China to a position behind the four dragons and ASEAN'[52]

[47] This motivation was described in the survey as 'supply parts to assembly manufacturers, including Japanese overseas affiliates'.

[s48] A 1994 study of Japanese FDI in East Asia concluded that creation of regional production networks was not a primary motivation for Japanese investors. See Edward M. Graham and Naoko T. Anzai, 'Is Japanese Direct Investment Creating and Asian Economic Bloc?' in Eileen M. Doherty (ed.), *Japanese Investment in Asia: International Production Strategies in a Rapidly Changing World*, Asia Foundation and University of California (Berkeley) Roundtable on the International Economy, 1994, p. 162.

[49] National Panasonic Press Release, 24 Dec. 1997, www. mei.co.jp/ corp/ news/ official.data/ data.dir/ en971224-3/ en971224-3.html. Matsushita's global sales revenue in FY97 was US$61.9 billion.

[50] Kyodo, 13 Nov. 1997 (FBIS-EAS-97-317, 17 Nov. 1997).

[51] In the year Japan and China signed their investment protection agreement (1988), Japan and ASEAN countries agreed on an ODA-supported ASEAN-Japan Development Fund and a Japan-ASEAN Investment Company capitalised jointly by the Japanese government and the Japanese private sector. See Leslie S. Hiraoka, 'Japan's Coordinated Technology Transfer and Direct Investments in Asia', p. 722.

[52] Jin Renshu, 'Japan's New Economic Strategy in the Asia-Pacific Region and the Direction of Sino-Japanese Relations', Chinese Economic Studies, July–Aug.

and that has not changed. In the 1990s Japanese firms located most of their FDI in developed countries. By contrast, for US investors China has been the second most sought after destination after Japan.[53]

Table 6.5. JAPANESE DIRECT INVESTMENT BY
COUNTRY OR REGION: SHARE (%)[54]

	1990	1991	1992	1993	1994	1995	1996	1997	1998
North America	47.8	45.3	42.7	42.4	43.3	45.2	47.9	39.6	26.9
USA	45.9	43.4	40.5	42.1	42.1	44.1	45.8	38.5	25.3
Europe	25.1	22.5	20.7	22.0	15.2	16.7	15.4	20.8	34.4
Latin America	6.4	8.0	8.0	9.4	12.8	7.5	9.3	11.7	15.9
Middle East	0.1	0.2	2.1	0.6	0.7	0.3	0.5	0.9	0.4
Africa	1.0	1.8	0.7	1.5	0.9	0.7	0.9	0.6	1.1
Oceania	7.3	7.9	7.0	5.5	3.5	5.5	1.9	3.8	5.4
Asia	12.4	14.3	18.8	18.5	23.6	24.1	24.2	22.6	16.0
Taiwan	0.8	1.0	0.9	0.8	0.7	0.9	1.1	0.8	0.6
Hong Kong	3.1	2.2	2.2	3.4	2.8	2.2	3.1	1.3	1.5
China	0.6	1.4	3.1	4.7	6.2	8.7	5.2	3.7	2.6
Asean-5	5.7	7.4	9.4	6.7	9.5	10.4	12.6	13.9	9.8
Indonesia	1.9	2.9	4.9	2.3	4.3	3.1	5.0	4.7	2.6

Since 1972, Japan has been an important investor in Taiwan and Hong Kong, often as a means to enter the China market with local partners (See Table 6.6). Some investment in China from Taiwan and Hong Kong is from Japanese subsidiaries in these countries,[55] which suggests that the official figures for Japanese FDI in China may be understated. Moreover, Japanese FDI is often made within the framework of a consortium. For example, one of the major power projects in the ninth five-year plan, a 600-megawatt station in Hubei, represented investment by a consortium in which the Japanese participant, Marubeni, held a minority stake.[56]

Views vary on whether Japanese firms will continue to see China as an attractive destination for direct investment. Profitability levels

1994, vol. 27 (4), p. 29, translated from *Shijie jingji* (World Economy), Oct. 1993, no. 10.

[53] Miyamoto, 'Discord in the Quartet of Japan, the United States, China and Russia'; and Ministry of International Trade and Industry, 'Charts and Tables Related to Japanese Direct Investment Abroad', Tokyo, Jan. 1998.

[54] Eximbank of Japan for 1990 to 1997; for 1998, Ministry of Finance.

[55] Shaun Breslin, 'China's Integration into the Regional Economy', pp. 101–3.

[56] *China Daily*, 10 Oct. 1997.

Table 6.6. JAPANESE DIRECT INVESTMENT IN
CHINA, TAIWAN AND HONG KONG:
VALUE (*US$ million*) AND SHARE (%), 1951–98[57]

	China	Share	Taiwan	Share	Hong Kong	Share
1951–79	14		323		939	
1980	12	0.3	47		156	
1981	26	0.3	54		329	
1982	18	0.2	55		401	
1983	3	negl.	103		563	
1984	114	1.1	65		412	
1985	100	0.8	114		131	
1986	226	1.0	291		502	
1987	1,226	3.7	367		1072	
1988	296	0.6	372		1662	
1989	438	0.6	494		1898	
1990	349	0.6	446		1785	
1991	579	1.4	405		925	
1992	1,070	3.1	292		735	
1993	1,691	4.7	292		1,238	
1994	2,565	6.3	278	0.7	1,133	2.8
1995	4,473	8.7	457	0.9	1,125	2.2
1996	2,510	5.2	521	1.1	1,487	3.1
1997	1,987	3.7	450	0.8	695	1.3
1998	1,065	2.6	224	0.6	602	1.5

of Japanese FIEs were said to remain low even in the late 1990s.[58] Moreover, Japan has lost some of the competitive edge it enjoyed in the late 1980s and early 1990s relative to US and European manufacturers in China.[59] Again, the uneven distribution of wealth in China and poor and uncompetitive distribution facilities have limited sales within China by Japanese FIEs. In addition, in the late 1990s, excess capacity emerged in the supply of household consumer goods of the sort produced by many Japanese FIEs.

While some observers argue that China's competitiveness will

[57] Based on information provided by Roger Farrell.

[58] Even in 1997, after the financial crisis hit Indonesia, Thailand and South Korea, productivity levels reported by Japanese companies in China were still lower than for most other major East Asian economies, except Vietnam. See Export-Import Bank of Japan, 'The Outlook of Japanese Foreign Direct Investment', 5 Nov. 1998, pp. 3–4.

[59] *Dempa shimbun*, 28 Oct. 1997, p. 3 (Comline) citing a Gallup poll. Japanese firms managed to retain ten out of the twenty most-recognised foreign brands, but dropped to only one in the top five compared with four in the top five three years previously. Three of the top five were from US-invested firms.

fade relative to countries such as Vietnam and India,[60] other studies suggest that provided the most influential factors (relative real wages and exchange rates, and economic integration represented by real exports and imports) remain strong, then FDI should continue to flow into China.

Whether that includes FDI from Japan depends on other factors as well.[61] The historic trends in China's position as a preferred location for Japanese investors according to sector has shown the pattern revealed in Table 6.7 which covers the period to 1995. Subsequent reporting from a variety of sources indicate that particularly favoured sectors in the late 1990s were telecommunications, information technology and automobile manufacture.

Table 6.7. CHINA'S RANK IN JAPANESE FDI LOCATIONS
BY SECTOR: 1980–95[62]

	Manufactures	Textiles	Steel-non-ferrous metals	Electrical	Machinery
1980	18	–	–	10	–
1981	18	–	–	–	–
1982	18	–	–	–	–
1983	18	–	–	–	–
1984	15	7	–	11	–
1985	15	5	5	10	8
1986	17	9	7	12	10
1987	15	6	8	8	12
1988	12	7	7	7	11
1989	12	8	12	9	6
1990	15	9	8	11	7
1991	10	3	11	5	9
1992	3	1	6	2	5
1993	2	1	3	2	2
1994	2	1	3	2	3
1995	2	1	1	2	3
1951–95	4	3	7	3	3

[60] Kiyohiko Fukushima and C.H. Kwan, 'Foreign Investment and Regional Industrial Restructuring in Asia', pp. 23–4.

[61] Geographic or social proximty was not a major determinant for investors from developed countries, but it was influential for Hong Kong, and Singapore investors. See Tao Qu and Milford B. Green, *Chinese Foreign Direct Investment: A Subnational Perspective on Location*, Aldershot: Ashgate, 1997, p. 141 Xiaming Liu, Haiyan Song, Yingqi Wei and Peter Romilly, 'Country Characteristics and Foreign Investment in China: A Panel Data Analysis', *Weltwirtschaftliches Archiv*, 1997, vol. 133, no. 2, p. 325.

[62] Based on information on values provided by Dr Roger Farrell.

Importance to Japan in the 1990s of private investment in China

The Japanese authorities have had a close working relationship with the country's private sector firms operating abroad, and have influenced the general climate for investment in foreign countries. For China, this has taken the form of measures like the 1988 bilateral investment agreement and associated Japanese support for legal studies aimed at reform of China's investment regime. The relationship between Japan's government and its private sector has however often been extrapolated to arenas of activity where it is not necessarily applicable. The relationship has been strongest in respect of the private sector persuading the government to press for sympathetic host country policies and to provide official financing of various sorts, but largely through the aid program, to support commercial activities in China.[63] It has been weaker in the reverse direction, when the government at the highest levels has sought the cooperation of the private sector to follow broader national interests that might conflict with specific commercial interests, especially where the government's interests have no legislative basis or enforcement mechanism. There is little evidence that governments in Japan today can shape investment decisions by Japanese firms in China to support strategic or foreign policy interests, except in the most generalised and limited ways indicated earlier.[64]

We are inclined to reject any suggestion that the Japanese government takes a strong directorial hand in development of private sector FDI in China in the interests of 'Japan Inc'. By the 1990s, the pattern of administrative guidance that characterised Japanese industry policy in the 1950s and 1960s has been basically replaced by one of providing information and infrastructure.[65] The government does react to the needs of the business sector by attempting to managing

---

[63] Including loans by Japan's Expo.t-Import Bank supporting foreign investment projects in China. In FY1997, the bank made nineteen loans to small and medium-sized Japanese enterprises for investment projects centred on China. See Export Import Bank, *Annual Report 1998* (WebVersion), www.japanexim.go.jp/98annualreport/asia.html.

[64] See T.J. Pempel, 'The Unbundling of "Japan, Inc"': The Changing Dynamics of Japanese Policy Formation', *Journal of Japanese Studies*, vol. 13, no. 2, 1987, pp. 271–306; and Bill Emmot, 'The Economic Sources of Japan's Foreign Policy', *Survival*, 1992 (summer), pp. 50–70.

[65] Jean-Pierre Lehmann, 'Corporate Governance in East Asia and Western Europe: Competition, Confrontation and Cooperation' in Charles P. Oman, Douglas H. Brooks and Colm Foy (eds), *Investing in Asia*, Development Centre of

undesirable or unexpected impacts of particular measures by the Chinese government or of adverse circumstances. To the extent that the Japanese government has provided oversight to the creation of regional production networks in the 1990s, it has done so in part by serendipity, but also in part with a strong vision of open regionalism – 'regional production networks that function in a world of global trade'.[66]

Profitability levels in China for Japanese FIEs are said to be relatively low.[67] If so, and since China-based production of Japanese firms remains a small part of their total activity, the direct economic gain to the Japanese economy of its private sector's investment in China is not large. In so far as Japanese manufacturing investment in East Asia as a whole creates an integrated and low cost production network, most notably in the electronics sector, the shift to production overseas has been critical to Japanese firms in maintaining their international competitiveness. In these integrated production networks, China is seen as playing some role, though hardly an irreplaceable one. But irreplaceable or not, profit is the goal of the Japanese firms, and while this is being achieved in China, the Japanese government will see itself as a beneficiary. After Asia's financial crisis, the potential importance of China as a partner in regional production networks may have been elevated in Japan's thinking, but that is not evident in the aggregate investment data. Other suitable sites exist outside East Asia to replace Indonesia, South Korea, Malaysia or Thailand, were new investors to shift their attention away from those countries. The big growth in new Japanese FDI was in Europe in 1998 and the USA in 1999.

Investments in China may have contributed positively to Japan's broader foreign policy goals. Yet, the additional bilateral trade flows

---

the Organisation for Economic Cooperation and Development, Paris, 1997, pp. 108–9.

[66] This point was made about Japanese FDI in general by Eileen M. Doherty, 'Japanese Investment and Production-Oriented Regionalism' in Doherty (ed.), *Japanese Investment in Asia–International Production Strategies in a Rapidly Changing World*, p. 20.

[67] On the positive side, the return on foreign investments in Asia generally has been increasing, and the sales of manufactured goods by Japanese affiliates overseas in 1997 surpassed the value of Japanese exports for the first time in 1997. Nevertheless, profitability for Japanese firms in China remains lower than in other major Asian countries, except Vietnam. See Japan, Ministry of International Trade and Industry, 'Highlights of the 27th survey of Overseas Business Activities of Japanese Companies', May 1998, www.miti.go.jp.

resulting from the investments have created tensions over trade deficits even as the FIEs have increased exports. Moreover, the quality and type of investment, and the terms on which it is made, are judged by the Chinese government as more important than the total value of the investment and China has in the past had concerns about quality. Moreover, China regarded Japan's lower levels of FDI in the region as a whole and its inability to stimulate the troubled economies during the Asian economic crisis through its import demand as a major policy failure on the part of Japan, and did not hesitate to say so.

When Japan's 'bubble' economy burst in the early 1990s and recession ensued, anxieties about 'hollowing out' of Japanese industry through the displacement of manufacturing to other countries emerged in Japan. Had Japan tried to restrict FDI as a consequence, China would presumably have responded negatively, although so far, Japan seems not to have moved to reduce overseas investment or restrain the outflow of Japanese manufacturing capacity. Such a move would only contribute further to Japan's loss of competitiveness but, in any case, the magnitude of the shift of Japanese manufacturing to China is proportionately small.[68]

The interplay between the priorities of the two governments in promoting particular sectors of the Chinese economy as targets of FDI has on occasion provoked comment about the strategic attitude of one government to the other. This has been so particularly for energy. On the one hand, it has been suggested that commercial decisions of private sector firms in Japan to invest in energy production activities in China, such as oil exploration or nuclear power, came from the policy requirements of the Japanese government to ensure long-term energy supplies for Japan.[69] There is certainly strong interest by Japan's energy companies in investing in China. For example, China is a major target of Japan's nuclear industry,[70] and the Japanese government has played an important role in the negotiation and finalisation of participation by Japanese companies in at least two nuclear power projects.[71] As noted earlier, the Japanese government

[68] Edward M. Graham and Naoko T. Anzai, 'Is Japanese Direct Investment Creating an Asian Economic Bloc?', p. 163.

[69] See for example, Taylor, *Greater China and Japan*, p. 69.

[70] *China Daily (Business Weekly)*, 10–16 Aug. 1997, p. 2 (FBIS-CHI-97-223, 12 Aug. 1997).

[71] Qingshan Phase Three and the general design of a 1,000mW pressurised water reactor.

has supported China's energy sector through ODA loans and the governmental Eximbank in Tokyo had funded some 49 energy-related projects by 1995.

There are important commonalities of interest between the Japanese government's requirement for security of long-term energy supplies and the Japanese private sector's desire to diversify their sources. There are also important strategic purposes to be served in procuring energy supplies from or through China rather than largely by sea from the Middle East. In September 1997, Japan's Prime Minister Hashimoto urged greater collaboration between Japanese and Chinese enterprises to address their longer term mutual interests in stable energy supplies, noting that China would probably be importing more energy than Japan by 2010.[72]

Yet the strategic interests of the Japanese government may be ahead of, or quite different from the sector choices made by Japanese private sector investors. Data for the years to 1992 show that the interest of Japanese investors in energy projects in Indonesia far outweighed their interest in projects in China, and that relative to Japanese investments in Indonesia in energy projects, their investments in Chinese energy projects were almost negligible.[73] As shown in Tables 6.1, 6.2 and 6.3, as of 1993 Japan's private sector invested more in fisheries development in China than in energy, and even then absolute values were small. Japan's interest in China's energy will increase, however, as Indonesia's export capacity diminishes and China's demand grows. Discussions about a pipeline from Russia's Kovytka gasfields through China to the Shandong peninsula and then to South Korea and Japan may well see a significant change in Japanese investments in energy projects in China in the coming decade.

China and Japanese FDI

Before 1978, China adhered firmly to doctrines of self-reliance or ideological isolationism so limiting any scope for significant private investment from capitalist countries, including Japan. In adopting

[72] Speech, 28 Aug. 1997: 'Seeking a New Foreign Policy toward China', www2.nttca.com:8010:/infomfa/ region/asia-paci/china/seeking.html.

[73] Kiyoshi Kojima, 'Dynamics of Japanese Direct Investment in East Asia', *Hitotsubashi Journal of Economics*, 36 (1995), pp. 121–4, citing official Japanese sources.

the 'four modernisations' policy and deciding to open up the Chinese economy in 1978, China indicated its preparedness to accept, if reluctantly, foreign direct investment.

In 1978 Deng Xiaoping met with the chief executive of Exxon in Beijing and invited his corporation to join China in joint ventures to develop offshore oil resources. The choice of sector was not accidental. Offshore oil development was just that – offshore. For this massive break with the past, it was important for domestic political reasons that there be no question of land-based or territorial control by foreigners, and that there be little risk that the everyday work of the foreigners in China would contaminate Chinese society. This was indeed the thin edge of the wedge for foreign investment, but it took another four years for China to draft and approve a law to govern joint ventures.

The shift to acceptance of foreign direct investment involved a difficult and slow learning process.[74] Each of its elements went counter to the communist party's long established beliefs, including beliefs about national identity and national purpose. For China, in the early post reform period, foreign capital itself was important as well as the associated technology transfer and export promotion. In moving from a self-sufficiency policy, China had to learn from experience how markets work; its initial belief was that foreigners would cooperate with Chinese firms to compete internationally to give export-led growth.[75] It also had to work out the balance between incentives to, and the benefits it should require from, foreign investors. Not surprisingly, that balance was often wrong.

Acceptance of FDI started experimentally in the special economic zones (SEZs). These coastal enclaves provided concessional regimes for foreign investment, but China's leaders conceived them as providing a mechanism for accepting foreign investment while putting clear geographic boundaries on its 'pernicious' influence. In those zones preference was initially given to 'compatriots' from Hong Kong and Taiwan although some provincial governments offered concessions to Japanese investors who tended to concentrate in northern China, as in Dalian. Japan was seen by China's leaders as the only Asian country to have successfully modernised and in this respect had something that appealed to the ideological dictates

---

[74] As Deng Xiaoping acknowledged. See Saburo Okita, *A Life in Economic Diplomacy*, p. 120.
[75] Rosen, *Behind the Open Door*, p. 160.

associated with attracting foreign investment that western countries could not offer, a view still held in the early 1990s.[76] The Japanese model held out the hope for China's leaders that, as an Asian country, China could follow suit.

At the beginning at least, significant taxation incentives applied generally. The establishment by China in 1984 of fourteen 'open cities', in addition to the four special economic zones, was important both symbolically and substantively in providing more attractive circumstances for further investment.[77]

The financial capital element has become less important, greater emphasis now being placed on the quality of investment. Technology remains a top priority interest of China's leaders. Moreover, with the greater understanding of the complexity of transferring technology, more importance has been put on management skills and on training that enables the Chinese to understand and manage the new technologies.

Given that for much of the reform period, FDI from other sources was more substantial than from Japan, China's government believed the Japanese government retained a significant influence on its business sector and in the 1980s in particular, contributed to the slow rate of Japanese investment in China. Chinese leaders frequently complained to Japanese leaders about the low level of Japanese FDI. Even so, when Japanese FDI first became significant in China, local level opposition emerged and in 1985 there were student demonstrations against the 'second Japanese invasion'. There were also complaints about Japanese workplace and employment practices, as well as more general complaints, including but not limited to the Japanese investors, about the competition with existing Chinese enterprises. These various complaints, while not absent, have diminished in importance.

The emphasis on exports reflected a view that access to the domestic market was more of a concession to attract investment rather than a benefit to China. This attitude has changed; eventually, China accepted not only that competition domestically was difficult to

[76] In 1992, Jiang Zemin still saw Japan, the only Asian country to have successfully modernised, as having something special for China that western countries could not offer. Cited in Taylor, *Greater China and Japan*, p. 58.

[77] In 1985, China opened up as development zones some of the delta regions, such as the Yangtze and Pearl River deltas. In 1988 the large island of Hainan off China's southern coast was declared a special economic zone and made a separate province.

avoid but also that access to the domestic market was now necessary to increase efficiency, notably of state owned enterprises (SOEs).

Compared with the 1980s, in the 1990s, China's leaders have gradually taken a more strategic view of FDI, but only after another major political battle and the intervention of Deng Xiaoping in 1992. Since Deng's 'southern tour' in 1992, many aspects of the old investment regime that had arisen in an atmosphere of hostility to foreign capital have been removed – foreigners were progressively allowed to own more than 50% of enterprises in additional sectors and, as already noted, foreigners were allowed into on-shore mining investment.

China continues to see FDI in general as vital for its economic development because of the technology and management skills it brings with it, but also for the strategic positioning in the international market that it allows. Only in the 1990s, however, did it come to understand fully, and to reflect that understanding in its policies, that investment decisions by foreign firms in general are commercial decisions made on the basis of potential profitability and that, if other conditions are not right, a large potential market, even as large as China, is not enough to attract foreign investment. Thus while China still makes make pointed references to the low levels of FDI from Japan, its comments tend to be more tempered.

Infrastructure investment has been a priority for the Chinese leaders but more in terms of international borrowing by government than for private investors. It is now trying to encourage private investment interest in infrastructure, particularly in areas outside the coastal zones. Japanese firms have been extensively involved in infrastructure projects in China but generally in association with Japanese aid or the international lending agencies and some of these firms have established locally to facilitate this. Japanese banks have been involved in lending for infrastructure projects co-ordinated by the Asian Development Bank or the World Bank. Overall, interest in the direct provision of infrastructure has been limited, although it has had some success, as in turnkey projects; one of the reforms of the early 1990s, for example, was that foreigners were actually allowed to operate Chinese power utilities on a thirty year lease basis.

The debate over foreign investment is not finished in China. The Asian financial crisis in 1997 and 1998 provoked shrill calls from parochial interests in China to constrain penetration of the economy by foreign investors from all sources, not just from Japan. In 1997, the

English language *China Daily* (*Business Weekly*) ran a series of four articles by an official of the Ministry of Foreign Trade and Economic Cooperation on the virtues of foreign investment, rebutting arguments that foreign-invested firms provided unnecessary competition or unfair competition to domestic firms.[78] The leadership firmly endorsed strategies of further liberalisation of the foreign investment regimes in the belief that through innovation and technology transfer it contributes to economic modernisation and through increased exports it provides necessary foreign exchange earnings. They have not, however, silenced strong voices within the Communist Party against these policies. Moreover, China, like most governments open to foreign investment, remains keen to regulate it, to channel it, and in some areas to limit it.

Importance to China of Japanese investment

For China, Japan is a major source of FDI, along with that from the US and EU, capable of contributing to industrial and technological advances on the scale and at a pace desired by China.[79] China's leaders pay special attention to the corporate leaders from Japan, and receive them regularly. As we have seen, compared with other countries, Japan is a significant but not major source of FDI for China (see also Table 6.8). Japanese firms contracted a total of US$28 billion worth of direct investment in China between 1979 and September 1997 – only some 6% of total FDI pledged in China in the period.[80] Even though Japan was a major national source of FDI, another 120 countries outside of the top four or five were by 1997 the source of between 5–7 times as much FDI as Japan, as Table 6.8 shows.

Total foreign direct investment in China as a proportion of fixed asset investment was just under 10% in the mid-1990s,[81] so in aggregate terms, the withdrawal of all new Japanese investment would deny China only about 1% of new fixed asset investment in a given

---

[78] The fourth article was by Liu Si, 'Official: National Industry, FDI Inseparable', *China Daily* (*Business Weekly*), 7–13 Sep. 1997 (FBIS-CHI-97-252, 9 Sep. 1997).

[79] The United States and Japan are the two largest, most technologically advanced, economies. No single EU member comes close, and this is reflected in relatively small investment flows into China by individual EU countries compared with those from the United States and Japan.

[80] Ministry of Foreign Trade and Economic Cooperation, Beijing.

[81] Zhang Xiaoji, 'Foreign Direct Investment in China's Economic Development' in *The New Wave of Foreign Direct Investment in Asia*, Singapore: Nomura Research

Table 6.8. IDENTIFIED NATIONAL SOURCES OF
CONTRACTED DIRECT INVESTMENT IN CHINA
BY VALUE (*US$ billion*)[82]

	1979–89	1990	1991	1992	1993	1994	1995	1996	1997	1998
Hong Kong	20.879	3.833	7.215	40.044	73.939	46.971	40.996	28.002	18.220	17.613
Taiwan	1.100	1.000	3.430	5.543	9.965	5.395	5.849	5.141	2.810	2.982
USA	4.057	0.358	0.548	3.121	6.813	6.010	7.471	6.916	4.940	6.484
Japan	2.855	0.457	0.812	2.173	2.960	4.440	7.592	5.131	3.400	2.274
Others	4.569	1.948	3.405	7.241	17.759	19.864	29.374	28.086	22.410	16.108

year – if a national average is considered.Yet, as we observed in Chapter 5, aggregate figures at the national level understate the importance of the contribution of FDI.

Foreign investment has contributed significantly to China's export growth, with the share of China's exports from FIEs rising from 0.11% in 1980 to 41% in 1995.[83] In China-Japan trade more than half of China's exports to Japan was produced in FIEs. By 1997, some 26% of output of Japanese FIEs in China was being exported to Japan.[84] The majority of China's exports from FIEs have however been in lower technology sectors or assembly operations and mostly from enterprises with Hong Kong or Taiwanese investment. Consequently imported equipment and input needs are high. Imports of FIEs still outstripped their exports but as local sourcing of inputs is increasing, the gap is diminishing.[85] Most FIEs continuously run

---

Institute and the Institute of Southeast Asian Studies, 1995, p. 224, gives a figure of 7.7% in 1992 and estimated a figure of 9% for 1993.

[82] MOFTEC cited by US-China Business Council (www.uschina.org accessed 12 Feb. 1999). Hong Kong figures for 1979–89 also included Macao, which provided about 3% or less, according to the Business Council. The Taiwan figures before 1992 are estimates by the US-China Business Council. The values are in current year dollars. China's MOFTEC estimates do not match Japan's MOF figures.

[83] Chen Chunlai, 'Foreign Direct Investment and Trade: An Empirical Analysis of the Evidence from China', Chinese Economics Research Centre, Working Paper 97/11, Aug. 1997, p. 35; East Asia Analytical Unit, *China Embraces the Market: Achievements, Constraints and Opportunities*, Canberra; Department of Foreign Affairs and Trade, 1997, p.140.

[84] Wu Delie, 'Absorbing the Impact of a Drop in Investment', *Guoji maoyi*, 20 Apr. 1998, pp. 23–5 (FBIS-CHI-98-159, 8 June 1998); see also Zhang Xiaoji, 'Foreign Direct Investment in China's Economic Development', p. 241.

[85] Wang Yong, *China Daily (Business Weekly)*, 11–17 June 1995, p. 2 (FBIS-CHI-95-112, 12 June 1995); Rosen, *Behind the Open Door*, p. 135.

trade deficits, with the deficit for all FIEs in 1994 said to reach US$20 billion.[86]

An important impact of international market forces, including FDI, on political structures in China may have been on the de-centralisation of decision-making. Japanese specialists now identify provincial and local authorities as important new targets of business initiatives and economic diplomacy. It is difficult to identify a nation-ally distinctive role for Japanese investors in this process of govern-mental change, however, different to that played by US or European investors.

Japanese investment, like all FDI, has a more substantial effect on regional development of parts of China, and on development of particular sectors of Chinese industry than on bilateral Japan-China economic relations at the aggregate national level. More generally, Japanese investors have concentrated their attentions on particular parts of China. By 1992, ten of China's 30 provinces or municipali-ties had received more than 80% of total FDI.[87] For Japanese invest-ors, where the requirement has been for locations with highly developed infrastructure and more highly skilled workers, cities on the coast of the industrial northeast have been most attractive, parti-cularly on the Sea of Japan (the Liaodong and Shandong peninsulas) and the Bohai Gulf. Japanese investors have invested substantially in Dalian, Beijing and in Shanghai, particularly since the opening up of the Pudong development. The Japanese presence in Dalian on the coast of the Liaodong peninsula is most conspicuous. By early 1994 there were reportedly about 500 Japanese companies with operations in some form in Dalian.[88] As much as 50% of Japan's FDI in China may have gone to the Dalian region by 1995.[89]

By 1997, a Sino-Japanese industrial park in Dalian had attracted 33 enterprises, most of which were wholly owned Japanese subsid-iaries.[90] As in the rest of China, Hong Kong and Macau investment in Dalian was greater than Japanese investment, but the Japanese interest had created a new Japanese population of 2,000 in the city.

[86] This has been documented for 1983–95 in Chen Chunlai, 'Foreign Direct Investment and Trade', pp. 15–16.

[87] Zhang Xiaoji, 'Foreign Direct Investment in China's Economic Develop-ment', p. 227.

[88] Kent Chen, *South China Morning Post*, 17 Feb. 1994, p.2, carried in FBIS-CHI-94-034, 18 Feb. 1994, p.8.

[89] Kyodo News Agency, 3 Feb. 1995 (FBIS-CHI-95-024, 3 Feb. 1995).

[90] Xinhua News Agency, 1 Sep. 1997 (FBIS-CHI-97-244, 1 Sep. 1997).

This is the second largest Japanese population in China after Beijing, and Dalian has its own Japanese primary and secondary schools.[91] In Beijing, by contrast, US investors had established a more visible presence by 1997, with about twice as many enterprises as Japanese investors, for a total commitment of about 50% more funds.[92]

Part of the attraction to Japanese investors in China's north is the familiarity left over from history, particularly from Japan's earlier occupation of Manchuria. Some Chinese specialists believe that it has been a clear policy of the Japanese government to promote private sector investment in North and Northeast China, with one source attributing the policy to a 'combination of economic, political and historic reasons'.[93] But as of the late 1990s, there were few publicly visible complaints from Chinese officials about this regional concentration. There is no clear evidence of strong political sentiment on the ground opposing the Japanese commercial presence and some in Dalian in particular favouring a welcoming attitude.[94]

Japanese investment in manufacturing in the northeast is creating new jobs in cities where they are desperately needed as many state-owned enterprises in China's industrial heartland shed large numbers of workers. In 1997, Japan and China were negotiating to make Dalian a model city for future bilateral cooperation in environmental technology transfer. In that year, the governor of Liaoning province, of which Dalian is the capital, was confident that it would expand its cooperation with Japan, especially with its big corporations.

A strong link between FDI and foreign trade is illustrated in Dalian.[95] One estimate indicates that in Dalian FDI accounted for 25% of fixed capital investment and that FIEs accounted for 20% of total manufacturing output, 50% of exports, and 45% of foreign exchange earnings in the early 1990s.[96]

While the province of Guangdong has received the most FDI overall, this has been in relatively unsophisticated industries. Beijing

[91] Mark O'Neill, 'China: Japanese Get Cautious Welcome Back to Dalian', Reuters, 21 Sep. 1994.

[92] China Economic Information, 26 Nov. 1997.

[93] Liping Deng, 'Understanding Japanese Direct Investment in China (1985–93): An Intercultural Analysis' in *American Journal of Economics and Sociology*, vol. 56, no. 1, Jan. 1997, p. 124.

[94] Interviews with Dalian and Liaoning officials.

[95] Chen, 'Foreign Direct Investment and Trade', p. 35.

[96] Ping Lan, *Technology Transfer to China through Foreign Direct Investment*, Aldershot: Avebury, 1996, pp. 129–31.

and Shanghai have been the favoured locations for the overwhelming majority of high value investments.[97] Japan's share of FDI in three of the most favoured provinces are shown in Table 6.9.

Table 6.9. JAPAN'S SHARE OF ANNUAL AND
CUMULATIVE CONTRACTED FDI
BY PROVINCE 1990–6[98]

	1990	1991	1992	1993	1994	1995	1996	1990–6
All China FDI								
US$m	6,596	11,977	58,124	111,426	82,650	91,282	73,276	435341
Guangdong: provincial								
share all China FDI	48.0	48.4	34.2	31.3	31.9	28.6	23.8	30.7
Guangdong: Japan's								
share provincial FDI	3.4	5.4	2.4	1.8	3.0	3.5	3.4	2.5
Shanghai: provincial								
share all China FDI	5.7	3.8	5.8	6.3	12.1	11.5	15.1	9.8
Shanghai: Japan's								
share provincial FDI	6.40	29.27	8.37	5.27	7.25	12.71	15.50	10.71
Fujian provincial share								
all China FDI	18.7	12.8	11.0	10.2	8.7	9.8	8.9	9.9
Fujian: Japan's share								
provincial FDI	2.0	0.7	1.2	0.9	1.6	2.5	1.6	1.5

The provincial preferences of Japanese investors in the period 1987–93 were: Liaoning (17% of Japanese FDI); Jiangsu (13.8%); Shanghai (12%); Guangdong (11.2%); Shandong (8.9%); Beijing (7%); Hebei (6.3%).[99] Despite the importance of Liaoning, however, over that period, it received more pledged investment from Hong Kong sources than from Japan (more than three to one) and almost as much from US sources (about two thirds of the Japanese total).

China has promoted certain sectors for foreign investment more vigorously than it has promoted particular regions but, overall, the sector choices of FDI have not been motivated primarily by Chinese government preferences. China maintains a range of discriminatory measures and policy instruments in place designed to channel FDI into certain sectors. The impacts on Chinese sector development of

[97] Gang Tian, *Shanghai's Role in the Economic Development of China–Reform of Foreign Trade and Investment*, Westport, CT: Praeger, 1996, p. 174.
[98] Ibid.
[99] Cited in Sun Haishun, *Foreign Investment and Economic Development in China, 1979–96*, p. 53.

FDI show up particularly in electronics and automobile production, where locally produced parts now form the larger share of intermediate inputs.[100] Table 6.10 shows the impact of FIEs in China's manufacturing industry for the eight sectors where FIEs have the highest shares of output.

Table 6.10. FIE'S ROLE IN CHINA'S MANUFACTURING
INDUSTRIES, 1995, BY SHARE (%)[101]

	% share gross output value	% share value added	% share pre-tax profit	% share employment
Total all industries	21.2	20.7	17.7	6.2
Electronics	60.0	58.8	60.3	27.5
Clothing, footwear	51.5	50.5	40.7	20.6
Instrument, office machine	39.6	36.9	44.7	11.9
Plastic, rubber	30.4	28.2	13.1	14.9
Furniture	29.9	27.8	25.5	12.2
Transport vehicle	24.6	23.5	13.1	6.2
Electrical	24.3	23.1	23.6	11.3
Food, beverage	23.0	23.2	26.6	8.5

While there is a mutually satisfactory match generally between Japanese investment decisions and China's development priorities, there are sectors of high priority to China in which Japanese firms have not made major investments, such as telecommunications and high technology industries.

Despite China's complaints over Japanese investors' failures to transfer technology, Japanese companies are increasingly seen as the most reliable foreign firms in fulfilling their investment commitments to China, and China continues to give particular encouragement to Japanese investment.[102] Chinese leaders regularly comment publicly on the high rate of success of Japanese funded joint ventures, the actual rate of use of contracted funds, and the vigour and interest of Japanese firms in China.[103] Chinese scholars often comment in a

[100] See Haishun Sun, *Foreign Investment and Economic Development in China: 1979–1986*, Ashgate, Aldershot, 1998, p.115; Gao Wei, 'High Level Visits'; and Zhang Xiaoji, 'Foreign Direct Investment in China's Economic Development', p. 233.

[101] Sun, *Foreign Investment and Economic Development in China: 1979–1996*, Ashgate: Aldershot, 1998, pp. 75, 77.

[102] Xinhua News Agency, 14 Sep. 1994, carried in FBIS-CHI-94-179, 15 Sep. 1994, p.12.

[103] Wu Yi, reported in, *Renmin ribao* (Overseas Edition), 11 Nov. 1997, p. 2 (FBIS-CHI-97-317, 13 Nov. 1997).

similar vein. Consequently, however small relatively, a view widely held in China is that the quality of Japanese investment is now high and contributes significantly to the economic and social rejuvenation of China.[104]

One assessment made in 1998 noted that Japanese FDI had helped turn China's economy into a market-based one; revitalised domestic industry; alleviated the shortage of investment funds; imported new industries and technology; increased domestic production; promoted exports, as well as increased tax revenue and employment.[105] While in national aggregate terms, tax and employment effects would be pretty marginal, FIEs overall provide a major source of foreign exchange earnings – one-third in 1994.[106] As already noted, Japanese FDI has made a particular contribution in that respect.

When Chinese leaders give special praise to Japan for its private sector investments in China, they are thinking of benefits in addition to the direct economic impacts. Some are common to all FIEs. The availability of concessional regimes for foreign-invested firms has encouraged many Chinese enterprises to sign up for joint ventures, so stimulating entrepreneurship within domestic industry.[107] A competition effect from FIEs also forced some of China's state-owned enterprises to be more outward looking.[108]

Some benefits tend to be more specifically related to Japanese FDI. These include: the associated transfer of technology, including management techniques; the important signal to investors in other countries given by the confidence shown by investors from Japan, the world's second largest economy and Asia's financial powerhouse; competitive pressures to other foreign investment in particular projects; important spin-offs for China in maintaining support inside

---

[104] Sun, *Foreign Investment and Economic Development in China*, 1979–96.

[105] Chen Jian-an, 'The Direct Investment of Japanese Enterprises in China and China-Japan Industrial Cooperation – To Commemorate the 20th Anniversary of the China-Japan Peace and Friendship Treaty', *Riben yanjiu jilin* [Collection of Japanese Studies], no. 1, 1998, p. 10. See also Sun, *Foreign Investment and Economic Development in China, 1979–1997*, p. 79, for similar conclusions.

[106] Stefan Kaiser, David A. Kirby and Ying Fan, 'Foreign Direct Investment in China: An Examination of the Literature' in *Greater China: Political Economy, Inward Investment and Business Culture*, London: Frank Cass, 1996, p. 51.

[107] Lan, *Technology Transfer to China through Foreign Direct Investment*, p. 139. Survey results for Dalian suggest that about one sixth of firms are less interested in the foreign firm's capital than benefits that flow from status as a foreign-invested firm.

[108] Bora and Chen, 'The Internationalisation of China and its Implications for Australia', p. 29.

Japan for business-like political relations with it; and in fostering Japan's often more sympathetic views of China within the councils of the advanced industrial nations. In addition, for China investment in the 1990s by large Japanese multinationals was particularly important since these are judged to be better sources of advanced technology, usually locating in bigger cities where unemployment is serious. To China's satisfaction, the investments in the 1990s have also been at a higher level of capitalisation than those of the 1980s.[109]

Japanese firms have contributed to capacity building in China through activities directed at community social needs (as we saw in Chapter 5) and by supporting a variety of public policy initiatives not directly linked to immediate commercial opportunities. Examples include NEC's sponsorship of a Sino-Japanese Software Research Institute in conjunction with the Chinese Academy of Sciences in 1994;[110] the 1997 sponsorship by ASN and NTT of Japan of a plan manager software system for China's Ministry of Construction to use in urban planning;[111] and a 1997 joint seminar between the national intellectual property associations of both countries.[112] But even some of these Sino-Japanese undertakings lose their bilateral complexion after a while, as they extend their cooperation to other large multinational firms.

Japanese companies invest substantially in training Chinese employees; for example, some 18,000 Chinese persons traveled to Japan in 1996 for vocational training, some 39% of all foreign trainees entering Japan in that year.[113] China, however, ranks low in terms of full integration in Japan's international business. In 1996, only 388 Chinese employees of Japanese companies were transferred from China to serve in Japan, less than from the Republic of Korea, but still 13% of all foreign persons entering Japan for that purpose.[114] The degree of localisation in Japanese companies operating overseas was lowest in China for major developing countries worldwide apart

---

[109] Liping Deng, 'Understanding Japanese Direct Investment in China (1985–93): An Intercultural Analysis' in *American Journal of Economics and Sociology*, vol. 56, no. 1, Jan. 1997, p. 124.

[110] *Keji ribao*, 15 Nov. 1994, p. 1, JPRS-CST-95-004, 15 Nov. 1994.

[111] Xinhua, 5 Mar. 1997 (FBIS-CHI-97-064, 5 Mar. 1997).

[112] Xinhua, 25 Mar. 1997 (FBIS-CHI-97-085, 26 Mar. 1997).

[113] Japan Immigration Association, www.netlaputa.or.jp/~nakaiofc/Status3.html.

[114] Ibid.

from Vietnam.[115] For Japanese firms, China ranks the lowest among its major investment destinations for the degree of local content (procurement of parts from local suppliers): about 40% compared with 45% for ASEAN; 50% for NIEs; and 60% for the USA.[116]

China competes directly with the ASEAN countries and the Republic of Korea (ROK) for Japanese investment.[117] These countries have already made efforts to counter the rising investment trends in China. They have been concerned not only about losing FDI, but also about changes in the consequent regional patterns of trade brought about by changes in FDI patterns.[118]

China's learning process about FDI has been extensive. Nevertheless, many Chinese officials who, as noted earlier, still see FDI as something China is more or less entitled too, believe that foreign investors have not borne the cost or risk of competition in the Chinese market, but have left those to their Chinese partners.[119] This view is compounded by a common Japanese practice, followed in China as elsewhere, of raising funds for their investments in the host country or with third country financial institutions.[120] According to a 1989–90 survey, almost as many new Japanese joint ventures were funded from Chinese financial institutions as were funded from the parent companies in Japan.[121] Hong Kong has been a large source of finance

[115] Yohei Nishiyama, 'The Outlook for Japanese Foreign Direct Investment and Promising Destinations', Highlights of JOI Review, no. 37, Japan Institute for Overseas Investment, Tokyo, 1998, www.joi.or.jap, figures 4.1 and 4.2.

[116] Yohei Nishiyama, 'The Outlook for Japanese Foreign Direct Investment and Promising Destinations', figure 3.4.

[117] Kiyohiko Fukushima and C. H. Kwan, 'Foreign Investment and Regional Industrial Restructuring in Asia', p. 17.

[118] Hideaki Ohta, Akihiro Tokuno and Ritsuko Takeuchi, 'Evolving Foreign Investment Strategies of Japanese Firms in Asia' in *The New Wave of Foreign Direct Investment in Asia*, Singapore: Nomura Research Institute and the Institute of Southeast Asian Studies, 1995, p. 62.

[119] Chen Bingcai, 'Relationship between Foreign direct investment and China's Technological Advance', *Guoji maoyi wenti*, 6 Jan. 1998, pp. 5, 13–17 (FBIS-CHI-98-077, 8 Mar. 1998).

[120] Shojiro Tokunaga, 'Moneyless Direct Investment and Development of Asian Financial Markets: Financial Linkages between Local Markets and Offshore Centers' in Shojiro Tokunaga (ed.), *Japan's Foreign Investment and Asian Economic Interdependence: Production, Trade and Financial Systems*, University of Tokyo Press, 1992, p. 153.

[121] Jian-An Chen, 'Japanese Firms with Direct Investments in China and their Local Management' in Tokunaga (ed.), *Japan's Foreign Investment*, pp. 261–5.

for Japanese parent companies setting up new enterprises in China. According to information from 1996, the share of financing provided by remittances from parent companies in Japan was higher for FDI in China than the Japanese global average: 67.4% from the parent, 24.8% from local sources, and 7.6% from local reinvestment.[122] But the share raised from local sources in China was also higher than the global average. By 1997, local financing had reached 37.2%.[123]

Some Chinese officials still believe that the Japanese government influences direct investment in China by its private firms, an influence manifested in levels of investment, types of projects invested and the geographical location of projects. Undoubtedly, specific interventions by the Japanese government have been very influential at certain times, such as through the provision of ODA loans, and in reaching a bilateral investment protection agreement. For some Japanese investors, influential roles have been played by their government, especially the use of high-level political access to help win certain competitive bids. Evidence on how important Japanese government interventions have been is as difficult to evaluate as is the evidence on how much influence Japan obtains from its aid to China. We noted earlier that government intervention by both Japan and China played a more important part in the 1970s and 1980s than in the late 1990s. At the same time, the government of China, through reform of its domestic investment regimes, through its domestic political actions, or its management of the domestic economy, has been the more influential in determining the direction and location of Japanese direct investment, and indirectly, its level.[124]

In the near future, economic conditions in both countries will influence the level and direction of Japanese FDI in China. Government policies in China will remain more important than those of Japan. In terms of micro-economic reform, China had done much by the end of the 1990s to promote new investment. Unilateral actions by the host country commonly create a better impact on investor sentiment than measures thrashed out during protracted negotiations at the initiative of potential investors.[125] Decisions taken

---

[122] Yohei Nishiyama, 'The Outlook for Japanese Foreign Direct Investment and Promising Destinations', figure 2.1.

[123] Eximbank official.

[124] See Zhang, *The Political Economy of the Japan-China Relationship*, pp. 148–9.

[125] Bora and Chen, 'The Internationalisation of China and its Implications for Australia', p. 45.

by China in international policy or macro-economic settings will also affect reactions to its domestic efforts. Thus not only membership of WTO but its compliance with WTO principles will be a major determinant in setting a favourable investment environment.

That environment is still deficient. Impressive as China's ability to attract FDI has been, one study of the period 1987–94 ranked it ninth among developing countries in relative performance, coming well behind Malaysia, Argentina, Madagascar, Paraguay, Singapore, Morocco, Egypt and Malawi.[126]

In starting this chapter we set out for consideration three areas of government interactions over foreign investment. The first concerned how each government approached the question of Japanese investment in China. When China instituted its economic reforms in 1978, both Chinese and Japanese governments expected Japan to be a substantial investor in China. Expectations were excessive, however, on both sides. China's inexperience in managing an economy no longer subject to total central control led to early problems of economic overheating and a consequent canceling of a large series of contracts, mostly with Japanese firms. The initial shock that this caused, and exchanges asserting lack of faith or lack of good will, brought the two governments together. Both governments were concerned to resolve the issue for the good of the economic relationship and eventually, at the governmental level, achieved a constructive settlement of the problem.

This loss of confidence for Japanese investors was less easily resolved. Together with the investment strategies followed by Japanese companies, it contributed to what has been a lower level of investment from Japan in the reform period than proximity, cultural affinities and the complementary nature of the two economies might have suggested. Other factors contributed, including China's investment regulations, and periodic belt tightening in China's economy, but these seem to have been less discouraging to investors from other countries. Particularly in the 1980s, Japan's low investment rate led to periodic, often strident, criticism of Japan by China's government. China suggested that Japan was not contributing as its economic

---

[126] Based on predicted levels of DFI according to a country's market size, economic growth, per capita income, efficiency wages, remoteness from the rest of the world, level of DFI stock and openness. Chen Chunlai, 'The Location Determinants of Foreign Direct Investment in Developing Countries', p. 45.

strength, benefits from its trade with China, and levels of FDI to other countries suggested it should. For its part, Japan made frequent representations to China over the problems its investors were facing under China's ever changing and often inflexible and arbitrary investment regime.

These criticisms were serious but by themselves seldom a major concern to the relationship. This was even more so after 1989 and the events in Tiananmen Square when China needed Japan's support, the investment regime was gradually liberalised, Japanese investment was increasing, and China came to understand better how market systems operated. Even so, at times in the 1990s for tactical political reasons, under pressure of conflicts arising from unforeseen domestic impacts, or to rebalance the balance of concessions and advantages, China's leaders have made important reversals in their efforts to attract FDI, and these reversals have had a discouraging impact. Nevertheless, in China, as in most countries, the domestic political debate about FDI is now largely about levels of control and regulation, harmonisation with international standards, and protective transitional arrangements for domestic sectors under threat.

Now both sides have achieved part at least of their hopes for the investment relationship. The government of Japan supported its private sector in its investment efforts in China to ensure that Japanese industry was well placed to benefit from the economic opportunities available there. Whether taken advantage of or not, those opportunities have arisen. China's leaders appreciate that the country has benefited from Japanese private FDI, with the manufacturing industry (textiles, machine assembly, consumer electronics and transport equipment) enjoying considerable rejuvenation. The leaders have shown relatively sustained commitment, often at some political cost, to the continuous reduction of disincentives to Japanese investment in China. From China's perspective, concerns remain about the inadequacy of technological transfer, but at least one major Japanese firm is now represented in joint venture production in China in most of the industries China considers strategically important.

Our second area of interest was concerned with the link between political relations between the two countries and investment patterns. Undoubtedly, the state of political relations between China and Japan has had an important influence on FDI from Japan. China's rapprochement with the west, the normalisation of relations between Japan and China in 1978 and Japan's increased concern with the USSR in the late 1970s provided a backdrop to an existing Japa-nese interest in developing economic relations with China, an inte-rest reciprocated by China. The periodic difficulties that emerged in the 1980s, discussed in Chapter 1, the events in 1989 in Tiananmen Square, and the coolness in 1990s over nuclear testing and the missile exercises in the Taiwan Strait added to the caution among many Japa-nese investors. These concerns were only partly overcome by the opportunities available in the domestic Chinese market from its high growth rates, liberalising investment regime and Japanese firms' needs for a more competitive export base. Clearly, problems of Japa-nese FDI have frequently been an irritant, but they have not them-selves been a major adverse factor in political relationships between the two countries.

Our third area of interest has a number of facets. Both govern-ments have had objectives for FDI beyond the straight economic ones. Although Japan has some concerns about the growing strategic weight of China, for Japan an economically struggling and therefore unstable China is viewed with even greater trepidation. Japan has been keen to aid China's economic modernisation because it fears the likely consequences of instability and political chaos on the Chi-nese mainland.

Both sides saw the economic interdependence that FDI implied strengthening the bilateral relationship through the increased con-tacts between the two societies that followed building not just good relations but vested interests in the relationship. China wanted to develop a constituency in Japan favourable to it, while Japan in the 1990s was keen to see China become integrated into the interna-tional system. In the decades since 1978, the penetration of China by international economic forces, including especially FDI, contrib-uted to the deeper integration of China into the global and regional community and served to further its domestic economic and poli-tical reform. Japan has played its part in this, and Chinese leaders have been willing partners.

Japan's share of total new FDI has been of the order of 10% on an annual basis, and of total fixed asset investment no more than 1%. That Japanese FDI is relatively small means that its contribution to interdependence is also relatively small. This also implies that the vulnerability that goes with interdependence is relatively small but not insignificant. Japanese investment in China is subject to the vagaries of investment regime changes but these have not caused major political tensions. Chinese reliance on the Japanese investment presence is not yet sufficient to create Chinese concerns about its vulnerability to Japanese dominance.

It is important, however, not to underrate the importance of Japanese FDI in China. After investments from Hong Kong and Taiwan, regarded by the leadership as Chinese and not foreign, Japan stands out in the statistics for national sources of direct investment either as the first or second most important after the USA. China's leaders know that a change in the value of new Japanese private sector investment would not reduce China's growth rates or export growth so substantially that aggregate national economic outcomes would be seriously affected. As we argued in Chapter 5, however, the marginal impact in China's financially constrained environment could be disproportionately large because of its budgetary problems and the limited capacity of its financial system to mobilise domestic savings for long term infrastructure investment. Moreover, China's leaders are acutely aware that Japanese FDI has contributed to a generalised dependence in certain sectors or regions on the output and external trade of FIEs.

A fall in new Japanese private sector investment to particular localities in China or to particular sectors may adversely affect trade growth, economic growth and therefore political stability in the affected localities. The Chinese government would not lightly risk such social costs in key industrial centres. There is also a symbolic importance to China of the trust inherent in Japan's decision to foster investment and to permit technology transfer, including in previously prohibited dual-use technologies. In current circumstances, Japanese investors may for this reason enjoy more potential for influence over Chinese leaders than the reverse although, in neither case is it a significant political issue.

Two decades of visits, informal discussions and formal negotiations over differences on investment policy have probably done much to break down pre-existing tensions. As the unfavorable features of the domestic investment regime in China have lessened in the opinion of Japanese investors and as new sectors have opened up to foreign investment, Japan's FDI has become a positive factor in forcing patterns of cooperation in bilateral political interactions. Japan's FDI has built up a degree of economic interdependence seen as valuable on both.

In the broad sweep of economic interactions between China and Japan, FDI is not a large part and may fall short of the test of contributing substantially to relations between the two countries so often alluded to in their rhetoric. On balance however it has been significant and increasingly positive factor in the relationship.

7

MANAGING COMPLEMENTARITY:
THE TECHNOLOGY GAP AND
ECONOMIC DEPENDENCE

Since Japan and China together account for three-quarters of East Asia's GDP, the conduct of the economic relationship between them will have a profound effect on each other and on neighbouring countries. In the two previous chapters we have discussed the aid and investment relationships between China and Japan. In this chapter we examine the implications for government to government relations of the two remaining components of the economic relationship – the transfer of technology and bilateral trade. For China, the ability to catch up with the West in technological capability is the key to its objective of national growth and modernisation, strategic as well as economic. China regards Japan, a country that has successfully achieved those goals, as a critical source of advanced technology. Bilateral trade, for its part, has carried much of the bilateral relationship in the postwar years. With export-led growth an important mechanism for China's development and China offering a massive potential market for Japan's export industries, trade remains a substantial element of the China-Japan economic relationship.

Government to government interactions on these issues have centred largely on two areas: problems over technology transfer; and government policies that have inhibited or stimulated trade. In both countries, however, implications for their relative strategic positions of developments in the economic relationship, and their mutual dependences, colour the policy thinking of both countries and shape their attitudes to the technology and trade relationships. Other aspects of these issues, such as the extent of cooperation or competition

242

between them in regional trade or in international institutions, are dealt with elsewhere in this study.

A strong body of academic thought, including among Japanese scholars, sees economic interdependence contributing to the development of peaceful relations between countries for various reasons. They include increased mutual understanding and reduced misperceptions that come from the interactions of those involved and the creation of communities with vested interests in the relationship that would press their concerns for peaceful and cooperative bilateral links upon governments. Such links also diminish the need for conquest to gain resources, and one resource now seen as central to power and prosperity – technology – cannot be obtained through conquest. Critics of these views see economic exchange, to the contrary, as often conflictual. The experience of the Japan–China economic relationship, despite often significant dissatisfactions, notably over technology transfer and trade imbalances, confirms the predominance of forces for cooperation over points of tension. Economic disputes between Japan and China, once seized upon by political groups in each country as evidence that the other was not a viable long-term economic partner, have become largely depoliticised. Disputes are now mostly settled so as to promote further a basic level of integration between particular sectors of the two economies and between particular sections of the two societies.

This chapter also highlights the underlying competitiveness and rivalry between the two governments, based in part on a determination in China to 'catch up' and in part on a fear in Japan of being 'overtaken'. These mutually reinforcing dispositions were given a substantial boost by Japan's sustained economic stagnation in the later years of the 1990s and by China's response to the Asian currency crisis. Yet the crisis also enabled Japan to demonstrate its economic power in a way that China as yet cannot, through the size of its financial support to affected countries.

Closing the technology gap: transfer or acquisition?

After 1978, successive national leaders in Beijing supported China's open door and reform policies in the hope that investment from the advanced industrialised economies would bring with it the advanced technologies they needed. Their goal was that technology transfer would deliver over a relatively short period a sophisticated technological base for the entire country. Japan's technological advance, both before the Second World War and subsequently, was an example for these leaders. Chinese leaders, therefore, placed special hope on Japan as a source of technological advance that they thought China could simply import, in the way they believed Japan had imported its technological advance. By the late 1990s, China's ambitions had not been met and technology transfer from all of the advanced countries, including Japan, had been limited and seen in China as 'second class'. Some specialists were advising the government that China should no longer pin its hopes on foreign investment for the transfer of high technology.[1]

The problems that emerged between the two countries were of two broad kinds – perceptions and realities. The perceptions included China's understanding of how technology transfer happened. In seeing advanced technology as something that could simply be imported, Chinese leaders had failed to understand the relationship between technological development and the domestic environment. For almost two decades after the open door policy was launched, many in the Chinese leadership equated technology transfer from a country like Japan with the export to China of machines, devices or processes that Chinese experts could with the appropriate training apply and manage.[2] The flows of high technology did not happen on the scale hoped for but most commentaries in the Chinese press continued to analyse technology transfer according to the value of import of equipment categorised according to technology level.

Some leaders placed great hope on replicating imported models or even by covert operations acquiring detailed specifications or design concepts for high technology equipment. Apart from their

---

[1] See, for example, Tang Shiguo, 'Sino-Japanese Technology Transfer and its Effects' in Charles Feinstein and Christopher Howe (eds), *Chinese Technology Transfer in the 1990s*, Cheltenham (UK): Edward Elgar, 1997, p. 156. Tang notes that some Chinese specialists have discussed the barrier that import of technology creates for the transfer of domestic R&D to industry, and so to national technological advance. See also the comments of a Chinese official, Chen Bingcai, 'Relationship between Direct Foreign Investment and China's Technological Advance', *Guoji maoyi wenti*, 6 Jan. 1998, pp. 5, 13–17 (FBIS-CHI-98-077, 8 Mar. 1998).

[2] Regulations promulgated by China in 1985 defined technology transfer in its internationally accepted sense as the transmission of scientific knowledge and production know-how related to a certain good. See Xu Jiangping, 'China's International Technology Transfer: the Current Situation, Problems and Future Prospects' in Feinstein and Howe (eds), *Chinese Technology Transfer in the 1990s*, pp. 82–3.

own complexities, reverse engineering processes can actually entrench technological backwardness, and considerable knowledge and experience is needed to work from blueprints. There was also little realisation that the operation of a command economy and large enterprises were counter-productive to the promotion of entrepreneurship and innovation that produce technological advance on the broad scale and in the short time frame that Chinese leaders had counted on.[3] Some of the more discerning leaders paid attention even at the earliest stages to the use of personal exchanges in promoting broad-based technological advance of the country as a whole but their ideas lacked effective support on the scale required. Moreover, Chinese enterprises are only slowly learning that they need to pay for the 'software' of technology assimilation (learning the 'why' as well as the 'how' of the technology) the cost of which in the case of Japan (and Korea) often exceed by many times the cost of the technology itself.[4]

A second perception problem reflected in China's disappointment with progress stemmed from a belief that its needs were for the most advanced technology and that anything less than that was selling China short. Yet the appropriate technology for China was often some way back from the most advanced technology, which was neither capable of being managed or maintained by local operatives and needed advanced laboratories and service centres for its support that were not then available, and still often are not.

Increasingly China's leaders began to fear that China was falling even further behind. Chinese productivity levels remain very poor. The World Bank has ranked China thirty-fourth out of forty countries surveyed in technological efficiency. The need to advance the country's science and technology base was put up as the long term unifying strategy or rationale for all government policy. The belief was expressed by China's president Jiang Zemin at the Fifteenth Party Congress and subsequently echoed by Prime Minister Zhu Rongji that advanced technology, understood in its broadest sense, was the

[3] An analysis of the evolution of China's growing awareness of the need to reform the social and economic foundations of technological advance is provided by Richard P. Suttmeier, 'China's Strategy for High Technology: Reform, R&D, and the Global Search for asset Complementarity' in Denis F. Simon and Hong Pyo Lee (eds), *Globalization and Regionalization of China's Economy: Implications for the Pacific Rim and Korea*, Seoul: Sejong Institute, 1995, pp. 195–227.

[4] Daniel Rosen, *Behind the Open Door: Foreign Enterprises in the Chinese Marketplace*, Washington, DC: Institute of International Economics, 1999, pp.73–4.

key not only to national strength in conventional military terms but also in terms of economic competitiveness, resilience and adaptability.

One aspect, the implications of which were only slowly understood in China, was that in countries like Japan, most technologies in which the Chinese are interested are owned by private firms with a commercial interest normally in transferring technology only in conditions under which they can retain control – in China this meant a wholly-owned or majority-owned subsidary, rather than through joint ventures.[5] But for most of the time since China opened itself to direct foreign investment, it insisted on joint ventures, with only minority control by the foreign partner.[6] With such a policy disposition, China simply was not attractive as an investment site for high technologies. The regulatory regime has since been relaxed such that under certain conditions a fully foreign owned enterprise or a controlling interest in a joint venture is now permitted.

A major obstacle in the past had been the failure of China to join international property rights protection regimes, and even after it did join, to enforce them. Action was gradually taken by China to repair its flawed record on intellectual property rights, leading at times to capital punishment for the crime, as there was recognition that this had to be a central part of an upgraded strategy to technology transfer.

The perceived vulnerabilities of China in relation to rapid technological advance in the United States helped galvanise political opinion in the leadership for major governmental administrative changes announced in March 1998. These moves included reorganising the State Science and Technology Commission into a ministry, and reorganising the Commission for Science, Technology, and Industry for National Defence (COSTIND) by increasing its powers, bringing under its wing powerful research and development capacities, and appointing a civilian head to direct it.

[5] Stephen Young and Ping Lan, 'Technology Transfer to China through Foreign Direct Investment', *Regional Studies*, 1997, vol. 31 (7), p. 670.

[6] Chinese sources report that Japanese firms either charge too much for technology transferred or try to control the technology of operations too closely, denying local workers the opportunity to experiment and innovate. By contrast, Japanese sources report that Chinese tend to undervalue the transfer of technology that does occur or over-estimate their capacity to absorb new technologies. See Jian-An Chen, 'Japanese Firms with Direct Investments in China and their Local management' in Shojiro Tokunaga (ed.), *Japan's Foreign Investment and Asia: Economic Interdependence, Production, Trade and Financial Systems*, Tokyo University Press, 1992, p. 264.

In addition, by the late 1990s, China's leaders had recognised that technology transfer, like the development of a national high technology base, is a broad ranging phenomenon rooted more in the domestic educational, economic and social order than in specific items of foreign hardware, no matter how advanced. This has also been reflected in the leadership's increased emphasis on reform in China's education system to encourage greater initiative and innovative capabilities. In the late 1990s, the Chinese government adopted some new policies on the foundations of national technological advance. These represent a realisation that the important process to focus on is 'technology acquisition' as a two-way process rather than on 'technology transfer' as a one-way transaction. China has accepted that the whole framework of China's industrialisation strategy as well as its education policy must be reformed if the goals of technological advance are to be met.[7]

Obstacles to technology transfer that were based on more immediate realities rather than perceptions have been of three basic types. These three often act in combination to influence commercial investment decisions of Japanese companies and the purchasing opportunities of Chinese enterprises in the field of high technology. The first is the potential effects on foreign-funded commercial operations of Chinese government regulatory regimes. As we have note elsewhere, these have diminished, including the move away from the requirement for joint ventures and for Chinese control where there are joint ventures.[8] Nevertheless they remain important. In meeting with Japanese business people in November 1997, China's Premier, Li Peng, acknowledged that China could do more with its domestic regimes to promote technology transfer and he was looking at policies that would be more conducive to imports of high technology.[9] The second, as we have also discussed, are the deficiencies in China's infrastructure, including the availability of appropriately trained personnel and the backup requirements of technical and scientific services. Between them, these two factors explain in part the limited

---

[7] On the industrial strategy see Tessa Morris-Suzuki, 'Japanese Technology and the New International Division of Knowledge' in Asia Tokunaga (ed.), *Japan's Foreign Investment*, p. 151.

[8] Incentive regimes for import of technology were often frustrated by other control mechanisms. See Pitman B. Potter, 'Law Reform and China's Emerging Market Economy' in United States. Congress. Joint Economic Committee. *China's Economic Future: Challenges to US Policy*, Armonk, NY: M.E. Sharpe, 1997, p. 240.

[9] Kyodo, 13 Nov. 1997 (FBIS-EAS-97-317, 17 Nov. 1997).

incentives for Japanese investors to consider China as a location for development of high technology industries. For the purposes of this study, however, decision-making by Japanese firms for technology transfer to Chinese enterprises are of interest only as they affect the interactions of the two governments or their policies.

A third factor, involving Japan's government directly, is Japan's participation in a multinational control regime designed to limit transfer of sensitive military technologies to China. On the broader strategic front, Japan has supported a coordinated approach by its major allies to prohibit the transfer to China of militarily sensitive technologies.[10] In the 1980s, the United States and Japan moved to liberalise technology transfer to China, and treated it differently from other communist countries which were allied with the Soviet Union or, like North Korea, still hostile to the United States.[11] This did not prevent suspicions from arising in China that Japan had a deliberate policy of withholding high technologies to ensure that China remained at least 20 years behind Japan's technology levels.[12] In any case, sanctions imposed by the United States and its allies on China after the 1989 Tiananmen Square crackdown put a partial stop to the liberalisation process, but through the 1990s, China still benefited from decisions by the United States on liberalisation of computer exports.[13] Some sanctions, such as those on science and technology exchanges, were still in place as far as the United States was concerned as late as 1999. And Japan has not had much pause for thought in

[10] For most of the time since China began its open door policy, Japan has been in the Coordinating Committee on Multilateral Export Controls (COCOM), which obliged it to follow policies agreed between the United States and its allies to restrict military technology development in the target countries. After the end of the Cold War, COCOM (the Coordinating Committee on Export Controls) was eventually wound up in 1994. It was replaced in December 1995 by the Wassenaar Arrangement, which tied together the former allies and Russia, and was directed toward restricting the flow of military and dual use technologies to a number of small states, such as Iran, Libya and North Korea. A number of other international agreements affecting technology transfer, such as the Missile Technology Control Regime or the Nuclear Suppliers Group, have influenced Japan's approach to the transfer of militarily sensitive technologies to China.

[11] Jing-Dong Yuan, 'United States Technology Transfer Policy toward China: Post-Cold War Objectives and Strategies', *International Journal*, vol. 51, no. 2, spring 1996, pp. 317, 320.

[12] Deng Yong, 'Chinese Relations with Japan: Implications for Asia-Pacific Regionalism', *Pacific Affairs*, vol. 70, no. 3, fall 1997, p. 377.

[13] Jing-Dong Yuan, 'United States Technology Transfer Policy toward China: Post-Cold War Objectives and Strategies', *International Journal,* pp. 320, 329.

joining the USA in restricting the most sensitive military technologies. For example, as recently as 1996, Japan actually tightened its restrictions on the export of encryption technology to most countries, including China. The atmosphere of hysteria in the United States through 1999 over the alleged leak of nuclear weapons secrets to China will guarantee that Japan remains sensitive to the allied security aspects of technology transfer even if it does not act as extremely as the United States.

Despite some easing of strategic restraints on technology transfer, Japanese officials continue to arrest and charge business people illegally exporting strategic technology to China. Moreover, even when Japanese companies obtain government approval to transfer advanced technology to China, they look over their shoulder at possible US objections. For example, in 1997, officials of Japan's NEC which had outbid US and EU competitors for China's largest semi-conductor project were concerned that the United States would complain about the transfers involved on the grounds of national security.[14] The concerns are justified in the light of experiences in the late 1980s. In 1987, after Toshiba of Japan exported naval-related technology to the Soviet Union, Japan succumbed to US pressure and suspended all high technology exports to communist countries (including China) for one year. As a result of this, a comparable incident in 1988, and then sanctions related to the Tiananmen repression, exports from Japan to China of 'technology' remained well below the 1986 level until 1991. Although the rebound was spectacular, reaching a high point in 1993, the figures again began to fall off in the mid-1990s.[15]

Technology transferred from abroad had been a factor in stimulating China's growth in the early reform period, much of it from Japan. The technology was largely unsophisticated, with many early FIEs being simply assembly operations. How far technological change contributed to China's growth in the reform period is part

[14] *Shukan Daiyomondo*, 7 June 1997, p. 14 (FBIS-EAS-97-155, 6 June 1997). The project, called '909', is directed at bringing China's semi-conductor industry to the same level as in major industrial powers. The project, based in Shanghai, will involve investments greater than US$1 billion by Chinese and foreign entities. As of the early 1990s, China's semiconductor products were limited to linear integrated circuits for colour televisions and specialty designs of industrial equipment. Most memory, microcomputers and logic integrated circuits had to be imported.

[15] Guo Li, 'The Current State and Future Prospects of Sino-Japanese Economic and Trade Relations', *Guoji maoyi*, 6 Mar. 1995, no. 3, p. 64 (FBIS-CHI-95-100, 14 Nov. 1995).

of an extensive and difficult to resolve debate, primarily because of the statistical difficulties associated with it. Krugman, in looking at East Asia as a whole including China, argued that growth had been mostly due to the increased application of capital and labour and not from increased total productivity growth based on technical progress.[16] Rosen concluded that total productivity growth was improving in China in the early 1980s but was decelerating in the 1990s.[17]

Technology transfer from Japan boosted productive capacities in certain industries, but they were relatively few in number. They included especially television manufacturing and textiles, but also other consumer electronics, some areas of machine production, metal casting and petrochemicals. But the range of technologies transferred has not produced the sorts of widespread renovation of China's industrial base that the proponents of the open door policies in 1979 expected. In fact, the levels of transfer have fallen far short. This will change to some extent in the coming decade if Japanese companies expand their investment in China's information technology sector to the extent that seems likely.

As we observed in Chapter 6, Japanese investors have begun to give greater weight to training components in their FDI programs. This meets some of China's criticisms about Japanese investors' unwillingness to provide technological 'software' and there are now numerous examples of limited technology transfer through technical cooperation agreements. In 1994, the Sanwa Group and the China Science and Technology Exchange Centre renewed for the third time an agreement on science and technology exchanges first signed in 1985. In the same year, Japan pledged a grant of RMB 1.8 billion to establish an advanced studies centre in Tianjin for teachers engaged in vocational training, with a further grant of ¥100 million to support technology transfer activities. In October 1994, the Kansai Productivity Center and the Japan–China Economic Relations and Trade Center sent a joint mission to China to inspect technology transfers and management–labour relations at local blue-chip companies as well as successful foreign enterprises operating there. Findings made by the group are being used to help Japanese companies move into

[16] Paul Krugman, 'The Myth of Asia's Miracle', *Foreign Affairs,* 73(6), 1994, pp.62–78; this debate is discussed at length in Heather Smith, ''Western' Versus' Asian' Capitalism' in Stuart Harris and Andrew Mack (eds), *Asia-Pacific Security: The Economics-Politics Nexus,* Sydney: Allen and Unwin, 1997, esp. pp. 60–6.

[17] Rosen, *Behind the Open Door,* pp. 124–5.

China.[18] In December 1994, Matsushita Electric Works established its third technology exchange agreement with Xian's University of Transport, to develop programmable controllers and associated software. As a result of such measures, as well as transfers associated with FDI, and other technology transfers arrangements, according to one study 28% of the technology imported by China in 1993 came from Japan, the largest single source according to Chinese estimates.[19]

For the Japanese government, dealing with the question of technology transfer to China has meant three things. It meant supporting Japanese firms in their efforts to persuade the Chinese authorities to amend their domestic commercial and legal regimes to facilitate the controlled transfer of Japanese technologies consistent with intellectual property laws, as well as to relax, and increase consistency, in the regulatory regime for FDI. It meant maintaining the appearance of cooperation (or normalcy) toward China by encouraging Japanese firms to transfer technology. It also meant balancing its interest in these two matters with its interest in restricting the transfer of the most advanced technologies to China. For China, the technology transfer issue has meant working in tandem with the Japanese government in the first two missions, while seeking to overcome Japanese government controls on technology transfer.

From the outset, the Japanese government's goals and policy settings with respect to technology transfer were much more limited in scope than China hoped for. One possible explanation is that these were shaped as much by non-commercial considerations as commercial ones. The over-riding policy attitude in Japan has been one of limiting technology transfer to China, and even as this disposition has weakened for some commercial technologies, it remains powerful. On the more narrowly economic front, Japanese authorities have been fearful of a 'boomerang' effect, where China became so well-tooled in industry through Japanese technology transfer that its economic power might threaten Japanese interests, either in general terms or in specific sectors of industry.[20] Moreover, as discussed in

[18] *Nikkei Industrial Daily*, 25 Oct. 1994 (NDB).

[19] Dai Ping, 'Seize the Historical Opportunity to Promote Trade and Economic Cooperation', *Renmin ribao*, 5 Mar. 1994 (translated in FBIS-CHI-094-044, 7 Mar. 1994, p.7).

[20] Martha Caldwell Harris, 'Technology Transfer and Sino-Japanese Relations' in Tamir Agmon and Mary Ann von Glinow (eds), *Technology Transfer in International Business*, New York: Oxford University Press, 1991, pp. 144–5.

Chapter 3, more Japanese politicians have become concerned in the 1990s with China's strategic orientation than they were in the 1980s. This has increased pressure in Japan for a more cautious policy on transfer of technologies to China that serve to enhance its overall national power.

Nevertheless, despite the Japanese government's caution over technology transfer, its sponsored cooperation in science and technology has been an important plank of bilateral diplomacy. 'Unofficial' exchanges began as early as the 1960s, but after 1972 a number of formal agreements were signed. By 1997 the two countries had cooperated on more than 170 projects throughout China in agriculture, metallurgy, oceanography, the environment, disaster prevention, earthquake science, biology and astronomy. There have been feasibility studies for more than seventy large projects and studies on the renovation of seventy medium sized enterprises.[21] Numbers of personnel going from China to Japan under these agreements remain small; fewer than 1,000 Chinese researchers, instructors or engineers entered Japan as temporary residents in 1996, compared with more than 4,500 from the United States.[22] The small amount of technology transfer that occurs under these government-sponsored programs does not meet China's main objective, the wholesale renovation of its productive base in all sectors of the economy, and even then its effect will take decades to be felt.

Nevertheless, the Chinese government regards such programs highly as a measure of trust and good faith. Despite China's concern about Japan's policies on technology transfer, Japan may have held a slight edge over other developed countries in the reputation of its companies to transfer technology.[23] This view certainly would have

[21] Xinhua, 28 Dec. 1997 (FBIS-CHI-97-362, 28 Dec. 1997): 'China: Roundup Views Sino-Japanese Cooperation'.

[22] Japan Immigration Association.

[23] Leslie S. Hiraoka, 'Japan's Coordinated Technology Transfer and Direct Investments in Asia', *International Journal of Technology Management*, 1995, vol. 10, nos 7/8, p. 729. See also Roy F. Grow, 'Comparing Japanese and American Technology Transfer in China: Assessing the "Fit" between Foreign Forms and Chinese Enterprises' in Agmon and von Glinow (eds), *Technology Transfer in International Business*, pp. 220–1. Grow found that the greater success record of Japanese firms was probably the cause not of some unique national characteristics of the Japanese firms operating successfully in transferring technology to China, but that there were more Japanese firms appropriate to the China market than appropriate US firms. A number of Japanese and Chinese specialists write of cultural differences between

been justified into the mid-1990s, but by then the movement into manufacturing in China of large US multinationals, such as Motorola, showed that the US companies could match, if not beat, the reputation of Japanese firms in transfer of some technologies, especially through licensed production and training of personnel.

That there appears to have been an increase in technology transfer from Japan to China in the 1990s is suggested by the lessened intensity of complaints by the Chinese government. Yet, despite the more relaxed relations, the Japanese government maintains a divide between the two countries so far as advanced technology is concerned. Complaints by China about the slow pace and restricted nature of technology transfer from Japan are not merely for rhetorical effect in Chinese diplomacy toward Japan. Japan's maintenance of strategic restrictions on exports of some more advanced technologies to China and the inability of the Japanese government to force any change on the commercial judgements of Japanese-owned companies are still viewed by the Chinese government as signs of less than cooperative behaviour. Even with the realisation that China itself must do more, lack of progress in technology transfer from Japan remains an irritant in China, and this irritant has added to other tensions related to the unequal economic status of the two countries and the strategic environment.

A Chinese specialist writing in 1997 observed that technology transfer between Japan and China remains 'particularly influenced by US-Japanese and US-Chinese relations'.[24] According to a news report, former Prime Minister Li Peng failed during a visit to Japan in November 1997 to persuade Japanese leaders to lift the bans on

---

Japanese and Chinese business practices that get in the way of smooth transactions. See Jian-An Chen, 'Japanese Firms with Direct Investments in China and their Local management' in Tokunaga (ed.), *Japan's Foreign Investment*, p. 271; and Tasuku Okubo, 'China and Japan–Financial Aspects', Tokyo: Sophia University, 1986, pp. 18–19. Another Chinese specialist noted that if cultural similarities or differences were important it was probably only at the early stage of market entry for a firm. See Liping Deng, 'Understanding Japanese Direct Investment in China (1985–93): An Intercultural Analysis' in *American Journal of Economics and Sociology*, vol. 56, no. 1, Jan. 1997, pp. 121–3. He identified the most important cultural trait of Japanese business people as their tendency to be risk-averse. But Deng also saw Japanese companies on the whole as being a little more sensitive to Chinese business culture than their US counterparts.

[24] Tang, 'Sino-Japanese Technology Transfer and its Effects' in Feinstein and Howe, *Chinese Technology Transfer in the 1990s*, p. 166.

advanced technology sales to China.[25] Li had expressed the hope that Japanese commercial interests would 'be able to win out among all other investors by bringing the latest technology and superior goods'.[26] In 1997, one Chinese commentator observed, perhaps for political effect, that Japan's ban on advanced equipment and technology transfers to China had weakened the competitiveness of Japanese products in China in that year.[27] The commentator was implying a threat that if Japan did not take a friendlier attitude on technology transfer, it could not expect its products to receive support from the government, state enterprises or consumers. This is likely, however, to be an empty threat.

Trade diplomacy and dependences

Trade was the principle basis for interaction between China and Japan in the early post war decades. In that period, Japan reached out to reassure China of its non-aggressive intentions and to restore something of the trading relationship that existed prewar.[28] As bilateral trade restarted postwar, it was originally based on barter, under a series of semi-official trade agreements. Japan was then the major export market for China, but the volumes were small. They only expanded substantially after China's reforms started to bite in the early 1980s. In that early stage, coal and petroleum made up about half of China's exports to Japan. Indicative of the broadening in the trade relationship is that they now account for only around 5% of a very much larger trade volume. At the time, as we discuss in Chapter 4, a major factor on the government to government trade relations agenda, implicitly if not explicitly, was the Taiwan issue. That has now largely disappeared from the bilateral trade agenda.

As part of the reform process, China moved from seeing trade not simply as filling unavoidable gaps in a basically self-sufficiency approach to economic management and as fundamentally exploitative

[25] Editorial, *Ming pao*, 17 Nov. 1997, p. D10 (FBIS-CHI-97-332, 21 Nov. 1997).

[26] *Nihon keizai shimbun*, 13 Nov. 1997 (NDB).

[27] *China Daily (Business Weekly)*, 10–16 Aug. 1997, p. 2 (FBIS-CHI-97-223, 12 Aug. 1997).

[28] Grow notes that China's imports and exports in trade with Japan in the 1980s reached the proportions of the 1920s Roy F. Grow, 'Sino-Japanese Economic and Technology Relations' in Denis F. Simon and Hong Pyo Lee (eds), *Globalization and Regionalization of China's Economy–Implications for the Pacific Rim and Korea,* Seoul: Sejong Institute, 1995, pp. 89, 92.

to recognising that it provided mutual benefits to the trading partners.[29] For China, it became accepted as an essential contributor to economic growth and modernisation. For the more than two decades since then, the progressively strengthening bilateral trade has been represented by both governments as proof of a fundamentally solid Japan–China relationship even through the low-points of bilateral political relations, through periods of low interest by Japanese investors, and through disputes over bilateral aid. Like other leaders before him, China's Vice President, Hu Jintao, saw bilateral trade as 'an important pillar for enhancing Sino–Japanese friendly relations'. Prime Minister Obuchi said in 1999 that 'Japan–China economic relations are the important foundation for bilateral relations'.[30]

Yet leaders like Hu and Obuchi only rarely elaborate on how trade enhances political and security relations between the two countries. In practice, compared with the early days of contract trade, which was overseen substantially by the two governments, the direct management of trade by the two governments has greatly diminished, with most change being undertaken by China. Governments on both sides still affect trade now by the conditions they impose but those conditions have become less important relative to the influence of the market, even for trade in a small number of commodities, such as oil or liquefied natural gas (LNG) where governments still have a direct role.

In moving toward that more market oriented framework, trade diplomacy has played an important part in loosening some of the governmental involvements in trade and in dealing with disputes as they arose. In dealing with the problems at these two levels, trade diplomacy between the two governments has not only been important; it has also often been difficult. The difficulties have commonly been entangled with other economic concerns, such as investment, technology and aid. A general problem has frequently arisen over Japan's trade surplus that periodically characterised the trading relationship. In the early 1980s, in particular, concern over Japan's

[29] Stuart Harris, 'China's Role in WTO and APEC' in Gerald Segal and David Goodman (eds), *China Rising: Nationalism and Interdependence*, London: Routledge, 1997, 134–55.

[30] *Xinhua*, reporting Hu's visit to Japan in 1998, 23 Apr. 1998, FBIS-CHI-98-115, 28 Apr. 1998; Obuchi's News Conference in Beijing, 12 July 1999, reported by NHK General Television Network (FBIS-EAS-1999-0710).

surplus was combined in China with the unhappiness among China's leaders over the low level of Japanese investment and the limited transfer of technology. Student demonstrations in the 1980s against a 'second Japanese invasion' added to the pressure on Chinese leaders on trade issues.

In the 1980s in particular, but continuing into the 1990s, trade from Japan to China was subject to significant adjustments in China's import regime, with its tariffs, import quotas and other non-tariff barriers simply tolerated by most other governments. Adjustments made from time to time in these mechanisms, and China's economic management measures to reduce overheating of its economy as well as to limit Japan's surplus, affected imports from Japan. This led to substantial instability in China's imports from Japan and Japan frequently raised the policies involved at government to government level. At the same time, the Chinese government was pressing Japan to import more from China to reduce the surplus.

Notwithstanding the tensions over China's trade deficit, the handling of the issue in the mid-1980s was one of the success stories of Japan-China economic diplomacy.[31] Japan and China had signed a semi-official official Long Term Trade Agreement in June 1978, based on the potential of the two countries to trade Japan's manufactures (mostly machinery for China's modernisation plans) for China's coal and oil (to diversify its coal markets and to alleviate Japanese dependence on Middle East oil). The strategic significance to Japan of this agreement was such that it was prepared in the agreement to commit itself to balanced bilateral trade. Over some years, China had complained about its bilateral trade deficit. As a centrally planned economy, with limited access to other sources of hard currency, China was committed to expand exports if it wanted to expand imports and, as a consequence, it sought balanced trade with each of its partners. China's inability to finance its projected import commitments flared up in 1979 and then again in 1981. We saw in Chapter 5 that the consequent cancellation of contracts with Japanese companies undermined the confidence of Japan's investors. They also provoked a re-think in Beijing about a more gradual, but more broadly based modernisation which took account of fundamental strengths in China relative to the rest of the world and was not limited

---

[31] Dong Dong Zhang, 'The Political Economy of the China-Japan Relationship in an Era of Reform and Liberalisation', Ph.D. thesis, Australian National University, 1997, pp. 87–8, 95–104.

to heavy industry. Japan's willingness to provide some immediate re-
medies through concessional loans and export insurance, helped
reinforce China leaders' acceptance of its reform program. Nevertheless, the implementation of credit controls, import controls and the
rescheduling or suspension of major new projects between 1979 and
1982 had a negative impact on the growth of bilateral trade.

These setbacks, including a still burgeoning bilateral deficit,
provoked important new efforts at trade cooperation between the
two countries. For example, in May 1986 Japan and China set up
organisations in each capital to boost Chinese exports to Japan.[32] By
1988, the deficit had fallen to a twenty year low, at less than US$200
million, and disappeared as a political issue. Over the decade, cooperation between the two governments was important in easing
some of the political burdens associated with the deficit. Various
influences eased these sources of tension. Zhang notes two. First,
China's reform measures (liberalisation of its domestic controls on
trade and borrowing) led by 1988 to a surge in exports to Japan.
Second, China encouraged trade diversification away from Japan to
lessen what was perceived in China to be too great an exposure to
this former enemy, which was also a capitalist country. In addition,
as we saw in Chapter 5, Japanese foreign investment was increasing,
as was its technology content. Moreover, not only was China moving
towards a greater market orientation of its trading system but the
learning process among China's leaders led to a better understanding
of the issues involved and the way the market system operated.

Nevertheless, in the mid–1990s, China became concerned again
about the trade deficit, which it said reached US$4.75 billion in
1994. The question was regularly raised in high-level meetings on
economic relations but China's improved economic conditions and
its considerably increased level of trade with the rest of the world
made a bilateral deficit of that size of much less political significance
than in the 1980s. China's officials were at times relatively relaxed
about it compared with the earlier decade. For example, a senior

[32] The Tokyo office which was called the Japan-China Trade Expansion Council,
brought together over 200 trading firms, and had ten subcommittees organised by
sector. The Secretariat of the Council was provided by MITI. The Council provided
technical assistance to firms operating in China's export zones and to other Chinese
firms interested in exporting. It also provided support for Japanese firms to meet
with potential suppliers in China to negotiate specifications for new export products. Japan's purpose in participating in such a venture was to make a contribution
to reducing its global trade surplus.

MOFTEC official expressed the view in 1995 that the deficit would persist because of the different levels of economic development in the two countries.[33]

Some of the disagreement over trade imbalances between China and Japan reflected different statistical understandings, with Japan at times arguing that it, rather than China, was the country with the deficit.[34] In 1997, Japan moved to reconcile its trade statistics with those of China because of these substantial differences. The Chinese statistics, which did not take account of goods trans-shipped through Hong Kong, showed that there was large surplus in Japan's favour between 1992 and 1995. Japan's trade statistics, which recorded goods shipped through Hong Kong but made in China as Chinese exports, showed a very large surplus in China's favour in the same years.[35] According to Japan's finance ministry, China's surplus was nearly US$14 billion in 1995.[36] The value of China's trade with Japan via Hong Kong was in the early 1990s almost as high as the value of direct Japan-China trade.[37] The Japanese government did not show any particular concern over any bilateral trade deficit it might have with China since it would be more than offset by Japan's large surpluses with most other countries. Moreover, it recognised that many of the goods imported from China were produced by Japanese ventures in China.

China will continue to face a dilemma over the trade deficit with Japan. If it continues to encourage vigorous investment by Japanese companies that, in itself, will increase the likelihood of a sustained deficit, an often inevitable burden for a capital importing country. Much of the current two way trade flow is a direct result of Japanese direct and indirect investment (the aid programs) in China.[38] Japanese-invested enterprises in China are likely to continue to import into China more than they export to Japan. Japanese firms investing in China bring plant and equipment in with them, and often

---

[33] *Xinhua*, 28 Apr. 1995 (FBIS-CHI-95-083, 28 Apr. 1995).

[34] *Kyodo*, 24 Jan. 1997 (FBIS-EAS-97-016, 27 Jan. 1997).

[35] The differences in Japanese and Chinese official statistics on the question of trade balance in the period to 1988 were not substantial for most years, but in some years were large. See tabulated data from both Japanese and Chinese governments for 1965–88 in Zhang, *The Political Economy of the China-Japan Relationship*, p. 86

[36] Jetro Homepage www.jetro.go.jp/FACTS

[37] Grow, 'Sino-Japanese Economic and Technology Relations', p. 93.

[38] Taylor, *Greater China and Japan*, p. 125 cites direct and indirect investment as the main determinant of the Japan-China trade between 1981 and 1994.

then bring in on a continuing basis inputs and components for their production activities. While the durability of the high levels of bilateral trade is not wholly dependent upon Japanese FIEs since Japan's exports and imports are not wholly linked to Japanese enterprises, much of it is associated with them in one way or another. A significant part of the raw materials, manufactures or other processed goods (some 25%) is exported by Japanese FIEs to Japan but many other producers, including Chinese enterprises, export to Japan. Government policies affecting investment therefore also influence the trade relationship.

This major source of the substantial growth in Japan–China trade was strikingly illuminated in 1997 in official Chinese statistics showing that exports and imports by foreign-funded enterprises in China accounted for more than half of the Japan–China trade for the first time – some 57.4%.[39] A downturn in two-way trade between Japan and China in 1997 was the result in large part of a drop of over 30% in capital goods imported from Japan by foreign funded enterprises.[40] By the first half of 1999, trade growth resumed (up by 8.5%), largely through new exports to Japan of production from Japanese-invested firms in China and Chinese imports of more finished products from Japan.[41]

Economic diplomacy and dispute settlement

The account in these three chapters of economic relations between Japan and China in the areas of development assistance, investment, technology transfer and trade has suggested a trend toward consolidation of normal economic relations over two to three decades. The chapters also show that the consolidation of normal economic relations has been buttressed by habits of consultation and dispute settlement. The two sides regularly sign new economic trade cooperation agreements. The creation of a variety of special consultative mechanisms, including those mentioned above, has also contributed to this normalisation of trade relationships. Other examples of special mechanisms include an annual meeting for China–Japan

[39] *China Daily (Business Weekly)*, 10–16 Aug. 1997, p. 2 (FBIS-CHI-97-223, 12 Aug. 1997). The figures reported were the for the first six months of 1997. Seasonal factors weighed the first half of the year in favour of this outcome since agricultural exports to Japan are more prominent in the second half of the year.

[40] *China Daily (Business Weekly)*, 10–16 Aug. 1997, p. 2 (FBIS-CHI-97-223, 12 Aug. 1997).

[41] *Nihon keizai shimbun*, 12 Aug. 1999.

economic exchanges established in 1980, which at its eighteenth session in 1998 attracted about 100 senior officials from both governments.[42] Others include the Japan–China Association on Economy and Trade, the Japan–China Trade Expansion Agreement Committee, and bi-annual bilateral economic symposia sponsored by the *People's Daily* and *Nihon Keizai Shimbun* (Japanese Economic News) since 1984.

Japan has been a firm supporter of China's admission into the WTO, both to ensure adherence by China to international trade rules, and to facilitate China's further integration into the international economy. Significant steps toward that were the agreement on market access for traded goods signed during Prime Minister Hashimoto's visit to China in 1997 and the agreement on services signed during Prime Minister Obuchi's 1999 visit to Beijing. The latter completed the WTO bilateral negotiations with Japan, making it the first of the G7 countries to reach such an agreement.[43]

There are several examples of disputes over economic relations that have been solved relatively amicably, such as a dispute over textile and clothing exports from China to Japan in the mid-1990. In that case, China's exports of textiles and apparel had grown rapidly, much of it coming from Japanese FIEs in China, to where by the late 1990s, clothing alone made up almost a third of China's exports to Japan. The increase in exports from China to Japan affected domestic Japanese textile producers, an industry in which Japan had been a major exporter in the 1960s and 1970s. China, through Japanese investment and through gradual application of new technologies to its cheap labour, came to be a competitor inside Japan for a struggling and remnant domestic industry. China benefited from Japan's early decision not to join the Multi-fibre Arrangement (MFA) as a result of which it did not face in Japan the restrictions it faced in MFA member countries on its textiles exports. In mid-1994, however, Japan's textile industry pressed the government to implement MFA restrictions on imports from China. Japan's Ministry of International Trade and Industry considered some protectionist measures to curb

---

[42] *Xinhua*, 6 Apr. 1998 (FBIS-CHI-98-096, 6 Apr. 1998).

[43] *China Daily (Business Weekly)*, 7–13 Sep. 1997, p. 2 (FBIS-CHI-97-252, 9 Sep. 1997). The Hashimoto agreement reduces tariff and non-tariff barriers and eases the inspection regimes for traded goods; Obuchi reached agreement on the services sector. Statement by Prime Minister Obuchi, *NHK General Television Network*, Tokyo) in FBIS-EAS-1999-0709, 12 July 1999.

the import surge. China was opposed but MITI conducted a series of studies over two years on the possibility of such moves.[44] In the end, Japan decided not to apply any further restrictions on imports of Chinese textiles. Important considerations included some concessional moves by China, lack of strong support in the Japanese government for such restrictions, opposition by parts of the industry which had invested heavily in China's production and the interest of both governments in setting an appropriate posture for their negotiations on issues related to the World Trade Organisation. It should not be taken for granted however that all such disputes will necessarily be easily resolved.

It is possible to detect a less confrontational attitude in Japan and China on economic disputes than that which characterises US trade policy in the 1990s. For example, in 1996, as pressures mounted for Japan to do something about copyright violations by Chinese firms of Japanese designs and trademarks in a wide range of products, the Japanese government sought to avoid a sanctions strategy similar to that adopted by the United States. It looked instead to provide technical assistance to China in strengthening its copyright protection regime. MITI was reported to have regarded a sanctions response as disruptive to trade and likely to prompt retaliatory measures by China.[45]

Economic relations with China remain a high strategic priority for Japan. In March 1996, Japan's trade ministry decided to upgrade its attentions to China in the belief that managing the economic relationship with that country would be one of Japan's biggest challenges in coming years. The Japanese government decided to augment its representative office in Beijing with an office of one its auxiliary organisations, the New Energy and Industrial Development Office. One of the principal missions of the new office would be to prevent the emergence of conflict between Japan and China in acquisition of energy.[46]

For its part, China clearly wants a greater sense of equality to condition the atmosphere of trade negotiations between the two countries. In 1997, China's trade minister stressed the need to focus on the long-term development of the two countries and on

---

[44] *Kyodo*, 24 Jan. 1997 (FBIS-EAS-97-016, 27 Jan. 1997).

[45] *Daily Yomiuri*, 19 May 1996, p. 6. The technical assistance was to include an English language patent database.

[46] *Nikkei Weekly*, 18 Mar. 1996, p. 20.

expanding cooperation 'based on the principle of equal footing and mutual benefit'.[47] She warned against politicisation of economic relations that she saw as running counter to this. While expressing some satisfaction with the trend in Japanese investment away from labour intensive manufacturing to value adding, she called for an improvement in the product mix of bilateral trade, and improvement in the quality and grade of commodities exported in both directions, and an increase in total trade values. Although the Chinese government has tried to play on its knowledge that Japanese companies retain strong interests in investing in or trading with Chinese counterparts, it has also come to accept that the conditions need to be right to attract this investment.[48]

The Japan–China trade relationship has been as sharply influenced by the differences in the political systems and their different stages of development as have other economic relationships. To the extent that there has been some convergence, important elements of political sensitivity have been reduced. On China's part, trade was originally pursued largely by the government and for different reasons from those that motivated private Japanese firms. At the same time, having passed since 1949 through self sufficiency and bilateral balancing phases, China's trade practices have moved toward a more open system where trade surpluses or deficits largely reflect underlying macroeconomic variables and real exchange rates and where motivations are much closer to those of Japan's private firms.[49] China is less open than Japan in terms of tariffs and import licensing or quotas. On present indications, however, it is likely to end up at least as open given that it has internalised the view that the internal benefits it gains from trade openness in terms of the economic efficiency and technological development are essential for its economic development. By contrast, Japan's trade policy is not based upon the principle of comprehensive open markets. Its liberalisation, while extensive, has come only under external pressures, notably from the United States and the GATT/WTO.[50] Substantial obstacles still exist to Chinese exporters

[47] Wu Yi, 'Finally Push Good Sino-Japanese Economic and Trade Cooperative Relations to 21st Century', *Renmin Ribao* (overseas edition), 11 Nov. 1997, p. 2 (FBIS-CHI-97-317, 13 Nov. 1997).

[48] Ibid.

[49] Nicholas Lardy, *China in the World Economy*, Washington, DC: Institute for International Economics, Apr. 1994, p. 37.

[50] This is also the thrust of the argument in, for example, Yumiko Mikanagi, *Japan's Trade Policy: Action or Reaction*, London: Routledge, 1996.

to Japan through various regulatory processes and domestic commercial practices. That, of course, is also true in China with respect to Japan's exporters.

Dependence

What constitutes dependence has several dimensions but in practice it is largely a subjective factor in terms of the concerns it raises. In a warm bilateral relationship, the strategic implications of a heavy economic reliance on the partner country may be of little concern; in a relationship characterised by mistrust the strategic vulnerability may seem substantial and lead to counter action to the extent feasible. We have noted that China has indicated at times its concern at its dependence on Japan for technology. In looking at dependence in the bilateral trade relationship, we need to start with the basis of trade.

For the two decades since 1980, Japan once again regained its pre-war position as China's largest trade partner, while for Japan, China has occupied the position of second biggest trade partner at least for the 1990s.[51] Whether and how far that relationship will grow depends upon many things, including political stability and sustained economic reform and structural transformation in China; and a resumption of economic growth in Japan, also dependent upon structural reform. It is generally accepted that the economies of Japan and China are sufficiently complementary, based on their respective factor endowments – Japan's capital and technology, China's low-labour costs and natural resources – for the conditions to exist for an expansive long-term trade relationship. Government leaders invoke the rapid growth in two-way trade, and the primary position of each in the other's total trade, as evidence of an emerging mutual dependence. Table 7.1 shows how the strength of the trade relationship measured in terms of each country's share of the other's trade has intensified during the 1990s. The importance of the Hong Kong factor, a reason for the dispute over the existence of surpluses or deficits discussed earlier, can be illustrated by the fact that through the 1990s Hong Kong increased the percentage share of Japan's exports to China by at least a factor of two (see Table 7.4), making it the second largest national outlet of Japan's exports after the US.

The complementarity that has emerged most strongly and looks likely to remain in place is that between Japan as a supplier of capital

[51] Grow, 'Sino-Japanese Economic and Technology Relations', p. 90 for China, 1980–93; for Japan, Ministry of Finance.

Table 7.1. JAPAN AND CHINA SHARES OF
EACH OTHER'S IMPORTS AND EXPORTS, 1991–8[52]

	1990	1991	1992	1993	1994	1995	1996	1997	1998
Japan's share of China's imports	14.2	15.7	16.7	22.5	22.8	22.0	21.0	20.4	20.2
Japans share of China's exports	14.5	14.3	13.7	17.2	17.8	19.1	20.4	17.4	20.7
China's share of Japan's imports	5.2	6.0	7.3	8.5	10.1	10.7	11.6	12.4	13.7
China's share of Japan's exports	2.1	2.7	3.5	4.8	4.7	5.0	5.3	5.2	5.1

intensive goods and China as a provider of labour intensive goods. Until the mid-1980s, China was not trading to its comparative advantage in labour-intensive goods, but even when it did so, it remained heavily dependent on imports of capital intensive goods. The bilateral trading environment has since become increasingly open and this means that the patterns of trade should more precisely reflect their respective comparative advantages. In Japan's case this will have been so for some time. For China, however, it seems increasingly also true. The evidence suggests that for China, commodity trade patterns are correlated with China's underlying international comparative advantage, a correlation that has improved over the reform period.[53] This comparative advantage lies in items such as coal, processed products and labour intensive manufactures such as clothing and processed foods.

After more than a decade of vigorous and rising trade with the advanced economies, China has approached world standards in the production of only a few classes of products, and the most advanced is probably textiles and clothing production that, together with footwear, accounts for over a third of China's exports to Japan. The composition of China's exports to Japan has changed over time with increased proportions of its exports consisting of processed goods, notably processed foods and elaborately transformed manufactures.

[52] DFAT, *The APEC Region Trade and Investment*, Nov. 1997, pp. 42–3, 46–7 for 1991–6. DFAT, *The APEC Region Trade and Investment*, Nov. 1998, pp. 44–5, 48–9 for 1997.
[53] Set out in a study by Xiao Ji Zhang cited in East Asia Analytical Unit, *China Embraces the Market*, Canberra: Department of Foreign Affairs and Trade, 1997, p. 150.

The share of China's exports to Japan taken by machinery and equipment rose from 3.5% to 12.5% between 1990 and 1996 while the share taken by raw materials declined.[54] China has therefore become competitive in the production of more capital intensive goods, such as in the manufacture of consumer electronics and personal computers, although the basic technology is normally imported with the assembly being undertaken in China[55]

Japan exports to China consist substantially of capital and technology intensive goods as well as inputs for further processing in China. Table 7.2 shows the most important categories by value in Japan's imports from China for 1990–6. Table 7.3 shows most important categories by value in Japan's exports to China for 1990–6.

Dependence is not simply the extent of trade, since it is the sensitivity of trade, reflecting the availability of substitute markets or

Table 7.2. CHINA'S SHARE OF JAPAN'S
TOTAL IMPORTS, 1990–6: BY CATEGORY
OF IMPORT (%)[56]

	1990	1991	1992	1993	1994	1995	1996
Food	15.7	16.9	16.1	15.5	16.9	12.8	12.2
Crude materials	9.4	8.4	6.6	5.4	5.0	4.1	3.9
Mineral fuels	24.2	16.6	13.5	10.3	7.0	5.8	5.9
Chemical products	5.4	5.2	4.1	3.6	3.4	3.7	3.4
Basic manufactures	13.6	15.2	12.7	12.3	13.5	15.2	12.5
Machines/equipment	3.5	4.7	5.1	6.7	7.6	11.3	14.4
Misc. manufactures	27.4	32.4	41.3	45.8	46.1	46.6	47.0

Table 7.3. CHINA'S SHARE OF JAPAN'S
TOTAL EXPORTS, 1990–6: BY CATEGORY
OF EXPORT (%)[57]

	1990	1991	1992	1993	1994	1995	1996
Chemical products	12.1	12.3	8.9	6.0	7.1	9.1	9.1
Basic manufactures	31.5	31.0	26.3	28.1	24.8	25.3	23.6
Machines/transport equipment	38.6	40.1	49.7	53.1	54.1	51.3	52.3
Misc. manufactures	11.4	11.2	9.5	7.5	8.5	8.2	7.9

[54] IEDB.
[55] APEC Liberalisation Study on Electronics; the example of Legend.
[56] IEDB.
[57] IEDB.

sources of supply, that define the vulnerability of a country to leverage from its trading partner. The extent of trade is, however, a reasonable first indication. That Japan provides a market for nearly one-fifth of China's exports is a significant factor in the relationship and while probably all the items are marketable elsewhere, and the vulnerability therefore limited, the economic costs that would be incurred were that to become necessary would be substantial. That is also true of Japan's exports to China.

There have been no major concerns expressed about the extent of strategic dependence by leaders in either country. In part this might be because the pattern of trade between Japan and China, that reflected a structural imbalance between the export and import trade of the two countries that makes a trade deficit for one partner inevitable, has also changed over time. While, as we saw, management of this deficit has been one of the most persistent issues in bilateral economic relations between Japan and China, it has been China that has been most concerned since it sees itself as having been the loser. As Zhang has pointed out, since Japan-China trade has been the largest single country share of China's trade for many years of this century, the bilateral balance has a proportionately large influence on China's overall trade balance.[58] Nevertheless, China has sought on many occasions not only to redress the trade imbalance but in the mid-1980s began to reduce its intensifying trade dependence on Japan which by 1985 had become the source of around a third of China's annual imports and was taking almost a quarter of China's annual exports.[59] China could perhaps feel vulnerable not just for its dependence on technology, referred to earlier, but due to the fact that through the inflow of Japanese investment it is becoming increasingly tied to Japan for plant and equipment and for inputs.

A degree of leverage would be potentially available to China to the extent that Japanese investment has fixed investment in place in China. Given that Japanese investment is still a small part of the total, the costs of taking advantage of that potential would not be so high. However, it is not conceivable that China would do so. Nor are there any signs that Japanese investors are concerned that their investments are at risk. Generally, for Japan the issue of vulnerability to trade pressure from China is less important overall. A perspective on the relative importance of China to Japan's export industries is given in

[58] Zhang, *The Political Economy of the China-Japan Relationship*, p. 85.
[59] Ibid.

Table 7.4 which shows that for some individual years in the 1990s, countries which might have similar market requirements to China, such as Taiwan and the ASEAN countries, provided larger markets for Japan.

Some sectoral dependences do appear to have been created by bilateral trade. For example, Japan takes some 30% of China's total exports of textile and clothing exports, and this share has increased from 12.4% in 1990.[60]

Table 7.4. MARKET DISTRIBUTION OF JAPAN'S EXPORTS AS SHARE OF TOTAL (%)[61]

	1990	1991	1992	1993	1994	1995	1996	1997
USA		29.3	28.5	29.5	30.0	27.5	27.5	28.1
EU		20.4	19.7	16.6	15.5	15.9	15.4	15.6
South Korea		6.4	5.2	5.3	6.2	7.1	7.1	6.2
Taiwan	5.4	5.8	6.2	6.1	6.0	6.5	6.3	6.5
Hong Kong	4.6	5.2	6.1	6.3	6.5	6.3	6.2	6.5
China	2.1	2.7	3.5	4.8	4.7	5.0	5.3	5.2
ASEAN[62]	11.5	12.0	12.1	13.9	15.4	17.5	17.8	16.6
Indonesia	1.8	1.8	1.6	1.7	1.9	2.3	2.2	2.4

In terms of Japanese imports, China has become a more important supplier for Japan than Taiwan in gross share terms during this decade, and has come close to matching Japanese imports from the EU and ASEAN, as Table 7.5 suggests.

Japan now accounts for roughly the same proportion of China's

Table 7.5. SOURCE DISTRIBUTION OF JAPAN'S IMPORTS AS SHARE OF TOTAL (%)

	1990	1991	1992	1993	1994	1995	1996	1997
USA		22.7	22.6	23.2	23.0	22.6	22.9	22.4
EU		14.5	14.5	13.7	14.1	14.5	14.2	13.4
South Korea		5.2	5.0	4.9	4.9	5.2	4.6	4.3
Taiwan	3.6	4.0	4.1	4.0	3.9	4.3	4.3	3.7
Hong Kong	0.9	0.9	0.9	0.8	0.8	0.8	0.7	0.7
China	5.1	6.0	7.3	8.5	10.1	10.7	11.6	12.4
ASEAN[62]	12.0	13.4	13.9	14.6	14.3	14.4	15.0	14.8
Indonesia	5.4	5.4	5.3	5.2	4.7	4.2	4.4	4.3

[60] IEDB.

[61] Tables 7.4–7.7: DFAT, *APEC Trade and Investment*, 1997 and 1998 volumes.

[62] ASEAN membership changed through the 1990s to include Vietnam. The ASEAN figures for 1992–7 are inclusive of Vietnam.

exports as the US but its share has tended to grow more rapidly, as indicated in Table 7.6.When the exports of China to Hong Kong that are re-exported to the United States are added in, the United States is clearly China's most important export market, has been for some years, and its importance is growing.

Nevertheless, there is therefore a considerable degree of interdependence between Japan and China. It is however, an interdependence that does not offer significant scope for either country to exercise direct political or even economic leverage over the other. Moreover there are no indications that the leadership in either country is concerned that the interdependence might lend itself to that purpose. Japan continues to believe that China's growing interdependence with Western countries is desirable as a means of reducing the risk of a destabilising China and Japan is willing to continue to play a full part in pursuing that end. An important consequence of this interdependence, moreover, is the increased interchange of Japanese and Chinese involved in the economic relationship, and the substantially increased numbers in both countries with a direct

Table 7.6. MARKET DISTRIBUTION OF CHINA'S EXPORTS
AS SHARE OF TOTAL (%)

	1991	1992	1993	1994	1995	1996	1997
USA	8.6	10.1	18.5	17.5	16.6	17.7	17.9
EU	9.9	9.4	13.4	12.8	12.9	13.1	13.0
South Korea	3.0	2.9	3.1	3.6	4.5	5.0	5.0
Taiwan	0.8	0.8	1.6	1.9	2.1	1.9	1.9
Hong Kong	44.7	43.9	24.1	26.8	24.2	21.8	23.9
Japan	14.3	13.7	17.2	17.8	19.1	20.4	17.4
ASEAN[62]	5.1	5.4	5.4	5.6	6.6	6.4	6.6
Indonesia	0.7	0.6	0.8	0.9	1.0	0.9	1.1

Table 7.7. SOURCE DISTRIBUTION OF CHINA'S IMPORTS
AS SHARE OF TOTAL (%)

	1991	1992	1993	1994	1995	1996	1997
USA	12.5	10.9	10.3	12.1	12.2	11.7	11.5
EU	14.6	13.3	15.2	16.1	16.1	14.3	13.5
South Korea	1.7	3.2	5.2	6.3	7.8	9.0	10.5
Taiwan	5.7	7.2	12.5	12.2	11.2	11.7	11.6
Hong Kong	27.5	25.1	10.1	8.2	6.5	5.6	4.9
Japan	15.7	16.7	22.5	22.8	22.0	21.0	20.4
ASEAN[62]	6.0	5.2	5.9	6.1	7.4	7.7	8.6
Indonesia	2.2	1.9	1.4	1.4	1.6	1.6	1.9

interest in the maintenance of cooperative bilateral relationships. This can be expected to lead to greater influence by domestic interest groups associated with the economic exchanges who want to see a cooperative relationship maintained and seek to press their interests on government policies accordingly. These are increasingly important in Japan, but their growth is most notable in China.

Asia's financial crisis and Japan-China economic relations

The Asian financial crisis, widely seen as a 'defining event in the economic history of East Asia',[63] provided fertile ground for the view that a new balance of power was being formed in Asia and that notions of interdependence of the sort that had underpinned the economic strategy of Japan toward China had been discredited.[64] This conclusion is open to doubt and, as we suggested earlier, strong bilateral economic relations with China remain essential for Japan's own policy priorities.[65] According to a US government assessment, Japan 'has clearly suffered a loss of confidence', and has developed an inferiority complex that contrasts strongly with its 'national feelings of economic superiority only a decade ago'.[66] This heightened anxiety identified in the US report will, in the light of China's sustained economic growth and its robust international posturing about its responses to the crisis, lead to some distancing by Japan from China, and an invigoration of Japan's economic diplomacy in other directions. This may have been the motivating force in a proposal by MITI in May 1999 to establish a free trade zone in East Asia involving Japan, Hong Kong, Taiwan, and South Korea.[67]

[63] Ross Garnaut, 'The East Asian Crisis' in Garnaut and Ross H. McLeod (eds), *East Asia in Crisis: From Being a Miracle to Needing One?*, London: Routledge, 1998, p. 21. The financial crisis may have threatened the biggest dislocation in the international economy stability since the oil shock of the 1970s which ushered in a long period of high unemployment in developed economies and which undermined support in developed countries for the concept of the welfare state.

[64] Paul Dibb, David Hale and Peter Prince, 'The Strategic Implications of Asia's Economic Crisis', *Survival*, vol. 40, no. 2, summer 1998, pp. 5–6.

[65] The regional impacts of the crisis are discussed in Chapter 8 but there have been important consequences for Japan-China economic relations.

[66] National Intelligence Council, 'Japan's Evolving Strategic Calculus', 16 June 1999, pp. 2–3.

[67] AFP, 23 May 1999. In late 1998 and early 1999, MITI undertook a major study of the appropriate strategic responses by Japan to the new international circumstances created by the Asian financial crisis.

The crisis had a marked impact on bilateral economic relations. As mentioned in the previous chapter, direct investment from Japan to China fell in 1997. In 1998 a substantial decline was posted in two-way trade – 10.7% – the first decline since 1990.[68] Japan's exports to China fell by 7.7%, and its imports from China fell by 12.3%. Japan attributed this fall to weak consumption and slower economic growth in China, and lower unit prices for principal Japanese exports such as steel. Japan also cited its own sluggish economy as a cause, noting that there had been a drop in imports of Chinese made clothing and associated products by Japanese affiliates. An early recovery was not expected. A Chinese specialist writing in early 1999 also expected the decline in Japan-China trade to linger, noting the lower prices available in Southeast Asia for competing products, and the slowing down of new Japanese investment in China.[69]

The downturn in some indicators of bilateral economic activity in 1997 and 1998 was accompanied by a negative turn in the atmospherics of bilateral economic ties. A number of Chinese leaders and economists were highly critical of Japan's role in bringing on the crisis through its failure to stimulate regional demand. As the crisis deepened, Chinese leaders argued that it was Japan's responsibility to pull the region out of its economic mess. China also sought to exploit a propaganda advantage over Japan by holding up China's responses, especially its own decision not to devalue its currency, as more imaginative and considered than those of Japan and as more of a national sacrifice than anything Japan had done. China criticised Japan for allowing the value of the yen to slide while China held firm its own currency. For its part, Japan was looking to lay some blame on China. In a 1998 White Paper on International Trade, the Japanese government sought to blame China in part for bringing on the crisis, by pointing to the rapid growth in Chinese exports to the United States at the expense of the ASEAN countries.[70]

While these bilateral tensions were evident, both governments

---

[68] Japan External Trade Organisation, Press Release, 2 Feb. 1999. The value of Japan's trade with China in 1998 was US$56.99 billion (exports of $20.1 billion and imports of $36.89 billion).

[69] *Xinhua*, 7 Feb. 1997, citing Wu Jinxia, a researcher at the China Academy of International Trade and Economic Cooperation. The decline in trade was not as substantial as represented in Chinese statistics as in the Japanese statistics, which may also reflect the effect of Hong Kong's economic difficulties.

[70] JETRO, White Paper on International Trade, 1998. See Table 9.

expanded their bilateral contacts in response to the crisis. The crisis had reconfirmed for them the absolute necessity of working together to overcome not just the regional manifestations of the crisis, but bilateral and domestic aspects of it as well.

Future economic relations between Japan and China

The scope of growth in the economic relations in the future will depend substantially upon economic growth in the two countries. In both countries, concerns over slow technological progress have solid bases. While Japan has been closing the technological gap between it and the United States and Europe, it is concerned at its continued dependence upon those countries for advanced technology and the possibility that it may not still be closing the gap.[71] This Japan–US gap is not likely to have a major impact on China's development, since China still has a major capacity for 'catch up' with Japan. Although technical progress seems not to have played a major part in China's economic growth so far, in the future growth will depend increasingly upon the application of enhanced technologies to available resources. Until China is able to generate its own technological advances, technology transfer will remain central to China's modernisation ambitions. As China enters the twenty-first century, however, it will have access to technology from a wider range of sources than in the 1980s and to some extent the 1990s. It will rely less on Japan and the technology transfer question will become less important. Yet much of its technology needs in the future will still come from Japan.

The advantage that China will retain, in its bid to attract Japanese technology transfer through direct investment, will be the size and purchasing power of its internal market, a bargaining leverage that other developing countries with low labour costs cannot match.[72] Together with proximity, the comfort of joining existing groups of Japanese FIEs in China, and China's continuing acceptance of the market system, China's domestic market will remain important in motivating Japanese enterprises with technology to transfer. In due course, moreover, China will increasingly possess some capacity through its own direct investment within foreign countries,

[71] Japan Science and Technology Agency, *White Paper on Science and Technology 1997 – Striving for an Open Research Community*, Summary, Tokyo, Mar. 1998.

[72] Young and Lan, 'Technology Transfer to China through Foreign Direct Investment', *Regional Studies*, p. 677.

including Japan, to acquire technology through acquisition of manufacturing firms in those countries.[73] Here, the barriers to investment in Japan experienced by other countries could become a new point of dispute between the two countries as China or its enterprises try to acquire a stake in technologically significant industries in Japan.

The Japanese government is likely to be able to count on a more positive attitude by Japanese investors towards technology transfer to China in the future. Paralleling China's learning about technology transfer, a learning process has taken place on the part of Japanese enterprises. This has led to a recognition that fear of the loss of intellectual property was perhaps an undue fear, particularly in advanced technology and in a dynamic context in which technologies are changing rapidly in any case. In addition, a growing number of Japanese investors appear to accept that the development of competing industries in China based on Japanese or comparable technology is 'if not inevitable, at least cannot be contained by any Japanese policy.' If they do not transfer their technology to China, finding the best way to do that for mutual benefit, their Western competitors will.[74]

We noted earlier that the trade relationship between Japan and China was expected to grow. China-Japan trade currently accounts for about 2% of world trade and studies suggest that it could grow to more than twice that share by the period 2010–15. One study suggested that China-Japan trade could by then match the 4–5% that the US-Japan trade represents. At present, Japan's share of China's exports substantially exceeds China's share of Japan's exports.[75] The study also suggests that that position may be reversed. Whatever the qualifications needed on such projections, the markets in the two countries have been taking increasing proportions of each other's exports. The probability is strong that the proportions will grow further, and thereby grow in political importance to them both.

The years of intensifying economic links since normalisation of diplomatic relations represent in many respects a normalisation of economic relations. This economic normalisation has been as faltering in its underlying fundamentals as it has been impressive on the numbers. This normalisation of economic relations is not yet complete, but that it has occurred at all is tribute more to the

[73] Ibid.
[74] East Asia Analytical Unit, *Asia's Global Powers: China-Japan Relationships in the 21st Century*, Canberra, 1996, p. 63.
[75] Reported in ibid., pp. 34–7.

convergence of economic systems, primarily through reform and an open-door policy in China than to sustained leadership attention in either country. Nevertheless, actions by both governments have on balance had significant positive effects on the trade (as on other economic) links.

The flowery rhetoric of the leaders of Japan and China is usually reserved for bilateral occasions and does not speak directly to the position that each country holds in the other's calculus of global interests, either economic or political. This dichotomy reflects a persistently difficult political dimension of the economic relationship, a dimension of the relationship still to be correspondingly normalised. By the 1990s, the economic and political circumstances of each country had changed fundamentally from twenty to thirty years earlier, but the nature of economic relations between them and the political aspect of these relations had assumed greater complexity. This new complexity has been demonstrated in many ways, beginning in 1989 with Japan joining its G-7 partners in economic sanctions against China after the 1989 Tiananmen Square suppressions. Even though Japan eased its sanctions ahead of some other Western nations and in advance of the twentieth anniversary in 1992 of normalisation, the politicisation of economic relations was clear, and has persisted. This was demonstrated in 1995 with its suspension of grant aid to China in reaction to the latter's nuclear testing, and with a policy committee of Japan's ruling Liberal Democratic Party calling in late 1996 for a more consistent conditioning of development aid to China because of its lack of progress on democratisation and its sustained military expenditures.[76] Japan's continuing refusal to lift all of its restrictions on technology transfer to China remains an important indicator that the levels of trust achieved by deepening economic relations remain relatively low. Trade has been less directly dealt with in this way but is tied to a degree to the political factors.

Just as importantly, however, the commercial contacts between the two countries, and the associated individual and social contacts between the two societies, have moved well beyond the exclusive purview of the two governments. Commercial considerations and individual choice now condition the majority of interactions between the two societies, a circumstance far different from much of the first two decades after normalisation. As Prime Minister Hosokawa

[76] *Japan Times*, 29 Nov. 1996 (NDB).

observed in 1994, economic relations between Japan and China have changed from vertical ties of the past to horizontal, cooperative ties.[77] Thus, while some basic issues of confidence in commerce remain to be resolved, the volume of economic contacts and the mechanical aspects of dealing with them have produced a degree of integration of some sectors of the two economies that is substantial.

Yet the question remains of just how far each government is forced by the scale of economic interaction to look more to serving commercial interests of its own nationals or national entities rather than subordinating these interests to broader strategic or political imperatives, as with the sanctions imposed on China in 1989. Both governments certainly retain a disposition to use commercial relations as a political weapon for broader strategic purposes. The independent power of the commercial or economic interests cuts the other way as well. Since economic processes are now major influences, then both governments have much diminished power to affect market impacts, positive or negative, at least in the short term.

Moreover, the narrowly bilateral aspect of the economic relationship – so prominent in the 1970s – has been overshadowed somewhat by the strengthening of both countries' economic ties with the international economy. Both governments now acknowledge that the global and multilateral aspects of international commerce and development aid have increasingly shaped the conduct of these activities between Japan and China.[78] Each government will recognise that its actions towards the other will be seen as a signal by the wider international community. In that respect, Japan has a stronger position than China. Of the two countries, it is China, as the supplicant for both aid and investment that is more subject to the vagaries of Japan's responses to the international market than Japan is in respect of China. But Japan is not immune from these vagaries, nor has it been free of strategic vulnerabilities in the shaping of its economic relations with China.

It has been politically convenient for the governments of Japan and China to paint the economic ties between the two countries in a

[77] Reuters, 22 Mar. 1994.

[78] See, for example, Prime Minister Hosokawa's remarks cited by Reuters, 22 Mar. 1994. See also Zhang, 'The Political Economy of the China-Japan Relationship in an Era of Reform and Liberalisation', p. vii.

positive light with representations of enduring complementarities or special consideration. The history of the economic relationship however shows a regularly adjusting balance of interests, with politics often intruding but with hard-nosed commercial considerations eventually becoming predominantly influential. As much as observers paint the two governments as equal partners, this has not been the case for much of the past five decades, as China has consistently been the much weaker partner. Both will be concerned to gain and develop markets but China's dependence on countries like Japan, but not only Japan, for advanced technologies as well as markets will remain a critical influence.

The claim that closer economic relations between any two countries will of necessity reduce misperceptions, enhance understandings and limit the likelihood of conflict is never unqualified. But the record of Japan-China economic relations is that some connection of that sort can be made in this case. The cumulative experience for both governments over more than two decades of opening up domestic markets to products from the other, the settlement of trade disputes, and the creation of standing mechanisms for trade promotion or dispute resolution has provided a solid foundation for normal relations in this area. Trust may be too strong a word, but there is certainly confidence on both sides that the other is predictable both in its reactions and in its willingness to solve difficult disputes. The work habits of consultation developed through a diverse array of trade negotiations and summit consultations on trade can flow over to a generally cooperative approach to solving bilateral political problems. More importantly, the size of the trade and its composition provide some incentives to each side to ensure that political relations do not sour enough to affect trade significantly. At the same time, the creation of regional mechanisms to promote open trade, such as APEC, and the enhancement of global regimes for open trade, through GATT and the WTO, has limited the extent to which Japan and China are likely to feel particularly threatened in political terms by developments in bilateral trade relations.[79]

Mutual predictability in economic relations is, however, not trust. The bilateral economic relationship continues to have its periodic troubles and is sufficiently unequal that it cannot in the medium term

[79] The participation of Japan and China in regional and global regimes is discussed in Chapters 1 and 8.

provide the counterweight to other bilateral political problems that both governments hope for. Whether economic ties over the next decade will provide a more solid foundation for integration in the longer term will depend on many factors outside the control of either government. This is discussed in Chapter 9.

8

JAPAN, CHINA AND
REGIONAL ORDER

Asia was the location of the most violent and protracted conflicts of
the Cold War. The major 'hot' wars took place in Asia – with Korea
and Vietnam the clear examples. And when the Cold War ended
in Europe, two civil wars in Asia that were shaped significantly by
it – in Korea and in China – had not been resolved, and the states
involved remained divided. Nevertheless, the major Cold War ideological divide in Northeast Asia that put Japan and China on opposing sides of the political fence disappeared in Asia in the mid-1970s.
Moreover, the dynamic of change in the Asia-Pacific since then, that
of economic development, has been one of considerable continuity.
Economic development has required a greater global participation
on the part of countries of the region, but has also led to increased
economic interdependence within the region. This has led not only
to a major increase in informal links among regional countries, and
a developed sense of regionalism, but also to the development of
regional institutions.

The power relativities in the region have changed substantially as
a result of the economic dynamic in place in recent decades but also
because of post-Cold War geopolitical changes. During the last decade of the Cold War, a three way 'united front' against the Soviet
Union had a harmonising effect on relations between Japan and
China and between each and the United States. With the end of the
Cold War, that effect disappeared; Japanese and US attitudes to China
changed as a result of the Tiananmen Square repressions and a diminished strategic need for China as a balance against Soviet power.
New anxieties began to emerge about the political and strategic

implications of China's growing economic power. China's concern with the region also changed but largely as a reaction to the US and other Western pressures. Japan has not found it easy to readjust to the new circumstances for domestic and international reasons. Compared with the last decade of the Cold War, the three countries had by the early 1990s 'lost their guideposts to unity'.[1]

The security concerns of states in East Asia, apart from South Korea, have shifted from immediate or fairly unambiguous threats to more ambiguous and less visibly threatening uncertainties. The dissipation of direct military threat has provided a substantial precondition for regional security cooperation but progress in dealing with the uncertainties in military security policy has been slower than in the economic arena, although some progress has been made in security cooperation more broadly defined.[2] The regional order, the systemic relationships through which the goals of the individual states in the region are achieved, is sustained by a mix of influences (balance of power, economic interdependence, and multilateral cooperation) and each regional state contributes to this order, but it is one that is substantially influenced by the United States. The relative importance of power, economics and cooperation for each of the countries differs markedly, and this also applies to Japan and China, yet since the early 1970s, there has been a wide acceptance – by no means unanimous – of the general principles of such an order in the region. In particular, for the first time in history, Japan and China have been working together in a regional order tolerable to both.

Particularly after the end of the Vietnam War, Japan's economic power provided a major stimulus to the development of a regional consciousness in non-communist East Asia and gave Japan a natural (if constrained) leadership capability. Japan has used this to facilitate, among other things, region-based economic cooperative processes. Japan is often characterised, somewhat inaccurately, as the leader in a 'flying geese' formation,[3] a conception that raises, among other

[1] Ryosei Kokubun, 'Delicate Japan-US-China Triangle Relationship', from SEKAI, August 1994 (FBIS-EAS-94-180, p. 27).

[2] In practice, the processes of economic cooperation in the region, whether ASEAN or PECC/APEC, have had important, if implicit, security dimensions. The development of these processes and their underlying motivations are discussed in Stuart Harris 'Policy Networks and Economic Cooperation: Policy Coordination in the Asia-Pacific Region', *Pacific Review*, 7(4) (1994), pp. 381–95.

[3] For a critique of the flying geese model see Mitchell Bernard and John Ravenhill, 'Beyond Product Cycles and Flying Geese: Regionalisation, Hierarchy and Industrialisation of East Asia', *World Politics*, 47 (1995), pp. 171–209.

things, a concern among regional states about Japan's economic dominance and political influence. Yet since 1951, Japan's regional influence has been substantially constrained not only by its bilateral alliance with the United States but also by the framework of US military alliances and strategic interests throughout East Asia. That framework remains a major influence.

As China has grown in economic importance its regional policies have been reactive rather than innovative, and early in the reform period its main concerns were to prevent any disadvantageous change to its security. Its main focal points have been: restraining the dominance of other powers, the United States in particular, a fluctuating ambivalence towards Japan as a US ally; and, most of all, a concern about Taiwan. Security considerations have also been visible, though less so, in China's gradual improvement of its relations with the Soviet Union in the 1980s and Russia in the 1990s. Only in the late 1980s and 1990s did China's regional policies begin to take on a more visible economic focus. Yet its position on East Asian regionalism, and its willingness to participate in regional cooperation efforts, changed in recognition not only of the economic benefits but also of the potential for countering adverse regional power relationships. This change was reflected in the endorsement, for the first time, of multilateralism as an element of Chinese foreign policy at the 15th Party Congress in 1997.[4]

Despite their constraints, and while bringing different influences to bear, China and Japan have both sought a greater role in shaping the regional order in the Asia-Pacific region. To some extent they have achieved that. In the economic field, the erstwhile hegemonic role of the United States has been displaced by regional multipolarity, although US economic influence globally still gives it considerable regional clout. In the security field, the United States remains the only country capable of projecting military and strategic power across the whole of the region. That is likely to remain so for a decade at least, even though more than a few states are developing military capabilities and strategic postures that will give the United States more pause for thought in the way it seeks to project its military power. Moreover, despite the still dominant influence of US-Japan and other bilateral links, and despite the Asia Pacific's limited historical sense of regional consciousness and no historical tradition of

---

[4] *Jiang Zemin's Report at the 15th Congress of the Communist Party of China,* Beijing: Sep. 1997.

multilateralism, the Asia-Pacific has developed a growing sense of region. Associated with that, an increasingly multilateral approach has been emerging in both economic and, if somewhat embryonically, in strategic fields.

This chapter asks a number of questions. After discussing the idea of regional order, and what constitutes the region, it asks about the future of Asian regionalism in so far as that affects China and Japan. It asks how they affect and are affected by the adjustments that will continue to be required to regional order and how far those adjustments imply leadership roles for China and Japan. It asks how that fits with the future US position in the region. Basically however the chapter's purpose is to see how answers to these questions will affect the China-Japan bilateral relationship in the future. While China and Japan have managed their regional roles without major bilateral crises to date, our interest is how far that will remain true in the future.

Two factors should be noted. First, what happens in the region depends in part upon influences from outside the region: the continuing pressures of convergence arising from internationalisation and from the changes occurring in the global order. These have been discussed in part in Chapter 1. Second, what constitutes the region depends predominantly on the range of interdependent interests that are involved. Advances in technologies and communications have transformed the importance of geography, while economic and strategic developments have changed economic and strategic interdependencies. Consequently changes in what is effectively the region, such as the growing involvement of South Asia in regional affairs, and the increased interactions with the CIS states, have occurred. China's involvement as a major regional influence, given its geographic centrality and strategic location, has also meant that that the distinction between Northeast and Southeast Asia has become less useful. A further sense of region comes from what countries have in common, even if only externally oriented: shared attitudes to others outside the region. Political, strategic and cultural interdependencies do not always accord with those of economics, and definitions of the region have become politically sensitive, as with the East Asian Economic Caucus (EAEC), and Asian membership of the Asia Europe Meeting (ASEM). While ostensibly about cultures and identities, judgements on these reflect as well instrumental and political factors.[5]

---

[5] As Katzenstein puts it, the concept of region is socially constructed and politically contested. See Peter Katzenstein, 'Introduction: Asian Regionalism in

East Asian regionalism

Although the various forms of East Asian regionalism are shaped by structural as well as strategic, political and economic determinants,[6] historically East Asia was a region largely around a Chinese centre. Although China was an important economy up to the Second World War, since the European influx in the nineteenth century, China had to conform to the political dominance of western powers. In Southeast Asia, and to a degree in Northeast Asia, British and then American dominance shaped regionalism. In the first decades of the twentieth century, an incipient sense of 'Pacific' regionalism started with non-government organisations, such as the Pan-Pacific Union and the Institute for Pacific Relations.[7] For Japan, however, Western dominance of China made it possible for Japan to conceptualise an East Asia order not centred on China and this eventually led to Japan's own regional dominance in the 1930s. Having become mired in China at that time, it moved militarily into Southeast Asia. While Japan has a tradition of regionalism not limited to the history of the East Asia Co-Prosperity Sphere, it had not been significantly concerned with Southeast Asia until the Second World War.

The dominant position of the United States after the Second World War and its imposition of a regional system based on a range of bilateral alliances, particularly those with Japan and Korea, slowed the emergence of a wider sense of region, notably but not only because of the communist/noncommunist divide. In addition, a consequence of colonialism and the post-colonial settlements was that linkages between new states in the region were limited, a limitation that took several decades to overcome.

Subregional developments buttressed the sense of regionalism in East Asia that came from economic developments at the national level, and created the need for the public goods that reduce transactions costs and enhance international economic interactions. In the case of China and Japan these developments included the eco-

---

Comparative Perspective' in Peter Katzenstein and Takashi Shiraishi (eds), *Network Power: Japan and Asia*, Ithaca, NY: Cornell University Press, 1997, p. 11.

[6] The evolving nature of the idea of region in Asia-Pacific is dicussed in Stuart Harris 'The Asian Regional Response to Its Economic Crisis and the Global Implications', *Pacific Review*, 13(3), Sep. 2000.

[7] Lawrence Woods, *Asia-Pacific Diplomacy: Nongovernmental Organisations and International Relations*, Vancouver: Univ. of British Columbia Press, 1993, p. 29

nomic growth and integration of greater China (China, Hong Kong and Taiwan), and Japan's links with Dalian, and then Shanghai through the Yellow Sea and the East China Sea. These were autonomous, largely privately driven processes of economic integration of the region. Efforts to develop other subregional processes in Northeast Asia have achieved only limited success.[8] This is despite the potentialities of the mix of low cost labour, natural resources, technology and financial capital that could come from China, Japan, Russia and the Koreas, and despite the strong desire on the part of China's northern provinces for easier access to the sea.

A lack of horizontal ties contributed to the limited development of subregional multilateral institutions in northeast Asia but more important constraints have been the unresolved political and economic uncertainties (especially in Korea and Taiwan). Although for China better subregional linkages could offer an alternative to wider US-Japan dominated regional processes and have security power balancing advantages as much as economic benefits, the Beijing authorities have not given them priority support. For Japan, the political and decision making uncertainties in these areas remain a daunting barrier to the use of its economic strength.

The regional involvement of both Japan and China, which are already important in their mutual relationship, can be expected to grow in the future. Since the starting point and policy responses of the two countries have been different, we begin by considering how their regional interactions have developed in the wider context of Asian regionalism.

Japan's resumed interest in shaping the regional order after the Second World War came first from its economic interests and then, as it developed political interests, from its economic strength. As already observed, in the post-Second World War years its attention was directed more specifically to Southeast Asia because of the Cold War divide in Northeast Asia. A desire to show an internationally cooperative attitude was also an early Japanese motivation for participation in multilateral activities.

Subject to its US relationship, and given its own economic success, Japan was able to grow in regional importance in Southeast Asia. Its relations with Northeast Asia were limited not only by the

[8] Gilbert Rozman, 'Flawed Regionalism: Reconceptualising Northeast Asia', *Pacific Review,* 11(1), 1998, pp. 1–27.

exigencies of the US Cold War position in respect of China and the various constraints affecting the Korean peninsula, but also by the regional legacy of colonialism and Japan's war history. Japan, moreover, needed markets and resources and these were more readily available in Southeast Asia. The Southeast Asian direction of its economic strategy was encouraged by the United States, and fitted the priorities of a business-oriented conservative government seeking economic growth within a developmental state orientation. Moreover, various Japanese prime ministers, from Kishi in the 1960s on, worked on the basis that while remaining within the US security umbrella Japan could exercise diplomacy in Southeast Asia that was independent of the United States.

From Japan's perspective, 'economic cooperation' was an important concept tying Japanese reparation payments and then economic aid to Japan's provision of goods and services or to Japanese demand for resources. Encouraged by Japanese government agencies, it was also linked to personal relations developed, often during the Second World War, between Japanese politicians and entrepreneurs and those in Asian countries, notably Indonesia, the Philippines and Burma.[9] Japan's economic relationships were a major factor in developing a sense of regionalism.

Leaving aside China's historic tributary system, largely a basis for economic exchange, China's regional involvement has been more recent than Japan's. From the PRC's establishment in 1949, China thought less in regional, than in global or bilateral terms. It had no specific regional economic or security policy.[10] Initially, China's involvement with the region was concerned more directly with its security concerns and the fear first of US linked encirclement and then that by the Soviet Union. Hence its support for North Korea, Vietnam and then its aid to communist parties elsewhere in Southeast Asia. It made an early attempt to enlist the overseas Chinese explicitly in its cause, but then reversed this policy in the face of regional antagonism. When it shifted from support for regional subversion and confrontation in 1974, towards cooperation with western allies

[9] Takashi Shiraishi, 'Japan and Southeast Asia' in Katzenstein, *Network Power*, pp. 178–9. It was the close alliances between Japanese firms and local politicians that led to riots in Bangkok and Jakarta when Japan's Prime Minister Kakuei Tanaka visited Southeast Asia in 1974.

[10] Weixing Hu, 'China and Asian regionalism: challenge and policy choice', *Journal of Contemporary China*, 5(11), pp. 43–56.

or sympathisers, it was motivated in part by a fear of the Soviet military threat and a concern for economic development that in the late 1970s led to the opening up of its economy to gain the benefits of economic modernisation. China's attention in pursuit of this goal was directed initially to the United States and Japan.

China looked to Japan for substantial assistance in its economic development, making much of the fact that it had not asked for reparations when it normalised its relations with Japan in 1978. Even after its normalisation with the countries of the region, China's concern over sovereignty, its geopolitical weakness and its suspicion of, and fear of dominance by, potential competitors, were important constraints on its thinking. For a time, in concentrating on economic development, it was comfortable with the concept of participation in the flying geese model. Yet, the implications in this model of Japan's position of leadership in the region became less acceptable to those opposing reform in China – and were part of the criticism of China's Premier Zhao Ziyang at the time of his fall in 1989.

As China's economy grew, increasingly another form of regionalism emerged – that of the Chinese diaspora, linked to greater China. A large proportion of investment in China comes from ethnic Chinese, primarily from Hong and Taiwan, but extending throughout Southeast Asia. China has consequently taken a greater interest in the region and now regards any development in the region as being of interest to it. Yet that appears to be driven less by a return to a great power or 'Middle Kingdom' mentality than by an interest in economic interdependence and, since the early 1990s, a reemerging fear of possible containment.

Japan and China may not have regional dominance objectives but they can be taken to have regional leadership ambitions and to be aware of the aspirations of the other. Those ambitions are, however, qualified. Japan is hesitant to be too forward in exercising leadership, and seeks to lead from behind.[11] China is still conscious of Deng's injunction not to be a leader,[12] again because of the fear of a reaction to China's historic, and potentially future, dominance. While both are sensitive to any attempts by the other to play a larger political role

[11] Alan Rix, 'Japan and the Region: Leading from Behind' in Richard Higgott, Richard Leaver and John Ravenhill (eds), *Pacific Economic Relations in the 1990s: Cooperation of Conflict?*, Sydney: Allen and Unwin, 1993, pp. 62–82.

[12] Quoted in Susan Shirk 'Chinese Views on Asian Pacific Regional Security Cooperation', *NBR Analysis*, 5(5), Dec. 1994. This is a useful discussion of the development of China's thinking on security cooperation.

in the region, mutual cooperation is usually necessary even if the needs do not emerge symmetrically. On balance, China's coopera- tion is essential for a wide range of political issues and for issues where scale – as with the environment – is involved, and Japan's for issues of an economic nature. It was galling therefore to Japan that out of the Asian economic crisis, China gained considerable status from its decision to hold firm its exchange rate and that of Hong Kong, parti- cularly when Clinton and Jiang, at their 1998 Beijing summit, to- gether sought to press Japan to reform its economy. Japan on the other hand was seen in the region, at least initially, as lacking both leadership capacity and regional sensitivity, although this was in part countered eventually by its subsequent provision of financial sup- port.

Despite inhibitions that both have about pursuing leadership objectives, Japan's overwhelming economic strength, its trade, aid, investment and official loans, and its technological capabilities, have created a substantially integrated regional economy and this will continue to give it important advantages in pursuing a leadership role. Yet that economic strength is not a total gain. Resentments re- main at Japan's economic dominance as do fears that regional econo- mies are being incorporated into a Japan-centered economic bloc. Not only does the idea of leadership reflected in the 'flying geese' model stimulate resentment, but Japan's only slowly liberalising market for the products of the region is also seen as a critical failing by a putative leader.

On the political side, Japan has sought to exercise leadership in the resolution of conflicts in Indochina and on the Korean peninsula and to extend the role of its SDF to enable it to participate in UN peace- keeping operations. It has also adjusted its aid policy to incorporate strategic, human rights and environmental objectives. For a time, it was also seeking regional support for its bid for a permanent UN Security Council seat although that subsequently seemed to receive a lower priority. Moreover, Japan and China have to compete with the United States, which starts with the support of much of the re- gion. Singapore's prime minister has said that a consensus among APEC leaders was that given the political and security implications of the growing economic power of Japan and China, there was 'a need to balance these two powers with a third – the United States'.[13]

---

[13] Goh Chok Tong, speaking at the 1993 APEC meeting, cited in Yang Razalia Kassim, *Business Times*, 23 Nov. 1993, p. 1 (FBIS-EAS-93-225, 24 Nov. 1993)

In projecting regional leadership, Japan has a harder position to sell than China. This is because of the sustained caution about any greater Japanese role in regional military security, a widespread belief that it wants economic dominance and the perception of its inability to offer effective and independent leadership. This is not helped by the United States wanting Japan to exercise leadership but in ways judged suitable by the United States. Yet the United States position is itself often inconsistent and unclear. Japan also has problems of its own ambivalence about how far it should emphasise its regional rather than its global (Western) role. It has been argued that Japan's inability to resolve the dilemma of its national identity construction between Asia and the West creates a 'legitimacy deficit' for its regional leadership role'.[14]

Japanese analyses have pointed for some time to the need for Japan to undertake substantial structural change in order to make international leadership possible. From the start of the Asian economic crisis in 1997 onwards, international pressure on Japan for domestic led growth and increased imports to lead the region out of crisis was intense. Yet this essential basis for any Japanese regional leadership was the clear message given in an official Japanese report (the Maekawa report) of more than ten years earlier.[15] Because of Asia's economic problems, and the heavy involvement of Japanese banks in the Asian crisis-affected economies, Japan faced problems in its regional, basically Southeast Asian, interests. The consequent political questioning in Southeast Asia – notably in but not limited to Indonesia – could affect Japan's future position, although memories in this field tend to be short.

More generally, Japan has viewed its global role as one of sharing responsibility for world peace and prosperity with the United States and Europe. In regional terms, however, this means that Japan needs a good political relationship with China and not only for its own wellbeing; without it, Japan 'cannot hope to win widespread acceptance as a leader elsewhere in Asia . . .'[16] Japan's history with China is of wider consequence outside the bilateral relationship in that it still interferes with Japan's efforts to lead a broader Asian region that

[14] Yong Deng, 'Japan in APEC: The Problematic Leadership Role', *Asian Survey,* XXXVII (4), Apr. 1997, pp. 362–3.

[15] *Report of the Advisory Group on Economic Structural Adjustment for International Harmony,* submitted to the prime minister, Yasuhiro Nakasone, 7 Apr. 1986.

[16] David Arase, 'Japan in East Asia' in Tsuneo Akaha and Frank Langdon (eds), *Japan in the Posthegemonic World,* Boulder, CO: Lynne Rienner, 1993, p. 123.

includes China. As the distinguished Japanese scholar, Masahide Shibosawa, with his colleagues argued, noting the absence of a moral undertone in Japan's postwar policies:

If Japan had been willing to face the cost of its conduct right from the end of the war, its perception of the world and its own role in it might have been very different.[17]

China does not support Japan's ambition to play a central role in the region,[18] but it also has barriers to its own easy regional acceptance. There is a regional desire to see a counter to the growing influence of China. Apart from hesitations others have about China's potential dominance, its many domestic problems limit its leadership capabilities. But China's acceptability in the region has, at times, been highly variable. More often than not China's desire to balance the power of Japan and the United States forces it into cooperative behaviour that regional states find acceptable. When China judges the US relationship as difficult, it tends to tilt towards Japan. When the relationship becomes more favourable, as it did following the 1997 and 1998 US-China summits, China gives more weight to its efforts to establish a 'strategic partnership' with the United States, thereby moving closer to fitting into the US bilateral framework.[19]

East Asian regional institutions

One manifestation of Asian regionalism is in its institutions. There have been two phases in the development of regional institutions in East Asia. These relate to the periods during and after the Cold War. In addition, the current institutional regionalism now has two significant dimensions. These can be seen, if too simply, as reflecting distinct economic and political impulses.

The first phase was that of the Cold War, during which there were many efforts under pressure from outside the region to buttress the range of bilateral security linkages with a regional grouping. These presumed adversarial relations between the western oriented nations

[17] Masahide Shibusawa, Zakaria Haji Ahmad and Brian Bridges, *Pacific Asia in the 1990s*, London: Routledge for Royal Institute of International Affairs, 1992, p. 126.

[18] Qian Jiadong, 'Security Trends in the Asia-Pacific Region' in *Disarmament and Security Issues in the Asia-Pacific Region*, Disarmament Topical Papers, 11, 1993, New York: United Nations, p. 38.

[19] Gaye Christoffersen, 'China and the Asia-Pacific: Need for a Grand Strategy', *Asian Survey*, XXXVI (11) (Nov. 1996), pp. 1067–85.

and the socialist countries. Their aim was for like-minded noncommunist countries to cooperate against the others. This essentially meant China. The major example was the South East Asia Treaty Organisation (SEATO), founded in 1954, and lasting until 1977. The Asia and Pacific Council (ASPAC) was an anti-Chinese organisation, set up at Korea's initiative in 1966, but which foundered and eventually ceased to exist in the 1970s. Japan belonged to both ineffective institutions.

The second phase saw the development of internally generated institutional arrangements. The first of any importance was ASEAN, established in 1967. This was not without its own Cold War stimulus, including as a counter to great power influence. The prime impetus, however, came from a mix of external security concerns such as disputes over boundaries, crystallised by the Indonesian confrontation with Malaysia, and the domestic importance of economic development as a security interest particularly in South East Asia. ASEAN has been important not only in limiting the conflicts among the original five members to peaceful resolution but, through its Treaty on Amity and Cooperation, it brought others into the 'peaceful' fold – notably Vietnam and Laos in 1992 and subsequently, in 1999, Cambodia. With stimulus from Japan among others, the ASEAN framework also led to the ASEAN Regional Forum (ARF). It provided a mechanism, therefore, and an experience that enabled other developments of a wider nature to occur. It is also the one regional multilateral arrangement, other than the Asian Development Bank (ADB), which has a degree of institutionalisation.

From the 1960s on, Japan had made a number of attempts to stimulate regional integration. These included initiating the Asian Development Bank and the Ministerial Conference on Economic Development in Southeast Asia (MCEDSEA). Although the ADB has become an effective institution, MCEDSEA did not and Japan's efforts faced regional suspicion of its motives and its power. As a result, Japan moved gradually to support institutional arrangements with a wider membership.

In addition, the Fukuda doctrine of 1977 made Japan's Southeast Asia policy essentially a policy of support for and increased links with ASEAN. Japan supported the ASEAN position on Vietnam and Cambodia, although it did seek some accommodation of the conflict and to maintain links with Vietnam. Given China's sustained support for the Khmer Rouge until well into the 1980s, this put Japan at odds with China on the issue.[20] Yet this seemed to have little effect on their bilateral relations. Japan became an early ASEAN post ministerial dialogue partner and subsequently a member of ARF.

The development of regional economic cooperation mechanisms had a separate but related path. In part they arose from growing trade relationships and shared economic problems internationally, including the emergence of the EEC as a significant trading bloc. Japan was an active participant in moves towards regional economic cooperation, including in the establishment of PAFTAD, PBEC, and APEC.[21] Early responses to the development of economic cooperation processes, however, reflected not only an interest in the public goods provided by dialogue processes; in addition, economic cooperation dialogue processes were seen as confidence and security building measures among countries with unresolved bilateral problems but limited horizontal linkages. Moreover, they contributed to economic development that was itself an essential security measure as a counter to the internal subversion arising from economic underdevelopment. Hence the emergence of various economic cooperation processes, notably PECC and APEC, with Japan's sustained support.

APEC helps Japan's objective of keeping the US interest in the region. As well as engaging China, it provides for a potential regional role for Japan's leadership. In the case of PECC and eventually APEC Japan's involvement was more comfortably, but not totally, accepted by the region since its influence was diluted. Japan supported and encouraged China's membership of these organisations. From China's opening of its economy in the late 1970s until the 1990s, this was essentially based on Japan's interests in helping China's economic development and to reinforce the opening up of its economy as a means of enhancing its stability and that of the region. Later it saw the growth of economic regionalism as an important counter to the fears emerging from China's military modernisation and its actions in the South China Sea.

[20] See Ken Berry, *Cambodia – From Red to Blue: Australia's Initiative for Peace,* Sydney: Allen and Unwin, 1997.
[21] Takashi Terada, 'The origins of Japan's APEC policy: Foreign Minister Takeo Miki's Asia-Pacific policy and current implications', *Pacific Review,* 11(3), 1998, pp. 337–63.

In 1979, China participated for the first time in PAFTAD, an economic conference process consisting of experts from regional countries. It had shown an interest in PECC from its beginning in 1980, an interest which was encouraged by Japan. Unlike the Soviet Union, China had not voiced strong ideological opposition to PECC prior to joining, although it had viewed the process as a largely Japanese inspired effort to promote Japanese economic prosperity, national security and political influence.[22] The potential for domination by Japan and the United States of the evolving institutional processes had also concerned it. Nevertheless, it joined PECC in 1986 and subsequently APEC in 1992.

China's experience in the regional economic institutions has been unproblematic except for the questions of nomenclature arising from Taiwan's involvement. China was more cautious in accepting membership of the security dialogues, and notably of the ARF, being concerned that it would be a group of countries collectively opposing China. Nevertheless, it became increasingly comfortable in the ARF dialogue, participating fully in the work of its subgroups. It also participates in the region-wide second track Council on Security Cooperation in Asia Pacific (CSCAP). It appears, moreover, to be embracing regional multilateralism in a way that is more than just lip-service, even though as a supplement to its bilateral diplomacy. The history of ASEAN, having given confidence to its members that no member will seek to resolve disputes with another member other than through peaceful means, gives rise to a growing wish to see a similar process established in Northeast Asia. Progress has been slow mainly because of North Korea, but China is now a constructive participant in CSCAP's North Pacific-working group, the only multilateral security discussion that includes all northeast Asian countries, including Japan. In the meantime, the ASEAN plus three – Japan, China and South Korea – meetings provide an opportunity for the leaders of three of the major Northeast Asian countries to meet among themselves.

In APEC, China and Japan cooperate without noticeable problems. Indeed, their economic interests, notably a lack of enthusiasm for agricultural trade liberalisation, are at times mutually reinforcing. Power relationships, although clearly in play in the economic institutions, are less so there than in the security field. Japan's regional

[22] Woods, *Asia Pacific Diplomacy*, p. 131.

security strategy, for example, includes support for the enlarged ASEAN includingVietnam as a counterweight to China, encouraging the United States and Europe to maintain their interest in the region and supporting US hegemony to offset China. For its part, China is concerned to ensure regional processes do not get involved in disputes over China's sovereignty issues, whether over maritime claims or overTaiwan. Even so, no major issues or tensions have emerged between China and Japan in regional security forums. In particular, none have arisen that flowed directly into their bilateral relationship.

As the major regional economic and political institution, APEC defines in one sense the Asia–Pacific region but in a way that defines it very broadly, not only institutionalising the links of East Asian countries with North America but also South America and Russia. In 1991, Malaysia's Prime Minister Mahathir proposed an East Asian Economic Group (EAEG) with a smaller membership of purely Asian members. Its aim was to counter what Mahathir saw as the formation of economic blocs among developed countries, and what in his view was the discouragement by the developed countries of economic development in the developing countries. Japan was asked, however, to take a leadership role.[23] Apart from Japan's own caution, the lack of enthusiasm by other Asian countries led to a less ambitious reformulation of EAEG as a caucus of APEC, now termed EAEC.

While China was an early supporter of EAEC, seeing it as a means of developing a counter to the pressures from the United States and the West on various fronts, particularly over human rights, Japan remained reluctant. In part this was a concern about the US position. It was also unclear about some of the EAEC's objectives – and its own ambivalence about its Asia orientation. Some in Japan saw EAEC as a logical part of Japan's Asian identity. Others saw APEC more coincident with Japan's Western and global identity and for a while therefore the global influence prevailed. Similarly, Japan did not sign the declaration that emerged from the Bangkok meeting preparatory to the 1993 UN Human Rights Conference which incorporated strongly the Asian values arguments then current, and which reflected similar motivations to those behind EAEC's

[23] Saburo Okita, *A Life in Economic Diplomacy,* Canberra:Australia-Japan Research Centre, Australian National University, 1993, p. 140.

development. Subsequently, after some clarification and adjustment of EAEC's objectives, Japan did become an EAEC participant.[24] While the EAEC was not a major factor as a purely regional dialogue body, it has become more central as a consequence of the emergence of ASEM with the Asian membership of ASEM coinciding with the EAEC membership and particularly the now formalised ASEAN plus three meetings.

Southeast Asia

With seeming resolution of the problems of Indochina on which China and Japan took opposing positions, perhaps the major source of potential differences between the two countries in Southeast Asia is in the South China Sea. China's actions there have several interests for Japan. These include its concern for the security of shipping lanes, particularly for its oil tankers, their implications for Japan's dispute with China over the Senkaku (Diaoyutai), and as a means to judge China's overall approach in the future. This is an area which one Japanese analyst notes is one of the few cases where Japan's 'national and security interests are evidently at stake . . .'.[25]

Japan has for some time had an interest in the area for oil exploration among other things, apart from its control of the Spratlys during the Second World War. Much of Japan's current interest in China's activities in the area concerns Japan's sea lines of communication (SLOCs), which comes from its heavy dependence on oil imports from the Middle east. Over 70% of Japan's oil imports pass through the South China Sea on route to Japan. Many analysts have argued that these would be threatened were China to dominate the South China Sea or were conflict to break out in the vicinity of the Spratlys. At the height of the international reaction to the Mischief Reef incident, some Japanese commentators argued that Japan could use economic sanctions against China to check China's 'naval adventurism'.[26]

In practice, interdiction of sea-lanes is more easily achieved at choke points rather than on open seas and there are alternative routes

[24] Nordin Sopiee, a close advisor to Mr Mahathir, set out a detailed list of what EAEC was not in an article in the *New Straits Times,* 19 Jan. 1992.

[25] Yoshihida Soeya, cited in Lam Peng Er, 'Japan and the Spratlys Dispute: Aspirations and Limitations', *Asian Survey,* XXXVI (10), Oct. 1996, p. 995.

[26] See, for example, Koichi Sato, 'The Japan Card', *FEER,* 13 Apr. 1995, p. 32.

that Japanese shipping could take which for high value cargoes such as oil would add little to the final product price.[27] Moreover China would also be vulnerable in conflicts over sea-lanes, given its increased dependence upon Middle East oil, a dependence that will inevitably grow. Under US pressure, Japan already has a stated policy of protecting sea-lanes up to 1000 nautical miles from Tokyo, although this policy is more symbolic than operational. While it is doubtful in any case whether Japanese domestic opinion would permit it, attempts by Japan to extend that policy to the South China Sea would be strongly opposed in the region by, among others, China. Although revision of the US-Japan defence guidelines raised speculation that they could cover the South China Sea, Japan's Prime Minister Hashimoto at one point excluded this explicitly by pointing to the definition of the Far East in the security treaty as being limited to areas north of the Philippines. The guidelines legislation passed in the Japanese Diet in May 1999, although ambiguous about the situations in which they will apply, does not provide for such activities.

Japan had not been unduly disturbed by earlier events in the South China Sea, such as China's occupation of the Paracel Islands. The passage of China's 1992 Territorial Waters Law included the Senkakus as well as the Spratlys as among the territories that China claimed and implied that a military defence of China's sovereignty in these territories could be warranted. This did stir Japanese anxieties since the Senkakus dispute remains an important problem in China-Japan relations. Japan consequently became more sensitive to China's overall attitudes to unresolved territorial issues, and China's apparent willingness to act aggressively.

For Japan it also seemed tied up with China's search for energy resources.[28] China, for its part, acknowledged at the Brunei ARF meeting in August 1995 that its actions had given rise to regional disquiet and China was subsequently more accommodating in discussing the issues with claimants, but not willing to discuss them with non-claimants. China recognises that an assertive position would be counter productive for it in various ways, including encouraging ASEAN countries to give more weight to joining with the United States in containing it. Consequently China sought to dispel tension

[27] David Coulter, 'The Economics of SLOC Protection: An Overvalued Mission', *Proceedings*, International Conference on SLOC Studies, Tokyo, 17–18 Nov. 1997.
[28] Lam, 'Japan and the Spratlys Dispute', p. 1001.

in the region by expressing the need for peaceful resolution of the disputes over the Spratlys. It has proposed the idea of joint development of the resources involved, with disputes to be settled through friendly consultations and negotiations 'in accordance with universally recognised international law'.[29] An agreed code of conduct in the South China Sea is likely to be agreed in due course to manage activities in the area.

Japan's support for the idea of 'joint development' in the Spratlys, in which Japan is not directly involved, could provide precedents for the disputes in which Japan is directly involved, such as the Senkaku (Diaoyutai), the Tokdo (Takeshima) or the Northern Territories.[30] Despite Japan's wish to participate in moves to reduce tensions in the South China Sea, it also has economic interests in any energy supply increases that might come from joint development in the Spratlys, whether or not Japan is financially involved. Its efforts in the ARF, and bilaterally with China, to be involved in discussions of the Spratlys in the Indonesian South China Sea workshops and elsewhere, however, have generally been unsuccessful. China has opposed them in part because it wants to limit discussions to claimants and in part to indicate its lack of support for Japan's political leadership aspirations.

Another aspect of China's relations with Southeast Asia concerns its links with Burma. Burma was, until 1990, a substantial recipient of Japanese aid. Although traditionally non-aligned and commonly xenophobic even towards the Chinese, China's influence in Burma nevertheless has a historical basis and has been a continuing source of competition with India. China's influence has grown, however, with the substantial international isolation Burma brought on itself with the rejection, by the then State Law and Order Restoration Council (SLORC), of the election results in 1990. China is one of the few countries not imposing significant embargoes on Burma, and Chinese military aid has been significant, meeting the special needs of a country with substantial internal conflicts still underway. Chinese economic influence has also grown with the economic development taking place in China's neighbouring Yunnan province, which sees Burma as its outlet to the sea. Beijing has an interest as

[29] Text of Joint Statement at the 1997 post ASEAN ministerial; see also *FEER*, 8 Jan. 1998, p. 32.
[30] Lam, 'Japan and the Spratlys Dispute', pp. 995–6.

well in controlling the drug traffic that moves across the Burma-China border.

China has helped Burma develop intelligence installations on the Andaman Islands which, although apparently Burmese rather than Chinese, are argued potentially to threaten sea traffic reaching the Malacca Straits.[31] It has been suggested, in particular, that this is a concern to Japan.[32] Japan continues to pursue a policy of constructive engagement, as do other members of ASEAN to which Burma was admitted in 1997, as a counter to undue Chinese influence. It has kept open its lines of communication to the Burmese government and some private investment and official aid, if at a lower level than before 1990, continues from Japan. While Japan is interested in providing an offset to China's influence in Burma, it has not been a point of major contention in Japan–China relations.

The North Pacific

In the north Pacific, adjustments since the end of the Cold War have changed national interests as well as power relations, and have affected China–Japan relations markedly. Interests are not now influenced by past ideologies except for North Korea's juche philosophy. Important among those interests for the various countries of the subregion is ensuring that some geopolitical balance is maintained. Not only China and Japan but also Russia and the two Koreas play a part in a complex balancing of relationships. In each case this involves policies countering movements within the subregion and also responding to events outside the region, notably shifts, or perceived shifts, in US policies.

In the north Pacific relationships the difficulties in general China–Japan relations discussed in Chapters 2 and 3 remain but they are not evidently sources of potential crisis. The need to maintain balance does, however, limit policy freedom for all involved. The changes have been numerous. As we have already observed, the Cold War eventually saw a China–Japan combination designed to constrain the Soviet Union. Subsequently, facing pressure from the United States and its Japanese ally, China moved closer to Russia. Giving greater

---

[31] Desmond Ball, *Burma's Military Secrets: Signals Intelligence (SIGINT) from 1941 to Cyber Warfare,* Bangkok: White Lotus, 1998, Chapter 11.

[32] Donald Seekins, 'Burma-China Relations: Playing with Fire', *Asian Survey,* XXXVII (6), June 1997, p. 537.

political priority to Asia gradually became Russia's own objective. Japan aimed to counter closer Russia–China relations. South Korea wants to avoid being squeezed between Japan and China, while North Korea attempts to survive. All impinge on each other as each country manoeuvres reactively.

In the north Pacific, China is likely to grow in influence, Russia may do so, but only in the long run, and Japan will find its position more difficult to sustain unless its economic strength can be brought to bear more substantially than feasible so far. What is also noticeable is that these developments are not supplemented in any significant way by autonomous activities at the regional level of sub-national actors, such as provincial governments. It is from Tokyo, Moscow and Beijing that the action stems. For Hokkaido, Primorski krai and even Liaoning, let alone Jiling and Heilongjiang, there is little action.

This balancing process is as important for its indirect implications for China–Japan relations as for their direct content. The underlying motivations involved in the cases of Russia and the Korean peninsula also need exploring.

China, Japan and the Korean peninsula

It has been suggested that Korea could be the point at which Sino-Japanese competition erupts.[33] So far, this has not been reflected in the basically cooperative behaviour of China, Japan and South Korea over the question of the Korean peninsula. Certainly, China and Japan both have important political and strategic interests in the Korean peninsula and they have not always coincided in the past. At the turn of the nineteenth century, Japan sought control over the Korean peninsula, fighting a major war with China and then one with Russia for that purpose,[34] but despite the bitter memories of the colonial period, Japan and South Korea developed close economic links after the Second World War through trade, aid and investment and Japan became an important model for South Korea's development.

Nevertheless, the animosity between Japan and Korea, not helped by the persistent claims by leading Japanese of the benefits of Japanese

---

[33] Michael Green, 'Japan and the Future of the Korean Peninsula', *Korea and World Affairs,* XXII (2), summer 1998, p. 203.

[34] Korea became a colony of Japan in 1910.

colonial administration, continues to influence relationships with Japan. It emerges in various forms such as arguments about compensation for comfort women and in the ongoing disputes over the Tokdo islands. It reemerged when South Korea shared with China its opposition to the revised US-Japan defence guidelines,[35] to which North Korea has also expressed strong opposition. South Korea believed that they gave Japan an unwelcome added security role in the region and hence support for an enhanced Japanese military, although subsequently South Korea softened its opposition, stressing rather the need for prior consultation.[36] It shares some of China's concerns, however, at Japan's interest in TMD. Japan has tried to counter the adverse Korean attitude to it through the provision of aid and specific actions such as setting up a fund to compensate comfort women. While, despite these actions, relations with Japan deteriorated under President Kim Yong-Sam, some improvement at governmental levels is evident following the Tokyo visit of President Kim Dae Jung in October 1998. During the visit, Japan gave a formal apology to South Korea for its past actions,[37] the first formally given by Japan to any country and not a gesture expected to be replicated for China. South Korea, for its part, removed the ban on imports of items of Japanese popular culture, such as films and TV programs.

China has a long border with North Korea, which it often likens to the US border with Mexico, in part because of the difficulty of administrative control, and with similar problems of illegal migration and trade. Although China lost perhaps half a million of its volunteer soldiers fighting in the Korean War on North Korea's side, during the Cold War it had to compete with Moscow for influence in Pyongyang. Since the collapse of the Soviet Union, however, it has been North Korea's principal, but not a wholly supportive, ally.

Japan supported the US Cold War commitment to defend South Korea against Pyongyang. Yet it has tried from time to time to develop closer relations with North Korea. South Korea has opposed these attempts on each occasion in the past, judging that such closer relations would strengthen North Korea and suspicious that Japan wanted to perpetuate the division on the peninsula. President Kim Dae-Jung has softened this approach, and South Korea welcomes the

[35] Young-Sun Song, 'Korean Concern on the New US-Japan Security Arrangement', *Korea and World Affairs*, XX (2), summer 1996, pp. 197–218.
[36] *Nikkei Weekly*, 31 May 1999.
[37] *Nikkei Weekly*, 12 Oct. 1998, pp. 1, 19.

improved relations between Japan and North Korea.[38] welcoming North Korean links with friendly countries, including Japan, providing they are in line with developments in the North's relations with the South. Korean sentiment towards Japan seems therefore to have eased but at the popular level it appears to remain closer to China than Japan.[39]

Given the potential for instability of this unresolved civil war, Japan and China have both sought to avoid any disturbance to the peninsula's cold peace. This became a matter of urgency when North Korea's nuclear ambitions became apparent in the early 1990s. China and Japan had similar worries, if for different reasons. Japan, which is within range of North Korea's missiles, feared that it could be a target of North Korea. China not only did not want another nuclear power on its border, but also did not want to give Japan an encouragement to develop a nuclear capability, nor for South Korea to inherit one if reunification occurred on South Korea's terms.[40] China and Japan, however, were both against the coercive strategy initially proposed by the United States against North Korea. Both believed that it could destabilise the peninsula, and cause the collapse of North Korea, leading to flows of refugees and possibly open conflict. China was also concerned about its control over the local administrations in its border provinces.[41]

Japan did eventually soften its opposition to graduated sanctions under US pressure within a UN Security Council framework, although the sanctions proposal was not proceeded with. Japan was not closely involved in developing the October 1994 framework agreement reached between the United States and North Korea, or the Korean Peninsula Energy Development Organisation (KEDO) that came from it. It has supported the Four Party talks, which Japan observes and has contributed substantially to the funding of the reactors and in the provision of food and other aid to North Korea under KEDO.

China's relations with South Korea have a substantial economic

[38] *Korea Times,* 21 Jan. 2000.

[39] Tae-hyo Kim, 'South Korea's Security Policy toward Japan: Balancing Perceived Costs and Benefits' in Ralph Cossa (ed.), *US-Korea-Japan Relations: Building Toward a "Virtual Alliance"* ', Washington: CSIS Press, 1999, 100–14.

[40] Leon Sigal, *Disarming Strangers: Nuclear Diplomacy with North Korea,* Princeton University Press, 1998, p. 57.

[41] Ibid., p. 58.

basis (investment as well as trade) but are also part of the geopolitical manoeuvring in the subregion, including ensuring that Japan does not reestablish a preeminent position. Moreover, establishing diplomatic relations with South Korea in August 1992 was important for China in breaking South Korea's diplomatic links with Taiwan. Historic factors favour China's links with South Korea over Japan's as economic factors overall favour Japan's links with South Korea. It is not necessarily a highly competitive process but anti-Japanese sentiment 'is proving to be a unifying force in Sino-ROK relations'.[42] Like China, South Korea focuses its security concerns on Japan, and regards good relations with China as crucial. The visit by China's Defence Minister Chi Haotian, in January 2000, the first such visit, was a significant move in peninsula relationships.[43] South Korea increasingly regards its relations with China as constructive and positive.[44] Yet it would not want to be swamped by China. For its part, China would not want such a close relationship that its own Korean-Chinese minority started to seek autonomy or that totally diminished its North Korean links.

China and Japan share a common interest in a stable, peaceful, friendly (and probably divided) Korean peninsula. They probably also agree on a continued US presence, although in China's case, in contrast to Japan, as a necessary evil in large part to maintain stability and to avoid Japan's remilitarisation. Were China to seek regional dominance, or Japan to pursue a greater military based role in the north Pacific, the present stable Japan–China consensus over Korea could be breached. But the existing compatibility in the relationship on this issue is likely to be sustained for some time. This would change were conflict to break out on the peninsula, but even then both sides would have strong interests in being very cautious.

Russia

When Japan signed its normalisation agreement with China and then its peace treaty, China tried to get Japan involved in its anti-hegemony campaign against the Soviet Union. In the treaty the two

[42] Oknim Chung, 'Regional Perspectives and Roles on the Korean Peninsula', *Korea and World Affairs*, XXII (2), summer 1998, p. 235.

[43] Sang-hun Choe, Associated Press, Seoul, 19 Jan. 2000.

[44] In-taek Hym, 'South Korea's Changing Strategic Thinking and the Future of Korea–US–Japan Relations' in Ralph Cossa (ed.), *US-Korea-Japan Relations*, p. 29.

countries opposed 'hegemony'. The Japanese accepted this since the wording was like that in the US normalisation communiqué and they were not willing to be drawn against the Soviet Union in the way China wished. Nevertheless, Japan's own fears of the Soviet Union, particularly as the Soviet military build up in the Far East in the late 1970s onwards occurred, facilitated improved relations with China. On the other hand, Japan's relations with Russia following the collapse of the Soviet Union remained cool, given that Japan raised the disputed territorial issue of the northern islands high on its foreign policy agenda.

Subsequently, in the initial Yeltsin period, especially after the 1991 coup attempt, Russia leaned towards the West and the United States in particular. This reflected the inclination of those then directing foreign affairs, and the hopes for Western support for Russia's democratic processes and investment and financial aid to assist the recovery of the Russian economy. Japan was part of the West in this approach, but Russia's relations with Japan remained limited. Lack of warmth in relations between Russia and Japan has a long history and relations were constrained by the Russian nationalist and military reaction to suggestions of concessions on the northern territories, and Japan's fears over Russia's military, particularly its nuclear capability and the potentiality of Russia as a long-term security threat. Russia's continuing economic problems, its unease at some Western policies that impinged on its own interests, its increasingly disgruntled military and a change in power relationships within the leadership in favour of the conservatives, led to a more assertive foreign policy and its shift towards strengthening relations with Asia. Initially this was towards Japan although conservative forces within Russia preferred China.

For Russia, the belief grew that Japan would need better relations with Russia and that Russian concessions on the northern islands were less necessary, at least at that time. Japan has in fact eased its position on the northern territories and both sides have moved to reduce areas of mistrust and to establish mechanisms of consultation and cooperation, culminating in the 1997 Hashimoto-Yeltsin agreement to move towards a peace treaty within five years.

Relations between China and Russia, despite the closer links established in the 1990s, have their problems. Some may come from the passing of communism but others hang over from history. The Chinese government of the day had hoped that the attempted coup against Gorbachev would succeed, the fall of the communist regime in Moscow being seen as a challenge to their own legitimacy.[45] It had close relations with the Russian military and with conservative elements among Russian elites, to the concern of Yeltsin. Nevertheless, when China saw a geopolitical need to draw Russia away from the West and Japan,[46] and to offset US unipolarity, China was able to improve relations relatively quickly with Yeltsin. Yeltsin visited China in 1992 and signed a number of important agreements which foreshadowed the concept of a 'strategic partnership' between the two countries and led to the 1994 multilateral security agreement between China, Russia and the three CIS states (Tajikistan, Kazakhstan and Kyrgyzstan). Subsequent exchanges of visits led in 1999 to the virtual completion of the negotiations on the disputed Sino-Russian border and substantial troop reductions on the borders and the development of closer military relations. The latter developed into an important supply relationship for Russian military equipment for China's military modernisation as well as some training of the Chinese military.

China still wanted markets in and investment from Japan and the United States, so it did not want to take its tilt towards Russia too far. Moreover, not all in Russia, including some in conservative circles, are comfortable with the close relations that have developed. Russian suspicions of China and its territorial ambitions are traditional and widely held, and only partly offset by the official policy that Russia will not sell the most modern Russian military equipment to China in order to maintain a capability edge.

On the other hand, China maintains contacts with the communists in Russia, and there are still sensitivities on the part of the Russian military, as well as by those in eastern Russia, to the strength of the Japanese and US militaries in the northern Pacific. China is generally positive about Russia-China cooperation in economic development, although gradually recognising its limitations. So too is Russia, although it is concerned about drug trafficking across the border from China, and the small Russian population in the Russian Far East (RFE) fears China's strategic dominance and potentially large population movements. The Russia-China strategic partnership

---

[45] Peggy Falkenheim Meyer, 'Russia's Post-Cold War Security Policy in Northeast Asia', *Pacific Affairs*, 67(4), winter 1994-5, pp. 495–512.

[46] Gilbert Rozman, 'Cross-National Integration in Northeast Asia: Geopolitical and Economic Goals in Conflict', *East Asia: an International Quarterly*, 16(1/2), spring/summer 1997, pp. 6–31.

seems to be 'lacking in internal motivation and highly motivated by the international environment'.[47] While there are solid reasons for both countries to have good relations, including with the CIS states, US policies have helped to encourage those relations.

The China–Russian partnership has not provided major gains in Russia's strategic or economic objectives in Asia, such as participation in discussions on Korea, and it has started to look again at Japan. The Russia–China partnership did, at the same time, galvanise Japan. Along with other regional countries, Japan expressed its concern over Russian sales of military equipment and technology to China as potentially upsetting the regional balance. It started to improve relations with Russia in order, among other things, to restore the balance in Northeast Asia. Japan knows that a nationalist government in Russia, while still constrained by its economic weakness, could be hostile to Japan, more supportive of North Korea, unpredictable about China and even less responsive on the northern islands. Nevertheless, Japan appears to a degree less concerned in overcoming the imbalance it envisaged emerging in China's relationship with Russia. Japan would also like to shape the course of future economic development in Siberia and the RFE, which would contribute to easing its concerns over future energy supplies. Moreover, by supporting planned Chinese–Russian cooperation in energy supplies, it would provide a three-way form of cooperation. The Japanese public is likely to remain sceptical, however, about Russia's political and economic governance, and to remain opposed to any major moves not based on an ultimate resolution of the northern territories issue.

The loss of the 'guideposts to unity' in US–Japan relations referred to earlier has led to arguments that regional economic ties will be the basis for improved relations and overcoming the problems in the bilateral relationships and enhanced networking processes.[48] Russia has regional leverage arising from its weak government, as a source of regional concern over proliferation, environmental, and regional stability. Its participation has consequently been accepted in regional security and other dialogue processes as a means of assisting with these problems, as with Russia's entry into APEC. Tokyo and Beijing,

[47] Yurii Tsyganov, 'The General Framework of Sino-Russian Relations', *Russian and EuroAsian Bulletin,* Contemporary Europe Research Centre, University of Melbourne, 7 (6), June 1998, p. 3; see also Herbert Ellison and Bruce Acker, 'The New Russia and Asia: 1991–5', *NBR Analysis* 7 (1), June 1996.

[48] Ryosei Kokubun, 'Delicate US-Japan-China Triangle Relationship', p. 29.

however, have started undertaking military exchanges, but both are concerned at possible future political changes in Russia where a military-industrialist controlled government could expand arms sales (including to North Korea) and be less constrained over weapons proliferation.

Regional interaction has increased in a number of contexts. KEDO and the negotiations leading up to it have involved greater regional interaction. Associated with that process has been a series of two by two discussions between the two Koreas, the United States and China. Proposals have been made for adding Russia and Japan to the two by two discussions. There have also been other suggestions: US and Japan have agreed to a three legged US, Japan and China dialogue but China prefers it to be it to be at a less formal, track two level. Such discussions, particularly if ultimately formalised, would help ensure that jockeying for balance did not lead to disputes because of misperceptions. That balancing process, perhaps better described as avoiding an imbalance, is itself certain to continue but the indications suggest only at a low level.

Russia's relations with South Korea are also 'part of a strategy of manoeuvring around Japan'.[49] The Russian military, while regretting the decline in Russia's relations with North Korea, and their loss of influence there, welcomed the closer relations with South Korea as a country which shared their concern about Japan. Yet Russia did not gain the benefits, economic or political, it hoped from its courting of South Korea and it had diminished its influence in North Korea. It has since been attempting to restore the balance.

The Persian Gulf and Central Asia

Japan's efforts at cooperation with China and the CIS states suggest a further expansion of the concept of the Asia Pacific region. We noted earlier that a high proportion of Japan's oil supply comes from the Middle East. This proportion is likely to increase as East Asian supplies dwindle and regional, especially China's, demands increase. Japan in particular, but also China, is concerned at their dependence on an unstable Middle East. As we have seen, the question of sea-lane security is also a matter of concern for both countries.

The emergence of the CIS states as independent entities has wide

[49] Falkenheim Meyer, 'Russia's Post-Cold War Security Policy in Northeast Asia', p. 506.

ranging implications for China. In the Japan–China context, however, the interest is primarily a question of the supply of energy – oil and gas. China had been an energy exporter to East Asia and to Japan in particular. As the economic reforms took hold in China, China's domestic energy demands increased rapidly. The evidence that China would become not only a net energy importer but a major participant in the world energy market raised concerns in Asia and in Japan in particular about the potential competitive impact on a region which still remembers the severe impact of the energy crises of the 1970s.

A number of threat scenarios have emerged from time to time about the potential rivalry between China and Japan in the Middle East or Central Asia that this would give rise to and the scope this gave for aggressive Chinese behaviour.[50] These scenarios tend to overlook the limited evidence of profitable resource possibilities in a number of the areas in question. They also tend to overlook the limited capabilities China will have have for a long time to act aggressively in prospective oil and gas areas close to home, such as the South China Sea, and to defend any installations against retaliatory terrorism.[51] Nor, for that matter, do they allow for the improbability of a country going to war exclusively for energy. For its part, Japan is concerned about China's impact on the global market but, as in its earlier resources policies, sees the solution in finding a way to increase global oil and gas production. Russia and China are among the logical areas since that would ameliorate the market impact of China's expanded demand while reducing dependence upon the Middle East.[52] These objectives it shares with China. Japan also has environmental interests. Not only does it prefer to refine its oil in China for environmental reasons but China's use of energy gives rise to acid rain from China's growing coal use. Thus, drawing on the gas resources of the CIS states for Chinese domestic consumption would also reduce the environmental threat to Japan.

Consequently, investment projects in which Japanese funds have

[50] Those using energy to support China threat arguments include Kent Calder, *Asia's Deadly Triangle: How Arms, Energy and Growth Threaten to Destabilise Asia Pacific*, London: Nicholas Brealey, 1996; and Richard Bernstein and Ross Munro, *The Coming Conflict with China*, New York: Alfred Knopf, 1997.

[51] See, for example, Stuart Harris, 'China's Quest for Great Power Status: A Long and Winding Road' in Hung-mao Tien and Yun-han Chu (eds), *China Under Jiang Zemin*, Boulder, CO: Lynne Rienner, 2000.

[52] Gaye Christoffersen, 'China's Intentions for Russian and Central Asian Oil and Gas', *NBR Analysis*, 9 (2), Mar. 1998, p. 31.

been involved or planned have included not just oil and gas exploration and development but also pipeline projects to or through China. China has benefited from the economic assistance that Japan has given in this respect, while Japan stands to benefit by reducing the sense of threat of energy scarcity.[53] Progress has been limited, not just through China's inaction, although Japan has expressed concerns about the slow decision processes in China in these energy developments.

South Asia

The South Asian nations have been generally marginal to the Asia Pacific region for much of the postwar period. India and China, in the early post-Second World War years, were leading members of the non-aligned movement. Their relationship deteriorated, however, as they clashed militarily over disputed borders in 1962, as India exploded a nuclear device in 1974, as India moved closer to Moscow while China moved in the opposite direction and as the several wars on the subcontinent turned the South Asian countries inwards. Although Pakistan was seen as a Western aligned nation, China's relations with it, as a third world country prepared to take an independent line, were warm.[54] India and China are competitors in the export field in labour intensive products such as textiles although this has not led to major disputes.

India was the first recipient under Japan's official aid program. Political relations remained insubstantial but polite except over nuclear issues and India's refusal to join the NPT and then its 1998 nuclear testing when aid was suspended. China's relations with India remained generally cool until Gorbachev indicated that Moscow would no longer expect to support India.[55] Following the subsequent Rajiv Gandhi visit to Beijing in 1988 a warmer atmosphere emerged in bilateral relations despite various ongoing irritants, such as China's non-recognition of India's absorption of Sikkim and India's belief that China's policy tilted towards Pakistan over Kashmir. In 1998, the assumption of government in India by the BJP party and the emergence of India as a nuclear weapon state cooled the links

[53] Ibid.

[54] Greg O'Leary, *The Shaping of China's Foreign Policy*, Canberra: Australian National University Press, 1980, p. 231.

[55] Russia's arms sales to India remain large – approximately double the value of those to China.

between India and China, as it did India's links with Japan. This cooling offset the suggestion of a convergence of interests between India and Japan over China's military modernisation.[56] China's relations with Pakistan have remained friendly and became closer as Pakistan became subject to sanctions by the US as a result of its efforts to develop a nuclear weapon to deter India.

China and Japan relations with South Asia have not featured significantly in their bilateral relationship. Two developments may change that. India's testing of a nuclear weapon led to criticism by both Japan and China but whatever the real reason for the testing in 1998, India's stated rationale was its fear of nuclear-armed China, the most saleable argument internationally, especially in the US Congress. Japan's criticism of India will have to take this into account. The second is that India is now a member of the ARF and is seeking membership of APEC and ASEM. Subsequent attempts to soften relations between India and China have been largely successful and thus Indian antagonism towards China need not cause undue tensions in those forums.

An Asian regional identity will continue to grow. The crucial manifestation of that regionalism is the continued willingness to pursue cooperative dialogue and the maintenance of institutions for that purpose. The Asian economic crisis affected ASEAN and APEC in several ways. Tensions developed in ASEAN in part through the political instability in several of the member countries, and leadership uncertainties. Yet the everyday activities continued. APEC was also faced with its limited ability to contribute to the region's financial problems and the trade liberalisation focus became somewhat blurred. Again, however, much of the less high profile activity of APEC continued and its contribution remained important. Security cooperation in ARF, although affected, faced fewer direct problems and was less affected.

What will constitute the region, however, is unclear. The Asia-Pacific is extending its boundaries, leading to efforts to develop an inner group of Asian countries. These objectives need not conflict. Not only is there a strong regional wish for this but the continuing convergence pressures of globalisation will reinforce it. Despite the

[56] C. Raja Mohan, 'India's Role in Southeast Asia' in Michael Everett and Mary Sommerville (eds), *Multilateral Activities in Southeast Asia*, Washington, DC: National Defence University Press, 1995, pp. 87–110.

inevitable setbacks from the Asian economic crisis for the existing multilateral institutions, functional activities in the region have grown and the trend to regionalism will reflect a wish for a greater say in regional activities. The countries in the region, China among them, will remain reluctant to move towards any formal European-type sharing of sovereignty, although the gradual acceptance of international involvement in internal affairs, already evident, will grow.

With the obvious exception of North Korea and the Taiwan strait, the regional order in the Asia-Pacific basically reflects a peaceful international environment and through the ARF, the countries in the region have subscribed to norms to that end. The evidence is that this is the preference of both China and Japan, as well as of others in the region. Strategic as well as economic uncertainties in the region remain and the region is still accommodating to the changes taking place or those it can foresee. In forming the developing regional order, China and Japan, both seeking great power status, will wish to be more involved, through consultation and engagement.

Nevertheless, they will both be constrained as regional leaders by a number of influences. The first is the continuing nature of the US presence. How far that will continue in its present form is hard to judge but even were there to be peaceful unification on the Korean peninsula or resolution of the Taiwan issue, any early change in fundamental commitment is unlikely although its form could change.

Second, China and Japan will both be hesitant about taking an assertive leadership role for various reasons associated with history. While China appears to have managed satisfactorily its many land border disputes, its maritime sovereignty disputes limit its regional leadership capabilities, among other things. It needs to maintain good relations with ASEAN members; it needs to maintain international support for its position, notably over Taiwan and as a counter to US antagonisms; it needs as well to overcome fears of its assertiveness which would affect its economic as well as political and strategic position. While anxieties that Japan wants to bring the entire region into a Japan-dominated economic system may have eased, concerns about its potential military power projection, while probably diminishing in part because of its leadership limitations, remain significant.

Moreover they will both have important domestic constraints in the structure of their economies and in their decision-making processes. Again, any leadership role they may play will have to be conscious of the other major players in the region, including Russia, South Korea, ASEAN and perhaps India. Finally they will be constrained by their limited leadership capacities. Leadership requires more than power, especially the capacity to exercise that power in support of ideas and to persuade others to accept those ideas. For some time to come the deficit in this direction for both Japan and China will remain.

Both countries, therefore, face challenges and constraints in their regional leadership aspirations. It means that strong leadership of a kind that will dominate in the region is unlikely from either. Moreover, we have argued that their regional influence will be enhanced by a stable and often cooperative political relationship between the two rather than a competitive or adversarial one. This differs from the view of some observers that unless regional cooperation is effective, historic rivalries and animosities might lead Japan and China to pursue a more autonomous approach to national security, probably involving strengthening of their defence capabilities, leading to a destabilising, and potentially dangerous competitive arms build up.[57]

While China–Japan relations will often be competitive, that competition seems unlikely for various reasons to fracture the peaceful order. Although the power relations between the two are factors that each will take into account as they do at present, the underlying economic pressures and needs will counter any tendency to extreme action. Moreover, China and Japan have already cooperated on a range of regional issues: in the UN, on Cambodia and on the Korean peninsula. They are likely to do so in the future, on a number of issues, including energy, if only because not to do so would adversely affect their claims to leadership.

In addition, the prime base of their regional power, economic in the case of Japan, and a Chinese diaspora in China's case, are not unrelated to each other. The expansion of Japanese business in Southeast Asia was greatly facilitated by networks that linked political and personal connections that had previously existed in Southeast Asia. These however were commonly linked to overseas Chinese businessmen or women.[58] We have also noted the further overlap of Japan's interest in enlarging the supply of oil and gas available to the region,

---

[7] Tsuneo Akaha, 'Security Policy' in Akaha and Langdon (eds), *Japan in the hegemonic World,* 1993, p. 98.
Shiraishi, 'Japan in Southeast Asia', pp. 169–94.

a policy area where collaboration between China and Japan is both necessary and in their common interest.

The geopolitics of power are likely to remain a factor in the region, particularly in North Asia. There the evidence suggests a desire by China and Japan to maintain a balance, not seeking superiority but not wanting others to be ahead. Moreover, any potentially destabilising aspects of the balancing of power, particularly in the North Pacific, are likely to be offset by growing economic interaction. To maintain stability, however, a continuing and expanded process of dialogue and the development of confidence building among countries in the region are critical. This will need to include other countries, such as South Korea, and Russia.

Japan China relations will be affected by these various factors but no overwhelming motivations seem likely to disturb the existing framework of those relations in a major way. That framework rests on a wish by both sides, based on geopolitical realities and not on sentiment, to maintain a carefully managed linkage. This assumes that the regional order proceeds with its adjustments without major unexpected developments. That appears to be what China and Japan would both prefer.

9

CONCLUSION

JAPAN AND CHINA AT THE START
OF THE TWENTY-FIRST CENTURY

This study has identified a wide range of bilateral interactions between Japan and China. Yet as central to the relationship as purely bilateral influences and bilateral relativities might be, they are often overshadowed by other influences. On the one hand, regional and global factors beyond the control of either Japan or China increasingly affect their mutual relations. On the other, as each government deals with those external influences, domestic goals and influences are becoming more important. In China in particular, the dynamics of interest group politics are changing rapidly and new interest groups are competing more effectively for power with traditional power holders. In addition, public opinion is providing growing pressure on governments in both countries across a broader range of issues, including foreign policy. Decisions of the two governments will remain the primary domestic determinant of bilateral relations but a variety of non-governmental interests increasingly compete to constrain, influence and on rare occasions dictate those decisions.

Taken together, the array of influences arising from these three sources (bilateral, international, and domestic) is making decision-making by Japan and China in respect of their bilateral relations more complex. Consequently, the governments of Japan and China will need to demonstrate considerable flexibility and responsiveness in keeping bilateral relations on a smooth path

In the external environment shaping the Japan-China relationship, three aspects are especially important. The first is the role of the

United States. By dint of its power and its relationship with both Japan and China, a three-way relationship has been established. The different objectives and different historical experiences of each of the three countries make for uncertain bilateral sets within what is often termed a 'strategic triangle'.[1] Nevertheless, the deepening interdependence of the three and the widening range of their common interests has strengthened regional and global order, and set limits on the room for manoeuvre of Japan and China relative to each other. Thus the cold reality of a strategic triangle has been warmed somewhat by an emerging sense of trilateralism on certain issues and by a diffuse range of other influences.

The second aspect is the evolution of world order under the influence of market economics and consolidation of post-war institutions, such as the United Nations, the GATT/WTO and the International Monetary Fund. Uncertainties about the nature of this order have resulted from the dissatisfaction of both Japan and China with their position in it as demonstrated by Japan's failed bid for reform of the UN Security Council and in China's long efforts to join the WTO. These uncertainties were aggravated by China's reaction to NATO's use of force against Yugoslavia over Kosovo in 1999 and the overt competition for influence between Japan and China during the Asian financial crisis that began in 1997. Nevertheless, both have demonstrated greater confidence in their capacities to pursue their interests within the evolving international structures without resort to radical measures. The economic relationships between Japan, China and the United States have strengthened the three-way interrelationship and the belief in each government that stability in the trilateral relationship enhances its national interests.

The third aspect is the general process of internationalisation.[2] We understand this to involve not just the increased flow of information, trade, capital and technologies across borders. It also includes the increased international influence of non-state actors and the growing international integration of markets. It involves as well a deepening sense of global community that brings together geographically

---

[1] For this reason, Seiichiro Takagi questioned the usefulness of a triangular analysis in *Japan Echo*, June 1990, pp. 18–19; Funabashi argued that such triangular relationships tended to be zero-sum and dangerous. Yoichi Funabashi, 'The Asianisation of Asia', *Foreign Affairs*, 72(5), 1993, pp. 75–85.

[2] As noted earlier we prefer the term internationalisation to the more commonly used 'globalisation'.

remote states in new economic and security relationships. In this sense, internationalisation has contributed to shifts in the foundations of both global order and domestic political order. Japan and China are not only accommodating these shifts – albeit at times with some reluctance and some resistance – but are making their own contributions.[3]

Just as global order and regional order profoundly shape Japan-China relations, the responses by each of these two great powers of Asia to the other increasingly affect in turn, and similarly profoundly, the international order around them. The combined economic and military power of Japan and China ensures that outcomes they deliver in their bilateral relationship affect not just neighbouring countries, but the farthest corners of the world.

This concluding chapter looks ahead to the global, regional and bilateral influences on how the two governments will approach each other in the coming decade. The discussion acknowledges two fundamentally different sources of change: dynamic and structural. The former, while not always unpredictable, arises sooner than expected or in a particularly destabilising and unexpected way. Such events can place unusual strains on normal decision-making processes and threaten the domestic political consensus that underpinned prior policy. They have the potential for radical change if handled badly. Predicting the dimensions of policy change in response to this type of event is more difficult than for those events that arise from gradual changes in underlying structures. Structural change – the unremitting pressure on governments from participation in the international society of states and from the domestic political imperatives of political order and prosperity – gives prediction of outcomes a more solid base.

Themes addressed in this chapter are, first, the identities and intentions of the two countries and the external influences on them. These influences include the interrelationships with the United States and the institutional and normative aspects of global order. How they respond to those influences depends upon their relative national strengths and vulnerabilities; we then consider how the impacts of those respective influences may work out in terms of their

---

[3] For example, in the economic sphere, and quite independently of their bilateral relations, Japan's surplus funds for foreign investment and China's cheap, semi-skilled labour force have together been profound influences for internationalisation not only globally but within the Asia Pacific region.

competition for regional leadership. The chapter concludes with a brief overview of how we see the future of the Japan-China relationship and its impact on global and regional affairs.

Identities and intentions

China and Japan share economic and strategic objectives common to most countries. As the new century opens, China will remain particularly concerned with economic development, Japan with economic competitiveness, and both with security. At the same time, it is only reasonable to expect two neighbouring major powers, with different, if related, cultures and with different military and economic capabilities, to have a complex bilateral relationship. That relationship can only be more difficult because of the bitterness of their history and by the impact of that history on the self-images of them both. Whatever the material circumstances of China and Japan, and their wider international interactions, how each relates to the other will continue to be influenced by their cultural and historically grounded understandings of themselves and what has happened between them.

For any country, national identity is shaped profoundly by their relations with other countries. Akira Iriye has argued that the modern destinies of China and Japan have been so intertwined that it is neither possible nor sensible to separate national identity issues from the bilateral relationship.[4] Their identities have at different times been defined almost wholly in terms of each other, though the West has emerged relatively recently as an additional factor in that definition. Since both Japan and China are societies in transition, especially in relation to their identities and the national goals associated with them, their bilateral relationship in the future is likely to be further affected by insecurities associated with national identity.

China's identity from 1949 on as a revolutionary state was not such a change from its general identity as a great power, a seat of culture and a source of ideas and values. Those values merely changed from Confucian to Marxist-Leninist. Having for fifty years denigrated Confucianism and with the failure of Marxism-Leninism, China now faces a challenge in establishing a new self-image. It is still a great power, still has a belief in the power of its cultural heritage but is less

---

[4] Akira Iriye, *China and Japan in the Global Setting*, Cambridge, MA: Harvard University Press, 1992, p. 7.

a provider of culture and values than ever before. In fact, it is now facing a need to defend its traditional cultural values, however undefined, against those of the West.

In Japan's case, the problem similarly is uncertainty. Japan's defeat in the Second World War, its concerns about its part in that war, and its subsequent dependence upon the United States for security, continue to pose problems for its self-image. For some time its acceptance by the international community as a major 'Western' nation, as an 'anti-militarist' power, and as an economic success story, offset much of the self-doubt that otherwise lay dormant. With growing international criticism of Japan's limited and risk-averse participation in world affairs, its economic achievement thrown into doubt by its economic crisis, and its uncertainties arising from the future of its aging and declining population, Japan's insecurity about its rightful place in the world resurfaced.

Towards the end of the Cold War, many Japanese showed an interest in their country becoming a 'normal' one but the idea of what constituted 'normality' remained vague. In part it was a question of moving from exceptionalism in international affairs to being like other countries but Japan still retained a unique identity as a global civilian power contributing to international security predominantly through indirect means.

National identity and mutual perceptions also relate to assessments of national security and military power. For both Japan and China, political and economic security are as important as military security but each still retains some concern about the other's military power. These concerns are at a substantially lower level than during the 1960s but through the 1990s each country rose in the threat perception of the other. In consequence, as we argued in Chapter 3, Japan and China have moved in the last decade to adopt a more wary strategic posture toward each other. We also argued however that the substantive foundations for such assessments of security threat from each other are quite weak. In fact, the main cause of heightened insecurity is the prism of considerable mistrust with which each views the other. They see each other through historical lenses and imagined futures rather than through military realities, and they are likely to continue to do so.

The future security interactions between Japan and China will depend largely upon the degree to which the determination to avoid a repetition of history overcomes residual prejudices left over from that history. The record so far and the underlying political trends in both countries suggest that the objective of non-confrontation will continue to have a powerful restraining effect on both. For China in particular, Japan's restraint in commenting on China's internal affairs, compared with the practice of the United States, is a positive factor. Japan's worries about the possibility of instability in China also mean it is less concerned about the continuing dominant role of the Chinese Communist Party than the more ideologically driven United States.

China is not presently oriented towards use of force unless its sovereignty appears threatened as, in its view, is the situation regarding Taiwan (and to a degree Tibet and Xinjiang). Even were China to become more belligerent, the disincentives for a military clash with Japan would be great. Japan is a major source of direct investment in China; it is the second largest market for China's exports; and Japan's allies could easily threaten China's interests in the diversification of energy markets and the protection of sea-lanes.

Similarly, Japan is not oriented towards aggressive international action and that too is most unlikely to change. Although developments such as the apparent danger from North Korea, particularly its missiles, exercise the minds of the Japanese population, and increase support for those wanting to enlarge Japan's military capabilities, there would still be substantial public opposition in Japan to major changes in its strategic posture.

Since the end of the Cold War, nationalist influences have become more evident in both countries, with nationalist groups in Japan seeking to exploit the uncertainty about national identity. In particular, they advocate a revisionist interpretation of the Sino-Japanese War in the 1930s and 1940s. They paint this war as a moral crusade against the imperialism of the West. To them, Japan's military expansionism was legitimised by the end of colonialism in Asia. For nationalists in China, the history of brutal aggression remains a signpost for the future. It will remain so as long as Japan declines to acknowledge both its own brutality and China's victory in a war in which Japan readily accepts its defeat by the United States. But other issues relating to nationalism, such as the territorial dispute over the Senkaku islands, will remain on the agenda. Economic issues will also increasingly affect nationalist impulses in both countries: in Japan's case, a declining confidence in the face of global pressures in the light of its structural problems; in China's case, an increase in confidence as long as its economy continues to post high growth rates.

In Japan, the strength of nationalist ideas is linked to various factors including the lack of independence and the belief that the constitution imposed on Japan was designed to keep Japan in an inferior status through the constraints on its capacity to defend itself. Thus the re-emergence of the nationalists in Japan is connected to the debate about constitutional revision. Given the issues of history, however, and associated with the state of transition that exists in both countries, in neither country is there a national consensus on the core symbols of their national identity. In Japan, its particular problem is that the ideals and symbols, for which there is a degree of nostalgia among the older generation, include the traditional emperor cult (and the Shinto religion), while other symbols tend also to be militaristic.

In China, nationalist impulses have been stimulated by pressures of economic internationalisation and, as suggested above, by the economic advancement simultaneously produced by internationalisation. The history and culture emphasised by the nationalists contrasts with the modernisers and westernisers who see a greater association with the international system as the way forward for China in order, among other things, to avoid future humiliations. Also important in the nationalist agenda is the restoration of international respect for China after 150 years of humiliation by Western powers and, even worse, by Japan.[5] Nationalist sentiment flared in China, as in Taiwan and Hong Kong, in reaction to the erection of a structure on the Senkaku (Diaoyu) Islands by Japanese nationalists.

The influence of reinvigorated nationalism is not likely to reorient the strategic policy of either country in the foreseeable future in the absence of a major societal crisis. In China, in spite of such public manifestations of support for nationalist impulses, the new national identity as a wealth-producing country increasingly accepting the norms of international society and seeking economic interdependence seems likely to hold. In Japan, nationalism has a stronger base. Nevertheless, even in Japan, the identity of the country as an anti-militarist society, averse to the risks of international involvement, with a continuing pride in its alternative approach to the exercise of power, seems likely to be maintained. Nevertheless, the nationalists do help to sustain the differences, notably over the war history, on the public agenda in the two countries.

---

[5] John Fitzgerald, 'Chinese, Dogs and the State that Stands on Two Legs', *Bulletin of Concerned Asian Scholars,* 29 (4), Oct./Dec. 1997, pp. 54–61.

The war history debate is not just about competitive nationalisms. This debate emerged a relatively long time after the end of the war with the schoolbook controversy in the early 1980s but it has intensified since the end of the Cold War. In Japan, the reawakening of the history issue is part of continuing debate about revision of the Constitution, especially Article 9 which was supposed to have prevented Japan from ever rearming. Liberal thinkers in Japan want the history discussed as a means of resisting any change at least to the nominal Constitutional ban on Japan's possession of armed forces. The Japanese Diet has established a committee to examine the possibility of revising the constitution, with Article 9 one of the clauses that will receive particular attention. Consequently, the issue will remain an important domestic Japanese matter, and it will continue to impinge substantially on the relationship with China, which wants Article 9 preserved in its existing form.

The bilateral relationship will remain one that lacks respect and warmth. The less than sympathetic attitudes of many Chinese or Japanese towards the other country will not improve rapidly. Such a change could develop eventually with the emergence of new generations relatively unaffected by the war and prepared to move on from the passions and emotions of their elders. Yet generational change alone is unlikely to be enough. A liberal change in the political system in China in particular would increase the interest among Japanese in China and give Chinese people more access to a greater range of informational and cultural products that could reduce their misperceptions and prejudices. While official exchanges would help, most impetus for change is likely to come from the universalising influences of cultural activities not specifically Japanese or Chinese, arising from both countries' integration into the world economy. The continued opening up of their own societies will therefore be the important factor.

International relations, however, are based largely, even if not entirely, on interests. We expect business-like relations to be maintained in such circumstances with the two countries getting most of what they want out of the relationship. The dilemma is that while better bilateral relations between China and Japan will depend upon coming to terms with the their histories, they will probably not be able to do that until there is a significant improvement in those relations. In turn that improvement may depend upon their establishing identities based more on universal values and reference to the world at large rather than ones based largely on reference to each other.

The United States and the triangular relationship

As long as the United States retains its position as sole superpower and its ideology as the 'indispensable nation', its relationship with Japan and China will continue as the major external influence on Japan-China relations. In the first place, Japan will want to maintain its alliance with the United States and will continue to support its alliances in the region. The United States will want to retain its alliances to maintain its forward strategic posture and to prevent any breakdown in regional 'stability'. Second, it will retain its commitment to support Taiwan against an unprovoked attack from China. This commitment, in circumstances of a continuing military alliance with Japan, will remain a core Chinese concern in its relations with the United States and a source of suspicion in China of Japan. Third, in the absence of conflict or sustained confrontation, the large-scale and deepening US commercial and societal involvement with the two countries will remain a major vehicle for continued mutually beneficial engagement of the three. The United States will remain a major market for both Japan and China, the single most important source of international investment funds for China (either through direct investment, equity investment, commercial loans, or international financial institutions), and a comparatively new source of direct investment for Japan. It will also continue as a major source of advanced technology for them both while, at the same time, continuing to develop military technologies far superior to theirs.

While the dominant structural trends in US-Japan relations will continue to be a force for stability in that relationship, there are potentially divisive pressures and incidents, such as the rape of a young girl in Okinawa by US servicemen, which can lead to a sudden upsurge in anti-Americanism in Japan. Such sentiments are complemented by periodic calls in Japan for a more independent foreign policy, not just from the nationalists, but also from mainstream analysts who nevertheless would see this as consistent with the alliance relationship. There is, at the same time, a fear in Japan that, despite the continuing strength of Japan's alliance links with the United States, Washington will in due course come to see China as the more important partner.

The Japanese government's response to these pressures has been to seek more freedom of manoeuvre both in economic and foreign policy contexts. Japan has sought to increase its influence in regional and global multilateral forums for its own sake but also to constrain US pressure on it over economic disputes and to limit US unilateralism in security affairs that Japan fears may involve it in some unwanted conflict.[6] Japan's reputation of being a 'follower power', although having some validity, underestimates Japan's existing regional independence of action, including with China. But just how far Japan has room for manoeuvre is open to question because of rising domestic concerns about regional insecurities, notably North Korea and China's emerging power.

Thus, the potentially divisive pressures (issues of the US bases, uneasiness about US closeness to China and the desire for greater independence from the United States) could conceivably lead to a complete break in the US-Japan alliance. But since Japan does not really have a feasible security alternative, such as alignment to another great power, a break in the alliance with the United States is quite unlikely for many years, absent some extreme and improbable turn of events.[7]

As with US-Japan relations, in US-China relations many of the structural trends look likely to consolidate the status quo. China is likely to remain committed to the domestic development strategy that demands good relations with the United States. Chinese leaders really have no choice but to deal cooperatively with the United States if China is to meet its needs for advanced technologies and investment capital. They know that any sustained disruption of China's economic growth would provoke a major political crisis in China. In the long term, despite the often troubled nature of political interactions, the United States will seek to maintain a constructive engagement policy toward China. This outcome may well be advanced

[6] See, for example, Denis Yasutomo, 'The Politicisation of Japan's "Post-Cold War" Multilateral Diplomacy' in Gerald Curtis (ed.), *Japan's Foreign Policy After the Cold War: Coping with Change,* Armonk, NY: M.E.Sharpe, 1993, pp. 323–46. See also Gregory Noble, 'Putting the Cork in the Other Bottle: alliance dynamics and multilateralism in Japanese foreign policy', paper to the American Political Science Association, Boston, 5 Sep. 1998.

[7] Takashi Inoguchi, in arguing for a more independent policy, has observed that since the arrival of Commodore Perry, Japan has simply allied itself with the most powerful country of the day which most recently has been the United States. *Nikkei Weekly,* Mar. 1999, p. 19.

if China is able to make further moves towards domestic political liberalisation.

In strategic policy, for the foreseeable future, China will continue to see important benefits in maintaining the status quo.[8] China will continue to accept Japan's security relationship with the United States as a means of containing Japan's already substantial military power. It also accepts that there are benefits for it in the US Navy's Japan-based presence for maintaining sea lane security. It will continue to balance qualified acceptance with pressure on Japan to limit any expansion in military cooperation with the United States. China's main fear of enhanced US-Japan military cooperation is that it would constitute a substantive policy of containment of China and, in particular, may affect its position regarding Taiwan. Its fears on these counts will grow if the United States and Japan continue to expand their military cooperation as they did in the late 1990s.

The dynamics of the US-China relationship have been less conducive to strategic stability than the structural factors identified above. And one fundamentally divisive structural factor – competing visions of domestic political order – causes serious bilateral aggravation. Rapid democratisation might produce more populist foreign policies in China and prompt it to shift to a more combative position relative to the United States. One powerful domestic constituency in China already favours this. At the same time, domestic US politics will remain a major source of volatility.[9] For these reasons the US-China relationship is more likely than the US-Japan relationship to be breached in the short term. Moreover, a breach would be as likely to arise from US actions, particularly over Taiwan, or from actions of the Taiwan government, as from China's initiatives. Any breach would have major implications for Japan-China relations.

We have sketched China's increasingly ambivalent view of the United States, and hence of the US link with Japan. Whether this ambivalence leads China onto a more combative foreign policy course will depend upon the way Chinese domestic politics evolve relative to China's perspective of the broader strategic canvas. Among the elements in this canvas are: China's perceptions of US interests

---

[8] Thomas Christiansen, 'China, the US-Japan Alliance and the Security Dilemma in East Asia, *International Security*, 23(4), spring 1999, pp. 49–80.

[9] Nicely elaborated in Owen Harries, 'A Year of Debating China', *The National Interest*, 58, winter 1999/2000, pp. 141–7.

and role in East Asia; how far it sees this vision supported in Japan; China's acceptance of the US capacity to remain for decades the dominant military power in the region; China's understanding of Japan's reactions to US unilateralism in global affairs; and attitudes in the United States to the costs of its East Asian military deployments.

The key element of China's strategic canvas, however, is how the US-Japan relationship affects China's interests in Taiwan. This has two aspects. The first is how US-Japan military cooperation would affect political choices in Japan in any military confrontation between the United States and China over Taiwan. We believe that Japan's response would be a matter of such domestic political contention as to be unpredictable before the event. On the one hand, Japan's general reluctance to become involved in US combat operations, and its strong desire to avoid a military confrontation with China are likely to enhance Japan's demand for a cautious and conservative US approach to the Taiwan issue. As Michael Green notes, despite the new defence cooperation guidelines, it will be easier for Japan to respond in support of the United States in a Korean conflict than in one over Taiwan.[10] On the other hand, the automatic involvement of Japan through US forces operating from Japanese territory against Chinese forces in the Taiwan Strait would confirm for many Japanese that they had little choice but to side with the United States.

The second aspect is the way in which US strategic power in East Asia, based in large part on the alliance with Japan, encourages actions by Taiwan to frustrate China's policies toward it. As long as Taiwan's leaders believe they can count on a security guarantee from the United States, backed up by likely Japanese support, they will be less likely to accommodate China. This was illustrated in the aftermath of the statement by Taiwan's President Lee Teng-hui in July 1999 that Taiwan's relationship with the mainland was a 'special state to state' relationship. While the United States and Japan were prompt to reassert support for the previous status quo of the 'one-China' policy, China's angry reaction to the statement only fuelled the growing mood in the Congress that the United States should strengthen its security guarantees to Taiwan. Should the trend of more regular affront by Taiwan to the concept of 'one China' continue to the accompaniment of a strengthening of stronger US security ties to Taiwan,

[10] Michael Green, *State of the Field Report: Research on Japanese Security Policy*, National Bureau of Asian Research, 1998, p. 8.

Chinese leaders will find it increasingly difficult for domestic political reasons to avoid resorting to an intensification of military coercion of Taiwan. If this occurred, and the US engaged Chinese military forces in response, Japanese support for the US would entrench an enduring hostility in China–Japan relations that would take many decades to overcome.

Thus China's estimate of how US power in East Asia and globally can be reconciled with its own international and domestic identity will be the dominant determinant of China's strategic posture toward Japan. As this discussion of the Taiwan issue suggests, the most dangerous variable in this calculation will be China's sense of security or confidence about its power in the face of sustained US political pressure on the legitimacy of Communist Party rule. This pressure is only continuing to mount – on issues like freedom of speech, political pluralism, freedom of religion – as well as on issues like the status of Tibet and Taiwan.

US power will also impinge profoundly on the issue of national identity in Japan and affect its strategic positioning relative to China. Support in Japan for the US alliance was always coloured by concern that the United States was dominating the country's international policy. Its booming economy in the late 1980s and some weakness and uncertainty in the United States gave Japan considerable self-confidence at a time when doubts were growing about US ability and willingness to stay engaged in East Asia. The end of the Cold War was seen initially in Japan as permitting a greater degree of independence in its relationship with the United States and this perception contributed to a flirtation with a foreign policy centred more on Japan's identity as an Asian country. The aspirations for a new identity of strategic independence were short-lived. The Gulf War's demonstration of the continued dependence of an oil-dependant Japan on US global power and the bursting of Japan's economic bubble progressively undermined the national mood of self-confidence and new security concerns emerged. Japan will continue to struggle with these questions of identity in foreign policy. Eventually Japan is likely to establish a more independent strategic influence in Asia through a gradual expansion of its military activities abroad. Because of regional sensitivities, however, any such expansion will only be politically possible within the framework of a close US alliance, a strategic posture that guarantees a certain sustained sense of estrangement or distance between Japan and China.

Institutional and normative aspects of global order

Japan and China will both continue to seek greater influence within the institutions of global order and will no doubt be more influential in the twenty-first century. Japan will retain for some years a more extensive global profile than China as a result of its economic interests, the world-class competitiveness of its enterprises, its financial power, the political influence of an aid program which is already global in its spread, and its increasingly active role in global institutions such as the G7 and the OECD. It has been moving from a short-term, interest-driven and therefore substantially reactive foreign policy to a longer-term policy, more principle-oriented one. It is likely to overcome, if only gradually, the constraints of its decision-making processes, which have undermined its aspirations for global leadership.

China will not quickly match Japan's economic influence, but its relatively small aid program is growing and its foreign direct investment, often in resource linked industries, is gradually expanding. Moreover, China will develop a more vigorous and creative diplomacy, especially in the one forum of global leadership where Japan is not represented – the UN Security Council. Achieving permanent Security Council membership will remain an important Japanese long-term objective but the impetus for such reform has slowed. Were Security Council reform to materialise, China has indicated that it would not block a consensus supporting Japan's membership. Nevertheless, since Japan's inclusion in the Council would diminish China's influence, it is not likely to take an active stance in pressing Japan's case.

China will continue to face constraints on its pursuit of more extensive international influence that Japan does not face. The first is its limited financial capacity. China will remain for some time a poor developing country in many respects, receiving billions of dollars of aid per year. In addition, it needs to avoid offending other countries in order to maintain their support in international forums on its major diplomatic concern: the status of Taiwan. It has also to ensure voting support to counter criticisms of its human rights record. China's involvement in the process of internationalisation also provides significant constraints on its foreign policy and these will grow. In particular, its high priority goals of political stability and economic development will remain dependent upon continuing foreign investment, bilateral aid, technology transfer and the support of the international financial institutions. It will also become increasingly vulnerable to the pressures of the international capital market. As a relatively new major player in the international economic system, China will face tougher tests of credibility in politics as well as economic behaviour than Japan.

With China's entry into WTO, the scope for excluding China from parts of the international system, however, is now very limited. Japan, while not wholly comfortable with China's growing influence, has consistently supported China's economic reforms and its international institutional participation, seeking to encourage social and political liberalisation in that country.

Japan and China are unlikely to be competitive in pursuing what they see as their global roles. There will be exceptions, as the issue of UN reform has already indicated, and as a latent rivalry over energy supply at some time in the future seems to suggest. The two countries will continue to seek influence in developing countries but not in sharply competitive terms. Both will compete in seeking a sympathetic international audience for their own view of the historical relationship with the other. Yet both are likely to moderate competitive instincts in pursuit of their global aspirations in recognition of mutual interests. These competitive instincts are, however, more visible in their positions on East Asian regional affairs. We return to those later in this chapter.

For both Japan and China, their capacity to significantly reorient or redefine the norms of international affairs will remain constrained. The main barriers are the lack of appeal of the unique aspects of their social systems, their history of belligerence, the expanded influence of other countries, and the greater power of internationalisation flowing from market capitalism and liberal pluralism. Leadership requires more than power. It needs the capacity to exercise that power in the support of ideas and to persuade others to accept those ideas. For some time to come both countries will experience an important deficit in this area.

Japan and China are unlikely to challenge the substance of international norms or seek to substantially reorient them. By contrast, they both will expand their adherence to international legal regimes because they both benefit from them, as they benefit from vigorous engagement in shaping the specific regulations within these regimes. Japan's diplomacy will remain a powerful buttressing force for contemporary international order, especially the principle of peaceful resolution of disputes. China is more uncomfortable with some aspects of international order – the role of NATO and the unilateralism of the United States – but will continue to look to the normative framework of the UN system to counter US unilateralism and to preserve positions it considers particularly relevant to it, such as sovereignty and non-interference in the internal affairs of another country. China's actions through the 1990s have, like Japan's, come to buttress the UN system and international order. Even though there will probably be occasional sharp departures from this buttressing effect (on issues such as Taiwan and human rights), the trend of greater intrusiveness of international norms on China's behaviour is now almost impossible to reverse.

Relative national strengths and vulnerabilities

For a considerable period, Japan will have a much larger economy than China, by whatever measure is used. Japan does face major structural problems in its economy, most notably in its financial system and in parts of its industrial structure, such as the construction industry, but also in its aging and declining population. It has been introducing its own reforms to address at least some of these problems. It has also demonstrated a capacity in the past to surmount major economic problems and it starts with a high level of economic and technological sophistication. Consequently, Japan will remain much stronger than China in economic power well into the twenty-first century.

The growth performance of the Chinese economy in the 1980s and 1990s was outstanding and if continued would gradually reduce the gap between the Japanese economy and its own – even without Japan's economic problems. By the mid-1990s, many forecasts suggested that China's economy would surpass in size not just Japan's in the early decades of the century but also at some later stage in the century overtake the US economy. This would make China once again the world's largest economy in GDP terms. But even before the onset of the Asian economic crisis in 1997, doubts were expressed about these forecasts. These doubts became more widely shared as the crisis progressed, even though China seemed for some time less adversely affected. We believe that China's prospective growth will be substantial, but a continuation of the high rates of economic growth achieved in the late 1980s and 1990s, already believed to be somewhat overstated, is unlikely.[11]

Deep structural problems face the Chinese economy and even if the radical reform measures announced in 1997 and 1998 are carried through in their entirety, progressively lower growth rates seem probable. One estimate suggests an average of 7% to 2020 but slowing in the later part of that period to around 5%, rather than sustaining a rate of 8–10%.[12] Among the likely causes would be lower returns from additional capital inputs, the declining impact of the shift of labour from agriculture to industry, a reduction in the scope for further 'catch-up' as a result of a closing of the technology gap, the costs of reform of financial institutions, and an aging population. More importantly, although China's economy will grow relative to that of Japan, and on certain assumptions could exceed it in magnitude by around 2020,[13] even then China would have a relatively low level of income per head by global and regional standards – only one tenth that in Japan. China would have increased power and influence but would continue to face major domestic challenges which would constrain its international influence.

In an economic relationship that is asymmetrical, China will remain considerably more dependent economically upon Japan than the reverse, both in trade and more especially in investment. But trade and investment relations between the two countries can be expected to grow and hence to expand the interest-based links that buttress the relationship. Japanese industry is increasingly integrating China into its production strategies. China's early sensitivity about competition from Japanese enterprises and the failure of Japanese business to transfer technology, while not totally absent, has consequently diminished. Problems in the economic relationship will arise from time to time, however, and China will remain sensitive to its overall degree of dependence on Japan. Yet given a continued

---

[11] A discussion of the technical reasons for the overestimation is in Nicholas Lardy, *China's Unfinished Economic Revolution,* Washington, DC: Brookings Institution Press, 1998, p. 9.

[12] World Bank, *China 2000:China Engaged: Integration with the Global Economy,* Washington, DC, 1997, p. 3; Lardy, pp. 214–16; Barry Naughton, 'The Chinese Economy Through 2005: Domestic Developments and their Implications for US Interests' in The National Intelligence Council, *China's Future: Implications For US Interests,* Washington, DC, Sep. 1999.

[13] World Bank, p. 30. (This is on the basis of purchasing power parity estimates of China's GDP.)

absence of balance of payments problems, these are likely to be relatively low-level concerns. Trade disputes are almost inevitable but such disputes in themselves do not necessarily affect significantly broader relationships.

The trend in Japanese investment in China will continue upwards, although annual growth rates will not uniformly show increases. Moreover, the quality of the investment will improve – it will become more capital-intensive and more technology-intensive. While most Japanese-invested enterprises in China are low-cost investments, Japanese firms will show increased interest in investing in higher cost projects. China appears to be improving the regulatory framework sufficiently to continue to attract new investment by Japanese (and other) firms[14] but China will also need to ensure that the viability of its economy as a whole is sustained if it wants foreign investment to continue to increase. This will be helped by increasing acceptance in China's domestic politics of the broader political and economic importance of proper treatment of foreign investors.

For Japan, investment in China will remain important, ensuring the competitiveness of some of its major industries and in gaining access to the Chinese market for some products. Japan will also continue to value investment in China for its strategic impact on Chinese society primarily through transfer of skills and workplace cultures, a policy objective Japan shares with the West.[15]

Tensions over foreign investment will not be absent in either country. Shifts by China in economic policies, particularly for foreign investment, will periodically cause friction in Japan. In China, tensions could well recur over complaints, valid or otherwise, that foreign firms are pushing out locals, and over resentments toward Japanese employment practices. These tensions will however probably be quite localised and therefore manageable in Beijing.

As we saw in Chapter 5, economic aid to China was a central element of Japan's policy in developing the relationship with China. well as a counter to Japan's substantial fears of instability in China helped to develop the Chinese market for Japan and eventually faci tated the foreign direct investment that contributed to a regic division of labour important for Japan's competitiveness. M

[14] Daniel Rosen, *Behind the Open Door: Foreign Enterprises in the Chinese M Place*, Washington, DC: Institute of International Economics, 1999, espe Chapter 7, pp. 231–58.

[15] Ibid., pp. 241–3.

generally, however, economic aid was part of a broader Japanese policy, opening up and modernising Chinese society, encouraging
cooperative rather than conflictual behaviour, ensuring greater prospects for stability in China, and bringing China into an integrated
relationship with the global community, supportive of the international system.

These broad motivations will remain important. For Japan, its
particular interests in maintaining its competitiveness in external
markets and in the growing Chinese market will also persist. Moreover, as the direction of its aid to China has shifted, the aid program
provides other direct benefits such as limiting adverse environmental
impacts from China on Japan. As we have observed, however, there
is increased criticism in Japan of the bilateral aid program. Ostensibly
on budgetary grounds, Japan has already reduced the growth in its aid
to China. It also stopped grant aid for short periods on two occasions
as a sign of its displeasure with China's policies. Further criticism in
Japan of the aid program will be unhelpful to the atmosphere of the
relationship.

China will be hostile to any major changes in the aid relationship.
The aid program has been seen by China not just a source of capital
and technology but also as a sign of confidence in the Chinese economy. There is also still some sense in Chinese minds of a Japanese
obligation to provide aid arising from its invasion and occupation of
China. A reversal would therefore have adverse consequences for the
relationship. Overall, despite the increased politicisation of aid on
both sides, there are no strong grounds for expecting significant
changes in Japan's aid program unless a major crisis in their relationship occurs.

In terms of the total relationship however, periodic difficulties in
the trade, aid or investment fields, will be dwarfed by growing opportunities for greater economic policy coordination at a strategic level
between the two countries. This cooperation will not only include
bilateral economic issues, but will extend to include cooperation on
China's WTO membership, on resisting trade liberalisation pressures
on their agricultural sectors, on combating protective or preferential
barriers to their exports in Europe and North America, on regional
economic forums such as APEC, and on energy procurement.

The potential strength of the Japan-China economic relationship
will be clouded somewhat by increasing perceptions of mutual
vulnerability or insecurity in military terms. Japan has a number of

advantages over China in non-nuclear military capability and these will persist for some time. For example, Japan has the second largest modern navy in Asia and its air forces, though smaller than China's, are much more capable for some scenarios than those of China. Japan has a sophisticated industrial structure capable of advanced weapon development and production, and an established supply line for large quantities of advanced US military equipment. It is also judged by many, including the Chinese, as being capable of moving fairly quickly to nuclear weapon production should it decide to do so.

China's defence industry is still relatively backward in most areas – one exception being in the field of missiles – and it relies substantially on imports for advanced technology. Its capacity to use the advanced military technology it has imported in a modern war context has yet to be tested but the general belief is that the 'software' (logistics, command and control, communication systems) to go with the hardware is still substantially deficient and will remain so for some considerable time. China's nuclear advantage may be important as a political symbol but it is of almost no operational significance to Japan as long as the US nuclear umbrella remains in place. Japan would only face nuclear attack or coercion from China in extremely desperate and most improbable circumstances.

Many in Japan have long been concerned about a potential threat from China – initially as an expansionist power proselytising communism and then as a nuclear power. Later, as its economic reform process started to work, and the subsequent process of military modernisation got underway, the Spratlys issue arose, the Taiwan issue heated up and nuclear testing proceeded. Concerns at China's growing military power became more extensively articulated in Japan. China's nuclear tests in 1995 and its missile exercises around Taiwan in 1995 and 1996 exacerbated insecurities in Japan about China's intentions.

Japan has not been passive in security policy. It has taken a number of steps that give greater weight and influence to the Defence Agency and the Self-Defence Force. These include more extensive patrolling of sea lanes and airspace around Japan, involvement in UN peacekeeping activities, development of increased intelligence and strategic planning capabilities, and revision of the guidelines for defence cooperation with the United States. Observers inside and outside Japan remain uncertain, however, about how important these steps are in terms of Japan's overall security policy and how much they run counter to Japan's defensive posture. Most observers remain confident that Japan's postwar anti-militaristic political culture will remain strong and act as a powerful constraint on the scope and purpose of any use of force by Japan.

There is less common ground among observers on the prospects for China's strategic posture. We have argued, however, that despite some belligerent flourishes since 1980, China's posture has been largely defensive as its leaders sought to give greater priority to economic development. Threat perceptions in China revolve more around China's ability to narrow the economic and technological gap than around order of battle comparisons or classic geopolitical considerations.[16]

China will continue its military modernisation at a relatively moderate rate, but its military capabilities will gradually improve in their sophistication. Its military capability gap with Japan will narrow in due course but given Japan's economic and technological strength and military potential, China has 'more than adequate reason to be apprehensive'.[17] On the other hand, Japan's geographic location and relatively small size do make it potentially vulnerable, if not to China's conventional weapons, to it growing missile capability. The dominant strategic reality though is that while the US alliance remains in place, neither Japan nor China has much reason to be apprehensive about the other as a source of unprovoked attack. Apart from China's available but limited nuclear missile capability, Japan and China have only limited power projection capability. Considerable time and redirection of priorities would be required for either to develop a more substantial one. It would also require a shift in strategic attitudes.

The bilateral security concerns of Japan and China will therefore remain at a lower level. Taiwan aside, China has long held a concern, albeit low level, at Japan's military spending and, initially at least, about its participation in UN peacekeeping activities. To this has been added its concerns at Japan's revision of the US defence co-operation guidelines, Japan's interest in theatre missile defence and the continuing pressure within Japan for constitutional revision. The

[16] Qimao Chen, 'New Approaches in China's Foreign Policy: The Post-Cold War Era', Asian *Survey,* XXXIII (3), Mar. 1993, pp. 237–51.

[17] Thomas Berger, 'Tangled Visions: Culture, Historical Memory and Japan's External Relations in Asia', paper to the American Political Science Association, Boston, 6 Sep. 1998, p. 4.

Chinese military in particular will remain especially watchful of the possibilities of rising militarism in Japan both in terms of its going nuclear and also in extending its interests in the island territories in the East and South China Seas.

Despite, or perhaps because of, this background, bilateral security cooperation will continue to expand. Their dialogue on arms control contributed to China's joining the CTBT and accepting commitments to the principles of the MTCR.[18] China and Japan have already cooperated on a range of regional issues: in the UN, on the Korean peninsula and, eventually, on Cambodia. The inauguration in 1998 of a trilateral US-Japan-China discussion on security issues was an important step in this field. Japan and China are likely to cooperate in the future on various issues, including energy, if only because not to do so would adversely affect their claims to leadership. But as long as Japan's alliance continues to evoke Chinese insecurity over Taiwan, and as long as China expands its nuclear and missile potential, bilateral security cooperation will remain somewhat cool and formalistic.

Regional competition in East Asia

We can expect the rivalry between Japan and China for leadership in the region to increase. This competition will remain somewhat indirect however since the two countries either cannot compete in the same spheres or choose not to. Japan's increased political influence will be a product largely of its overwhelming economic strength, its related presence throughout the region, the appeal of an economic model that has been both very successful and Asian. For China, increased influence will come from its growing strategic power, the Chinese diaspora and China's size and centrality in the region. Japan may have been more successful than China in overcoming historical problems with regional countries. For Japan, while suspicions will remain and its overall power will still be eyed warily, its generally constructive and low key approach will ensure it has a role, including as an offset to China. Countries like Vietnam and the Philippines will remain more wary of China than of Japan. China's continuing threats of war with Taiwan, continuing maritime disputes, and the inevitable fear of a large power will remain a constraint for China. Any regional

[18] Robert Manning, 'Burdens of the Past, Dilemmas of the Future: Sino-Japanese Relations in the Emerging International System', *Washington Quarterly*, 17 (1), 1994, pp. 45–58.

sense of assertiveness by China in these areas will adversely affect its economic as well as its political and strategic position.

Nevertheless, China has increasingly gained acceptance as part of the regional order. With problems of ideological communism and support for insurgencies in the region largely overcome, its status grew. This was buttressed by its largely successful efforts in resolving the many boundary disputes on its land borders, and by its increasingly cooperative participation in the international system. That status will almost certainly continue to grow.

As already noted, the regional ambitions of both will be constrained by continuing US influence. The record of Japan and China in East Asia will also remain a constraint on major initiatives by either in the region. Both will have to settle for more passive roles as Great Powers in East Asia, and continue to play second fiddle to the United States.

China will continue to see the United States rather than Japan as its major competitor for influence in East Asia, yet it will be unable to match it, given US global power, notably military power, and influence. Were it to try to match the US regional capabilities through its modernisation process, it would face the problem that the more it succeeded, the more it would increase regional apprehensions about its intentions. In practice, China will probably accept that the United States will continue preeminent in the region politically and militarily for some considerable time and accommodate to it. This is in part due to its recognition that, apart from its concerns over Taiwan, it will continue to benefit from the peaceful international environment of the status quo and in part because of its internal needs to maintain economic growth to avoid domestic political instability.

Added to the limits both face to their leadership aspirations are the often differing interests of the other major players in the region: Russia, South Korea, ASEAN and perhaps India. Consequently, strong leadership of a kind that would dominate the region is unlikely from either Japan or China. Moreover we have argued that the regional influence of each will be enhanced by a stable and often cooperative relationship between the two rather than a competitive or adversarial one. This differs from the view of some observers that unless regional cooperation is effective, historic rivalries and animosities might lead Japan and China to take a more autonomous approach to national security. This would probably involve strengthening their defence capabilities, resulting in a destabilising and potentially dangerous competitive arms build up.[19]

Japan, in playing a more active role in the region, will still 'lead from behind', in part to avoid being seen as contending with the US political predominance. Until the 1997 economic crisis, Japan's role as the 'locomotive' of East Asian growth was not in question; indeed, the apprehensions in the region were of the economic dominance of Japan. With the 1997 crisis, however, Japan was extensively criticised for failure to offer economic leadership. This resulted mainly from its failure to take up a role as a 'consumer of last resort', due to its own economic weakness, but also from its refusal, under US pressure, to follow through on its proposal for an Asian Monetary Fund. While much of this criticism was less than just, the feeling of a weak leadership capacity in Japan will diminish only slowly.

However, the United States has also been seen as deficient in the economic field for offering little itself and for strong backing of IMF 'solutions' which were, at least initially, especially contentious, and which have had qualified success. In fact, Japan contributed substantially more than the United States to the recovery programs of the affected countries in the region. Moreover, Japan sought to recover some of the lost ground by resurrecting the AMF in another form, as the Miyazawa Initiative, offering loans of up to $US 30 billion to the crisis-affected countries. Japan's leadership ambitions may benefit more though from its move to internationalise the yen.[20]

Despite the global role that China and Japan both seek, and despite their rivalry in the region, they both have Asian starting points, with 'different assumptions and sensibilities' to those of the west.[21] Underneath their acceptance of the international system is a shared belief in the distinctiveness of Asia. While the perceived 'urgency of forming a new Asian order'[22] diminished with the economic crisis, and

[19] Tsuneo Akaha, 'Security Policy', Tsuneo Akaha and Frank Langdon (eds), *Japan in the Posthegemonic World,* Boulder, CO: Lynne Rienner, 1993, p. 98.

[20] For a more extensive discussion, see Christopher Hughes, 'Japanese Policy and the East Asian Currency Crisis: Abject Defeat or Quiet Victory?', University of Warwick, CSGR Working Paper, no. 24/99, Feb. 1999, pp. 49–50.

[21] Ronald Dore, *Japan, Internationalism and the UN,* London: Routledge, 1997, p. 124

[22] Se Hee Yoo, 'Sino-Japanese Relations in a Changing Asia' in Gerald L. Curtis (ed.), *The United States, Japan, and Asia: Challenges for US Policy,* New York: W.W. Norton, 1994, p. 310.

there was in any case little evidence of action to bring this about, both Japan and China (with South Korea) participate in an ASEM process that reflects at least a geographic sense of Asian community. This has led to the formalising of the related hitherto informal summits of ASEAN plus the three Northeast Asian countries, providing an opportunity for Japan, China and South Korea to meet annually.[23]

In the absence of a central balance of power at the global level, ideas about the need for a regional balance have emerged. Classic power-balancing, however, has not been a major motivation for Japan or China, but there are some signs of it. Both Japan and China, to a degree, see Russia as a balancer to each other, as well as to the United States. However, in the light of Russia's weakness any reliance on it as a balancer will be almost indistinguishable from pursuit of less systemic interests, such as security of borders, hoped for economic gains, and energy cooperation. Both Japan and China certainly see the United States as a balancer in their relations but this is only occasionally understood in a classic balance of power shift, which implies the flexibility to change allies in order to adjust to changes.

Given that both Japan and China have concerns about US hegemony, the suggestion that they could come together in a 'strategic partnership' has at times surfaced in Chinese thinking. It was proposed by among others, He Xin, of the China Academy of Social Sciences (CASS) and published in authoritative journals such as *The Beijing Review*. The idea was dismissed at the time, however, as an 'extreme leftist' and impractical proposal.[24] The latter at least could be expected to remain the dominant view. Ronald Dore has argued, however, that it is not impossible in certain circumstances in the future – such as being on the receiving end of joint and adverse US and European action – that Japan and China might join together in a defensive alliance.[25]

Overall, the evidence suggests a desire by Japan and China to maintain a low level equilibrium among countries in the north Pacific, not seeking superiority for itself but not wanting the other to be

---

[23] Japan, China and South Korea held a separate meeting during the November 1999 summit. *Far Eastern Economic Review,* 9 Dec. 1999, pp. 22–4.

[24] See Ian Wilson, 'Sino-Japanese Relations in the Post Cold-War World' in Stuart Harris and Gary Klintworth (eds), *China as a Great Power: Myths, Realities and Challenges in the Asia-Pacific Region,* Melbourne: Longman/New York: St Martin's Press, 1995, pp. 91–106.

[25] Dore, *Japan, Internationalism and the UN,* p. 124.

ahead. Even if either were to show signs of greater interest in a new balance of power, the potentially destabilising aspects of this interest would be offset by growing economic interdependence, particularly in oil and natural gas investment and trade.

Although China has only recently reemerged as an important economic power in the region, there are concerns in Japan about the impact on its regional influence of Greater China (the mainland, Hong Kong and Taiwan), as we discussed in Chapter 4. But the success of Greater China is part of Japan's continuing success story. Japanese enterprises, having increasingly moved their production facilities offshore, have created structural economic interdependencies with much of the region, including China. Japan has a substantial interest in the economic fortunes of East Asia, including Greater China, its emerging structural interdependencies often overlapping with rather than replacing the existing Chinese framework. China's growing economic power can often be traced directly to Japanese enterprises, and the expansion of Japanese business in East Asia was itself greatly facilitated by personal networks among overseas Chinese businessmen.[26]

Economic and political realities suggest however that the conception of Greater China, while having a rhetorical appeal, overlooks the degree of independence of Taiwan from China and the position that Taiwan occupies between Japan and China. The concept of greater China is one that resonates positively in China but many in the leadership fear that the reality is actually turning out quite differently. As far as Japan is concerned, China suspects that it is basically opposed to China's reunification with Taiwan even though Japan would not move away from the 'one China' policy without considerable provocation from China, or a major policy change by the United States.

Japan, and more recently China, are supporters of multilateralism. For Japan, the UN was 'a source of its own legitimacy in the community of nations'[27] and for a considerable period, its preferred arena for its diplomacy was in multilateral institutions. Much of its later political activism after the Cold War was UN-oriented. As its diplomatic focus has shifted to Asia, it has looked to pursue its policy goals

---

[26] Takashi Shiraishi, in Peter Katzenstein and Takashi Shiraishi (eds), *Network Power: Japan and Asia*, Ithaca, NY: Cornell University Press, 1997, pp. 169–94.

[27] Yasuhiro Ueki, 'Japan's UN Diplomacy: Sources of Passivism and Activism' in Curtis (ed.), *The United States, Japan, and Asia*, p. 347.

substantially within a multilateral context, where it has often played a leading role, and is likely to continue to do so. Regionally, Japan's diplomacy will remain active in APEC, ARF and in the ASEAN Post-Ministerial Conferences.

Although these forums, and notably the ARF, do not provide security as such, they do contribute in providing for increased transparency, developing confidence and reducing misperceptions and misunderstandings and developing norms of behaviour, such as the peaceful resolution of disputes. They enable both countries to put pressure on the other in a non-confrontational way, and in both cases to counter US pressure. In practice the various economic forums, while having their own value in providing public goods, also contribute to security through developing a sense of region and common interests and understandings.

We have argued that there are many things dividing Japan and China and in some respects those differences will remain or grow in importance. The periodic eruption of disagreements based on these differences will continue to attract attention in the media in the two countries and in the West. The sensationalism of the newspaper headlines will however be increasingly deceptive. Overall, what has been important is that despite such substantial differences, both governments have sustained a business-like approach to the other. It is likely that this will become more difficult, given the greater concern of public opinion in both countries about the relationship, but both governments will not abandon this approach except under extreme duress. We have noted that whatever the public feelings towards each other, there is no domestic constituency in either country for a belligerent military posture. Moreover, across the wide range of interrelationships we have considered, the two countries have adopted policies that provide substantial constraints upon such a posture. Aspirations for greater influence in the international order (and in international society), unsatisfied ambitions for acceptance in the regional order, and the range of bilateral dependences in aid, investment, technology and trade will not guarantee, but will all reinforce, the non-confrontationalist approach. We can still expect the bilateral relationship to be based on avoidance of military confrontation and characterised by a mix of cooperation and competition.

Although both will have to respond to continuing international change, the underpinnings of the international policies of the two countries are reasonably well laid out. Both countries have in large part been follower countries, either of the United States or an international system substantially influenced by it, and that is unlikely to change rapidly. Both countries, however, will want scope to play a more substantial part in the international system. If this does not happen, more serious tensions could emerge. But since each has moved to play an active and mostly constructive role in that system, the international community is likely to make some adequate adjustments to maintain Japan and China in this pattern of behaviour.

Of course, the possibility exists Japan and China will act differently in the future. The transitional processes under way in China will be particularly influential on the future of Japan–China relations. Japan faces less obvious pressures but in responding to its structural and its identity and security challenges, major adjustments will be required. Adverse domestic factors could emerge. For example, China's economy and society already face major problems and the possibility of social disintegration is the great fear of Chinese leaders. For Japan one would have to postulate a sustained economic downturn and the emergence of a much larger unconservative movement before it sought a more adversarial, as distinct from a more assertive, approach to China.

But the forces most likely to promote an abandonment of the cooperative behaviour by Japan and China are more likely to be beyond the control of the two countries. The region has a number of major powers all of whom, with the exception of the United States, are powers in transition: Russia, North Korea, South Korea, and Taiwan. The two major potential security flash points in the whole Asia-Pacific region – the Korean peninsula and Taiwan – are adjacent to both Japan and China. It would not be too difficult to manage the relationship in the event of a Korean peninsula conflict. That would be more difficult in the event of a conflict over Taiwan. Military conflict over Taiwan that set them against each other would divide them in such a fundamental way that the consequent bitterness would be massive and long lasting.

Against this, the growing involvement of Japan and China in the global order will be a powerful and stabilising influence on Japan–China relations. And despite US interests and actions often being disliked by both countries, and despite their common interest in greater independence from US influence, they both know that in their future relationship with each other the US role will be vital. Whether Japan and China like it or not, the rules for this three-way relationship will, for the most part, not be set by either of them, but will come either from the United States as the strongest of the three or from the broader social milieu of international society. This study suggests that even were the Taiwan authorities to provoke some sharper confrontation between Japan and China, there are powerful constraints at the international, regional as well as the bilateral level that would help constrain them and prevent escalation. The demonstrated pragmatism of the leadership of the two countries would also reduce substantially any risk.

The commitment of Japan and China to avoid war with each other will remain the fundamental underpinning of their future relationship. While this commitment does not rule out friction and tension, often quite deeply felt, it does ensure considerable opportunity for a very bright mutually beneficial future.

BIBLIOGRAPHY

Government reports and documents

Australia, Department of Foreign Affairs and Trade, *The APEC Region Trade and Investment*, November 1997.

——, November 1998.

——, East Asia Analytical Unit, *Asia's Global Powers: China-Japan Relationships in the 21st Century*, Canberra: Department of Foreign Affairs and Trade, April 1996.

——, East Asia Analytical Unit, *China Embraces the Market: Achievements, Constraints and Opportunities*, Canberra. Department of Foreign Affairs and Trade, 1997.

China, *Jiang Zemin's Report at the 15th Congress of the Communist Party of China*, Beijing, September 1997.

Japan, 'The Modality of the Security and Defense Capability of Japan', 1994.

Japan, Defence Agency, *Defense of Japan 1978*, Tokyo: English edition, 1978.

—— *1979*, Tokyo: English edition, 1979.

—— *1988*, Tokyo: English edition, 1988.

—— *1990*, Tokyo: English edition, 1990.

——— *1990*, Tokyo: English edition, 1990.

Japan, Export Import Bank, *Annual Report 1998* (web version), 23 November 1998.

——, 'The Outlook of Japanese Foreign Direct Investment', 5 November 1998.

Japan, Japan Information Network, 'Cities that Japanese desire to Visit Sometime, as of 1994', Tokyo: Rikuruto KK, 1994 (electronic source).

——, 'On Japanese Overseas Air Travellers', Advertising Department of Mainichi Newspapers, 1994 (electronic source).

————, 'Top 10 Overseas Travel Destinations, as of 1994', *Annual Report of Statistics on Legal Migrants*, Tokyo: Judicial and Research Dept, Ministry of Justice, 1994 (electronic source).

Japan, JETRO, White Paper on International Trade, 1998.

Japan, Ministry of Foreign Affairs, *Japan-China Joint Declaration on Building a Partnership of Friendship and Cooperation for Peace and Development*, 26 November 1998.

————, Consular and Migration Affairs Department, 'Annual Report of Statistics on Japanese Nationals Overseas', November 1998, http//:jin.jcic.or.jp/stat/stats/21MIG33html.

————, *Diplomatic Blue Book 1995* (electronic version).

————, *Japan's Official Development Assistance, Annual Report, 1997*, Tokyo: Association for the Promotion of International Cooperation, February 1998.

————, Prime Minister Ryutaro Hashimoto, Speech on Japan's Foreign Policy toward China, 28 August 1997.

Japan, Ministry of International Trade and Industry (MITI), 'Charts and Tables Related to Foreign Direct Investment in Japan', Tokyo, January 1997.

Japan, Ministry of International Trade and Industry, 'Highlights of the 27th Survey of Overseas Business Activities of Japanese Companies', May 1998, www.miti.go.jp.

————, Charts and Tables Related to Japanese Direct Investment Abroad', Tokyo, January 1998.

Japan, Ministry of Justice. Judicial System and Research Department, 'Annual Report of Statistics on Legal Migrants', 30 June 1998, http//:jin.jcic.or.jp/stat/stats/16EDU62.html.

Japan, Prime Minister's Office. Public Relations Office, 'Opinion Survey on Foreign Affairs', January 1998.

Japan, *Report of the Advisory Group on Economic Structural Adjustment for International Harmony*, submitted to the Prime Minister, Yasuhiro Nakasone, 7 April 1986.

Japan, Science and Technology Agency, *White Paper on Science and Technology 1997 – Striving for an Open Research Community*, Summary, Tokyo, March 1998.

Japan, The Japan Foundation, *Overview of Programs for Fiscal 1991*.

————, *The Japan Foundation Annual Report 1997*.

Osaka, Junior High School Textbook, International Society for Educational Information Inc.

Tokyo, Shoseki Junior High School Textbook, published in translation by the International Society for Educational Information Inc., Tokyo 1994.

United States, National Intelligence Council, 'Japan's Evolving Strategic Calculus', 16 June 1999.

Non-government reports

Australian Pacific Economic Cooperation Committee, 'Switching On – The Effects of Liberalisation in Asia's Electronics Industry', Canberra: Studies in APEC Liberalisation, 1998.

Keidanren, 'Promotion of Privately Funded Infrastructure Projects in Developing Countries', 27 January 1998.

———, *Reforming Official Development Assistance (ODA) in Japan*, April 1997.

Books and journal articles

'Sino Japanese Relations: Achievements and Prospects', *China News Analysis*, 15 February 1993.

Agmon, Tamir and Mary Ann Von Glinow (eds), *Technology Transfer in International Business*, New York: Oxford University Press, 1991.

Akaha, Tsuneo and Frank Langdon (eds), *Japan in the Posthegemonic World*, Boulder: Lynne Reinner, 1993.

Asia Pacific Economic Group, *Asia Pacific Profiles 1998: Northeast Asia*, Canberra, 1998.

Austin, Greg, 'Japan and China in the Asia Pacific Region The Southeast Asia Dimension', *A Conference Report*, Canberra: Australia Japan Research Centre, 1997.

Austin, Greg, and Diana Betzler, 'Gulfs in Sino-Japanese Relations: An Evaluation of Japan's Cultural Diplomacy toward China', *Journal of East Asian Affairs*, summer/fall 1997, pp. 570–613.

Ball, Desmond, *Burma's Military Secrets: Signals Intelligence (SIGINT) from 1941 to Cyber Warfare*, Bangkok: White Lotus, 1998.

Benedick, Richard Elliot, *Ozone Diplomacy: New Directions in Safeguarding the Planet*, Cambridge, MA: Harvard University Press, 1991.

Berger, Thomas, 'Norms, Identity and National Security in Germany and Japan' in Peter Katzenstein (ed.), *The Culture of National Security: Norms and Identity in World Politics*, New York: Columbia University Press, 1996, pp. 317–56.

———, 'Tangled Visions: Culture, Historical Memory and Japan's External Relations in Asia', paper to the American Political Science Association, Boston, 6 September 1998.

Bernard, Mitchell and John Ravenhill, 'Beyond Product Cycles and Flying Geese: Regionalisation, Hierarchy and Industrialisation of East Asia', *World Politics*, 47, 1995, pp. 171–209.

Bernstein, Richard and Ross Munro, *The Coming Conflict With China,* New York: Alfred Knopf, 1997.

Berry, Ken, *Cambodia – From Red to Blue: Australia's Initiative for Peace,* Sydney: Allen and Unwin, 1997.

Bora, Bijit and Chen Chunlai, 'The Internationalisation of China and its Implications for Australia', Chinese Economies Research Centre, University of Adelaide, Working Paper, 97/5, 1997.

Breslin, Shaun, 'China's Integration into the Regional Economy' in Sam Dzever and Jacques Jaussaud (eds), *Perspectives on Economic Integration and Business Strategy in the Asia-Pacific Region,* Macmillan: London, 1997.

Brown Weiss, Edith and Harold Jacobsen (eds), *Engaging Countries: Strengthening Compliance With International Environmental Accords,* Cambridge, MA: MIT Press, 1998.

Buckley, Roger, *US-Japan Alliance Diplomacy 1945–1990,* Cambridge: Cambridge University Press, 1992.

Bull, Hedley, *The Anarchical Society: A Study of Order in World Politics,* London: Macmillan, 1977.

Buruma, Ian, *Wages of Guilt: Memories of War in Germany and Japan,* London: Vintage, 1995.

Calder, Kent, *Asia's Deadly Triangle: How Arms, Energy and Growth Threaten to Destabilise Asia Pacific,* London: Nicholas Brealey, 1996.

Cassen, Robert *et al.,* *Does Aid Work,* 2nd edition, Oxford: Clarendon Press, 1994.

Chang, Iris, *The Rape of Nanking,* New York: Basic Books, 1997.

Chao, Charles, 'Peking-Tokyo Relations Over The Past Year', *Issues and Studies,* 14 (4), April 1980.

Chen Chunlai, 'Foreign Direct Investment and Trade: An Empirical Investigation of the Evidence from China', *CERC Working Paper 97/11,* University of Adelaide, SA, August 1997.

———, 'The Location Determinants of Foreign Direct Investment in Developing Countries', *CERC Working Paper 97/12,* University of Adelaide, SA, November 1997.

Chen Jian-An, 'Japanese Firms with Direct Investments in China and their Local Management' in Tokunaga, Shojiro (ed.), *Japan's Foreign Investmentand Asian Economic Interdependence: Production, Trade and Financial Systems,* University of Tokyo Press, 1992.

———, 'The Direct Investment of Japanese Enterprises in China and China-Japan Industrial Cooperation to Commemorate the 20th Anniversary of the China-Japan Peace and Friendship Treaty', *Riben yanjiu jilin* (Collection of Japanese Studies), no. 1, 1998.

Chen Qimao, 'New Approaches in China's Foreign Policy: The Post-Cold War Era', Asian *Survey,* XXXIII (3), March 1993.

Christensen, Thomas, 'China's Realpolitik', *Foreign Affairs,* 75(5), September/October 1996.

Christoffersen, Gaye, 'China and the Asia-Pacific: Need for a Grand Strategy', *Asian Survey,* XXXVI (11), November 1996, pp. 1067–85.

———, 'China's Intentions for Russian and Central Asian Oil and Gas', *NBR Analysis,* 9(2), March 1998.

Chung, Oknim, 'Regional Perspectives and Roles on the Korean Peninsula', *Korea and World Affairs,* XXII (2), summer 1998.

Clough, Ralph, 'Taiwan – PRC Relations' in Robert G. Sutter and William R. Johnson, *Taiwan in World Affairs,* Boulder, CO: Westview Press, 1994.

Coulter, David, 'The Economics of SLOC Protection: An Overvalued Mission', *Proceedings,* Tokyo: International Conference on SLOC Studies, 17–18 November 1997.

Craig, Gordon and Alexander George, *Force and Statecraft: Diplomatic Problems of Our Time,* New York: Oxford University Press, 1983.

Curtis, Gerald L. (ed.), *The United States, Japan, and Asia: Challenges for US Policy,* New York: W.W. Norton 1994.

———, *Japan's Foreign Policy After the Cold War: Coping with Change,* Armonk, NY: M.E. Sharpe, 1993.

Deng Liping, 'Understanding Japanese Direct Investment in China (1985–1993): An Intercultural Analysis', in *American Journal of Economics and Sociology,* vol. 56, no. 1, January 1997.

———, 'Understanding Japanese Direct Investment in China (1985–1993): An Intercultural Analysis', in *American Journal of Economics and Sociology,* vol. 56, no. 1, January 1997.

Deng Yong, 'Chinese Relations with Japan: Implications for Asia Pacific Regionalism', *Pacific Affairs,* 1997, fall, vol. 70, no. 3, pp. 373–91.

———, 'Japan in APEC: The Problematic Leadership Role', *Asian Survey,* XXXVII (4), April 1997.

Dibb, Paul, David Hale and Peter Prince, 'The Strategic Implications of Asia's Financial Crisis', *Survival,* vol. 40, no. 2, summer 1998, pp. 5–26.

Dore, Ronald, *Japan, Internationalism and the UN,* London: Routledge, 1997.

Dower, John, *Japan in War and Peace,* London: Fontana, 1993.

Ellison, Herbert and Bruce Acker, 'The New Russia and Asia: 1991–1995', *NBR Analysis* 7 (1), June 1996.

Emmot, Bill, 'The Economic Sources of Japan's Foreign Policy', *Survival*, 1992, summer, pp. 50–70.

Ensign, Margee, M., *Doing Good or Doing Well? Japan's Foreign Aid Program*, New York: Columbia University Press, 1992.

Falkenheim Meyer, Peggy, 'Russia's Post-Cold War Security Policy in Northeast Asia', *Pacific Affairs*, 67(4), winter 1994–95, pp. 495–512.

Farrell, Roger, 'The Political Economy of Japanese Foreign Direct Investment, 1951–95', Canberra: Pacific Economic Papers, no. 295, Australia-Japan Research Centre, December 1998.

Feinstein, Charles and Christopher Howe (eds), *Chinese Technology Transfer in the 1990s*, Cheltenham, UK: Edward Elgar, 1997.

Fitzgerald, John, 'Chinese, Dogs and the State that Stands on Two Legs', *Bulletin of Concerned Asian Scholars*, 29 (4), October/December 1997.

Fujita, Kimio, 'China and Its Asian Neighbours' in Michael Ying-Mao Kau and Susan H. Marsh (eds), *China in the Era of Deng Xiaoping*, Armonk, NY: M.E. Sharpe, 1993.

Fukui, Haruhiro, *Party in Power: The Japanese Liberal Democrats and Policy Making*, Canberra: Australian National University Press, 1970.

Fukushima, Kiyohiko and C.H. Kwan, 'Foreign Investment and Regional Industrial Restructuring in Asia' in *The New Wave of Foreign Direct Investment in Asia*, Singapore: Nomura Research Institute and the Institute of Southeast Asian Studies, 1995.

Funibashi, Yoichi (ed.), *Japan's International Agenda*, New York University Press, 1994.

———, 'The Asianisation of Asia', *Foreign Affairs*, 72(5), 1993, pp. 75–85.

Garnaut, Ross, 'The East Asian Crisis' in Garnaut and Ross H. McLeod (eds), *East Asia in Crisis: From Being a Miracle to Needing One?*, London: Routledge, 1998.

Garver, John, *Face off: China, the United States and Taiwan's Democratisation*, Seattle: University of Washington Press, 1997.

Glaser, Bonnie S., 'China's Security Perceptions: Interests and Ambitions' in *Asian Survey*, vol. 33, no. 3, March 1993.

Graham, Edward M. and Naoko T. Anzai, 'Is Japanese Direct Investment Creating and Asian Economic Bloc?' in Eileen M. Doherty (ed.), *Japanese Investment in Asia: International Production Strategies in a Rapidly Changing World*, Asia Foundation and University of California, Berkeley, Roundtable on the International Economy, 1994.

Green, Michael, 'Japan and the Future of the Korean Peninsula', *Korea and World Affairs*, XXII (2), summer 1998.

————, *State of the Field Report: Research on Japanese Security Policy*, National Bureau of Asian Research, 1998.

Greenfield, Jeanette *China's Practice in the Law of the Sea*, Oxford: Clarendon Press, 1992.

Grow, Roy F. 'Comparing Japanese and American Technology Transfer in China: Assessing the "Fit" between Foreign Forms and Chinese Enterprises' in Agmon, Tamir and Mary Ann Von Glinow (eds), *Technology Transfer in International Business*, New York: Oxford University Press, 1991.

Gurtov, Mel and Byong-Moo Hwang, *China's Security: The New Roles of the Military*, Boulder, CO: Lynne Reinner, 1998.

Harding, Harry, *China's Second Revolution – Reform after Mao*, Washington, DC: Brookings Institution Press, 1987.

Harris, Stuart, 'China's Role in WTO and APEC' in Gerald Segal and David Goodman (eds), *China Rising: Nationalism and Interdependence*, London: Routledge, 1997, pp. 134–55.

————, 'China's Quest for Great Power Status: A Long and Winding Road' in Hung-mao Tien and Yun-han Chu (eds), *China Under Jiang Zemin*, Boulder, CO: Lynne Reinner, 2000, pp. 165–82.

————, 'Policy Networks and Economic Cooperation: Policy Coordination in the Asia-Pacific Region', *The Pacific Review*, 7(4), (1994), pp. 381–95.

Hatch, Walter and Yozo Yamamura, *Asia in Japan's Embrace: Building a Regional Production Alliance*, Hong Kong: Cambridge University Press, 1996.

Heginbotham, Eric and Richard Samuels, 'Mercantile Realism and Japanese Foreign Policy', *International Security*, 22(4), spring 1998.

Hicks, George, *Japan's War Memories: Amnesia or Concealment*, Aldershot: Ashgate, 1997.

Hidenori, Ijiri, 'Sino-Japanese Controversy since the 1972 Diplomatic Normalization', *China Quarterly*, no. 124, December 1990, pp. 639–62.

Hiramatsu, Shigeo, 'China's Naval Advance: Objectives and Capabilities', *Japan Review of International Affairs*, vol. 8, no. 2, spring 1994, pp.118–32.

Hiraoka, Leslie S., 'Japan's Coordinated Technology Transfer and Direct Investments in Asia', *International Journal of Technology Management*, 1995, vol. 10, nos 7/8.

Hodder, Rupert, *The West Pacific Rim: An Introduction*, London: Belhaven Press, 1992

Hu Weixing, 'Beijing's New Thinking on Security Strategy', in *The Journal of Contemporary China*, no. 3, summer 1993.

————, 'China and Asian Regionalism: Challenge and Policy Choice', *Journal of Contemporary China*, 5(11), pp. 43–56.

Hughes, Christopher, 'Japanese Policy and the East Asian Currency Crisis: Abject Defeat or Quiet Victory?', University of Warwick: *CSGR Working Paper*, no. 24/99, February 1999.

Ienaga, Saburo, *Japan's Last War*, Canberra: Australian National University Press, 1979.

Inoguchi, Takashi, *Japan's International Relations*, London: Pinter Publishers, 1991.

Iriye, Akira, *China and Japan in the Global Setting*, Cambridge, MA: Harvard University Press, 1992.

Jacobsen, Harold and Michel Oksenberg, *China's Participation in the IMF, the World Bank and the GATT: Towards a Global Economic Order*, Ann Arbor: University of Michigan Press, 1990.

Jain, Rajendra K., *China and Japan 1949–80*, 2nd edn, Oxford: Martin Robertson, 1981.

Japan Forum on International Relations, 'The Policy Recommendations on the Future of China in the Context of Asian Security', Tokyo: The Forum, 1995.

————, *The Policy Recommendations on the Future of China in the Context of Asian Security*, Tokyo, January 1995.

Jin Renshu, 'Japan's New Economic Strategy in the Asia-Pacific Region and the Direction of Sino-Japanese Relations', Chinese Economic Studies, July–August 1994, vol. 27 (4) translated from *Shijie jingji* (World Economy), October 1993, no. 10.

Johnson, Chalmers, 'Containing China: US and Japan Drift Towards Disaster', *Japan Quarterly*, October–December 1996.

Johnston, Alastair Iain, 'Engaging Myths: Misconceptions about China and its global role', *Harvard Asia-Pacific Review*, 1997–98.

————, 'International Structures and Chinese Foreign Policy' in Samuel Kim (ed.), *China and the World: Chinese Foreign Policy Faces the New Millennium*, Boulder, CO: Westview Press, 1998, pp. 55–87.

Jun, Kwang W. and Saori N. Katada, 'Official Flows to China: Recent Trends and Major Characteristics' in Kui-Wai Li (ed.), *Financing China Trade and Investment*, Westport, CT: Praeger, 1997.

Kaiser, Stefan David A. Kirby and Ying Fan, 'Foreign Direct Investment in China: An Examination of the Literature' in *Greater China: Political Economy, Inward Investment and Business Culture*, London: Frank Cass, 1996.

Katzenstein, Peter and Takashi Shiraishi (eds), *Network Power: Japan and Asia*, Ithaca, NY: Cornell University Press, 1997.

Kee Pookong, Yayoi Nakada, and Hironbu Take, *Japan's Aid Program:*

Trends, Issues and Prospects, A Report Prepared for the Australian Agency for International Development, February 1996.

Kibata, Yoichi, 'Japan's Search for Identity in Asia', paper to a University of Tokyo/University of Sydney International Symposium, 2–3 October 1998.

Kim, Samuel (ed.), *China and the World: Chinese Foreign Policy Faces the New Millenium*, Boulder, CO: Westview Press, 1998.

————, 'Behavioral Dimensions of Chinese Multilateral Diplomacy', *The China Quarterly*, no. 72, December 1977, pp.713–42.

Kinoshita, Toshihiko, 'Japan's Direct Investment in China: Current Situation, Prospects, Problems' in Kui-Wai Li (ed.), *Financing China Trade and Investment*, Westport, CT: Praeger, 1997.

Kissinger, Henry, *The White House Years*, London: Weidenfeld and Nicholson and Michael Joseph, 1979.

Klintworth, Gary, *New Taiwan, New China: Taiwan's Changing Role in the Asia-Pacific Region*, New York: St Martin's Press and Melbourne: Longman, 1995.

Koasi, Yutaka and Kenji Matsuyama, 'Japanese Economic Cooperation', *Annals of the American Academy of Political and Social Sciences*, no. 513, January 1991.

Kojima, Kiyoshi, 'Dynamics of Japanese Direct Investment in East Asia', *Hitotsubashi Journal of Economics*, 36 (1995).

Kokubun, Ryosei, 'The Delicate Triangle in the Post-Cold War Era: Sino-Japanese Relations and the United States', manuscript.

Komiya, Ryutaro and Motoshige Itoh, 'Japan's International Trade Policy 1955–84' in Takashi Inoguchi and Daniel Okimoto (eds), *The Political Economy of Japan*, vol. 2: *The Changing International Context*, Stanford University Press, 1988.

Koppel, Bruce M. and Robert M. Orr, *Japan's Foreign Aid – Power and Policy in a New Era*, Boulder, CO: Westview Press, 1993.

Kreisberg, Paul, 'Asian Responses to Pressures on Taiwan' in Parris H. Chang and Martin L. Lasater, *If China Crosses the Taiwan Strait – The International Response*, New York: University Press of America, 1993.

Krugman, Paul, 'The Myth of Asia's Miracle', *Foreign Affairs*, 73(6), 1994.

Kuriyama, Takakazu, 'Some Legal Aspects of the Japan – China Joint Communiqué', *Japanese Annual of International Law*, no. 17, 1973.

Lam Peng Er, 'Japan and the Spratlys Dispute: Aspirations and Limitations', *Asian Survey*, XXXVI (10), October 1996.

Lan Ping, *Technology Transfer to China through Foreign Direct Investment*, Aldershot, UK: Avebury, 1996.

Lardy, Nicholas, *China in the World Economy*, Washington, DC: Institute for International Economics, April 1994.

———, *China's Unfinished Economic Revolution*, Washington, DC: Brookings Institution Press, 1998.

Lee, C., *Japan Faces China: Political and Economic Relations in the Postwar Era*, Baltimore, MD: Johns Hopkins University Press, 1976.

Lehmann, Jean-Pierre, 'Corporate Governance in East Asia and Western Europe: Competition, Confrontation and Cooperation' in Charles P. Oman, Douglas H. Brooks and Colm Foy (eds), *Investing in Asia*, Paris: Development Centre of the Organisation for Economic Cooperation and Development, 1997.

Lewis, John Wilson and Xue Litai, *China's Strategic Seapower: The Politics of Force Modernization in the Nuclear Age*, Stanford University Press, 1994.

Li Genan, 'A Great Change in Japan's Stance on Asian Security Measures' in *Waiguo wenti yanjiu* (Studies of Foreign Affairs), February 1993.

———, 'The Reorientation of Japan–US Security Assurance Mechanism', *Waiguo wenti yanjiu* (Studies of Foreign Affairs), Changchun, 1996, no. 2, pp. 1–3.

Li Luye, 'The United Nations at the Turn of the Century', *CCIS International Review*, no 3, 1996, pp.1–18.

Liu Jiangyong, 'Facing the Challenges: China-Japan Relations Crossing the Century', in Yuan Chengzhang and Cheng Feng, *The International Environment of China's Modernisation Development Crossing the Century* (in Chinese), Beijing: Chinese Communist Party University Press, 1998.

———, 'Japan's Diplomacy after the Disintegration of the Soviet Union', *Xiandai guoji guanxi* (Contemporary International Relations), 1992, no. 00, pp. 25–30

———, 'My Preview of Japan in 1997', *Shijie zhishi*, 16 February 1997, no. 4, pp. 8–9 (FBIS-CHI-97-080, 16 February 1997).

———, 'My Preview of Japan in 1997', *Shijie zhishi*, 16 February 1997, no. 4, pp. 8–9 (FBIS-CHI-97-080, 28 April 1997): 'China: Scholar Previews Japan in 1997'.

———, 'Sino–Japanese Relations facing the 21st Century', Paper to an International Workshop held at the Australian National University, 27 August 1996.

Liu Xiaming, Haiyan Song, Yingqi Wei and Peter Romilly, 'Country Characteristics and Foreign Investment in China: A Panel Data Analysis', *Weltwirtschaftliches Archiv*, 1997, vol. 133, no. 2.

Long, Simon, *Taiwan: China's Last Frontier,* London: Macmillan 1991.

Lu Huiru, 'An Analysis of Japan's ODA Loans to China', *Riben wenti yanjiu* (Studies in Japanese Affairs), 1998, no. 1, pp. 18–22.

Lu Zhongwei, 'Post-War Japan at Fifty', Contemporary International relations, vol. 5, no. 7, July 1995, pp. 2–3.

Manning, Robert 'Burdens of the Past, Dilemmas of the Future: Sino-Japanese Relations in the Emerging International System', *The Washington Quarterly,* 17 (1), pp. 45–58.

Martha Caldwell Harris, 'Technology Transfer and Sino-Japanese Relations' in Agmon and von Glinow (eds), *Technology Transfer in International Business,* New York: Oxford University Press, 1991.

Mikanagi, Yumiko, *Japan's Trade Policy: Action or Reaction,* London: Routledge 1996.

Ming Wan, 'Human Rights and US-Japan Relations in Asia: Divergent Allies', *East Asia: An International Journal,* 16(3/4) autumn-winter 1998, pp.137–68.

Miyamoto, 'Discord in the Quartet of Japan, the United States, China and Russia'.

Mohan, C. Raja, 'India's Role in Southeast Asia' in Michael Everett and Mary Sommerville (eds), *Multilateral Activities in Southeast Asia,* Washington, DC: National Defence University Press, 1995, pp. 87–110.

Muller, David G. Muller, *China as a Maritime Power,* Boulder, CO: Westview Press, 1983.

Nathan, Andrew and Robert Ross, *The Great Wall and the Empty Fortress: China's Search for Security,* New York: W.W. Norton, 1997.

Naughton, Barry (ed.), *The China Circle: Economics and Electronics in the PRC, Taiwan and Hong Kong,* Washington: Brookings Institution Press, 1997.

Nester, William R., *Japan and the Third World – Patterns, Power, Prospects,* New York: St Martin's Press, 1992.

Nishiyama, Yohei, 'The Outlook for Japanese Foreign Direct Investment and Promising Destinations', Highlights of JOI Review, no. 37, Tokyo: Japan Institute for Overseas Investment, 1998 (www.joi.or.jap)

Noble, Gregory W, 'Putting the Cork in the Other Bottle: Alliance Dynamics and Multilateralism in Japanese Foreign Policy', Boston: Paper to the American Political Science Association, 5 September 1998.

O'Leary, Greg, *The Shaping of China's Foreign Policy,* Canberra: Australian National University Press, 1980.

Ogata, Sadako, 'The United Nations and Japanese Diplomacy', *Japanese Review of International Affairs*, 4(2), fall/winter 1990.

Ohta, Hideaki, Akihiro Tokuno and Ritsuko Takeuchi, 'Evolving Foreign Investment Strategies of Japanese Firms in Asia', in *The New Wave of Foreign Direct Investment in Asia*, Singapore: Nomura Research Institute and the Institute of Southeast Asian Studies, 1995.

Okita, Saburo, *A Life in Economic Diplomacy*, Canberra: Australia-Japan Research Centre, Australian National University, 1993.

Okubo, Tasuko, 'China and Japan – Financial Aspects', Tokyo: Sophia University, 1986.

Olsen, Edward, 'The Role of Taiwan in Asian Multilateral Security: Towards the 21st Century', *Journal of East Asian Affairs*, XII (I), winter/spring 1998.

Ozawa, Ichiro, *Blueprint for a New Japan: The Rethinking of a Nation*, Tokyo: Kodansha International, 1994.

Park, Choon-ho, 'China and Maritime Jurisdiction: Some Boundary Issues', *German Yearbook of International Law*, vol. 22, 1979.

Peek, John, 'Japan, the United Nations, and Human Rights', *Asian Survey*, XXXII (3), March 1992, pp. 217–29.

Pempel, T. J., 'The Unbundling of "Japan, Inc"': The Changing Dynamics of Japanese Policy Formation', *Journal of Japanese Studies*, 1987, vol. 13, no. 2.

Potter, Pitman B., 'Law Reform and China's Emerging Market Economy', in United States Congress, Joint Economic Committee. *China's Economic Future: Challenges to US Policy*, Armonk, NY: M.E. Sharpe, 1997.

Qian Jiadong, 'Security Trends in the Asia–Pacific Region', in *Disarmament and Security Issues in the Asia-Pacific Region*, Disarmament Topical Papers, 11, New York: United Nations.

Quansheng Zhao, *Interpreting Chinese Foreign Policy: The Micro-Macro Linkage Approach'*, Hong Kong: Oxford University Press, 1996.

Rix, Alan, *Japan's Foreign Aid Challenge: Policy Reform and Aid Leadership*, London: Routledge, 1993.

Rosen, Daniel, *Behind the Open Door: Foreign Enterprises in the Chinese Market Place*, Washington, DC: Institute of International Economics, 1999.

Ross, Robert, *Negotiating Cooperation: The United States and China 1969–1989*, Stanford: Stanford University Press, 1995.

Rozman, Gilbert, 'Cross-National Integration in Northeast Asia: Geopolitical and Economic Goals in Conflict', in *East Asia: An International Quarterly*, 16(1/2), spring/summer 1997, pp. 6–31.

Rozman, Gilbert, 'Flawed Regionalism: Reconceptualising Northeast Asia', *The Pacific Review,* 11(1), 1998, pp. 1–27.

Rubinstein, Alvin Z., 'Assessing influence as a problem in Foreign Policy' in Alvin Z. Rubinstein (ed.), *Soviet and Chinese Influence in the Third World,* New York: Praeger, 1975, pp.1–22.

Ryosei Kokubun, 'Patterns of Cooperation in Chinese Foreign Policy towards Japan since 1972', unpublished paper.

Seekins, Donald, 'Burma-China Relations: Playing with Fire', *Asian Survey,* XXXVII (6), June 1997.

Self, Benjamin, *Confidence-Building Measures and Japanese Security Policy,* Washington, DC: Henry Stimson Centre, 1998.

Shirk, Susan, 'Chinese Views on Asian Pacific Regional Security Co-operation', *NBR Analysis,* 5(5), December 1994.

————, *The Political Logic of Economic Reform in China,* Berkeley: University of California Press, 1993.

Shojiro Tokunaga, 'Moneyless Direct Investment and Development of Asian Financial Markets: Financial Linkages between Local Markets and Offshore Centers' in Tokunaga (ed.), *Japan's Foreign Investment and Asian Economic Interdependence: Production, Trade and Financial Systems,* Tokyo: University of Tokyo Press, 1992.

Sigal, Leon, *Disarming Strangers: Nuclear Diplomacy With North Korea,* Princeton University Press, 1998.

Simmons, Katherine, 'Japan's Reaction to the Tiananmen Square Incident: Challenging the Conventional Wisdom', MA Thesis, Canberra: Australian National University, June 1997.

Simon, Denis F. and Hong Pyo Lee (eds), *Globalization and Regionalization of China's Economy – Implications for the Pacific Rim and Korea,* Seoul: Sejong Institute, 1995.

Sino-American Cooperation on the Korean Peninsula, Conference report, Hawaii: Asia Pacific Centre for Security Studies, May 1998.

'Sino-Japanese Relations: Achievements and Prospects', *China News Analysis,* 15 February 1993.

Smith, Heather, 'Western Versus Asian Capitalism' in Stuart Harris and Andrew Mack (eds), *Asia-Pacific Security: The* Economics-*Politics Nexus,* Sydney: Allen and Unwin, 1997.

———— and Stuart Harris, 'Cross-Strait Economic Relations: Dependence or Interdependence?' in Greg Austin (ed.), *Missile Diplomacy and Taiwan's Future: Innovations in Politics and Military Power,* Canberra: Strategic and Defence Studies Centre, 1997.

Söderberg, Marie (ed.), *The Business of Japanese Foreign Aid: Five Case Studies from Asia,* London: Routledge, 1996.

Song Shaoying, 'Establishment of a New Economic Order in East Asia and Sino-Japanese Economic Relations', Chinese Economic Studies, July–August 1994, vol. 27 (4) translated from *Shijie jingji* (World Economy), March 1993.

Song Young-Sun, 'Korean Concern on the New US-Japan Security Arrangement', *Korea and World Affairs*, XX (2), summer 1996, pp. 197–218.

Story, Greg, 'Japan's Official Development Assistance to China', Canberra: Research School of Pacific and Asian Studies, p. 35.

Sun Haishun, *Foreign Investment and Economic Development in China: 1979–1996*, Aldershot: Ashgate, 1998.

Suttmeier, Richard P., 'China's Strategy for High Technology: Reform, R&D, and the Global Search for asset Complementarity' in Simon, Denis F. and Hong Pyo Lee (eds), *Globalization and Regionalization of China's Economy – Implications for the Pacific Rim and Korea*, Seoul: Sejong Institute, 1995.

Tao Qu and Milford B. Green, *Chinese Foreign Direct Investment: A Subnational Perspective on Location*, Aldershot: Ashgate, 1997.

Tarte, Sandra, *Japan's Aid Diplomacy and the Pacific Islands*, Canberra: Asia Pacific Press, National Centre for Development Studies, 1998

Taylor, *Greater China and Japan: prospects for an economic partnership in East Asia*, London: New York, Routledge, 1996.

Terada, Takashi, 'The origins of Japan's APEC Policy: Foreign Minister Takeo Miki's Asia-Pacific Policy and Current Implications', *The Pacific Review*, 11(3), 1998, pp. 337–63.

Terrill, Ross *A Biography: Mao*, New York: Harper and Row, 1980.

The Policy Recommendations on the Future of China in the Context of Asian Security.

Theater Missile Defense (TMD) in Northeast Asia: An Annotated Chronology 1990-Present, East Asia Nonproliferation Project, Center for Nonproliferation Studies, Monterey, 1999.

Tian, Giang *Shanghai's Role in the Economic Development of China – Reform of Foreign Trade and Investment*, Praeger, Westport, 1996.

Toshiyuki Shikata, *China, the United States and Japan: Implications for Future US Security Strategy in East Asia*, Alexandria VA: Center for Naval Analyses, 1997.

Tow, William, 'China and the International Strategic System' in Thomas Robinson and David Shambaugh (eds), *China's Foreign Policy: Theory and Practice,* Oxford University Press, 1994.

Tretiak, Daniel, 'The Sino-Japanese Treaty of 1978: The Senkaku Incident Prelude', *Asian Survey*, vol. 18, no. 12, December 1978.

Tsyganov, Yurii, 'The General Framework of Sino-Russian Relations', *Russian and EuroAsian Bulletin,* Contemporary Europe Research Centre, University of Melbourne, 7 (6), June 1998.

Ueki, Yasuhiro, 'Japan's UN Diplomacy: Sources of Passivism and Activism' in Gerald Curtis (ed.), *Japan's Foreign Policy After the Cold War: Coping with Change,* Armonk, NY: M.E. Sharpe, 1993.

Wakasugi, Ryuhei, 'Japan's Trade and Investment Policies towards Asian Countries', Paper to an international workshop on *Japan and China in the Asia-Pacific Region,* Canberra: The Southeast Asia Dimension, ANU, August 1996.

Wang, Qingxin Ken Wang, 'Toward Political Partnership: Japan's China Policy', *Pacific Review,* vol. 7, no. 2, 1994.

Whiting, Allen *China Eyes Japan,* Berkeley: University of California Press, 1989.

Wilson, Ian, 'Sino-Japanese Relations in the Post Cold-War World' in Stuart Harris and Gary Klintworth (eds), *China as a Great Power: Myths, Realities and Challenges in the Asia-Pacific Region,* New York: St Martin's Press, and Melbourne: Longman, 1995, pp. 91–109.

Woods, Lawrence *Asia-Pacific Diplomacy: Nongovernmental Organisations and International Relations,* Vancouver: UBC Press, 1993.

World Bank, *China 2000: China Engaged: Integration with the Global Economy,* Washington, DC, 1997.

Wu Yanrui, 'The Performance of Foreign Direct Investment in China: A Preliminary Analysis', discussion paper, Dept of Economics, University of Western Australia, 1998.

Xia Liping, 'Some Views on Multilateral Security Cooperation in Northeast Asia', *Xiandai guoji guanxi* (Contemporary International Relations), 20 December 1996, no. 12, pp. 12–15.

———, 'Some Views on Multilateral Security Cooperation in Northeast Asia', *Xiandai guoji guanxi* (Contemporary International Relations), 20 December 1996, no. 12, pp. 12–15 (FBIS-CHI-97-074, 20 December 1996).

Yasutomo, Denis, 'The Politicisation of Japan's "Post-Cold War" Multilateral Diplomacy' in Gerald Curtis (ed.), *Japan's Foreign Policy After the Cold War: Coping with Change,* Armonk, NY: M.E. Sharpe, 1993.

———, *The New Multilateralism in Japan's Foreign Policy,* London: Macmillan, 1995.

You Ji, 'Missile Diplomacy and PRC Domestic Politics' in Greg Austin (ed.), *Missile Diplomacy and Taiwan's Future: Innovations in Politics and Military Power,* Canberra: Strategic and Defence Studies Centre, 1997.

Young, Stephen and Ping Lan, 'Technology Transfer to China through Foreign Direct Investment', *Regional Studies*, 1997, vol. 31 (7).

Yuan Jing-Dong, 'United States Technology Transfer Policy toward China: Post-Cold War Objectives and Strategies', *International Journal*, vol. LI, no. 2, spring 1996, pp. 314–38.

Yuan, Paul C., 'China's Offshore Oil Development: Legal and Geopolitical Perspectives', *Texas International Law Journal*, vol. 18, no. 1, winter 1983.

Zhang, Dong Dong, 'Political Economy of the China-Japan Relationship in an Era of Reform and Liberalisation', PhD thesis, Australian National University, Canberra, 1997.

Zhang Guang, 'The Trend of China's Post-Cold War Foreign Aid Policy', *Riben xuekan* (Journal of Japanese Studies), 1993, no. 4, pp. 35–54.

Zhang Taishan, 'Japan's Military Strategy for the New Era', *International Strategic Studies*, no. 3, 1998.

Zhang Xiaoji, 'Foreign Direct Investment in China's Economic Development', in *The New Wave of Foreign Direct Investment in Asia*, Singapore: Nomura Research Institute and the Institute of Southeast Asian Studies, 1995.

Zhang Yongjin, *China in International Society since 1949: Alienation and Beyond*, London: Macmillan and New York:St Martin's Press, 1998.

Zhang, Dong Dong, 'The Political Economy of the China-Japan Relationship in an Era of Liberalisation and Reform', PhD thesis, Australian National University, July 1997.

Zhao Quansheng, *Interpreting Chinese Foreign Policy: The Micro-macro Linkage Approach*, Hong Kong, New York: Oxford University Press, 1996.

Zhao Quansheng, 'Japan's Aid Diplomacy with China', in Bruce M. Koppel and Robert M. Orr, *Japan's Foreign Aid – Power and Policy in a New Era*, Boulder, CO: Westview Press, 1993.

Newspapers and news agencies

AFP (Agence France Presse)
Associated Press
Beijing Central Television
Central News Agency
Beijing Review
Nihon keizai shimbun
China Daily (Business Weekly)
Bungei Shunjyu
Cheng ming

China Daily
China News Digest
China Pictorial
Chuo koron
Dempa shimbun
Detroit News
Far Eastern Economic Review
Gaiko Forum
Guangming ribao
Guoji maoyi
Guoji maoyi wenti
Hong Kong Standard
Japan Echo
Japan Times
Jiefangjun bao
Jiji Press Newswire
Keji ribao
Kyodo
Liaowang
Look Japan
Los Angeles Times
Mainichi shimbun
Ming Pao
New Straits Times
Nikkei Weekly
Renmin ribao
Renmin ribao (Overseas edition)
Reuter
Sankei shimbum
SEKAI
Shokun
South China Morning Post
The Australian
The Guardian
Shukan Daiyomondo
Tokyo Shimbun
Xinhua
Yomiuri Shimbun
The Nikkei Industrial Daily
Zhongguo qingnian (China Youth)
Zhongguo qingnian bao (China Youth Daily)
Zhongguo tongxun she

Databases

International Economic Databank
Japan Immigration Association,
OECD Development Assistance Committee, On-line Statistical Data-
    bases
OECF On-Line Data Base

INDEX